On the Way to NowHere

On the Way to NowHere

Komala Lyra

iUniverse, Inc.
New York   Lincoln   Shanghai

On the Way to NowHere

iUniverse books may be ordered through booksellers or by contacting:

iUniverse
2021 Pine Lake Road, Suite 100
Lincoln, NE 68512
www.iuniverse.com
1-800-Authors (1-800-288-4677)

First edition 2004 published in the USA by iUniverse

Grateful acknowledgement is made to the following for permission to reprint copyrighted material:
Osho International Foundation, Switzerland (www.osho.com) for quotes from Osho from
The Great Secret
David Whyte for excerpt from *The Poetry of Self Compassion* recorded 1991. Copyright © 1991
by David Whyte. Used by permission of the author (www.davidwhyte.com)
Coleman Barks and Maypop Books for translation of Rumi quotes excerpt from
The Essential Rumi and *The Illuminated Rumi*
Karma Chagmey Rinpoche for quote from *The Union of Mahamudra and Dzoghen*

Editing by Anila Manning and Nishant Matthews
Cover photo by Komala Lyra
Design support by Dirk Ananda

Scorpio Moon Press
38 Miller Avenue PMB 204
Mill Valley CA 94941 USA
www.scorpiomoonpress.com
scorpiomoon@sammasati.net

ISBN: 0-595-33480-6

Printed in the United States of America

Dedication

To my friends…

Bia, Lia, Bebeth, Neyda, Ora, Angela Loureiro, Inez, Sylvia, Lucia Naegli, Ana Margarida, Claudia Saladini, Beth Vaz, Maria Inez Penna e Costa, Beatriz Ballerini—my childhood friends. The heartful innocence of our friendship has been with me, beyond distances and time.

Claudia, for being my sister, and to Pedro, Joao e Ana Carolina.

Monica and Heloisa, I still see us hanging out at the university, discussing the infinite possibilities of making this planet more beautiful, more esthetic, lively. We chose unique ways to design our lives…

Angela Oak, my dearest friend, delighted to have you in my life… I write for you and for Sushma. Let's dance!

Sandra, Lucinha, Sergio, Ferrazinho, for being part of an important time of definitions, uncertainty, questions, decisions…

Eduardo, your passion and intention motivated me to search for the sparkle within…

Paulinho, you happened to push me over the fence without even knowing it… Thank you.

Ignez, my mother, for your sensitivity, intuition, care, appreciation of beauty, generous love, joy of gifts and surprises, willingness to review, mother warmth, sincerity and Tagore's poems that touched my heart.

Waldyr, my father, for your intensity, sense of adventure, laughter, and the strong genes that allowed my body to go through many challenges and Indian times. And for galloping on our horse Beija Flor with me in your lap!

Guy, my brother, first friend, for all we have shared bare feet in the countryside. I appreciate you coming down to play with me, the piano we have never learned, the joy and the fights shared with a sense of humor that we can read in each other's eyes, your sensitivity now translated in the beauty of your moving images… "Pelo atalho se chega mais depressa…"

Julia, my niece, with the tenderness that you deserve to flower…

Vovo Juju, Vovo Augusta, Bisa, Tia Guida, Tia Zeze, Tio Arnaldo, Toca, Zeca, Tia Dora, Tio Hugo, Hugo, Caique, Paulinho, Tia Alice, Tio Bitar, Bel, Mauro, Tia Chola, Idita, extended childhood family.

My grandfathers, Alvaro and Joao, who I never met.

Miguel, for our friendship in times of freshness and wonder.

Enric, lover, passion, inspiration, husband, you moved me a thousand lifetimes.

Beti, for the mystery of our meeting, the courage of your sincerity and trust, and daring to look further...

Chico, for opening the doors of mystery and magic and Zen.

Prageet and Gyaneshwar for walking me through the ashram for the first time.

Digs, for being my brother and sweetest friend.

Tosh, for the gift of your love and generosity.

Digant, for your kind love and friendship, and the beauty of your paintings.

Dhyana, Varsha, Neera, Mayoori, Anando, Renuka, Madhuma, Chaitanyo, Vasumati, Puja, Sajeela, Lani, Pratima, Adina, with whom I have shared sisterhood in many different ways.

Michael, beloved friend, for that flower vase delivered in the midst of the night...

Chintan, for the infinite heart space...

Hareesh, for the moments of serendipity and lightness, and music I still cherish over the years.

Bharat, for showing up magically again and again.

An offer to all other friends whose expressions inspired my journey, whose names I cannot remember, who invited me into unknown lands, and gave me strength to be truthful. For the moments we have lived with an open heart, casual meetings, a one-night stand, a waltz or a tango, each piece is meaningful...

Especially to Isa, Judy Bahnson and Kaveesha.

Nish, beloved. The tenderness of our love stays precious.

In gratefulness to Osho, who initiated me into trust.

CONTENTS

On the Way

Earth and Sky

In Time

Beyond Time

Acknowledgements

Thank you...
Bia, for asking me to write.
Nish, for your presence in my life.
Anila, for your enthusiastic response and editing.
Anastasia, for being my first reader.
Len and Hillary, for your kindness, friendship and love.
Brian and Josie, for inviting the invisible connections...
Andrea, for your feedback and suggestions.
Abhar, for being around while I was writing.
Ashira, for receiving me in your house with so much love.
Katrina, for the flowing river of our sharing and intention.
Laurie, for welcoming me in your home.
Venu, for our connection beyond words.
Sudipo, for your intelligence and friendship.
Karmen, for the fullness of your heart and my retreat time at your home.
Premda, for your sincere comments and caring friendship.
Eve, for the inspiration and focused intention.
Adina, for your angel wings.
Goldie, for your earthy love and care.
Siddhena, for your creative joy and the mystery...
To Premal and Miten, Chaitanya Hari, Jai Uttal, Krishna Das, Caetano Veloso, Joshua, Al Gromer Khan, and many other musicians whose sounds inspired my time at the computer.
Sajeela, for our time together at Haramara.
Mahima, for your friendship, hospitality, and care always present.
Rhea, for your presence and warmth.
Chohan, for the inspiration to follow through with this project.
Nidhi, for your voice opening my heart.
Ahado, I so much appreciate your care with me.
Kate, for finding the lovely home we have shared.
Enid, for silence, tamboura and reminding me not to wobble.
My clients in Mill Valley, for holding the ground while this writing was happening.
Shaan, for taking me to Parimal where I finalized this editing.

INTRODUCTION

Looking back at my life, I wonder. Words and phrases float above my head. Surprised, I listen. I sit to write. As the letters appear in the screen, I get a glimpse of what they convey. Linking something inside myself, re-connecting with friends.

On a hot summer day, a girl was born. A twenty-year-old mother, a professional father. Black haired with brown eyes, like many others born in that same day in the large city of Rio de Janeiro.

This girl turned playful, sensitive, no stranger to tears, sharp in her perceptions, enjoying the beauty of tropical nature and the easiness of an extended family including one brother, friends, and household maids. What began so ordinary turned into a life of intensity and introspection, fire and water, rebelliousness and search.

I grew up in Brazil, where the Old Portuguese got an African accent and lots of slang expressions. Language... Mine is peculiar. Not exactly ruled by grammar. Rather sensuality, warmth, with sun and ocean and moon and sand tossed in.

Living around the world, my tongue played with different idioms. Soon it became clear that they were not enough to say the essential.

In time, the dancer, the painter, the wife, the lover, the healer, the friend, the traveler, revealed the many forms that a soul can take. The thread of endless expressions was a spirit awestruck with the beat of a life without edges, flickering multicolored.

Somewhere there was trust. I really did not know then, don't know now, where does it come from. What makes me keep daring? This trust took me out of my family and native country at an early age; this trust brought me wakeful nights, dear friends, unusual strangers, caring lovers. This trust made me learn and continuously open to perceptions beyond logic.

I learned art and design. I learned to express things I could sense unseen, and translate them into forms of beauty and practicality. I learned to touch people with my hands and heart. I learned to love with totality and spirit. I learned to follow my ability to see the potential and water it to seedling, hanging in there not knowing if it will ever turn into a tree, or a flower, or simply remain in incubation. I am still learning patience and forgiveness. I followed the stars and the moon, and the sun, and the waves in the ocean. I ran after butterflies and galloped on wild horses. I sat under trees and took airplanes over the oceans.

Most people are intrigued by the outer form of beauty and love. Most artists are enchanted with their art; most lovers are entranced with their beloveds. I am too. At the same time, I have looked for the source. The place where beauty and love come from. This search took me into art, healing, and love affairs. Creating and destroying form, again and again, through intention, commitment, heartbreak, fresh beginnings. Inexplicably, I have always been called to that deeper place.

I have searched for the source of art, the source of love—giving myself to life without reserves, meeting, letting go, present to the risks and opportunities of each encounter. I let myself be taken. By my own sensitivity, my thirst for truth, instinct for love… I was offered dreams, gold, flesh, exquisite beauty, affection, passion, deceit, illusions, realness, honesty, the naturalness of sex, the warmth of conscious touch, bliss, the coldness of unconsciousness, pain, sharpness, silence, noise, and much more. I drank it. Sometimes in a gulp, sometimes sipping it slowly. The outer forms became a kaleidoscope of people, places, movement. The foreground of changing shapes enhanced the background of stillness and watchfulness.

Responding to the appeal of love I discovered something in myself that I had intuited in art and poetry—the underground texture of life that paintings and words can point to. Through relationships I started living it, sensing its blueprint inside my own body, feeling its pulse inside my heart. I learned that I could fall in synchronicity with life's rhythm by dissolving into each moment and each person without holding to definitions of who I was, who I was supposed to be, who I was expected to be. Life came forward with surprises, not always pleasant, but always expanding my ability to receive it. I learned that merging, initially with men and ultimately with life, led the way to my inner lushness, to the land of no-boundaries, to wordless relaxation. The gentle circuitry of my inner world switched on, re-aligned, waking up a vibrant woman, undefined, responsive, resourceful. My body started interacting with life as co-creator of the mystery that had been hanging on museum walls, or living in stained glass windows of ancient churches. I gained maturity, focus and sensibility.

The fragrance of my soul has been released as time takes me through life. I listened to the soul of the dancer, the soul of the lover, the soul of the artist, the soul of the healer, the soul of this woman who rides a bike around town, who can move with the waves of ecstasy and hold the precision of intimacy. With others, with life itself. I touched the essence that does not have a name.

Difficult to tell stories within a frame. I am a Pisces. The ocean has no top or bottom, left or right. I easily get lost in time. Liquid shapes rearrange themselves in synchronicity with the whispering breeze. Strength and imperfection in silent communion.

I sit at the computer and put on my reading glasses. My paintbrush is the keyboard. When I am here, I forget how it is there. When I am there, I have no memory of being here. The stream of vague reminiscences contrasts with sharp and clear images.

Gratefulness, plenty. My eyes reflect it when the first star glides.

Love, as an inner bathing, embracing and yet bypassing romance. Like a cloud that has density, though no substance. Through the love I treasured and cared for, I got here alone. Disconcerting.

My path has been intertwined with fire and water. I learn with intensity and challenges, sensitivity and quietude.

The fire kept aflame my search, made me move fast and respond with passion. It burnt attachments and desires, cleansed my body in sickness, flashed my mind with inspiration, gave me sharp intelligence to discriminate and learn from life's heat. It has taken me to ashes, beginnings and endings, transformation.

The water guided me into relaxation, the raw material of delight. It bathed my heart with gentleness, teaching me to wait, rest, and be permeable. It made me dive into the depth of relationships, unafraid of emotional sways. The water invited me to merge in intimacy and sensuality. It whispered softness, offering me protection in fluidity and resilience.

This blending generates steam and clouds, waves and volcanoes, rain and thunders. I watch my innermost nature, accept its limitations. Sometimes I compare, and wonder…where is the earth I can build my home in?

I notice friends making sure the ground is solid before they take each step. I observe how, with each move, they leave clear footprints for future reference with a serene confidence strange to my legs.

I see myself somersaulting, stumbling, flying, swimming. I don't know how to walk on a straight line. I sniff the abyss, come sharply near the edge, close my eyes and jump! Free falling incites fascination. I know I have a choice, yet I don't. Absolute trust, sheer stupidity, or an astrological consequence of having moon in Scorpio? Once in mid-air, the demons come close, uncertainty stirred.

Doubting that somewhere in the dark, there will be a bottom. Hoping I won't get too hurt. Unsure that I will ever stand up again.

Often it does hurt. It always takes longer to reach the ground than my comfort zone extends. Landing is never as smooth as I anticipated. Swiftly, I find myself in territories that I had no idea existed. Once I reach firm terrain, its density gives me comfort. Hummm! This process takes blood and guts, but it delivers freedom from fear.

I am learning how to walk, one step at the time. I am not naturally humble or patient. The way doesn't end where I'd imagined it would. Each "one more step" leads to more space ahead, and around.

These are stories of my personality searching for something that does not belong to it. Absurd! Though the echo of its form has not yet dissolved into source, the longing of the soul has dipped me into silent realms. I dwell in between worlds. Avoiding pain seems to suffocate life's roots, though tenderness nourishes them as much. The flower blossoms when the sun dries out dew caresses.

The experiences I lived were discarded as fast as they were savored. Like a butterfly without a cocoon, I have enjoyed the transparency of being with no expressions attached, the wind blowing leaving no traces. I have disdained the value of articulation. Words and images thrown away like dead corpses. Now, while writing, my mind affirms the irrelevance of past events, yet recognizes their imprints. A strong force keeps me focused.

When I left home, I did not know that my journey had no way back. I did not know that it would entail cliffs, and edges, and mountains, storms, and coming close to death a few times, and having my heart broken. I was too young and too determined to see it. However, tenderness stayed within me, through difficulties, through pain, through doubt. With its guidance, I write.

I did not know that I would meet a master who would look straight into my eyes and beam my heart. I did not know that he would invite me to dance, strip off pretense, fear, hesitation. I did not know that his presence would unite old and new, weaving sundry stories into a rich mantle. I did not know that he would serve as a bridge, and then vanish.

I did not know that I would have many homes, and none. I did not know that I would find home in the aliveness of the heart-spirit.

I followed invisible threads, that only much later became visible as stepping-stones. I often felt alone, being able to see in the dark, when nobody else could apprehend what had not yet taken form. Sometimes I was met with trust, others with incredibility.

Searching for the alignment that would force me to meet life in its totality, I sensed movements that placed my body in precise places. I stretched between union and separation, emptiness and fullness, offering and receiving. I still veer with the sniff of the rain. As the years have passed, this movement is mostly internal, outer circumstances became less relevant. The sequence of places and events enhanced the crispy quality of the inner world—spaciousness.

I have savored wondrous beauty and mystery, solitude and potential. These allusions are alive within, even when there is nothing outside that reminds me of them. Like light diffusing straight and round lines, blurring reason, pointing to the source of freedom. Freedom that makes this moment translucent.

"Saying it" brings vulnerability and also shame since I have nothing in my hands to show off, hold on to, or account for. Nakedness, susceptibility, mistakes. Freshness. Recycling life, exposing, I give out this narrative.

A circle drawn in the air, a healing journey, a turning myself inside out, a wild ride! No beginning or ending. Unexpected events keep weaving the mystery. Friends invite trust, when nothing else seems to make sense. I am grateful.

Memories seem to be intrinsically emotional. So, others involved in events I am relating may describe the facts otherwise. Names have been omitted or changed in recognition of privacy and the subjectivity of my account.

May this story enrich your life. May it warm your heart, may it dissolve what is old and hard, bring light to what is hidden and shy. May it persuade you to dance. May it bring forth renewal in your life, as in mine.

Timeless Time

"Being born as a man was only the introduction; life has not yet begun for you.
So far you have only been involved in the preparation; you have not yet begun the
pilgrimage—you have only been preparing for the journey.
Your luggage is ready—you have arranged all your things very carefully; the trunk,
the bedding, the provisions are ready for the journey—but you have not yet set out.
Man is at this point, at this stage.
If you want to understand clearly what man is and where he is going, then look at
him as someone who has made all the preparations necessary for a journey but is
sitting beside his luggage because he has forgotten where he has to go, because he has
forgotten why he has made all these preparations.
Your condition is the same.
All your preparations are complete; you are now a completely evolved human being.
Now you can only jump into your pilgrimage; now there is nothing lacking in you.
The instruments are properly tuned; you only have to start playing your music."

OSHO   *The Great Secret*

THE JOURNEY

Death has always been close. The ephemeral quality of bodies and things... Instinctive knowing.

As a child, I often sat under a large pine tree, my eyes closed, protected and restful with my back against its bark. I knew then, I had to leave alone, step out of the circle—family, comfort, security.

At the age of eleven I saw young men and women being killed on the streets of my hometown. The army took over the government. I witnessed hundreds of young students protesting, being beat up and shot to death. These scenes instilled urgency in my heart.

At fifteen, I met Edu. Parties, movies, kisses in the dark, sweet hugs, walks in the botanical garden. His sensitivity threw my defenses loose. I was shy and not sure how to behave. My intelligence was inspired by his intensity and determination. The longing became tangible in my body.

My friends dreamed of marriage and children. Inside, this voice... There is something else, you will never be content with a man and children, risk, explore!

Growing up in a wealthy family, I had no ambition for money. Surrounded by successful professionals, I had no desire for a career. Observing how couples related and treated their children, I desired no family. I soon realized that politics and sociology led nowhere. I could see abuse of power, lack of understanding of human sensitivity, of intelligence and above all, of creativity.

Family, children, career, politics were the basics of most people's lives. I perceived compromise, unspoken agreements and subtle lies, misuse of words and bargains. People abiding by self-restrictions in order to survive, living in cages designed by their ideas and commitments, ignoring the potential life had to offer. No! Life could not be reason, dreams, biology, gestation, birth, death, getting old and disappearing, continuously trying to hide the fear. What was left?

Nature and primitive cultures called my soul.

I was gifted with artistic talent, a sharp mind, the ability to respond to life joyfully, and a beautiful body. I was restless, unhappy. I lived in material luxury, my parents were willing to discuss openly, and extend a long way to meet me. The longing was clearly inside, and pushing me... As I did not know where to move towards, I kept moving away from what was not giving me the answers.

Occasional sounds and images triggered a faded remembrance. Nothing I could pinpoint. Faraway music...just a note was enough to evoke a familiar melody. Like a warm voice cuddling my soul. Resting quietly, hearing my heart beating and the pulse inside my head, I could see images in pastel nuances hardly distinguished. A cloud passing by slowly…still the veiled form was alive and dancing. Trying to hold or pierce through it fostered anxiety.

Sometimes my body-sense expanded, I felt huge, outside the contour of my physical shape, notably light, almost floating. I looked at people and they appeared tiny. I was a giant watching them staring at me. This unusual shift of perception evoked curiosity, and an almost compulsive desire to be still. I knew there was a calm place of knowing within.

I foresaw the explosion of love, and newness with every day, liveliness in freedom, the relaxation of trust. I dreamed of a place where my creative spirit could play unleashed, uncensored.

I sensed constriction inside my chest, the anguish of knowing what to say without knowing how to be. I was ready to pay any price to discover LIFE!

I looked for hints and answers. Marx, Kafka, Nieztche, Ionesco, Sartre, Proust, Camus, Artaud soaked with lots of Greek mythology (in French!) inhabited my late nights, emphasizing the absurdity and woe of life. Shakespeare brought a little buoyancy for dessert, just a sideline. A "Yes!" gusted inside with a book called Siddhartha, by Herman Hesse. I may have been thirteen… Though I knew nothing about India, its recollection was unquestionably familiar. This was a story of a lost time still alive in my soul. Nostalgia. How to get there now? How to retrieve its essence?

Who explains synchronicity? Apple falling off the tree, gently touching the ground.

Breaking loose

Sitting in the airplane, I reclined in relief. Rings of restriction disappeared. My belly sensed all limitations were unreal. Life was ahead, to be discovered through my own experiences.

I was sixteen. My first European tour.

Paris was home. Memories of times I was intimately familiar with. I walked with assertiveness, intuitively knowing my way around.

Visiting Frankfurt. Ancient pain, imprints of terror and panic. I hid in the hotel room, crying while my friends wanted to go shopping!

In the South of France, I visited Nice and Carcassonne. The landscape evoked remembrance, harmony and commotion. Like the colors of a painting I had seen once before and knew to be significant. I wanted "that" attunement inside, so clear and yet, indefinable, evasive, unsubstantiated.

Returning to Rio: I needed to leave Brazil as soon as possible. Though I could not identify my dormant potential yearning to unfold, I had heard the music that caressed it.

I investigated possibilities to study abroad, just as a good excuse to leave. I shared my intention with Angela, a dear friend. I appreciated her creative spunk and I was determined—she "had" to come with me. We sent our portfolios to a Graphic and Industrial Design school in Milan. We were both accepted. Angela left, while my father vetoed my plans. I was held back, but not discouraged.

I was working as a colorist with Leon, an illustrator who had an artistic agent in Milan. We played with a tender complicity. He understood my desire to find new ways, encouraging my traveling and offering practical leads to make my transition possible.

Many late nights silk-screening tee-shirts provided for part of the money I needed. Recognizing my determination, my father finally offered his support. The only arrow was pointing OUT!

It was January, hot summer in Rio. My suitcases were packed, the ticket booked for the next day. My belly broke out into one large blister. I was leaving my family, my friends, my country, and I knew there was no return.

My boyfriend, who was in medical school, cared for my wound understanding my emotional state. There was gratefulness and appreciation for his love, simplicity and down-to-earth way, the joy and sweet moments we shared so young, the experience of making love for the first time, our efforts to find ways to meet and relax. He offered his heart with tenderness, my first love-dance partner. I cherished his sincerity and dedication. His sense of humor always brought us back together after intense fights, his care was nurturing, and yet... I sensed freedom and love beyond our meeting.

As I passed the gates after customs, I saw my parents, my brother, a few friends, my friend-sister Claudia, and my boyfriend, waving in line behind the glass doors. Next to them was Leon, who only made himself visible after I had passed the passport control, smiling as I walked towards the airplane. With laughter, I received his love and encouragement. He had a special way to be charming. Delighted with this farewell, I approached the plane waving with mixed sadness and joy. The melting of deep emotions warming my body assured me that my blister would clear up soon.

Arriving in Milan, Angela was waiting at the airport and hosted me in her tiny studio near Porta Venezia. The first days were fully engaging—winter fog, cold nights, snow, subway rides, a new language.

Through the eyes of my Brazilian conditioning, life had to be physically pleasant; I needed to be in nature, hear the birds singing, feel the sun in my skin. Gray days and austere aesthetics made me turn inward. In the beginning, this experiment of physical and emotional breakthrough was uneasy. My mind did not comprehend my decisions. However, something else was guiding me and I disregarded inner voices shouting old lullabies.

At university, our teachers dressed up in butterfly ties and suits, way different from Rio de Janeiro professors. I enjoyed the universe of art and experimentation.

Studying was not a priority, just a good excuse to keep me away from the familiar, and create the space I needed to identify my deeper needs. Though I had to keep on my feet to follow up with reports and homework in a language I was just learning, I did well and learned fast.

Leon moved to Milan a few months later with his wife, Joy. Their friendship supported my grounding.

Finding an affordable place to live was challenging. At first I stayed with an Italian family. Soon I got bored.

Searching for another option, I met a Russian woman who worked as a diplomatic translator and had a nice room to rent. I decided to move there. However, her late nights with different men and suspicious activities forced me to move out in a few weeks. Temporarily, I stayed at Leon's house while looking for another place.

Unexpectedly, my boyfriend came for a short visit. I was overwhelmed by this surprise. It was difficult to stay open to him while trying to create space alone to find out what I really wanted. The day he left I went to the emergency room at the nearby hospital with unexplainable belly pain. Again, my body was sending me signs that my mind was beginning to listen to. Though I doubted that we were to get married as planned, we kept our relationship going through letters and phone calls. His love was so faithful that it was difficult for me to trust my own needs.

During summer time, my mother came for a visit. For the first time we met out of the family context. We went together to Paris and London, enjoyed museums, movies, walking and shopping, laughing as good friends. Recognizing a level of connection beyond mother and daughter, we started moving from animosity, fights and complaints to meeting with respect and understanding.

She was concerned with my housing situation and insisted that we go check out a Christian monastery with rooms for rent. Certainly the last place I would choose. We rang the bell… A conventional nun dressed up in a costume opened the gate. She guided us into the atrium of a large building. My mother, who was learning Italian, proudly explained that we were looking for a room. There was absolute quietness. The nun whispered the rules: no coming in after ten, no visitors, no music, no this, no that. Suddenly, we simultaneously burst into a loud laughter. Unable to contain our giggles, we walked fast towards the door, leaving the nun astonished. Soon after this event, I rented an apart-hotel, tiny and clean, in a convenient location.

I started experiencing a freedom of movement that made my focus in life clearer. I had to work to afford doing what I liked. Through the Brazilian Consulate, I got jobs for simultaneous translations during diplomatic conferences, trade shows and legal consultations. Well-paid and easy work considering that I fluently spoke five languages. By then, I had learned to speak, read and write in Italian. I was growing up in an independent and adventurous way.

I enjoyed traveling, using my *Europe on Ten Dollars a Day* book. In London, I delighted in Persian and Egyptian art, Carnaby Street, as well as Sir John Gielgud playing Shakespeare. Paris was my hometown and any excuse got me there. Around Italy, Florence and Venice especially got my attention. The beauty of the landscape and art nourished my soul.

My closest friend at university was from Bolzano, a small town in the north of Italy. Sabine had a strong German character, but we got along well beyond the differences of our cultural upbringing. We had a great time studying together. Milan was a gray and boring town in the eyes of a young girl from Rio. Looking for sun and ocean where there was absolute fog, serious people rushing downtown, and a prevalent snobby attitude in the air was frustrating. The Alto Adige was far more enjoyable. Fresh air, open spaces, horse riding, long walks, beautiful homes, learning to ski, enticing landscapes, good wine to start the day, or a strong cognac to warm the blood. To make it better, there were often train strikes. A good excuse to extend my stay!

During my holidays with Sabine, I spent time with one of her close friends. He was a warmhearted man who worked as a court journalist. We moved together from court cases to informal restaurants in the countryside, and occasionally stayed overnight in a rustic mountain cottage. Wood stove, snow and coziness. As I did not speak German, I had the opportunity to flavor life without my mind's interference. I enjoyed his fluidity and spirit. Being with someone with whom I did not have much in common, no future plans, no romantic dreams, but sharing the joy of silent moments, making love, cooking, appreciating the beauty of remote nature, being lazy... I started to experience inner spaces that I had long known were possible. Each day was fresh.

PASSION

One year had passed, and I was expected to return to Brazil.

My boyfriend was finishing medical school and getting ready for our marriage. I felt pressured by his determination. I doubted that I would ever find what I yearned inside. I knew nobody that could relate to my longing. And more, there were no words to define what I was looking for. Yet, a taste of possibilities had been awakened, scratching a surface that started to reveal under layers. Curious burning. There was kindness and appreciation for him in my heart, but not enough. I wondered why was I so demanding, what did I really want?

Through being in contact with people from different countries and cultures, and being alone, I started to look at my conditioning and relationship with my parents. They thrived in opposite qualities, but were not able to recognize their differences as an opportunity to support each other and their potential as complementary. Their relationship never found a point of integration, but often became discord and irritation. I observed from a distance the source of my conflicts with them and consequently, with myself, and began to settle my own grounding independent of their opinions and expectations.

My basic nature stretched to both sides—fast movement and relaxation, action and care, intensity and softness, creativity and receptivity, risk-taking and acceptance, mind sharpness and intuition. Life seemed to request that I take in both sides, integrating their beauty and lessons. Understanding that my personality traits could be traced to their influence, education and genes was freeing and challenging. The next step was to bring awareness into situations where I felt trapped, and take responsibility for my choices.

Did I need to have a particular environment to flower on my own way? Could I just use different opportunities to learn? I was not sure.

My boyfriend insisted that we get married at the end of the year. In uncertainty, I decided to return to Rio at the end of November. I sensed our marriage was not going to last long! Anyway, I enjoyed shopping for our new home, getting Italian-design dishes, decorations, bedding, and what else I could afford and ship in a reasonable container.

At the end of October, Angela invited me to drive to Paris with her Italian lover and a common friend. An opportunity to say goodbye and enjoy my last days of "freedom." A Volkswagen Beetle, autumn landscape, the beauty of the South of France. Enchantment! A few hours on the road, and suddenly, the engine stopped! The car was towed for repair and we decided to take a train.

A few days in Paris, the simple pleasure of walking in this city was enough to energize my body and rekindle my heart's contentment.

As Angela and her boyfriend had to pick up the car, our friend stayed with them, I decided to return alone.

In the midst of holidays, Milan was dead. Leon and Joy were in Lucca, a small town in Toscany, for a film festival. Over the phone, they encouraged me to catch a train and meet them there.

I arrived for dinner. Friends, artists, agents, an ambiance of creative flair. Only then, Leon told me there was no room for me to stay. "Something will come up. Now you are here!" After dinner we went to a nightclub. As I was dancing, Joy announced that she had found a room for me.

Derek, an artist from Barcelona, had been given a suite with two rooms. I had seen him from far away autographing a book. An elegant tall figure wearing a fur coat over jeans. His presence had an impact that called my attention, neither hiding, nor showing off.

We were introduced under the lights of the dancing stage. He smiled with a sense of approval. I was twenty years old, rather slim, dressed in a stylish flowing skirt and black high-heeled boots. We walked to the hotel together. It was cold and he naturally embraced me. He was charming, friendly, and unusually familiar.

At the hotel, we entered a majestic, baroque, large suite with two bedrooms and a small entry. There were four beds. My host came out of the bathroom wearing perfectly ironed pajamas. I innocently laughed. I had never seen a man in pajamas, moreover with such a sophisticated attitude. He was a bit embarrassed, trying to be polite to the young girl who had showed up in his bedroom. He was then thirty-two. We were both a bit bewildered, but only for a few moments… Fast enough we were naked in bed discovering the sweetness of touching each other. In a flash I thought of my future marriage and decided to enjoy this one-night stand. We made love with gentleness, and a passion that I had not experienced before. I was memorably relaxed.

That night soaked my yearning. Suddenly there was no longing. Natural simplicity erased wonders. Timeless time. I rested within. Unexpectedly, I was invited to the gateways of my heart and pushed further. My soul bathed in serenity and murmurs.

The morning after, we walked around appreciating the beauty of autumn colors and the walls around the old town protecting our meeting. We were not strangers. We sat quietly holding hands. Surprisingly, he asked me to marry him. We had hardly talked until then. His voice was determined. I had heard from Leon that he was more of a playboy, who had many women. However I knew he was sincere and we were to live together. I said yes, firmly and clearly. I explained that I had a ticket to return to Brazil and planned to get married in a few weeks, but had no doubts that he was to be my husband. He smiled and hugged me, turning me around in the air. The blur of colors washed my mind. We rested on each other's arms for a long while.

What was to be my first "one-night stand" changed the course of my life. Derek lived in Barcelona, his hometown, however he decided to return to Milan with me. We drove back with Leon and Joy.

We moved together into my small studio. I called my boyfriend in Brazil and announced my change of plans. I told my parents that I had met the man I truly wanted to marry. I hardly knew anything about him and could not give many details. I was doubtless. That was enough.

Derek stayed with me for a month or so, and we moved into a larger apartment. Then he went to Barcelona to pick up his car and some of his belongings. He had decided to keep his apartment there for occasional holidays. Meanwhile, I went to Rio.

My state was of passionate clarity. There were no explanations needed as the facts were settled with no room for negotiation. My boyfriend was hurt. I was caring towards him and certain that this was the best for both of us. My parents were too astonished to make further comments. I wasn't open to hear anyway.

I had experienced my heart's infinity and wanted to live in its vastness.

Magic in the Air

Derek and I got married on a snowy day in Bellinzona, Switzerland. We arrived late. The judge had left the courthouse and we traced him back home.

We celebrated the event during an informal lunch at a local restaurant and later with a dinner at a friend's house in Milan. Derek's parents and mine, Leon and Joy, another couple of friends, Angela and her boyfriend were our guests.

I had resisted the idea of a legal marriage, as I believed love could not be bound by a social agreement. Our life bond happened the day we met. No need to make it outspoken. There was a sense of privacy and intimacy that I wanted to protect. Derek insisted. Coming to appreciate his intention, I agreed. When we formally said yes to this commitment, I felt relaxed and embraced in an unexpected way. He was my husband, and I understood in my heart what this vow meant. I was ready to honor it for life. Rather than bound, I was freer and lighter.

Derek gifted me with an exquisite piece of art-nouveau jewelry. Its delicacy and beauty symbolized the life I saw ahead for us. The natural pendant pearl and the diamonds sparkling around it brought a new awareness to my heart. There was a special attention in my movements when I wore this necklace.

This day opened to years of discoveries in intimacy and love, and a lifetime of keen friendship. I was "on track." There was a sense of destiny and rightness beyond concepts and my mind.

The following months brought moments of alertness, electrifying excitement, ethereal pulsing. Passion, porous love merging without bounds. Trust unveiled absolute and flawless, making me taste the essence of tenderness, forcing me to listen to undulating quietness inside.

We moved to a beautiful apartment in the outskirts of Milan. Surrounded by gardens, a distinguished setting with a clubhouse, swimming pool, tennis courts, and restaurant. A truly bourgeois lifestyle. But we were not settling for that...

A few months later I suspected to be pregnant. Exciting! Derek was delighted and had already chosen names: Sarah or David. Finally, I got my period, and felt relieved. From there on, the idea of having a child didn't catch our desires. We were fulfilled with each other, rather enjoying our intimacy without extra company.

Our life was passionate. Derek invited my sexuality into flowering. Making love was natural, tender, ardent, spirited, blissful. Our rhythm was essentially fluid. We worked through the night, cigarettes and whisky on the side; at sunrise we had breakfast, a bath, and then made love until we slept in a warm embrace. The mornings in Milan were often gray and foggy. Days were for walks, meeting friends, making love again, playing tennis or hanging out together. This bohemian life style fitted us well.

Derek spent his days painting, I decided to complete the last year at university. My graduation thesis was on "The effects and psychological influence of colors on human behavior". This research used different cultural elements, from ancient times to modern-day advertising, to understand the effects of color on the body, emotions and mind. It presented various experiments that reflected specific reactions to the spectrum of colors. I dreamed of an ideal community where design and graphic arts would support a healthy life, rather than seduce and conquer for profit. My projects intended to bring more sensorial acuity into daily life, and develop new flexibility in thinking patterns. I planned to integrate the aesthetic of primitive cultures with the resources of modern technology.

Soon my idealistic views met disappointment. After a few job interviews, it was clear that I had to find my own way. I decided to focus on photography, also part of my training. The power of my images was to be unconstrained.

Socially, we related with an elite of artists, writers and publishers. Our conversations were work-related and stayed polite, superficial, mostly political or analytical. We often received written invitations to formal parties with precise time of arrival corresponding to the time when the risotto would be perfectly cooked. The guests knew to wait at the door, only ringing the bell exactly on time. Funny and absurd. I missed my Brazilian girlfriends, and human spontaneity.

Once during an exclusive party at a friend's house, we both got bored with the diplomatic tone of the conversations. It was a large house in Padova, made with heavy stones. We went to the bathroom, locked the door, undressed, filled the huge bath tub with warm water and jumped in, sure that our hosts were wondering about us...

Derek was irreverent with life though genteel and gracious. We shared a sharp sense of humor. His intelligence captivated me.

During summertime we drove to Barcelona. I loved its lively spirit. We both savored warm days and cold drinks outdoors, a few friends who had no set time for dinner, and would come to visit unexpectedly. We considered moving to Spain; however Franco was still in power and Derek had a clear political position against his government. His writings and illustrations were known for their spiky criticism and he was not welcome in the country.

During one of our vacations we visited Salvador Dali, who lived in Cadaquez and was Derek's friend. This little town was enchanting, and windy! Dali's universe was as absurd as his paintings, in tune with constant motion and perceptions beyond logic. During this visit I recognized that many of our artistic friends lived in a permanent state of neurosis; their expressive cosmos was disjoined from their lives and emotions. Where did life and art meet? I could see that extraordinarily talented artists were not at peace, did not live a satisfying life. Though art had always represented the most profound insinuation of life's mystery, and the creative process fascinated me as a life path, I was really interested in LIFE. I listened to Dali and his voice was disconnected from his heart, his mind was fast and bright as one can be. However, there was no silence, no rest, no human warmth, no sense of meaningful connection. Questioning and wondering were incited in Cadaquez. How to live from the fullness of my heart?

Derek had reached a peak in his career, praised by publishers and art critics. My young impetus despised his pride and success, provoking his soul to find what would be really meaningful to live for. Certainly not fame and recognition. I did not know any better myself, but intended fiercely to keep looking, until there were no doubts. I was restless.

One day I looked at his illustrations and felt in my body that I could paint exactly as he did. While Derek was out for a few hours, I took a large Schoeller paper and started using watercolors in his manner. Easy! I don't know if my motivation was jealousy, empathy, or the savor of the future on my lips.

There it was, in a few hours! His style was unique and sophisticated, with the éclat that I had magically captured. I placed the illustration on top of his working desk visible from the entrance.

Derek came back accompanied by a well-known publisher, a snobby and selective man, who was hiring him to illustrate a book about the Inquisition. I was surprised by his visit. In a Milanese ultra-polite way, he said "Piacere, tanto piacere, Signora Sio!" He followed by emphatically commenting about this new painting. Derek looked at it for the first time puzzled. I was quiet. They sat on the living room to discuss the details of the publication. Derek signed the contract.

As the publisher left our home, Derek looked at me mystified about the painting. Intuitively, he knew my mischief. He had never seen me paint before, except for well-defined graphic design projects. Arrogant and provocative, I said, "See, anybody can do what you do, even I can do it! Paintings are dead as soon as you finish them. You can only be unique when you are alive!" He disregarded the point I was trying to make, astonished and pleased to recognize my gift. However, I was inquiring into the possibility of living every moment of our lives with the same sensitivity that his images expressed. I was desperately trying to push us both beyond being "artists," towards being artful humans. Could we use our resources of intelligence and sensibility beyond the confinements of a painting? Could we set our core priority towards the quality of our lives, our love, our learning to be free from others' recognition, expectations, demands, and the value that we attached to these parameters? I sensed the gap but could not articulate it, nor envision how to bridge it except through destructive criticism.

He encouraged me to continue painting. We shared long nights over white canvas, letting the forms reveal our feelings and intentions, wonders and dreams, ideas and discoveries, going to sleep with the pleasure of creative birthing.

His book about the Inquisition was published a few months later, dedicated to me. It included an illustration of a burning witch using my body as a model.

Milan was a conservative town, inclined to intellectual and artistic endeavors. Our friends were much older and the Milanese style was rather formal. At twenty-two, enjoying red overalls from Fiorucci, that was not much fun...

In the evenings, I played Signora Sio going to concerts, the Opera, elegant dinner parties, wearing long black velvet capes, fur coats and charming hats, French silk dresses, high heels. I felt imprisoned in this social role. Caught in the narrowness of a culture that had well-defined limitations, I could not see my way through it. I could not see myself expanding on ongoing terms in that environment. I was awkward and unsatisfied, experiencing depressive moods, not knowing in which direction to move. I had everything: a man who adored me and who I adored, a nurturing sexual connection, a beautiful apartment, work I loved, a lifestyle with leisure, a maid to care for my home. Though my life with Derek was vibrant and fulfilling, I felt isolated. I could not relate to ambition, a career, planning for a family or building up a "concrete" future like everybody else. I wanted to live in nature, enjoying a simple life with creativity and easiness. I called that being "real." The same old voice inside was cooking for changes.

This inner state of dissatisfaction started to manifest in fights for silly reasons and sudden high fevers, leaving me tired and a bit delirious.

At that time, an accident taught me a useful lesson. While cooking a roast beef, I was rolling a large piece of meat inside a pot filled with boiling oil. In a moment of distraction, the fork slipped from the meat and the oil splashed on my face causing severe burns. Derek took me to the hospital for emergency care, and for a few weeks I had a blistered face. Being young and beautiful I was used to get looks of appreciation. Suddenly, with a swollen burnt face, I observed other people reacting towards me with avoidance and disgust. How fast the change! I realized the ephemeral quality of the body, the illusion of identification with physical traits, how relationships were established according to judgments from appearances. This incident motivated me to look beyond the surface, further inside. Whenever I sat somewhere in a public place or in meetings with friends, I searched for the emotions behind the faces, the perceptions beyond the aspect of the physical body. This turned into a constant exercise; just looking, straight into the core, letting the outer dissolve and reveal the original face. I started to detect subtleties of moods, the lies of social conventions, the heart's desires behind the façade, and to pay more attention to my own judgments.

As the winter extended way too long for my Brazilian body, my mind would go into sudden pirouettes of despair. I dreaded those moments, looking for reasons that would justify such dissatisfaction. I blamed it on the too-cold weather and the fact that life in a city was insane at a basic level. Once a year, when the cold and snow were overwhelming, I flew alone to Brazil to soak in the sun, bathe in the ocean, satisfy my need for intimate friends. I missed Derek, but returned recharged.

Derek's working visa in Italy was tied to an advertising company in Treviso, a town near Venice. Each month we "had to" spend a few days there to update his visa.

Charming time: walking through the canals, observing the melancholic look of residents in synchronicity with the weather, listening to classical musical concerts outdoors in Piazza San Marco. We eagerly waited for our monthly outing, sometimes adding a few extra days in Tuscany. We stayed at El Toula Relais di Campagna, a refined bed and breakfast in the midst of a winery: linen sheets, silver trays for breakfast in bed, crystal glasses for the best wine, gourmet food, and the serenity of the landscape. These days of indulgence and pleasure refilled our reservoir of energy, making it easier to endure the gray days back in Milan.

We lived richly though our income was unstable. Derek's work was unpredictable, but we had no concern for the future. We trusted our creativity in a natural and uncompromising way. Our expressive waves pour onto paper and our daily life, consuming our energies with totality and joy. We had no time to be bothered with mathematics. We never considered any savings nor calculated our expenses in relationship to what was on our bank account. We took decisions from a space within that was expansive and teeming with possibilities.

Derek used to say that it was necessary to spend in order to have empty hands open to receive. We did abide by this rule! Once we ran out of food, no cash to fill our gas tank. We lived for a week on the bread that was delivered daily to our door and billed at the end of the month, and many bottles of Veuve Clicquot champagne that we had stored for special occasions. Suddenly, a contract was finalized and we had enough to live for another year.

Our home was decorated with care for the objects we chose, antiques, art pieces, and rare, out of print, art books. We appreciated the best of everything. We drove an Alfa Romeo, dressed impeccably, ate deliciously, drank the finest wine. Derek had a noble soul, his gestures were magnanimous and legitimately kindhearted. We were both at ease in refined environments, but simply embraced restrictions with a playful attitude. This way, that way, we danced together.

Three years after our marriage, Derek came with me for a vacation in Brazil. We flew to Paris for a few days on the way to Rio. We were happy absorbing the vibrancy of this city, its eclectic environment. We indulged in movies, exhibitions, concerts, bookstores, and late night pubs for an Irish coffee.

Sitting at a cafe at Rue du Bac, we shared our desire to move to Paris. We had signed a six-year lease for our apartment in Milan, and that meant "commitment." It was unthinkable to break a contract, as we would have to pay for one year's lease. However, our dreams did not account for practical details. We had decided to move to Paris!

We enjoyed the mountains and the ocean while in Rio. Having Derek "home" with me, meeting my friends, was comforting and added a new dimension to our relating.

Derek returned earlier to Milan to meet a work deadline, while I flew to Barcelona to visit a friend and his parents. A few days later, he let me know that he had been invited by the director of Larrousse to move to Paris, with a two-year contract to illustrate a series of books. Our moving expenses paid, great salary, work he loved. We were exhilarated.

I was floating through Barcelona and the winter did not matter. Arriving back in Milan, Derek picked me up at the airport and we went directly to a restaurant to celebrate our luck and future adventure. I remember walking in Brera, so drunk I could hardly see straight. Arriving home we made love all night. Sleep was not needed in such state of contentment. Life was showering on us!

The best came a few days later. We were considering how to approach our landlord. He was Fellini's assistant, living in Milan and often spending time in Rome. A bit uptight, he was a kind man in his early forties, though his movements and behavior mimicked an old man. The phone rang and, surprisingly, he was on the line. Cautious, looking for words, he asked to come and see us. We were curious... Shy and embarrassed he explained that he was moving with his family to Rome and needed to sell the apartment. He was forced to break our contract and as a compensation for this distressing request, he offered us one year's rent. He asked if we could leave within the next three months. Oh! He would also pay for our moving expenses. He understood the inconvenience and was very sorry, but would do his best to make things easy for us.

We barely kept up the conversation, trying not to laugh.

Derek signed the contract with Larrouse and I flew to Paris to look for an apartment.

I sat at the same cafe I had been with Derek a few months earlier and opened Le Monde. My eyes caught an ad for an apartment for rental *"sur la rive gauche, pres de la Seine, 86 Rue du Bac."* I called immediately. The agent was showing the place in a few hours. Looking out the glass door, I saw the large carriage entrance on the building across the street with the number 86. A typical Parisian building, solid, made with stones from a few centuries before, large windows and the care that was usual in that neighborhood. I drank my café au lait, counting the minutes for my appointment.

I walked up the stairs to the first floor. A few people were already waiting in the atrium. I was twenty-three, light-framed. Though I was wearing a fur coat, my presence was not solemn. The other candidates were much older and "respectable." The rent was high, more for a family budget than for a young couple.

As the door opened, I was sure that was to be our home. This beautiful apartment was especially grand: two oversized living rooms and two bedrooms, all with beautiful marble fireplaces, several windows opening to a courtyard, lots of light. The kitchen was large, bright and clean. The floor plan was perfect for us, though not suitable for families with children. I was glad to watch others leave.

I filled out the application confidently and our contract was settled an hour later. I called Derek from the café. He said, "I knew you were going to find our home fast!"

We received a substantial check from our landlord and went out dancing to celebrate. I was fast to hire an international moving company to pack our house. As I opened the door to the movers, a tall guy asked me to call my mother, I could not be "la signora." What a thrill to see this huge truck taking our things away.

We drove our car a few days later, enjoying a vacation in the south of France, stopping leisurely to visit Picasso's museum, and quaint villages under the soft sun of the Midi.

Paris

Paris in the springtime was pure indulgence. Sun warming up, the colors of fashion, voices humming, outdoor cafés, the verve of different characters, from kids to old beggars, the cycle of life renewing, reminders of hope and merry possibilities. Buoyancy was in the air.

Our new home was decorated with beauty and intent. On a crazy impulse, I transformed the living room with a coat of dark maroon paint, which gave a distinctive feeling to the space, enhancing our art on the walls. As there were several large windows on both ends, and mirrors above the fireplaces, the color accentuated the light coming in. I moved onto lacquering our bathroom with royal blue.

Derek was absorbed in his project on the history of France, a series of Larousse volumes illustrated by different artists (still in print nowadays). His work was truly appreciated and he was glad to get paid regularly. That was an unusual deal for an independent artist.

On a daily basis, we found balance between work and relaxation. We enjoyed idle time, often outdoors. With our cameras, comfortable shoes, good bread and cheeses, we headed to the countryside. We enjoyed making love in the woods. Unexpectedly, wildly, gently, rolling over the leaves on the ground, unconcerned about anything else.

Museums appealed to us. Especially the Jeu de Paume, the Louvre, Rodin's home, Monet's house, a lovely jewelry museum on the outskirts of Paris. We sat for hours in front of single paintings, letting their colors and magic sink inside. One of my preferred places was the Musee des Arts et Metiers, near the Bois de Boulogne, containing ordinary objects created with outstanding sensitivity. At each visit, I wondered about the people who created such works of beauty and love, sensing that they might have been truly content.

Surrounded by the culture we enjoyed, with magnificent forests close by, resting in a lovely home, I wished nothing else.

Helo, one of my closest friends from Brazil, moved a few blocks from our house. Having fallen in love with a Dutch artist, she was commuting between Paris and Amsterdam. Her presence was emotionally comforting. Still intimate friends, we were discovering the nuances of relating with our men with the passion we had longed for since our teenage days.

Life was offering many avenues for expression and learning. I went back to university to study architecture and then anthropology. I painted, colored Derek's illustrations and created my own professional photo lab at home. I presented my portfolio to a prestigious agency and was immediately hired. I loved photographing fashion shows, portraits, and exclusive sports. It required sharp awareness to respond to situations with swiftness and accuracy. Besides there was a human contact that I cherished, artistry and flexibility that fitted my personality.

A lightness of being bathed our lives and opened deeper realms of love and intimacy. I wondered why so many people looked unhappy. I had completely forgotten my own discontent, not so long ago.

Our marriage was a communion of bodies, interests, heart and soul. I got lost in the darkroom, developing my photos, producing prints with special effects, perfect contrast. Derek painted away through the night. Our togetherness weaved independence and merging. We had our separate worlds of discoveries, learning and creating, embracing our individuality without restrictions, at the same time, melding in the sweetness of our love.

Sex was the core energy for expressing our love and life force, as well as inspiration for creative impulse. Derek's paintings were elegantly sensuous. The gentleness of his images was alluring. They transmitted his body's sensibility in a direct and instinctive way. Each line and color reflected precision and fineness. Making love was like painting. Our bodies drew colors in the air. I could see it! Magnificent compositions, glowing, swirling effects. Motionless motion stirring ancient passion. He was my companion-lover-friend. I had no doubts that we were made for each other and we had met at the right time.

First zen master

While living in Paris, I met people who stimulated my senses and inspired creative inquiry. My attention was focused in my inner world, and through fine arts I connected with a sensitivity that guided me inward. Photography, painting, movies, and dance opened the doors to the universe of beauty and awe that facilitated introspection.

I loved going to movies, frequently watching three or four in a row. The effect of the accumulation and stimulation of images flowing through my vision field opened an extraordinary inner dimension.

I continued to paint and was invited to exhibit a series of women's faces expressing the many nuances of my own feelings, at an art gallery in the Marais where they all sold. Even though that was a major achievement for someone my age, I did not make much of it. My sense of inner purpose was my only guidance.

Enjoying the variety of my assignments, the vivacity of journalism through imagery, as well as the contact with other professionals, I photographed for two international agencies.

I met Chi at *Manchete*'s office, the largest Brazilian weekly magazine with European headquarters near the Madeleine. My friend Helo, who was working as their fashion correspondent, introduced us formally. He was their photographer in Paris and was looking for a temporary substitute while going away for vacation. She suggested that I take the job.

Chi was an unusually striking man, Brazilian Indian blood, tall, long black hair, large dark eyes, yummy lips, a musketeer in style and charm. His seductive appeal was absolutely relaxed. I remember the beauty of his hands and the deliciousness of his touch on my hair as we met for the first time. He had a way to see through women, and to call forward their hearts and beauty. He saw my longing for expansion, the potential ahead, and called me on. I responded resolutely.

He handed me the job without great explanations. I said yes, without thinking. When something comes my way, if it feels right, I receive it…and then reflect. Chi's trust and confidence set me on. Soon, I realized that I wasn't prepared to work in such a professional level without guidance. No space for mistakes, within deadlines and the responsibility of a large publication. Too late…

I found myself inside the Louvre Museum with the task to photograph a seasonal exhibition of rare Impressionists. Chi had handed me a Hasselblad large-format camera, umbrellas for shading and reflecting light, and sophisticated light meters, but I was not quite familiar with this equipment. I had a few hours to complete my job, working with a special permit given to selected publications. One chance to get it or lose it.

There were two other photographers working in the same room. I carefully observed their movements, watching them from a distance, then coming closer and asking a few questions. I had to play safe and make sure to get the photos with the right light, angle and definition. The only way was to use ten times more film than regularly needed, repeating the same shootings with different settings. To my relief, several full pages with large color photos were published on the next issue of *Manchete* with my name in the credits.

This episode encouraged my self-trust and pushed me a step further into daring to learn through life experiences, bridging my intuition with professional skills.

Years later, I heard a story that clearly illustrated my feelings at that time.

> A master thief was getting ready to die soon, and needed to pass on his lifetime skills. He was the king of thieves, a magician with rare expertise, known to have entered the royal palace and stolen the most valuable jewels without leaving a trace.
>
> One day he approached his son, "Tonight I will teach you my art." The son was excited. The night came... Father and son left the house together moving cautiously towards the king's palace. The father requested total silence. The son was to follow his steps without questioning anything. So, they climbed walls, tricked armed guards, passed ferocious dogs. The son was breathless... Suddenly they were inside the royal chamber, and the father with amazing aptitude opened the door of the large vault where the jewels of the kingdom were secured. The son was mesmerized by countless precious stones, and dazzling diamonds. His father moved fast... In a split second, he was locked inside the safe and his father was out making a loud noise, banging the door of the king's room. Left alone inside the dark vault, he heard the king calling for help.
>
> The father escaped easily and went back home laughing. He was deeply asleep when the son returned, furious, screaming at him, "How did you do that to me? I could have been killed inside the palace, I am your son!" The father smiled, opened his eyes and asked "Didn't you manage to get out? That is the way an art is transmitted. I trust you, my son! From now on, you take my place."

A few other tasks with similar challenges were left on my plate. Somehow I managed to find my way out and learn.

When Chi returned, many of my photos had been published weekly. He was cool about it, like the thief father. He had no doubts. The fact that he trusted me so bluntly deepened my own trust. From there we became close friends.

Chi was intentionally charming and inviting. He had a girlfriend, Lena, a beautiful Brazilian woman who I also had met through Helo. However, it was clear that he spent time with other women and she accepted it as his way.

We started to spend days together, photographing around town.

One afternoon, I went to his apartment to eat and rest. He lived in a small studio on the fifth or sixth floor near the Beaubourg center, and we had to climb by stairs. Once up in the house, it was natural to be lazy. The afternoon turned into night and our resting together turned into a sensuous play. We made love without any other consideration of circumstances, others or time. I fell into profound silence. He held me for hours in a gentle embrace. His energy was strong and still. This was new and different than my connection with Derek.

Chi had a large bathtub close to his bed, and as I opened my eyes coming back from this astounding state, he was inside the bathtub waiting for me. There were no words, we moved like cats. My body was light as a feather and opened from inside out. We spent a long time in the bath. As I write now, the physical memory of this evening is back in my cells, as an initiation. It was like a new color never seen had been presented and my eyes could not yet distinguish it, much less name it. I was taken by this silent spell, lost in time and space. At some point, we moved out of the water, and I said goodbye. Certainly, way past midnight...

I drove home and found Derek over his paintings, curious to find out where I had been. I described my experience to him, he held me on his arms and I felt his love beyond conditions. He told me that Lena had come to visit me in the afternoon. She was hanging out in the house waiting for me, it was getting late, so she called Chi to see if he wanted to meet her for dinner but he did not answer. They both had a feeling that we were together. In an intuitive impulse Derek and Lena decided to go out for dinner and later to her house. They made love in a friendly way. She was cute and pleasant to be with, but not really his type. Derek was glad to receive me back home. We went to bed cherishing our love, relaxing into opening to others as well.

Chi played with confidence and inner calm. Our first evening opened the space for further intimacy and time together. His presence nourished a space within that I always knew existed but had only tasted before in sadness, never in joy. Joy had always been rather bubbling, fulfilling, energizing. Never empty or silent. He pushed me into a still point, serenity, soulful depth. His body had an aliveness that turned me on absolutely, and yet, in the background, there was silence.

It was enough to lie together for hours. I did not understand what "that" was, but drank of its nectar. He played with me straight and sincerely, at the same time, provoking and seducing. When we were together his presence was undivided.

One evening he called me late, must have been close to midnight. Derek and I were painting as usual, and Chi asked if I wanted to come and spend the night with him, we had not seen each other for a while...

Mid of winter, snowy night, I drove to his house, climbed the stairs and a woman opened the door. Surprise! As I came in, Chi gave me a warm, long hug and took me directly to bed. Candlelight, soft music, silk sheets, bubble bath, champagne, and a few other women elected for that evening in concert, easy and mellow, sharing the beauty and sensuality that this man was able to create. My mind did not question anything; my spirit was being showered with the kind of lessons and sense of love that was not in my schoolbooks, nor in my parents' conditioning.

Back home, I was happy to be with Derek again. Resting in bed together, he held me close to his chest and caressed my hair while I shared with him my discoveries and feelings. He was twelve years older than me, and had had a life full of adventures. His maturity in relationships made him understand my needs and impulses. He was able to support me with care and easiness. I felt loved, embraced and unafraid to explore.

While making love with Derek I experienced intensity that made me lose the grip of my sense of self; delicacy and constant fluidity. It was sensuous, absurdly natural, strongly sexual, intentional, passionate, alive. It was tender, very tender. We expressed our love with gentleness. We made love often, fresh and anew. Our closeness was boundless. No footprints left behind, but a sense of continuous life impulse moving through. We met in balance and expansion.

The stillness I experienced with Chi was attractive in a different way, magnetic, magical. His presence called upon silence, though he was very active. Making love was never focused on sex. It happened unexpectedly. Sometimes after we had been together for several hours, or in the midst of a photo development session, or after we had fallen asleep for a while, waking up early in the morning… It was impossible to ever anticipate anything with him. He did not allow it. He continuously created unpredictable situations, making it impossible to hold on to expectations. His ability to break patterns of thoughts was impeccable. If he was conscious, or not, of what he offered, it did not matter. I received his presence in gratefulness for what it encouraged and appreciated the insights it provoked. There was only one-way to be with him: openly and non-judgmentally. If I was open to "see what may happen out of this situation," then…

Being with Chi made me more aware of my own aloneness. Our meetings were complete every time. I was fascinated to discover what was revealed of my inner works at each time I responded to his invitations.

Being with Derek made me more fluid and open. Our connection was eternal. There was no way to choose one over the other; my heart was touched impartially.

Chi called my spirit forward and reinforced its connection with my heart. The silence I experienced in his presence was new for me, and yet an ancient feeling. Finally, the longing, the search for something unknown, was fulfilled in those moments of intimacy. He often stayed inside my body without ejaculating, simply merging, embracing, going nowhere, resting in alertness and presence of body and heart. The delight of relaxing into dissolution, neither going nor coming, but the turning of passion inwards, collecting energy instead of dissipating.

Sometimes the four of us would go out together, as Lena relaxed with our relationship and enjoyed when Chi was available for her. Lena and I were good friends and made it light and caring, sometimes calling each other to find out whose night it was to be with Chi. He was a master, gracefully holding the scene. Our lifestyles supported this flow.

One afternoon, we agreed to meet in front of the Beaubourg. He took me by the hand and we walked slowly towards the Halles, a prostitution zone. Chi seemed at home with the women who nodded at him. We stopped to chat casually with a few of them, and were invited into a bordello where he had an acquaintance with several young prostitutes. We spent the afternoon there while clients would come in and out. I noticed my judgments and how easily I tended to classify others in a glimpse. I noticed my fears as well as my delight. In the course of conversations, I suddenly captured the "spirit" behind prostitution. The women we met were simple at heart. They talked about their jobs with ease, sometimes with sarcasm, or boredom, sometimes in tedious details. I heard passion and courage, a giving out that required a quality of love. Yes, I dare to say that.

I recognized the innocence and naturalness of these women. They had a matter-of-fact quality that surprised me, no romanticism about sex, often pleasure and fun, indifference or disgust. There was frank authenticity on the way they moved and talked. We left late into the night and went for dinner. No comments. The experience was enough.

On another occasion we walked around the Jewish neighborhood. Revelations of faces and characters, men with their religious hats, chatting with neighbors, children and mothers, restaurants that were an extension of their homes. We walked through the streets unhurried, waiting for a captivating scene to place itself in front of our eyes. Later, coming back to the studio, there was always an enchanting time in the darkness. Our reflections sprouted into images, revealing more than forms and light, the uniqueness of our sensitivity and keenness of observation.

Every time I went out with Chi a new level of awareness related to conditioning became further evident. I sensed myself more able to absorb and relate to a wide range of people. There was a fresh understanding growing underneath my mind settings. At every opportunity I dove deeper, impossible to back off. I wanted to know what was undeniable.

One morning, lying naked on the small terrace above his studio, summertime in Paris, he told me the story of a Japanese Zen master. Though I do not remember his words, they evoked intimacy and recognition. The sun touching my skin, his voice touching my soul...

Chi's beauty, trust, craziness, defied my heart. My first Zen master.

LONGING

My relationship with Derek grew passionate, loving, and as sincere as we knew how to be. We dared to look and talk without fears.

He made me experience the connection between my heart and my sexuality. I often cried while making love, tears of softness and joy. My heart tingling with a myriad of subtle sparkles, resting in serenity. My thirst was satisfied. His sexuality was assertive and fully given, and yet extremely gentle. He preserved our intimacy with care, sometimes with jealousy asking questions or making comments which revealed he was comparing himself to Chi, feeling threatened by the "other man" who sexually shared his woman. In the richness of our experiments we were closest friends, romantic lovers, creative partners. In trust, we danced together. He was my husband and life companion.

The candor and subtleties I experienced through sex seemed unusual. I often fell into silent spells, content in stillness. I was inexplicably blessed, gifted with a sense of overflow and natural expansion. I had never met anybody who spoke of such experiences. Surely none of my friends. No books I had come across mentioned the potentiality of sex as a doorway to the lightness of the spirit. What else could be more eloquent than expressing love through the body?

We both enjoyed spontaneity without schedules—free of obligations, we moved with no plans. We dove into life headfirst, creating experiments of pleasure, joy, amusement, surprise, investigation. Yes, sometimes we met in pain, confusion and disagreement, lacking of emotional maturity. However, sooner after a fight or difficulty, we cuddled on each other's arms, remembering the love that brought us together. We expressed what was alive inside unconditionally. I trusted that our bond was unquestionable. It was unnecessary to protect our relationship, hide, or make myself smaller in order to keep him at my side. This certainty encouraged my impulses to explore well-hidden feelings, expose my fears, discover who was this woman growing up in this foreign land, wanting eagerly to understand life's intricacy.

I had an instinctive sense that there was more to life than the happiness we lived in. A hunger inside scraping my belly. Yet, I still didn't know what would satisfy it. The old longing to further expand, to fully embrace the vastness of life's potential...

Derek's open mind and intellectual sharpness offered me support to inquire, doubt, and cope with life beyond rules or expectations. In gentle moments, he confessed his fear of losing me, concerned that I might decide to move back to Brazil. As this was the furthest possibility in my mind and feelings, I disregarded his comments.

During these years I came across Henry Miller, Anais Nin, Simone de Beauvoir, Sartre, Lawrence Durrell, as well as artists like Antonin Artaud, and Robert Doisneau, who lived during the Second World War. Oh! Suddenly an explosion happened while devouring all books I could find by these authors, especially Henry Miller and Anais Nin.

Henry Miller stirred my guts. He urged the rawness of life without boundaries, the ardor of love disregarding social rules. He expressed vibrancy in the fullness of body-soul, defying, provoking, taunting. His verve was enmeshed in blood and sweat, dance and songs. His voice was loud and lucid, non-compromising and piercing. He endured the consequences of his integrity with dignity and humor. Pain was as real as joy, laughter as resonant as tears. He pointed to the unreality of limitations, pushing the boundaries of life to the realms of undivided pleasure, and unwavering commitment to honesty. I wanted to live in the wideness he implied.

Anais Nin invited the subtlest layers of my sensitivity to surface, find expression. Her sensuous femininity was familiar to my heart and my skin. The texture of her emotional responses balanced warmth with fierce perception. The alertness of her responsiveness to life merged with the delicacy of her body. The nuances of her love translated natural joy.

These people dared to LIVE! I wanted to meet them. Sadly, I found out that Anais Nin had died a few months earlier. Henry Miller was on his late eighties and living in California. I wrote him a letter and received a formal response from his caretaker, letting me know that he was in retreat. On a separate piece of paper, a note: "Live with passion!" hand signed Henry Miller. These words lit my heart.

I recognized passion as the imprint of love in action, reflection of courage in words and movements, expansion without tracks, trust unraveled from the core, unwavering soulfulness.

Relationships recalled my passion. Other people's spark ignited mine. Therefore, I chose to be close to people who expressed love and beauty in inspiring ways, who touched my heart while sharing simple tasks, who untied fear with the softness of their care and appreciation. They enticed me to dare, risk, look inside, feel, respond, break loose. As nothing else made any sense, my life priority was relating.

The idea of communal living had been with me since long. As a teenager, together with my closest school friends, I planned to bring this concept into practical reality. We conceived of a place integrating our professional skills, care for each other, utilization of natural resources, and social consciousness. We discussed details of housing, organization, work and relationship between us. This vision stayed alive within.

One evening, I talked about it with Derek. We both were ready to share our creativity, love and intimacy with others. Where to start? We decided to invite Derek's closest friend, for our first communal experiment. A risky adventure!

He was a movie director from Barcelona with a fierce character. He made me laugh heartily with his charm, irreverence, non-conformism, and remarkable intelligence. His response was, "We may never talk to each other again afterwards, but if we don't try, we will never know what our friendship may stand for. When do we meet?"

We arranged for a marathon week in Barcelona. Living together twenty-four hours a day, we moved with hearts and guts, allowing our desires, sexuality, words, movements, and feelings unfold without censorship. We faced different emotions: jealousy, fear of losing each other, anger, insecurity, vulnerability. We doubted each other's intentions and sincerity, as well as acknowledged our courage bypassing the mind's social control. We were in the mid-70s and did not know of anybody else moving along on the same lines. My friends in Brazil were married, having babies, and our European friends were rather conservative. Pioneering as evolving human beings, we had no instructions to follow.

Returning to Paris, we were happy to be alone again, a bit hurt, unsure how to proceed, gentle with a new space inside and in between us, more emotionally attached to each other. I sensed our love was strong and grounded, and trusted its solidity even when we were shaken by what was still unclear, undefined, in process.

During the winter of 1977, one of my childhood's friends visited us for a few weeks. We talked again about our intention to live communally. One afternoon, I went to work and upon my return I realized that Derek had made love with her while I was away. I was surprised not to have been included. She was very beautiful and had a furtive personality. I felt left out, uncomfortable with their approach. Derek's sensitivity was mostly alive when relating with women, especially while making love. Beyond my jealousy, I saw his beauty and fullness when he was free to follow his sensuous impulses. As much as I was trying to free my creative and love force, I was supporting him to find his own way. Using this opportunity to expose our concerns and wishes, we talked through it and met again at the core of our love for each other. Our experiments were solely guided by an inner sense of direction.

After this incident, a great desire to change something struck me again. I was still looking for the essence of love, and ways to live it intently.

I considered city life as insane. Country living always talked to my heart. I started looking for bucolic villages in France, for places where it would still be possible to live at a slower pace.

In my search, I read about Greece's smallest island called Anafi, reachable by boat only, with about three hundred inhabitants. Suddenly the impulse to leave Paris got clear. I talked to Derek about it, but he was not enthusiastic about my plans. I talked to Chi about it. "Go! Try your own way, do not waste time doubting!" As I was sitting naked in his lap, hugging me warmly, he transmitted the trust I needed to decide. He held me for the longest time, his silence became mine, indicating the space within from where my own guidance would always come.

I decided to take the Orient Express train from Paris to Athens, and invited Ela to come along. Derek was sad, surprised though supportive. My idea was to find a place to live very simply and invite him to join me as soon as possible. He could keep doing his work long distance. We were irritable. There was sadness in his eyes when we hugged at the train station. I was crying, but determined.

January. We took very little with us, imagining the ocean and sunny landscapes. We left Paris in the midst of a blizzard, and as the train moved east, the snow got worse and worse. As we reached Yugoslavia, the train stopped. Cold, so cold! We spent uncountable time in Yugoslavia locked in a room guarded by policemen; our passports were taken away and we had no food. Outside the window was pure white, impossible to distinguish earth from sky. Our adventure turned into a nightmare. Finally the train moved again. Most people were angry and hungry, the bathrooms were disgusting...

We arrived in Athens, exhausted, confused and starving. I missed Derek and Anafi sounded too far and primitive. We were dying for good food, a warm bath, and a cozy bed with fresh sheets. Without second thoughts, we took a taxi from the train station to an elegant hotel in town. We registered for the night with advanced payment.

I danced madly in the huge room, finally out of the jail-train. Room service and gourmet food! Civilization was well worth celebrating! We drank wine and slept soundly. I walked around Athens confused, trying to figure out how to go to Anafi. A few days later I called Derek. The phone connection was scratchy. He was upset, asking me to go back home. Abruptly, we got disconnected. I was left suspended in the air, feeling I had taken a stupid decision. Why had I left anyway? After all, what did I have to complain about? I was living in a city of beauty and charm, my husband was waiting for me, I had a gorgeous home, and work I enjoyed. Ela did not know what to say, she was also in a moment of transition and doubt. We went to the ruins of temples and walked around town, nothing interested me.

I sat quietly in front of the ocean, looking at the waves. Unexpectedly, a profound peace touched my body, my heart turned liquid, and my mind stopped chatting. I knew then this state was within me. I had to learn to access it. That simple! I was looking all over for something that I had within. I did not need to go anywhere, but keep finding the way back inside! I thought of Chi...

We took a bus to the airport and bought a charter ticket back to Paris a few hours later.

Arriving in Paris, I was ashamed. I could not justify my frustrated adventure. I needed a few more days to digest it before going back home. Ela and I took a student's room in a tiny hostel near the Sorbonne, with a shared bathroom at the end of the corridor. In a state of shock, I slept long hours.

A few days later I called Derek. He picked us up. Such a relief when he hugged me, warm and welcoming.

We reconnected with much tenderness. We held each other and talked. I did not know what I was looking for, more than this love and connection that I delighted in. As we started to make love, our bodies became surprisingly violent in an enticing way. He held me with dominance and strength, as if that was his way to say he missed me. I was startled and shaky. He was bold, wild. My body shook with pleasure and pain, no line in between. Another inner boundary was crossed. We played out our emotions in a theatrical interaction, embracing new expressions of liveliness. I experienced breakthrough with fierce totality, ups and downs and ups and downs!

I was unsure how to restart my life in Paris. I knew I had to learn to access this inner space of silence beyond circumstances. That was my secret key. Chi had opened the door to my own home! Now I had to live inside it.

Just after my return from Greece, my body started to concern me. I was constantly exhausted and had intense sciatic pain. I disregarded those signals until they became loud enough to disrupt my daily life. Forced to go see a doctor, I discovered that I had an extraordinary high level of white blood cells, indicating an infection. I spent the following months trying to determine what kind of infection I might have. Unusual examinations and medical tests showed no precise results, though I was still always tired and my blood count was getting worse.

My daily routine included several hours a day in different hospitals. I took my Nikon with me, developing an interesting series of black-and-white photos in the waiting rooms. My attention was called to faces and bodies in pain, apprehension, desolation. As I was born in Brazil, I was directed to a hospital specialized in tropical diseases, where I was most often the only white person in the room. However, nothing was detected there either.

From being impatient and wanting to find out what was disturbing my body's usual healthy flow, I moved into a reflective and restful mode. While waiting, I relaxed. During these hours in limbo land, I started to connect my emotional moods with my state of health and became convinced that they had a close relationship if not an inseparable link. I was a stranger in a place of demand, ambition and competition. I was stretched between the push to strive for success on one side, and romantic family ideals on the other. I did not belong to either. No wonder why my body was refusing to move.

As I sat and waited, I observed the lack of human care prevalent in medical facilities. Cold, practical, "scientific" attitudes did not help me to be more in touch with my own body, nor healing for that matter. I examined my life choices. I let the longing scream inside louder and gave it more space on a daily basis. I spent time walking alone, sitting for hours near the Seine, or in the gardens, at Rodin's house-museum, drinking from the beauty I so much appreciated.

My back was increasingly painful, to a point that I could not work anymore. I was directed to the American Hospital in Neuilly to receive a series of physiotherapy sessions, including massage and breathing exercises. I drove there every day and each session lasted about two hours. The woman who cared for me was probably in her forties. From my young perspective she was old! Proper American look, short curly hair well kept with stiff spray, makeup and a nurse-type uniform that made her incredibly unattractive. Her smile was superficial and phony, and her tone of voice hit me too high. However this woman had a transforming role in my life. She guided me into slow movements coordinated with deep breathing techniques. Her hands were soft and supportive and she was determined to make me feel better at each time, making sure in her broken French that I was perfectly following her instructions.

As I moved into my own body with increasing awareness, I started experiencing a new sense of pleasure. Often during the sessions I got into an orgasmic state, which the woman seemed to be unaware of, continuing through her instructions, unfazed. I opened my eyes and looked at her in awe. How was it possible to have an orgasm without a partner? In fact, guided by this homely woman? I had no logical answers, but a tremendous curiosity to discover the basis of my own health and body functioning was set in motion.

I came out of the sessions stoned out! This trance-like state hit me every time. I sat on the wall near the parking lot and gazed into the trees, listening to the birds around. Every color was scintillating. The sounds were precisely distinct. The sensuality of the surroundings surprised and pleased me.

For a few months this routine engaged my senses. My attention focused on observing the subtleties of my body's chemistry, moods, modes, emotions, the way my mind judged and reacted, selected and decided. How did these waves influence my body's health and performance?

Slowly my body movements started responding to direct sensorial perceptions, rather than following mental or emotional impulses. I naturally paid attention to where my feet stepped, how my back extended or bended, how I carried my photographic material on my shoulders, and everyday chores turned into dance rather than mechanical tasks. With the combination of these treatments and self-observation, my flexibility increased, my body started to heal, become more aligned and enliven. The pain subsided, the blood tests reverted to normal, and I was ready for summer!

This experience opened to a lifetime inquiry into the body and subtle energy realms, and later to my professional development as a healer and teacher.

During this time I met Therese Bertherat, whose revolutionary work emphasized the connection between the physical and emotional bodies. Her "anti-gymnastic" method integrated William Reich's understanding of energetic anatomy with somatic education. Recognizing the uniqueness of each individual, her approach supported neuromuscular reorganization focused in postural realignment, balance, flexibility, and spontaneity. Bringing awareness to breathing patterns while encouraging verbal expression of sensorial perceptions, the body was invited to move with precision and gentleness, engaging forgotten muscles thus generating new neurological pathways, and releasing accumulated tension in the different layers of tissue. I further learned to listen to my body's messages of pain or easiness, and bring attention to areas of discomfort or emotional memories.

I continued to dance at the studio of Joseph Russilo, an extraordinary teacher. His skills and dedication inspired deeper levels of emotional expression, making inner grace visible through the movements of the physical body. Dance became a doorway to the silent space, one that I could access alone and at all times.

As my health was restored, I resumed my work as a photographer with ongoing assignments.

Hot air balloons were fashionable. I was asked to cover an international balloon competition, taking place in a country club a few hours south of Paris. I spent a few months following their adventures in the air, resulting in a series of articles with beautiful photographic illustrations. My weekend trips to this club paced my life with flair and pleasure, strengthening my professional confidence. The ambience was festive, even when we had to sit for hours waiting for the right wind to blow. Meanwhile, good wine and stories.

The club members were enthusiastic, mainly men and couples from a traditional, aristocratic background. They were particularly curious about this young woman, competent, playful and able to maintain a conversation with ease in a foreign language. From both sides there was attraction and learning. I enjoyed bathing in different environments, losing boundaries and identity. After long waiting, when the balloons were finally able to take over, I had to be on my feet and fast! Eyes full of marvel, I was absorbed by the intensity of the course of action. Fire, wind, jumping in at the exact moment! Then…calm and silence while flying majestically over the land. A nourishing extravagance of pure joy. I sipped of this luxury. My photos were admired as unique and published in several magazines. Indeed beautiful, audacious shots with colors in movement, evocative abstractions, unusual. This series brought me an invitation to work for National Geographic.

I loved my hours in the dark room, at home or with Chi, learning to be meticulous with precise details while printing, refining my expression of just the right light or composition. I published a book with a series of photos taken at the Marche aux Puces. These were pictures of colorful beauty, taken with infrared film. Sensitive to the heat emitted from objects, they revealed nuances of unusual colors, which translated the various degrees of heat emission, beyond what the eyes could see. These images had a mystique and peculiar magic. People, dolls, objects, seen anew. That was a big deal for someone as young as I was, Paris being a place of artists and great competition. I tended to despise outer recognition, sensing it as an obstacle, hindering what I felt to be truly meaningful for my life. I had seen that prestige and success did not bring great happiness, so could not see the point of following that path…

During the years I lived in Paris I was enrolled at the architecture university. I chose to study buildings and sociological structures in primitive cultures. One of the teachers was an earthy man in his mid-forties, who had traveled all over the world. His enthusiasm, idealism and intelligence made me drive a long way for his classes. This course was particularly interesting—it reinforced the intelligence of community. I was fascinated by primitive cultures, for their sense of harmony and human respect, simplicity, beauty, intelligence and creativity, qualities that continue to this day to be meaningful in my life.

For two years I went to university. Nevertheless, as much as I added information and experiences to my life, at twenty-four years old nothing seemed to hit me at the core. I kept hoping that sooner or later I would find my own expression, my own language.

Besides my study, work, home and love life, I often sat alone and closed my eyes. That state of rest gave me comfort. Simply closing my eyes and doing nothing? Stopping going around busy with all there was to be done! I had no choice. This sitting quietly happened on its own timing, it took over my will as a compulsive non-action. Nothing I ever came across referred to this state, except the description of catatonic and comatose people.

As this was happening more and more often, I doubted my mental sanity and felt scared. I could just be crazy, and sooner or later would be locked in a madhouse. That was a perspective that I perceived as a real possibility. Fearing others' judgments and actions, I started studying psychology to get familiar with the types of people I might get locked in with. I decided to get further acquainted with the works of the mind, and what madness was about.

I met a remarkable man, Bruno Bettelheim. He was in his sixties, soft-spoken; a truly kind man, who had been working for years with children medically classified as schizophrenic or dysfunctional at an unrecoverable level, often called "poupee de chiffon" which means "rag doll." These children had no motor coordination and no speech ability, so were kept in hospitals with minimum care, usually alive for a few years. He developed a program to support those children, based on his belief that their disease was caused or induced by lack of understanding and love in their early years. He believed these children needed an environment with a different consciousness that would give them inner confidence to relax and open up, learn and grow. Several families participated in this project—mostly well-educated couples. They adopted some of these children, offered their love and care, and reported regularly on their development, with Bruno's guidance and support. All was documented progressively over several years, and gathered in a series of movies. The resulting images were unforgettable. Children and their original families were interviewed initially, though most were not able to speak or move at that stage. Later, the children were followed with their new families, living in the countryside, actively participating in simple tasks such as milking cows, making bread, cooking a meal together. They were interviewed as they became more integrated, able to speak and move, revealing amazing intelligence and insights. These documentaries reinforced my feelings and views of society, as well as the need for alternatives that were more humanly caring, able to recognize the soul beyond the manifestations of the body and mind.

I was not aware that my restlessness reflected the longing of my soul trying to break through the confinement of mind-body identity. A dull feeling in my chest, my eyes looking for something I could not find, the meaningless actions that I observed myself performing, and the spin of the mind doubting it all. At the same time, a delicate thread of beauty touching my body from inside, obliged me into silent moments of awe and rest, a susceptibility into the future that was not yet ready to be exposed.

Different circumstances increasingly intensified this yearning. Guided by strong intuition, I "coincidentally" participated in events or met people who were instrumental in realigning my life and taking me to a turning point.

One evening, Derek and I went to a book presentation. Inside a crowded room, I spotted a woman who called my attention for her penetrating dark eyes. In her late thirties, she looked like a gypsy with Parisian sophistication on top of it! We met like sisters. She was the author of the book being presented *"The Girl Who Ate Flowers,"* as she explained, an account of her life. She was born a gypsy in Yugoslavia. Traditionally given for marriage at an early age, she was determined to evade this arrangement and move on to search different ways. Within her tribal customs, to be able to leave, she needed to ask permission from her grandfather. However, if he agreed and she decided to leave, she would never again be allowed to go back to her original family, or any other gypsy tribe. That was a lifetime decision with no return. Her grandfather blessed her and she left before meeting her future husband. She walked across Europe alone, managing to cross borders, tricking policemen, begging for food, eating flowers and whatever she could find along the way, sleeping outdoors, hiding wherever she could find shelter. Eventually she arrived in Paris. For a young child, that was a long way. She was found begging on the streets in Paris and adopted by a family with means to send her to school. Her presence infused me with inspiration.

On a regular basis, dance performances induced me into states of awe and silence. I went to a Japanese traditional Noh and Kabuki theater, and was impressed by the transmission of energy during the acting. The faces and bodies of the actors hardly moved, and yet a universe of feelings and intentions were conveyed. I merged with this transmutation of energy without action, merely evoked with inner intention. I returned to the theater several times, to sip over and over the subtleties of the actor's performance, their faces and expressions delicately vehement.

I stumbled upon a traditional form of Indian dance, as I was invited to a private home to view Ms. Louba Schild perform Kathakali. Her exquisite sensitivity awakened empathy, provoking tears of recognition and sadness, strangely mourning a joy long lost. This was an all-night long act, with brief breaks in between, when snacks and tea were offered. Throughout the evening, people maintained a quiet attitude. Soft voices, not much talk. Silent appreciation made me feel at home and relaxed.

The beauty and dignity that I sensed during this dance mystified my eyes. I recalled reading Rabindranath Tagore's poems as a child, in my mother's handwriting. While she was pregnant with me, she translated his poems from English into Portuguese, collecting them into a booklet, which she later bound with a nice leather cover. Again and again I read through those pages in rapture. The same climate, the same sweetness of the words now translated into gestures and movements. I remembered reading *Siddharta*. Those images and landscapes were imprinted in my heart. The vision of those dances brought those dormant memories alive. That night I decided to go to India.

During this evening, I met a woman who had traveled overland to India and Nepal. She looked like a plain French housewife. However, what she described stirred my guts and imagination. Yes, I knew what she was talking about. The ambiance of India was under my skin. The music, the movements, nothing was new. Ancient reminiscences were revived. I sensed that soon I would break through my life-dream, another reality was piercing my consciousness.

Derek had no interest in these events. My comments and vivacity did not ring a bell for him. India, Japan, that was too far away. He was involved with Spanish political affairs, Franco's death and power struggles for free Catalunya, his paintings and our life together. And, by the way, what are we having for dinner?

On the other hand, Chi listened to me attentively, without saying much. Together we photographed a few performances, including a superb Japanese modern ballet. A couple with their bodies painted white, wearing only a cache-sex, danced on black stage with shimmering light arrangements. Their minimalism and plasticity captivated my attention. Their focus and precision left me breathless. Our photos translated the grace of their movements in a dynamic way, describing body forms, nuances and shapes, light and shadows, as magical lines in the air. I went to this staging four times. The awe of orgasmic silence embraced me again and again. I wanted that intensity of beauty permanent in my daily life.

These experiences overlapped my master thesis on Anthropology, "Rituals of Birth and Death in Primitive Societies," another chapter on self-inquiry.

Earth, Water, Air and Fire, elements of transmutation and integration, were the core of my research and writing. They represented doorways in and out of this visible play, and had been used since ancient times to welcome and release the spirit's dance within the body. Different worldly rituals converged at the point where community represented integration of body, heart, soul and spirit, where individuality was accepted as a reflection of the multifaceted vastness of essence. The wisdom of each one of these particular energy aspects supported the grounding of life in its many forms, as well as pointed the way back to the source when the time was ripe.

I started to bring awareness to these natural cycles inside my own body. I recognized an array of symbols constantly pointing towards creation and dissolution, and the need to let life guide me through their momentum.

These classes brought my life more into focus, opening my senses to recover the vastness of LIFE. I started to observe daily cycles of completion, each let-go, even in simple things like eating a meal, kissing my lover goodbye. Ordinary acts of creation, my paintings and photos became more meaningful; my attention to minute details grew in refinement.

As a child, I was unusually aware of death. I carried a sense of urgency within, sensing I could die suddenly. I consciously focused in completion, choosing to do what I wanted and felt was important regardless of outer demands or requests. I kept my cupboards and room always clean, writing my thoughts and needs for communication, whenever it was not possible to convey them personally. During these years living in Paris, this need for completion intensified. A redefined sense of priorities pointed to questioning again and again. What if I suddenly die? What is at the core? I kept asking and daring to experiment.

JUMP

Autumn afternoon... I was driving to a photographic assignment in the countryside, a few hours south of Paris. I noticed someone standing by the side of the road. Nothing around and no traffic. Slowing down, I saw a guy holding a walking stick, long hair, penetrating blue eyes, loose clothes, a small bag crossed over his chest. I could not guess his age. I offered him a ride, letting him know my direction. He silently nodded, opened the door and sat next to me. He closed the door carefully. I said hello and accelerated back on the road. He said nothing. For an hour or so we drove, no words, he looked straight ahead. His face was ancient, some wrinkles, bright eyes. At first, I was uncomfortable with his lack of communication or connection. Soon, I relaxed. His silence was making me breathe slower. Arriving to my destination, he nodded again and got out of the car, kept walking straightforward on the road. The strength of his presence stayed with me as I moved on for my work assignment.

I was at an international parachuting competition as a photographer on duty for the agency I worked for. There was a festive atmosphere preceding the flight. All men and women gathered in their gear, excitement and jokes. I had already received instructions for this adventure, and the helicopter was waiting for me. The guys cheered me up. They called me "bicket" which means a young female deer, as I was young, slim, and could move very fast to catch speeding images. It was a small helicopter and I sat next to the opening from where I was to jump. We took off, flying over beautiful fields. I checked my cameras. Just a moment, I am in the air!

How long was it? I have no idea. The shift inside happened in a split second. Visions, feelings, insights, flooded my consciousness in that second. Pain in my chest, a gutsy scream cutting the air. Pungency.

No photos! I was just there, coming down as the parachute opened, I can't remember how. A new perspective of life was coming my way, as fast as the ground was approaching. No more photos, no more observing. Metamorphosis. In that instant, the throbbing of life bursting out of my pores demanded urgency.

The spaciousness around converged into a sense of core priority. I needed to simplify my life. In a flash, I perceived my lifestyle as senseless, my life force constantly outgoing. I wanted to live in nature, have more time to be quiet, less outer distractions, more space to focus on my inner world, nurture intimacy. I was an observer behind my Nikon's lenses, capturing events, forms, movements, but not living at the center of my own life. I was scared to stand alone, and follow my own sense of direction, especially because it was not outer, or goal oriented. Rather demanded introspection, letting go, exposure.

This was an abrupt wake up call. Its sound burst my ears. My eyes were wide open. My own voice arose from deep inside, clear and doubtless. Time to make a shift! There was no how, no logic…

I landed in the field and got picked up by the staff, no talking. I went directly to the hotel. I was in tears. I collected my belongings, no goodbye. I got into my car and drove back to Paris, though I was supposed to work for a few more days.

Driving at high speed, my mind was swamped with astounding clarity. My body was hypersensitive. Turning point. My heart beating fast, thoughts racing, my whole life got reduced to one point. I have to maintain the vibrancy of this honesty at any cost. I must sustain the courage to live in this lucidity! No drawing back.

I drove directly to my agency to drop the films. I resigned formally from my work. The owner, a friendly Dutch guy, thought I was joking.

Speed driving through town back home, not always easy to find a parking spot, there it was! Close enough!

I walked up the stairs to my apartment. I opened the door excited with the idea of surprising Derek two days early. He was usually eager for my return whenever I had to work away from home. He was focused over his table and colors.

I don't remember how we hugged and kissed. I remember walking into our room and looking at the bed undone, seeing objects that didn't belong to me lying on the side. It was obvious that someone else had slept there.

Liza, a close friend from Brazil, had been our guest for a few days. As I got an unexpected call to photograph this parachute competition, she stayed at our home while I was away.

As I entered the room, I sensed that they had made love in our bed. My heart sniffed the pain and the breakthrough of what would come next.

The following hours and days imprinted my memory as a waterfall of events, emotions, conversations, shock, despair, excitement; absurd, overwhelming intensity. I can't remember the sequence of facts.

They had spent a few nights together. Everything I believed, expected, knew and trusted suddenly disintegrated at light speed. I was impotent and, paradoxically, helping this process. Like throwing myself from a high bridge, knowing that there would be water under, at the same time, feeling the vertigo of the fall.

Facts didn't have consistency. I talked about my feelings, my certainty about another way of living, relating that was sincerely meaningful. My voice was like a river flowing towards the ocean. I was trying to convey the taste of that split second of awareness, the parachute fall, the light that came through my consciousness and I did not want to shut again. I was a madwoman, bubbling with words that did not mean much to them. Neither Derek nor my friend seemed to relate to my cascade of sounds. Though I hoped to be met in this impulse, I did not try to fit their mind setting. It was a long night. There was no way back. I had stepped towards that moment, and now I had to face it. Yes, I was afraid, sad, angry, clear, confused, strong, and vulnerable.

We spent time together, made love in different combinations and emotional tints, shared what we envisioned, voiced what we feared, and protected what we could not deal with. I was pushed ahead of time and the sway was stronger than my mental or emotional resistance.

A week or so may have passed. I felt immense complicity with Liza. Her beauty, innocence, openness and sensuality touched me in a way I had not experienced before with another woman. I was sincerely welcoming her into my life and relating with Derek. I could see the richness and potential of us living together. Derek continuously affirmed that he was with me, and Liza would soon leave to Brazil. But I was not relaxed. There was a hollow feeling in my belly.

We talked about moving together to the countryside, possibly in the south of France. I meant it. I took action to turn this dream into reality. As a photographer, I had worked with Kenzo and other fashion designers and had special access to their warehouses. It would be easy to fill a few suitcases with fashionable clothes, and sell them in Brazil. That would add some six months of extra cash flow, and make it easier to find another place to live more simply. I decided to fly to Rio with Liza, who was then due to return home. She would make arrangements to come back as soon as possible.

We left Paris on the same flight, both fragile, moving as if pregnant with a gentle secret. I could not imagine talking about these last events with anybody else. That was way beyond my friends and family's understanding or view of life. Coincidentally, Liza lived two blocks away from my parent's house, where I was staying. It was easy for us to meet and stay connected. May be two or three days later, we said good night at my house and planned to meet the next morning to go to the beach. I woke up expecting her phone call, but it got late and I did not hear from her. I called and the maid informed me that she had gone to the airport. I was surprised. Did she go to pick up someone unexpectedly? No, she went to Europe, her mother took her to the airport, reported the maid. Are you sure? Oh, yes, she had all her suitcases ready since yesterday...

It took me a few seconds to realize that she had left to meet Derek. When it hit me, I called him. He said that he did not want me to interfere with his decision, therefore hadn't told me anything about it. He asked her also not to talk to me about their plans. He was cool and distant, letting me know that he always expected me to leave him and return to Brazil. Now I had the opportunity to stay in Rio and go on with my life alone. He felt it was better this way, and he wanted to live with Liza. He asked me not to call or disturb them.

I could not believe that I was talking to the person with whom I had lived with for the last four years. Just a few days ago he had asked me to return as soon as possible, expressing how meaningful our life together was for him. My mind was twisted a hundred times. I did not know what to say. I felt empty, hurt, paralyzed. I cried in disquiet. Strangely, there was certainty that this shake up was needed for a shift to happen, for my aching finally to be transformed into consciousness. My gut feeling kept me centered through agony and deception.

Betrayal. I did not compare or evaluate myself related to Liza. We were born in the same town, a few days apart on a Pisces month; we had the same name, went to university together and were now sharing the same man. My connection with Derek was rare; he was the man I married, I honored that intention and was shocked with his behavior. Their partnership in deceitfulness dazed me. He had encouraged me to experiment and find my own way, and now as we were at a crossroad, he pulled the carpet from under my feet!

Crudely, I was shaken by this test. Derek's support and love had nurtured solid trust within, to a point where it was crystallized and irreversible. I could stand the pain and move on.

My mother was nearby while I talked to Derek on the phone. We had a psychic connection and I knew she was suspicious of my surprising visit. She saw me bursting into tears and came close to ask what was happening. I resuméd the last events. She listened, loving me with no comments. I told her I needed to be alone and did not want to be disturbed.

I spent about two weeks in my bedroom, which had a glass door to a terrace with views to a forest. Most of the day, I stared at the trees. My eyes were swollen. The maid would bring me fresh orange juice and leave it outside the door. I lost weight, feeling lighter and lighter. I decided to live this situation to its bottom; the pain was intense. My mind made efforts to see through the details, figure out solutions, possibilities, but there was pitch-black space ahead. Crying was all. I was irritated, desperate, angry, sad, hopeless, hurt, heavyhearted, depressed. My body was aching. Through these waves, there were moments of calm, especially late in the night when everybody went to sleep. I would go out to the terrace and lie in the hammock. It was warm and there was a flowering jasmine tree. Its sweet scent brought me back to a restful space, where I was clear, ready to move on. The next morning the pain nagged back. Waves came and left, I had no power to interfere.

As the days passed by, I started to see the events as detached from myself. There was my self-image in the middle of this plot, being active part of it and yet a spectator. I laughed alone in my room. Then, the next wave of sobs would come by and remind me of the beauty of the love I had shared with Derek, could it dissolve just like this?

In the same way that my meeting with Derek generated the impulse to let go of a planned marriage and a regular family life, this separation was forcing me into another adventure, not yet defined. I sensed the expansion of what was to come next.

One day, I woke up laughing, fresh and bright. I was ready to relate again. I had a few suitcases full of clothes to be sold and friends to connect with. I called my friends, but did not talk about what had happened, it was like a distant story.

Ela invited me to travel to Minas Gerais, with her brother. We spent a week driving and visiting small towns. My eyes were clearer, colors seemed brighter and I was looking at everything in a different way. I was skinny, and food had also a different flavor. I was gentle with myself. Life was just starting.

I photographed a diamond mine on the way. Even though I was using my Nikon again, I was not "behind" the lenses. I penetrated the images with my body, I was inside them. I sensed resilience and richness, increased patience and understanding. I listened with increased accuracy, finding newness in old phrases. I was not certain about anything.

I went back to Rio ready to return to Paris. I booked my ticket and called Derek to let him know of my arrival date. I asked him to move out of our apartment. He was surprised to hear my plans; he expected me to stay in Rio. It was clear for him that our apartment was still my home. He guaranteed they would move out before my arrival, agreeing to leave the keys with the concierge. I asked to talk to Liza but he said she did not want to talk to me.

Wearing camel-colored corduroy pants, a cozy cashmere sweater and my fur coat on the shoulders, way too loose for my rather slim body, once more walking towards the airplane, waving goodbye...

FRESH BEGINNING

Arriving at Rue du Bac, the taxi driver was kind enough to help lift my suitcases up the flight of stairs. The concierge abruptly informed me that my husband was at home. My heart fluttered, hoping that he would be waiting for me alone.

I rang the bell. The door opened just enough for me to see Derek's face behind the crack. He stepped out into the hallway and saluted me as if we had never been apart. However his words, his smile and the way he hugged me did not have the same energy. He was apologetic suggesting that I find a hotel or another place to stay. He did not let me in the house. My throat suddenly went dry. We discussed the fact that he had agreed to move out. That was my home, someone else was using my things, sleeping in my bed. I asked him to be reasonable, but he was not willing to negotiate. He called a taxi to take me to a hotel...

I went to a small hotel room near the Seine, a few blocks down from my house. I cried, and slept, and ordered food in the room, and cried and slept...

November, snowing and cold. One evening I went out to the English-style pub I used to go with Derek and asked for an Irish coffee. Its heat and richness gave me a lift. I walked in the snow to another café, this time to have a cup of tea and write, trying to get more clear. I wrote a letter to Derek and Liza expressing my feelings and trying to understand the recent events. Bottomless ocean of emotions and wonders, dreams and delusions, certainty and doubts, clouds and blue sky. The waiter kept asking me to pay for the couvert, as usual in Paris. At every request, I needed to order something else, and the night slipped by. When I finished writing the letter, the sun was rising. I walked out of the cafe towards the post office. Suddenly, an acute pain in my belly made me stop. I fainted on the street. I woke up with a woman holding my arm and trying to talk to me. She helped me into a taxi. I went to my hotel room, slept for several hours, waking up with the ringing phone.

Anne Sophie had called me at home, and Derek gave her my hotel number. She was a lively French girl and her friendship was loyal and sincere. We met for dinner and she invited me to move into her apartment. She had recently married and they were both dear friends. We had spent vacations together and shared many meals over the last years. Their house was comfortable and they were caring and supportive. My energy level increased and I reached to connect with other friends. I completed my master's degree in anthropology, realizing that the theme of my thesis was now entwined with my life experience. I was dying and birthing.

Chi encouraged me to keep moving with what was truthful inside. He used words and concepts familiar to my heart, though nobody else I knew could relate to. I knew he was pointing to the "right" direction: no direction. Wait…listen to your heart. We spent days and nights together, no holding, no future, no expectations, always surprising and loving, easy, enriching.

A few weeks later, Derek agreed to meet me. My heart still hoped for a shift. Looking into his eyes, I saw again my beloved. We walked hand to hand. I sensed our connection beyond time. Instead of feeling hurt and brittle, I was restful and strong. Our conversation was not relevant, understanding happened in between the words. Surprisingly, I was certain that we were not to be together anymore. I had glimpsed another possibility within. Life was delivering me a message that had no reference to mental reasoning. It was not black and white clarity, rather a spiral-spin taking me slowly into a different awareness of my choices. My love for Derek was doubtless, but the basic trust between us was broken and I could not mend it. I came to rely on my own sense of direction and was ready to take other risks.

I realized that Derek had an unusual ability to invite me (and other women) into ecstatic states of energy. He made love with the same totality that he painted. However, we did not know how to sustain that capacity consciously in daily life. We did not know that it required care and inner strength, as it pounded on dormant potential. We were suddenly inundated with extra life-spark and had burned ourselves with it. Observing our contradictions, search and inner process gave me clues to understand my needs, and make further decisions. Only much later I fully grasped the dynamics of our attraction, the complexity of our relationship and the blessing that it represented in my life.

Weeks later, Liza asked me to meet her at a restaurant. Could the three of us live together? She was ready to try. No, going back was not possible. We talked over dinner, then sat on a bench on the street, freezing, wrapped inside our fur coats. I embraced her as a beloved friend, but our lives had come to a crossroads, and we had chosen different directions. I was peaceful. We said goodbye late into the night.

I started looking for apartments to rent. It was not easy to find a studio in Paris, lines of people going up stairs leading to tiny cubicles. I could not see myself living in a box, looking at snow falling on the roof. Sometimes my dramatic mind would imagine moving into a studio and dying there, an easy solution! But not even that I managed, as by the time I applied for the lease, someone else had already been approved. This game was tiring and pushed me to explore other possibilities. I had desired to live in the countryside, now I was free to choose where to go. Hey!

Through Lena I met Bruno, a friend who lived on the flat above hers. He was going away for a few weeks and offered me his studio. I had some illustration work to complete and his place was just right.

Bruno returned and extended his offer to continue sharing his flat since he often stayed overnight at his girlfriend's. We became good friends. At the end of winter, they invited me over for a week at their countryside house. Perfect timing!

They came to pick me up. As I opened the car's door, there were five Persian cats waiting to share the back seat with me. Bruno and his girlfriend gave me a hug and helped put my suitcase inside the trunk. I was staring at the cats in a blank. They noticed something was off. "I don't like cats!" Bruno laughed. He had green cat's eyes... 'They will love you, come in!" His easiness made me relax.

Immediately, the cats came around me. Their long fur and soft bodies pleasantly touched mine. How could I have missed this seductive sensation? Their gentleness rubbed against my skin. I closed my eyes sensing gentleness, making friends with myself as much as with the cats.

Arriving at the countryside, the sun was setting, the colors were magnificently pastels, the smell of earth was stimulating and we went out to get wood for the fireplace. The cats moved with me everywhere. I dug potatoes and carrots for dinner. The fireplace was flaming. I slept in a large bed with the cats. These lovely animals taught me to trust my own softness. We were easy and relaxed with each other, going for walks, cooking and hanging out in front of the fire. By the time we returned to Paris, I was ready to move out of town.

A few days later I saw a photo in a magazine. I wanted to live there! The house pictured was located in Ibiza, a Mediterranean island off the coast of Spain. I walked to a travel agency, looked at some more photos, and bought a ticket. I called Derek to let him know that I was moving to Ibiza. He had been there several times. "You will like the place!" My plan was to go for a few weeks, rent a house and then return to pick up my household for the final move.

Bruno gave me a tiny kitten to take with me. I hid this small creature inside my handbag, not knowing that it was against the rules to carry a loose animal inside the airplane, nor considering the difficulty of keeping her quiet during the flight...

We landed safely late in the night, a few days before Christmas.

IBIZA

Walking out of the airplane, salty smell in the air, I was in the right place! I could not see much in the dark, but the ride to the hotel through bumpy roads, the fragrance of earth and rosemary was enough. Recognition.

I took a room with ocean view at a hotel in Santa Eulalia, roaring waves sound. Speaking fluent Spanish, I moved with ease. I had to hide the little cat, "No Animals Allowed" sign on the registration form. I had no idea of what cats like to eat. Milk, yes and Maria biscuits, but by the second day she was unhappy. Soon I found a neighbor with a child eager to have a little kitten.

Ibiza was a small village with a friendly and welcoming population. I started to connect with people on the streets, at the small health food store and at the cafes around town. It was exciting to be alone and explore a new environment, natural resources and a population who cared to conserve them. The native people spoke Catalan, which was Derek's mother tongue. I had learned the basics with him, and could easily understand it, speaking well enough to get by.

I met Ana walking on the beach. She took me to her "finca," a simple adobe farmhouse with a well outside and no electricity, where she lived with her five-year-old daughter. Originally from Barcelona, a single mother, she moved to the island following her desire to live closer to nature in a modest way. She designed and manufactured clothes, selling them at the seasonal market. Most local residents made their living selling merchandise to tourists during the summer and enjoyed resting during the winter.

We drove through the countryside looking for places to rent. She introduced me to hidden spots and warm people. I was thrilled with the beauty of the place!

I found a lovely house, on top of a hill between Santa Eulalia and San Pedro, both villages connected with the main road leading to Ibiza center. The owner was an old farmer who had lived there his entire life. In the rental agreement it was established that he would come every day around five in the morning to care for the veggies and fruits growing on the property and share with me his fresh produce, as well as almonds and home-made goat cheese. I was enchanted.

Prices in Ibiza were reasonable. I paid for one year's rent with the cash I had, keeping enough savings for food and other basics. Life was to be simple. I moved in with my small suitcase.

The house was made of adobe, thick walls, white, cozy and comforting. I was at home at once. Downstairs there was a large living room, an atrium, and a bedroom. Adjacent was the kitchen rustically furnished with a large wooden table, a stone sink, a wooden stove and a fireplace, which offered heating for the whole house. Upstairs was a large veranda and a bedroom, which became my retreat. Through a tiny handcrafted wood window in my bedroom I viewed a large almond tree, the rolling-down hill, sheep grazing, the ocean in the distance. Located about one kilometer away from the road, the silence was absolute.

As I settled, I called Derek and asked him to leave the apartment for a few days, so I could come in and organize my things. He agreed and decided to go to Barcelona for that time.

Back in Paris, it was cold and strange to be "home" after about five months. It was difficult to see the space I had shared with Derek turned into another scenario. I slept in our bed, crying again, but this time consciously acknowledging my part in the choices that led to our separation. Their behavior still hurt; however I was grateful for the opportunity that was forcing me to review my own choices.

I decided to leave all home objects and furniture, selecting only a few personal items and special gifts. I was ready to move on.

I said goodbye to Paris, walking around with immense attention for the beauty and richness of this city, sitting at my preferred restaurant and getting drunk with white wine over Belon oysters.

I danced full hearted to the sound of Ravel's Bolero, celebrating the space that served me as a home. My body expressed what was ready to dissolve. I had no idea if I would ever return to Paris, or see Derek again.

Vision

Back in Ibiza, mid January. I loved my new home! The heaviness of the walls gave me ground. Having no electricity offered quietness and the atmosphere to rest within. I closed my eyes and sat without concerns. Nobody to relate, nothing to do. No ahead. Collecting water from the well in a bucket and bathing outdoors, making bread everyday, cooking in the large old stove...

Sense of time was soon lost into the rhythms of nature. The birds woke me up, the full moon kept me alert, the dark nights cuddled me to bed, cold weather held me at home enjoying the warmth of the fireplace!

There was still sadness; at the same time, freshness inside. I desired nothing. I stared at the walls, appreciating the hands that built it.

The mail was slow and inefficient. I had no phone and no acquaintances in town. I rarely left the land. I let my body rhythms move me mindlessly.

The ocean at walking distance. My playground was a nudist beach set on a round bay with gentle waves. There I started meeting men and women who had left a "regular" life to experiment with other ways to create and relate. For the first time I assisted a birth. Beauty and rapture, seeing a baby coming out of his mother's womb, received by friends singing, welcoming this tiny body rather full of life. I helped to wash him in the ocean. Life was offering its bounty! No longer could I imagine going back to subways and traffic, shopping and rushing through crowded streets. My body expanded to include the landscape and the waves and the sky.

Paper and colors. I started painting again. Whatever would come through my movements and hands was unanticipated. Time vanished into creativity. Sleepless nights, elated by kaleidoscopic inspiration, letting the colors tell me about love, passion, pain, being a woman, distant lands, the songs of my heart expressed in thousand nuances.

Slowly, a distinct recognition of joy matured. Slim and beautiful, my body became increasingly alive and sensuous. I spent most of my time naked, either at home or at the beach. This sensation of physical pulsation spilled over my wellbeing. A new sense of vibrancy became tangible. Doubts subsided. THIS was what I was pointing to when I trying to share my love, THIS was what I was trying to define and find ways to express, THIS was more meaningful than art, THIS was ARTALIVE!

I had left formal art and was learning to transform it into artful living. Bliss was not hanging on the walls, but visible through the radiance of my eyes and skin. My emotional experiences no longer needed to be translated into images, but were rather fluidly washing my heart, and legs, and voice. My paintings released transparency and enchantment, emotions and mystery.

I was meeting myself in unforeseen modes, allowing various expressions to take over. No censorship, no comments, no judgments. I danced when dance took over my limbs. I screamed whenever a loud sound scratched my throat. The herds of sheep communed with me from a distance, sounding as lost as I was. I cried when sadness visited me. I sang when I woke up happy! I laughed and talked aloud whenever humor knocked at my door. An array of emotions and expressions took over. I had nobody to refer to, I had no idea of what life was about—only the subjective reality of each moment was relevant. No ideals, no hopes. Within conventional parameters, I went crazy. No fear. Instead, relief!

Waves of responses, events, memories and creations, people coming and going. No precise season can delineate this cycle. Winter, and spring, and summer, and autumn…

My connection with Derek was continuously present in my heart. He had moved back to Barcelona and Ibiza was close by. I was certain that sooner or later he would come for a visit. Months later, I collected several of my paintings and writings and mailed to him with an invitation. On a phone conversation, I was disappointed to hear that he had no interest in coming by. His sarcastic comments about my primitive lifestyle hit me hard. Walking home in a cold night, the stars were flashing in the dark sky, the wind was keeping me frisky and dashing down the road. I threw up on the sidewalk…

I climbed the stairs to my bedroom and blasted the gas heating to warm it up. While undressing, I noticed a strong smell in the air. I considered the gas might be leaking. My state of mind was not actively suicidal, but passively enjoying the possibility of slipping out. Lying in bed exhausted and dazed, I closed my eyes. I was awake, though stunned, immobile. My body slowly turned floppy and calmer. Idly, I was aware of becoming more and more limp, disassociated from my ability to watch physical sensations and my mind. Profound peace. Colors moving in my inner vision, gently, languidly, gracefully, continuously… At once my perception shifted to embrace liquidity and spaciousness. Soft lights, undistinguished sounds, whispers… I saw my body flat in bed. I was floating way above it, with no connection with its physical reality, inert and dull. My next memory jumps to touching my face and stickiness of warm blood coming out of scratches on my forehead. The cat that I cared for since moving into the house was insistently meowing next to me. The door of the room was open. He had cracked it open with his weight and some fresh air was starting to circulate inside. This sweet wild animal woke me up from the trip out in space. My body was groggy. I slowly moved and opened the window, put my face out to inhale some invigorating clean air. It was very cold. I went out to the veranda, and fell asleep inside my hammock.

I woke up surprisingly content. The beauty of the surroundings impressed me anew. I went for a long walk, sat on top of a hill to watch the ocean far away. Spring was approaching and the island's trees were flowering…

A few months later, Sylvia, a Brazilian friend who lived in Paris joined me. She was sturdy and intelligent, sharp humor, easy to be around, creative, practical and down-to-earth. We effortlessly shared our house tasks, and soon came up with an idea to generate income.

We created a business partnership, designing and sewing silk clothes. I borrowed a sewing machine from my landlord's daughter, our large wood stove became a dyeing factory, and soon we had piles of skirts ready for the summer season.

The market was fun, a large field set with tents and tables, wood and fabric screens to protect from the intense sun, lots of exchange between the merchants, mostly selling articles brought overland from India, Nepal, Morocco, Bali and Thailand. I loved the esthetics of the East and started to dress more like a gypsy, with my long hair framing my body. Faster than we imagined we had a regular income, and our skirts imprinted with stars were seen around town...

At the peak of the season, Bruno came for a visit. He had separated from his girlfriend and we became lovers in a warm way. Enjoying the beauty of the summer, we drove around together, spent days at the beach, made love in aliveness and sensitivity, cooked at the house, rested on the hammock together, and said goodbye with appreciation for each other. During the following years we maintained an intimate friendship.

My parents also came for a visit. I was happy to offer them a taste of my inner and outer world. Our relating was based in respect for our differences and choices. I was patient and caring, for the first time consciously appreciative of their qualities and gifts, letting go of old grudges and blame. They seemed glad to see me alive and happy.

At the end of the summer, Liza came for a few days. We cleared our feelings about the way things had happened in Paris. I was in peace with my choices, fresh perspectives within. Life had forced a core shift, and a strong kick seemed to have been necessary. Her life with Derek was a far-away reality for me.

Our connection sprang from deep inside my heart and triggered a dimension of love beyond our personalities' issues and identifications. The perception of a vaster realm, beyond personal definitions, became magnified a thousand times. As raw and unconscious energy, it took us to places where we encountered challenges as well as the potential for growth and understanding. Later, I realized that this quality needed to be nourished and brought down to earth with intentional awareness, rather than burned out through the passion of its intrinsic impulses. However, then, we were still learning...

As she left, I was unclouded.

Slowly I became more social. Ibiza was a meeting-point of freaks, colorful people, wild children, interesting music as well as drugs—an international gathering of visionaries who hid in the mountains and lived colorfully.

Having no car, I either walked or hitch-hiked. Usually, a bit of both. Sometimes a local, others a tourist or a freak who was better off and had a van offered me a ride. There was a family-like network throughout this small island and we crisscrossed.

The relaxation of social rules was evident. Gatherings were respectful of each person's moment and movements. If I was in the mood to close my eyes and sit quietly while others were talking, playing music, or cooking, that was ok. If someone decided to wash clothes while others were smoking dope or making love...that was a choice, hey! Every mood was honored, relating happened in the wisp of the moment.

Most of my friends had open relationships, playing with different partners, accepting and inviting others into intimacy. Sex was unfettered, spirited, and truly close to the natural elements. Oftentimes I would make love on the beach, as the sun was setting and the sand was still warm. I came close to men of different backgrounds, cultures and races. Enjoying these meetings without expectations or romantic fantasies took me into another realm of sexual exploration. Enjoying sex and being in love did not have to be packed together. Sexual energy was alive on its own and manifested in varied forms of expression. Yes, it turned into lovingness, but not necessary into romanticism. Yes, the openness in my heart always prevailed. But it was no longer attached to one person. I started recognizing the partner as a mirror of my own energy, reflected in different lights.

Fascinating to observe the infinite qualities revealed through different interactions, kinds of touch, body types. I was rather enticed by the resulting revelations about myself than by the men who delivered them. I watched my judgments about appearances and personalities. My parents' critical voices were loud and clear, though I was living thousands of miles away from them. I intentionally decided to spend time with a man who I judged strongly. He was a talented visionary artist, probably fifty or older. How could I possibly make love with a man as old as my father? He was a world traveler with endless stories. I enjoyed listening. I let my guards down and used our time together to watch my own resistance. I was self-conscious while meeting him in public places, guessing others would comment about it. Slowly, I relaxed, receiving his silence with appreciation. He could sit next to me for hours in stillness. I had no clue of what he tried to convey through words, his mental and imaginary universe was from another galaxy. Silence was once more the gift.

Other encounters, brief and longer, were colored with similar elements of self-exploration.

Laughter, mellowness, and friendliness made the climate for these meetings. Often casual, true initiations, rarely lingering for "I want more." I do not remember feeling incomplete or upset. There was care and amiability. Communication, though not sophisticated, was tinted with heartfulness. Meetings at houses or on a one-to-one basis had an intrinsic quality of amazement, as it was impossible to predict outcomes. Sometimes, as I was walking to the beach a stranger would pass by and give me a ride...in the course of the conversation we would decide to visit someone else...and from there, I got invited for a meal at another place...before long, I had spent several days in pilgrimage between here and there, eventually landing on the beach a week later. Talking about being flexible! My sensorial perception became radically fluid. Sounds, touch, tastes, colors, smells permeated my consciousness unfiltered. The hardness of the mind's holdings gradually melted away. Unique insights and refreshing inspiration manifested in simple details. Habitual thoughts gave space to new opportunities.

My closest friends were components of a music band. In time, my house became a meeting point for the musicians in the island. I loved coming and going, and finding my home animated with joyful resonance, a group of naked friends intermingling cooking a good meal with the latest soundscapes. I especially enjoyed making love in this environment and two of the guys in the band became my alternate lovers. Both Latin-blooded, Spanish and Portuguese. I was learning to play between the flute and the piano. The sense of collaboration and creativity that they shared spilled over our personal lives and love affairs. Young and adventurous, we were a crazy family, maybe only for that summer time, but surely totally for that summer time!

At the end of the season, after a morning shopping at the market, I sat at the downtown marina with Michella, an Italian girlfriend. It was mid-afternoon, the sky was bright blue and we talked about going out sailing sometime. Soon, two good-looking men approached us in a flirting manner. They were both French, in their late thirties. They were setting out that evening to sail towards Morocco. Would we like to come with them? We both laughed! They really meant it! The owner of the boat was a restaurateur in Paris and his friend was an actor. They were on vacation and would be glad to have company. We looked at each other and said yes! We drove in their rental car to my house. These two guys, from a much more conservative background, had never seen such a scene! Music, food, naked bodies in easiness.

Summer nights in Ibiza diffuse sweet scents, the earth exuding warmth and nourishment. We had dinner outdoors, got to connect with the guys a bit more and they stayed overnight at my house. The next morning we sailed away before the sun got too high. They had a month free. We had no time frame...

This first night on the open sea enforced a distinct sense of humbleness. Four insignificant people floating inside a small boat above this huge ocean. I sat outside alone, speechless. No boundaries. Awe, delight, peace, overwhelm, emptiness. Exhilarating and scary, ultimately ecstatic. I moved like a cat. The guys were easy. I shared a cabin with the owner of the boat and a few nights later we made love rocked by the waves, in a caring way. Detached from my body and actions, and yet wide open, I felt connected with everything around. The sky and the ocean and the stars and the sun and my body and other's bodies were not separated in any way, a continuous sense of interweaving.

I spent most of the time sitting in silence, drinking of turquoise and darkness. In between, I dove in and out of the magnificent ocean, letting its motion shake my bones. Waves and waves and waves...

The idea of arriving in Morocco was appealing. Its colors and mystery... However the moment to moment in the ocean was stronger than the anticipation. A few days later, we docked for the night in the south of Spain and the boat hit a rock, something got damaged. The part needed for the repair was ordered and deliver was promised in a few days... A week later, it was boring to stay in the boat waiting. I took a train to Barcelona from the nearest town.

I called Derek and he invited me to stay at his apartment. Liza was back in Brazil. I stayed with him for a few days. He was open-hearted, our love and connection was intact, we were sure to be friends for life. Our cycle was complete. I returned to Ibiza, glad to be back home for another song.

The summer was winding down...the population in the island decreased visibly as autumn approached. Many of my friends were getting ready to go to France to pick grapes and asked me to join them. Others were getting ready to travel to Morocco, India, Nepal and Thailand, to buy items for next season. Another crossroads.

My musician friends left for a tour in Europe, Sylvia returned to Brazil, the house became quiet. I went for walks, made jam with seasonal fruits, sat at the veranda watching the clouds...

It was time to renew my rental agreement. My landlord had decided to give the house to his granddaughter who was getting married. I was sad to let go of my nest. I loved the isolation and the beauty of the old house.

On a soft afternoon, someone took me along to a rather remote house. As we got there, I realized that they were having a heroin party. I did not want to try it. I was invited to sniff it instead, which I was told was much milder. What stayed in my memory was an afternoon that could be accounted for eternity. I was lying on the floor, quietness inside. My heart was big and warm. My body light and soft, I could not move nor speak. The voices around were soothing, cuddling me into numbness and delight. I vividly remember my thoughts almost as balloons hanging in the air. There might be another way to get to this state of perception without drugs. I do not want to destroy my body. I want to live in this tranquility! That inner voice made me decide to move until I would find my way to undisturbed peacefulness.

During my last month in the island, I met Carlo, a fierce Spanish man in his late fifties who had been a professional drug dealer for long years. His girlfriend was a small, delicate woman, an angel as his caretaker. I invited them to move into my house while my lease lasted. He was a joy to be around. I got a bit scared opening the kitchen cupboards and finding kilos of hashish bars stacked neatly. He had been in jail for many years and had some of his toes gangrenous as a consequence of extremely cold weather and poor living conditions. So, he sat outdoors every morning with his feet in warm water—a scene that I avoided watching. We cooked hearty meals and laughed sitting around the fireplace. I enjoyed listening to his stories, his courage and roughness, but above all, the fullness in his heart and wicked humor. I have learned from his integrity— impeccable, though expressed in oddity.

As the winter turned into spring, I decided to go for a visit to Brazil, almost six years after I had left home. I did not want to have any strings attached in Europe. I was interested in re-discovering the country I was born in, with less veils in my perception.

I exchanged my bicycle and other house articles for coral pieces to be made into necklaces, knowing I could sell them when needed. I gave away most of my clothes, keeping my grandmother's fur coat and one of my Nikon cameras just in case...

I said goodbye to the land that had generously fed me, danced in the veranda as the sun was setting, feeling light and grateful. Opening my wings for another flight!

I landed in Rio unannounced, taking a taxi from the airport directly to a coffee shop in Ipanema. The smell of the ocean was familiar and pleasant. I asked for a fruit smoothie, and called my mother. She was surprised! I had learned from her the joy of unexpected gifts.

Darkness in the ocean

Dazed with the sudden change of landscape, I rested at my parent's home. Space and comfort, views to the ocean and the swimming pool to wash my jetlag.

A few days later Carlos came for a visit. We had been friends since our teenage years, and shared a heartfelt sincerity. I was confronted with old expectations from my family and friends, trying to protect the gentleness of my inner space, feeling pushed and pulled at the same time. It was relaxing to relate to someone I trusted. As I allowed words to unlock my feelings, my body started shaking uncontrollably. My friend held my hand, helped me pack a small carry-on bag and place it into his car. I did not ask where we were going…

We drove to Buzios, a charming village a few hours north of Rio, where he had a simple house. What a relief! I could breath and let uncertainty shake me. Simple life, resting in the hammock, cooking, walking along the white sand beach, swimming, sleeping well…

One afternoon while walking on the beach, we heard a voice singing, moaning… We walked closer to a rock where the sounds were coming from. Surprisingly, we found a young woman giving birth alone, near the shore. Carlos, who was a doctor, moved towards her and helped a baby girl to come out. We both washed her in the ocean. This magical event brought the three of us close in an innocent and loving way. The mother was originally from an Indian tribe in the center of Brazil and had been living inside a small rock cave nearby. She had left her tribe curious about life in the big city. Getting work as a maid in Rio, she started to learn the ways of a large town, with different social rules. She had been pregnant before, but had to give the child for adoption. Now she wanted to keep this baby though she was not sure where to live or how to survive. She was relaxed and clear. Coming from the extreme opposites, we met at the same point. How to live in integrity and love? I kept in touch with her for the following months, until she decided to return to her tribe. Her beauty, trust and naïve stand was a true gift. Her strength helped me to feel more grounded and ready to move on.

Back in Rio, I called my cousin, Toca. He was getting ready to film a documentary about the Yoruba community located in Itaparica, an island off the coast of Bahia. This was an exceptional venture considering that they had never allowed white people inside their land. Did I want to come with him as part of the crew? YES! A few days later we were taking a boat to the site.

The Yoruba people came to Brazil as slaves during the early eighteen hundreds. As a royal African tribe, they treasured their inheritance and protected their tradition with wholeheartedness. When slavery was abolished in Brazil in eighteen eighty-eight a core group gathered on this island. They worked as domestic servants to assure economic survival, but maintained their community closed to strangers, conserving their tribal rituals with genuine pride.

Juanita, a passionate and ambitious Argentinean anthropologist, was married to one of the direct heirs of the oldest chief. He had moved to Salvador to study at the university, therefore was more open to new influences. She had been planning this project for several years, and through him, indirectly progressed into approaching the elders of the tribe, finally receiving their consent to produce this documentary. My cousin was one of the photographers, and the crew involved three other guys. I was thrilled to be part of this undertaking.

Staying at this idyllic island was a bonus, on top of this exceptional chance to be part of an anthropological camp. My interest in connecting with the spirit of primitive cultures had been stirred while studying in Paris, though remained theoretical. I longed to experience daily living in a community where human integrity and communion with nature were still untouched by Western civilization. A rare opportunity that I intuited would answer my existential inquiry.

We shared a simple brick house, furnished with a few mattresses on the floor, Brazilian-style hammocks and a kitchen counter. The guys were easy and enthusiastic. I enjoyed helping with small tasks. The job was fulltime, as we had to be present at tribal rituals during the day and almost every night.

Beauty, intelligence, wildness, instinctual ways, simplicity, vibrancy, sexuality pulsating in the air, majestic tropical nature, naturalness in the everyday flow, graceful dignity scintillating through the women, strength and intensity blasting off the men, exuberance expressed with every child, and fresh food. Permeating restfulness suspended in time. My body responded instantly to this energetic vigor. I felt gentle and shaky, often frightened by the incredible pull of the ocean. Coming close to the shore, I feared to be swallowed by the waves. I imagined my body walking through the waters towards the horizon. This illogical image had a magnetic force that made my body shake every time I was at the beach. Fire meeting water, the sun setting and the waves merging with it. An irreversible transformation was happening inside.

Male polygamy was one of their basic social rules. Political power was asserted by virility and patriarchal hierarchy. As a white, young, beautiful woman, I provoked interest. The men looked at me with burning desire, though it was clear in a tacit way that they could not approach me sexually. However their energy was afire in my skin. As much as I wished to have a taste of this wild and untamed quality, I knew that it was impossible to even sniff it. We kept mutual respect, while I participated as a tribal member in their daily activities and was often invited for a drink with the guys.

Every evening a special ceremony took place—a ritual of spiritual significance and the highlight of tribal life. We were honored to be invited and take part as one of them.

Men and women gathered in the meeting hall, a large space, with no furniture or chairs, cement floor and a wooden double-entry doorway. At the same time, the elders of the tribe conferred inside a tiny room at the back of the main space. They were a few men over one hundred years old who had been born in Africa. Quietly, we waited. Suddenly, the loud sound of drums and percussion jolted our bodies inviting motion. People started to dance letting the drumming move their joints like the wind moved the palm trees. The precision and intensity of the rhythm intended to call the spirits and invoke their guidance.

The room was usually crowded with about two hundred people at a time. We mingled with the audience, stirred by the entrancing beat.

Abruptly, the door of the small room where the elders gathered would burst open and a large figure would come out. Recognizable by its characteristic dress, speaking manner, and movement, these figures were believed to be disincarnated spirit guides, who manifested according to the momentary needs of the tribe. They were very tall, two meters or more. Each one had a characteristic head mask and garment, truly resplendent, made with psychedelic combinations of bright colors, decorated with beads, shells, adornments, feathers, tiny pieces of mirrors. They had a distinctive style of dance, sometimes frantic, sometimes mellow and wavy. Mostly fluid as they swayed, the materials floating in the air described lines and undulations in constant movement. Their very manner conveyed a kinesthetic language beyond grammar and the qualities represented by that entity. It was fascinating to watch this energetic burst come out of a little cabin. As the only people allowed in the small room were the elders, it was hard to imagine that those men could dance with such vigor for long hours.

The spirits moved wildly and nobody was allowed to step over their tracks. A master of ceremonies was appointed for the honorable job of clearing the path. He followed their movement and speed. Holding a long stick on his hand, he beat it on the ground at the spots where the spirit had just passed, making the way clear for the audience to move on. An intricate choreography. Waves of human bodies swirling in spiral patterns around the room, feet pounding, attentive listening. Unexpectedly there was a hasty stop! Everybody froze wherever they were. The spirit stood still in a listening position. That indicated that anyone could come forward and ask questions. The spirit listened and offered advice. This interaction happened in Yoruba language. The sincerity of their exchange surpassed verbal meaning. I perceived its rawness and heartfelt intelligence without understanding a word.

Successively, various spirits came out to dance. When the evening was over, usually at sunrise, we walked back home drinking of the soft ocean waves designing the shoreline.

Later in the day, the women translated the main topics discussed by the spirits while I helped them wash clothes outdoors. Jealousy, disease, pain, relationships, competition...the usual human concerns. The issues were resolved with intuitive wisdom in a compassionate, almost mythical way. Nothing was ever turned into a problem although they moved through emotional states, got sick and needed to sort family issues. Trust in the flow of life was at the core.

Once a spirit rushed out the door, running madly around the building. We followed him up and down the hill, towards the ocean, around again and again for many hours. At dawn, the spirit calmed down, and returned inside the room. Later, I was told that he represented freedom, reminding people not to be confined inside their thoughts. The directness of this kinesthetic experience electrified my blood and spirit.

These evenings required engagement without resistance. Even though we did not sleep much, I felt refreshed, awake. The fullness of this lifestyle was teaching me to allow the vibrancy of the universe beating inside. What a strong taste!

I spent sunsets with the women and children, sitting on rocks alongside the lagoon, washing clothes, singing. The bright sun moving ever so slowly, while the sounds rose and modulated in harmony. I felt fortunate to join them, blessed by their feminine kindness. Surrounded by dark and glistening eyes, I was showered with rare innocence.

At the end of our stay, the eldest man in the tribe suddenly died. He was way over a hundred and the patriarch of all. Born in Africa, he had kept the stories of his motherland alive and was revered by tribal members as their noblest ancestor. His death represented the beginning of a new era and triggered internal political struggle. We participated in funerary ceremonies, thus completing the documentary.

My search for the primitive backfired. I was caught between two realities: the genuine experience of life's richness still preserved by an environment and culture in the imminence of destruction; and the understanding that it was not possible to conserve the past. I had to live from my unique placement in the evolutionary momentum.

Through this tribal lifestyle, I had experienced consciousness as all-including, all-accepting. It was impossible to avoid or dissect its reflections; instead, I needed to integrate them.

I had a sophisticated education, my mind strived for understanding, my body requested refined sensitivity, I was a white, European offspring. How to embrace my given attributes, my genetic background as well as my potential as a human being? My unwavering questioning rattled stronger.

Leaving was not easy. I cared to preserve the preciousness of this time and was cautious.

Stars. Palm trees. Warm wind. Sun turning into laziness…people passing by… I am quiescent. I cannot look. I cannot see myself. I want nothing. No strength to move. Where to go? What for?

The pain is gone. My sense of self dissolved. I am not in a hurry. I don't know who I am. Fiery juice is running through my veins. Alertness joins quietness. How to live in the harmony of opposites merging, contrasting colors blending?

Grey sky. Guitar sounds. Harmonica. Firefly. Solitude. Stillness. Hidden moon. I listen. I do not command words. My voice is heavy. Silence. Resonance.

A song on the radio "the best place is to be happy, it does not matter where I am going, the best place is where love can be..."

One impulse—to go out and buy food! I am hungry. I move mechanically. A friend had given me an address of someone in Salvador. I took a bus to knock at this woman's door and she offered me a room to stay. I moved around selling my coral jewelry to local boutiques. In a way or another I always had what I needed.

I photographed without a camera. Focusing, cutting images in my mind. Colors brilliance, teeth, smiles, ocean, bodies soaking my eyes. Carnival. Loud music. Rhythm Bahia. Mangoes. Guava. Bananas. Pineapples. Indolence of ripe fruit falling from trees. Green coconuts full of water inside. Fishes in the ocean. Why seed anything? Fruits grow everywhere. Oranges. Sugar cane.

People pushing and pulling inside a crowded bus. Cheap perfume. Sweat. Buttocks and breasts. The accelerator jerks. Wait a minute! One more to get out, man! Every day the same routine. People coming and going to work jammed into buses. Nonsense city. I have nothing to do with this. Though I am inside this bus. A young woman sleeps and wakes up, with every curve, then reports aloud that she even dreamed meanwhile. Time to get out!

Beach days, making love with people I meet here and there, experimenting with my sensitivity rather than getting lost into the man's body, emotions or desires. I was strong, alone. My connection with people did not carry into the future. Each meeting was teaching me to stay centered within. I sat quietly, never sure where I was going to sleep the next night. It was warm and bananas grew everywhere...

Sensuality awakening, flowering pleasure, listening carefully, lightly touching, sniffing each other in subtlety. Drawing with my hands on someone else's body, transported by details, eyes meeting, mouths coming close, tasteful. Merging senses, neither inside nor outside. Neither me or you. No hurry, no fixed intentions, stretching gently. Enjoying.

Living fearless, in the absurdity of any day...the lack of time-sense was such. Gypsy way! The following month took me around Bahia, listening to stories, watching people.

JUNGLE TIME

Taking it easy and moving with the flow, I ended up in a small fishing village. Porto Seguro was defined by an oceanfront street with colonial, colorful small houses set in a row, a restaurant, a bed-and-breakfast and a grocery store. Behind the main street, there were other poorer, sparser houses, merging with the jungle in the background, unpaved roads, and an outstanding white church.

I got there hitchhiking. I had the address of a young couple who invited me to stay in their spacious, modest house. In Brazil, even in the poorest places, there is natural generosity in sharing and inviting guests into a home. They had just moved from Salvador intending to live closer to nature and create a friendly community. I was happy to sleep in a hammock viewing the coconut grove and the ocean.

Farther I moved away from the buzz of towns, friends and activities...closer I felt to an essential quality of creativity and relaxation within. I had no ambitions other than live with friends in a creative and harmonious interaction. Space for silence, art, beauty, love. Space for dance, space for joy. The same words being repeated, trying to find their meaning in bones and rivers, flowers and sky, not as ideas hanging on a cloud far away, but as intimate states visible in the walls of my home and body.

The natives were soulful and friendly, naïve and earthy. The alternative population, twenty people or so, had moved from larger metropolitan areas with the intention of starting something new, based on valuing and utilizing natural resources. Visionaries and adventurers, they shared a desire for a relaxed pace and harmonious co-creation.

Set in the main street, there was a large house transformed into a restaurant by a couple from Belo Horizonte. He was a medical doctor and his wife was a nurse, both prepared and served food. A stained-glass artist opened a small boutique, and set her studio at the back. A couple of young, vivacious women transformed a lovely house into a bed-and-breakfast. A few others, in the same way, were starting small businesses.

I got close to Diana, a journalist, a bit reckless, straightforward and full in her belly. We rejoiced in laughter, at the café sipping sugar cane juice, talking about nothing. She introduced me to a few people who lived further hidden into the jungle, including an European couple who made bread and specialty cookies. They distributed their production door-to-door with the help of a mule, large baskets placed on each side of the animal.

I met Nando at the café. We connected in an amiable and sensual way. A few years earlier, during a sailing trip, he had stopped at Porto Seguro. He fell in love with the place and decided not to go back to his lawyer career in Rio. He lived simply, wearing old shorts, naked chest, barefoot, toasted by the sun. He owned a small guesthouse, and offered me a room there. His smile was delicious, letting see through his heart. Sincere, earthy, caring. We enjoyed making love outdoors. My preferred spot was a protected sand beach formed by the meeting of the river and the ocean, our bodies caressed by warm, sweet water and soothing salty waves.

The extraordinary beauty of the environment made me happy. Kilometers of empty white sand, magnificent turquoise waters, warm enough to invite bathing with no goose bumps. Nobody around. Barefoot, wrapped in a sarong, sitting at the restaurant sipping a fresh juice, swimming, long hours playing with the waves, walking on the beach, watching unusual birds, wild animals…

Early in the morning and after sunset I painted, receiving what was in front of my eyes. I carried my crayons and watercolor around even when I had nothing more than a small handbag.

I explored the trails and hidden alcoves of wilderness. A few hours walk along the coastline took me to an even smaller village—Arraial D'Ajuda—with no more than twenty houses arranged in two lines facing each other. Time to lay immobile and get cooked by the sun. I enjoyed being alone listening to what was truthful inside, letting my rhythms find their own cadence…

The roughness of human characters highlighted the timeline between conscious and unconscious, in a raw, daily way.

I watched Mara, attractive young woman. "She is not good in her mind!" People commented as she passed by. Children screamed, trying to scare her. I only noticed the soul in her eyes, her smile. Bright red dress, sleek lipstick, tanned skin, large hat. Daughter of local people, the family was ashamed. "She is crazy! We do not take any responsibility!" She went into the boutique, stole some clothes, got out through the window. Her brother said that she had burned them all at home. The boutique owner didn't like that, but said nothing, afraid of the large fisherman's knife she carried on a belt around her waist.

She approached me, "Miss woman, if there is need for me to whack a man, I will finish with him. Everyday I pray to God that there is no need!"

She arrived at the bar, sat, listened to music, stayed put in the corner. She slept, holding her face with one of her hands, elbow on the table. Suddenly she peed on the floor, not even awake, just the noise called people's attention. When the bar was ready to close, someone shook her up! Time to go! She stood up and walked in front of the ocean, clumsy, in torpor, very pretty. She was maybe twenty years old.

One day a movie crew arrived. They were looking for a "real" Indian. They found Ezequiel at the nearby federal Indian reservation.

The film happened in Troncoso, a hippie settlement. Ezequiel drank hallucinogenic tea, smoked marijuana, fucked a white woman and announced aloud, "Today I had sex with a hairy pussy woman!" Not exactly the behavior they expected from an actor.

The movie was over, and Ezequiel stayed in the village. "I am property of the federal government! Do not touch me! I do not want any problems!" he repeated, and drew on his indemnity to act crazily. As he intruded into other's lives, he got beat up more than often. After a while, no real facts were necessary. If someone would fight with his wife and got upset, better look for Ezequiel to smack! Any excuse was enough. Some chicken disappeared... Ezequiel was blamed! Another spank!

One day it was his day for revenge! He took advantage of a situation and knifed another man. People tried to separate the fight, run, escape, blood! Ezequiel got afraid of his friends' retaliation. He disappeared in the jungle, pretending to be dead until moods cooled off. Then he returned to his original reservation.

The guy who was knifed lost a lot of blood, some came around him to pray for his life. There was no doctor in the village, a girl who was a doctor's daughter came to help, she ended up staying to take care of him, and arranging for his removal to the nearest hospital. That was a full day's gossip with people discussing who was right or wrong...

The horses kept munching the grass peacefully, the dogs continued to bark, the men still drank in the bars, the women had babies, the children with intestinal parasites did not stop eating from the earth. I watched it like a movie. Detached from identification with the stories, I observed emotions and boredom, novelty and routine, eccentric and well-mannered behavior, social compliance and rebelliousness. I did not fit anywhere, anyone.

I spent my twenty-sixth birthday alone, walking on the beach, drinking spaciousness and a royal blue sky. I slept outdoors on the sand.

Ideas, wishes, bubbles. I was impatient. Content. Simple was simple. Nothing else to understand. What was I supposed to do? Suddenly I smiled feeling ready again to invite the beloved into my heart.

Someone asked me, "Do you like to read?" "No, I like to live!" Life was my school, the ocean I bathed, surfed, dove, floated! The waves were breaking high!

THE UNPREDICTABLE

One afternoon I was sitting at a restaurant when a handsome guy came in and asked if he could sit with me. I was glad. Paulo was especially attractive, early thirties, tall, elegant body, serene face, well-designed features. Something about him was trustworthy and real. His dark brown eyes expressed uncommon penetration and shine. During our first conversation we found out that we had been neighbors in Paris; we had lived in the same street, a few blocks apart, exactly at the same time. He had suffered a deep shock that forced him to reflect on life's values. Having decided to let go of his business career to try something else, he abandoned his family's readymade path and moved to Caraiba, a remote beach about a day's walk from Porto Seguro. In partnership with a friend, he had purchased several kilometers of beachfront property with the idea of creating a community.

We walked together at sunset, then made love on the beach until it was dark. We sat in silence outdoors looking at the stars...

The day after, I went with him to Caraiba. The area was designated as an Indian reservation, almost decimated, where a few native families lived with scarce resources. Adding to this thin population, there were a few "white" landowners who planned to rebuild the village.

The location was magnificent. Splendid trees, and a large river flooding into the ocean gave rise to dancing waves in tones of turquoise and green. Once in a while a canoe passed by, a man standing on it, stirring calmly down the river.

Paulo lived in a small cabana, made with sticks and mud, palm roof and earth floor. There was no electricity or tap water. A bed made with local wood was the only piece of furniture. And a hammock, of course... Cooking happened outdoors in the open fire and the toilet was a large hole on the ground, lime powder on the side. We talked about our dreams, and how to make them real. He had the financial resources, plus a private plane to transport people and materials. We focused on planning the development of a community, discussing minute details, using my studies in design and architecture combined with his business and financial skills. A few weeks later we had a precise budget, timing schedule, and an itemized account of the grains, spices and seeds needed to begin a vegetable garden. We planned for materials to construct a few more houses and a proper toilet, baking supplies, good tools, pots and pans, and what not. As fruit trees abounded in the area, there was plentiful food reserve. We spent days organizing this first step, and sailing off the coast. Nights making love with candle light, caressed by warm breeze...

Paulo and his brother went on to Sao Paulo to shop for our basic needs.

I needed to be independent. I wanted to make sure that there would be no hooks for me with Paulo, maintaining my ability to move freely, separately from him. I gathered some jewelry inherited from my grandmother and sold it for cash, collecting enough money to buy the materials to build my own house and to live there for a few months. In those days, that was not much… Caraiba was at the end of the world!

A few days later, we returned with a full load of miscellaneous goods.

We arrived in Porto Seguro late in the afternoon. I felt lousy, tired from the long journey. We had to leave the car there, and take a boat or his private plane to reach our destination. From Porto Seguro to Caraiba there was a small dirt road through the jungle, accessible to trucks only, if it was not raining…

It was pouring rain, an authentic tropical storm. No boats or planes could go anywhere. We stayed at a bed-and-breakfast, hoping for better weather the next day.

In the middle of the night I was burning in fever and could hardly move with unbearable back pain. Paulo took me to the doctor, the owner of the restaurant, who had an emergency room in the back of his kitchen. By the time we got there, I could not say a word. The severity of the pain knocked me out. I had a violent kidney infection, in a well-advanced state. Alarmed, the doctor told me I had about twelve hours to live. His resources were not enough to care for me. He urged that I get removed to an intensive care unit in a regular hospital.

Oh, yes, making love in the river had probably given me a bladder infection, which had moved into the kidneys.

We were miles away from any hospital, and the weather was impossible. I was getting increasingly relaxed in this state of separation from my body, vaguely distinguishing sounds and sensations. I did not want to go anywhere. If I was to die, I could not wish for a better place. I spent the night under his observation, on a drip with some medication, lying on a cot in a tiny room. The sound of the rain, my breathing, eyes hardly opening, body so weak, I was ready to go…

At sunrise the weather cleared and Paulo arranged for a private plane to take me to Rio. My mother took me directly to the intensive care unit at a hospital. The doctor in charge was adamant—I was going to die soon! We were getting closer to the twelfth hour. I had been raised with homeopathy and my body was too sensitive for other drugs. My mother, who strongly trusted her instincts even in alarming situations, decided to call our homeopathic doctor. He immediately came to the hospital and took responsibility for moving me to my parents' house.

I did get much worse and then started to recover. For a couple of weeks, I lay down, looking at the ocean at a distance, enjoying the paragliding crew constantly flying over the house from the mountain just behind it.

This calm sense evoked images of India. No logical explanation. I knew then that I was heading East as soon as my body would recover. Life had its own ways to point me the path forward. My parents were upset and the ambiance at the house was not pleasant. I was impatient to move on.

Once more my body was showing me the way. I felt so connected with its wisdom and capacity to heal, that it was easy to follow its indications. It was as if my decisions originated from my cells. My mind had no power to interfere.

Paulo came for a visit. Our coming together had ignited his movement and set him clearer on his intention. He was going back to the land and I had decided to go to India. We said goodbye.

While in bed, I took time to connect with my old school friends. We shared our shifts and turns, our lives unfolding through different experiences, their realities quite unlike mine, though a sense of love and closeness was always present. They were having children, divorcing, marrying once more. Our heart connection was beyond time and formality. I tried to convey my discoveries and longing while accepting their choices.

As soon as I was able to walk, I moved to a friend's house. I needed to make money. I got a job translating a boring book on transpersonal analysis. "I am ok, you are ok." If you repeat this long enough, you will get the point. I wished it to be that simple… I sat in front of the typewriter and completed this project as fast as possible. To keep sane, I baked bread every day and sat quietly.

One night I had a vivid dream… I was sewing a beautiful dress, designed with patches of different materials cut in a precise way, long and flowing. In the morning I went for a walk with the colors still in my mind. At the park nearby, I met Sonia. She had lived in London for a few years working as a fashion designer, and we had met in Ibiza several times. What a surprise! We were both glad to run into each other, she was living two blocks down the road. I talked to her about my dream. We decided to collaborate and sew these dresses for sale. Like lightning, we went to buy fabric, and the following days and nights on her atelier. The dresses were unusual and strikingly colorful. Money was flowing while we were having a blast! I bought a one-way ticket to Madrid/Ibiza.

Goodbye again! I was grateful for the beauty of my native land and its lessons.

LETTING GO

Arriving in Madrid on a hot day, I checked in at a hotel near the Prado Museum. Art always inspired my directions in life. I walked around some paintings I loved, especially befriending Goya's vision.

I flew to Ibiza two days later. No idea where to go, or what to do. Getting out of the airport in the evening, the scent of the ocean in the air, fresh breeze, dark sky full of stars, I was thrilled. I decided to walk towards Santa Eulalia, as I only had a backpack. I counted on finding a small motel in town for the night, or just hanging out on the beach, sleeping cuddled by the ocean sounds. I was glad to be alive!

The road was empty, already late into the night. A few minutes later, a car approached and stopped next to me, someone calling my name... That was Juan, an Argentinean friend. Glad to meet him, I got into his home-van and we drove to a remote beach where we slept. Early morning, we bathed in the ocean, nobody else around. He was an intense guy, blond with big blue eyes, energetic and vital, straightforward, a true freaky vagabond with a huge heart. We made love, earthy and mindless.

The following days were idle, enjoying the day by day in a lazy way, staying at a friend's house. Time in Brazil had shaken me up, and my body needed rest to spring back.

On a sunny morning, I went to town to buy a ticket on the ferry to Barcelona, planning to hitchhike to Rome, then fly to India. On my way back, I got a ride with a guy whose face was wild and handsome. There was a steadiness and radiance about him that was instantly attractive.

He invited me to his house—a typical Ibiza "finca" set on a hill with ocean view, almost no furniture. His bedroom had French doors opening to a lovely garden with a center round well. We spent the afternoon making love, eating fresh fruits, occasionally going outdoors to get water for a refreshing bath. In front of his bed there was a large photo of a man with dark eyes and the most penetrating look I had ever seen. His face emanated quietude, stillness coming from deep within. I could not take my eyes out of this portrait.

I was utterly relaxed, yet it was clear I was to leave the following day. He asked me to stay longer, but I was set! I kept looking at the picture on the wall...those eyes were piercing my soul. Go! Do not postpone. We spent the night together and I left the next morning.

During the boat trip I sensed "rightness" in my belly with no explanation attached. I looked at the waves crashing on the side of the boat; that movement mesmerized me all the way to Barcelona.

I went to lunch with Derek and Liza, in Barcelona. They could not relate to my decision of going to India. Liza asked questions about my traveling plans. Not much to say. I was moving on intuitive impulse, no reasonable aim... I described to them the eyes of the man on the photo. Yes, I knew I was going to find that peace in India. Liza listened. Our psychic connection was always strong. We hugged goodbye. I understood how the pain of breaking through my marriage had fueled my questioning and was moving me forward.

I started my journey with luck, getting a ride with a German couple. Through the coast of Spain, towards France. I reclined in a leather seat, watching the landscape, loose thoughts... They dropped me somewhere a few hours later. The trip followed smoothly.

On the way, I stopped to visit Michella, who was living at the island of Elba. She was running a café with her boyfriend right in the main plaza. Her apartment was large enough to take me in. I helped them at the café for a week or so. At her house, I read a book containing a poem with the story of Chiyono, a woman Zen monk who became enlightened one night, as the bucket of water she was carrying from the well suddenly broke. *"No Water, No Moon"* was the title of the book. I was impressed with the meaningfulness of this story; it touched something inside that confirmed my need to keep moving.

Back onto the ferry, one more ride and I got to Rome hungry! Not knowing anybody in town, I planned to spend a night there and get a ticket to India the next day.

I had lunch at a nice restaurant. As I came out, there was a familiar figure standing next to me. Pedro! My musician-lover-friend from Ibiza. We laughed in surprise. What was I doing there? He had been in Rome for while with his band, playing at a nightclub. Would I like to stay with him? An invitation from heaven...

We drove to his apartment—an empty living room with his piano, a bed on the floor, good food in the kitchen. His presence and music sweetly touched me.

Rome was a party, and I forgot about India for a while. I enjoyed this bohemian life in the city. Days hanging out in bed, Pedro playing the piano for hours, I painted letting the music guide my hands. Dancers in movement appeared out of large pieces of watercolor paper, insinuating graceful forms. In the evening we went together to the club where he played. I became part of their troupe, dancing with another girl to the sound of their vibrant music, a combination of Latin-Eastern rhythms. We drove back home every night like kids after a nice treat.

Another girlfriend was working as a stage designer in a theater. I enjoyed helping her create props and light effects. I found an excellent modern dance teacher and spent a few hours a day in dance classes. The river of life was rushing steadfastly.

I was surrounded by musicians and artists, and immersed in the beauty of classic art works. I took time to go to the Sistine Chapel, admiring Michelangelo's genius. Museums, street artists, sculptures, paintings and historical monuments made my days.

I submerged in intimacy with Pedro. His sensitivity and talent nurtured me. India could wait. A month or two passed.

One night Pedro asked me if I would be ok if he would spend the night with another girlfriend. I agreed... A friend who was having dinner with us, invited me to his place. He was a Brazilian football player who had been hired by one of the major Italian teams, married with an Italian stewardess. They lived in a lovely flat with their small baby. She was often traveling and their relationship was open.

I remember well his face, his athletic soft body, yet strong, agile and flexible. His smile was sincerely candid. It was natural to be naked in bed with him, his baby crawling in between. Before we got together he called his wife to let her know that he was going to spend the night with me. He was straightforward, his mind was simple. I could feel it in my body, his touch, and the sensations it provoked—harmony in flawless motion. We made love in and out during the night, slept embraced with his baby hugging both of us. Nothing could have been more ordinary, and yet...

We cooked breakfast in the morning, speaking Portuguese mixed with Italian slang. We went for a walk in the park and hugged goodbye. I was ready to fly!

Who am i?

Walking downtown, I found a travel agency and asked the lady at the counter when there was a flight leaving for India. "Ah si, India, ma dove? Signorina, l'India e un paese molto grande!" I had no idea of India's geographic design. In fact, it did not matter at all where I was landing. India called my soul. Though I had almost no information about this country, I could smell the flavor of its spices.

Since my sickness in Brazil, I was ready to die. At the same time, I realized the need to find fullness in life, no time to waste. The sweetness of that experience left me fearless. The silent stillness that visited me then, had a magnetic pull and sprinkled my heart with a precious texture. I wanted to contain it permanently. I had tasted it through sex, sickness, and while alone in nature. In those moments, there was no longing, no desire, nor wonder, but absolute rest within. That silent orgasm kept calling my attention.

Through sex, I had experienced it with different men. And in nature, alone. I knew it did not depend on others, nor was a physical occurrence. I perceived it as a consequence of a precise inner tuning, of my own ability to open to life without defenses. When this state happened during a sexual embrace, it was a consequence of my taking refuge inside rather than losing myself in the other. Different relationships had melt away layers of self-definitions. While embracing others' unique qualities, I learned to offer my body and soul without holdings, in innocence beyond personal attraction.

Though several men had been with me in this space of emptiness and bliss, many did not seem to value or recognize it, nor be able to stay present to its force. It was confusing, but recognizing this fact did not dissuade me. Those moments of communion beyond words were infused with contentment.

I had experienced silence pouring from infinite source. Behind it, I sensed love without hesitance. I wanted to integrate my discoveries into a lifestyle and companionship that would support and nurture this inner space. I needed to find this silence as a constant source of inspiration and nourishment. It could not be just a flickering flame, visiting me at its own will. I was looking for a silent lover. Someone who would meet me in overflow, someone with whom I could rest and be quiet, with whom I would dive together into the space I experienced when I closed my eye.

I wished to find a place where death was received naturally. When my turn would come, I rather have people singing a sweet farewell than doctors rushing around trying to "save" me. That "in between" space imparted the twilight of beatitude. I wanted to taste it again. If only death would take me there, I was ready to go.

India invoked magic and madness. Absurd familiarity. India united extremes—vibrancy and lassitude, colors and void, noise and harmony, horror and grandeur, life and death in unison. I was leaving Europe "forever."

"Just give me a flight anywhere." The woman looked at me as if I was crazy, probably doubting I had the money to pay for the ticket. She asked if I had a visa. No, had not thought of it. "Bene, signorina, lei avra bisogno del visa!" She made a temporary reservation for my flight, gave me a paper to take to the consulate, and the address. Clearly impatient and upset, she conveyed the feeling that she was wasting her time on me.

I walked to the consulate. Luckily, not so far away. Good that I did not know much about Indian bureaucracy; I had no idea what to anticipate. I was granted an entry visa to India in a few hours, with time enough to go back to the travel agency. The lady received me surprised. I paid for the ticket and confirmed the details for the next flight leaving to Bombay, via the Emirates, on Kuwait Airlines, two days later.

I walked to a park nearby, sat for a while on a bench, appreciating the purplish sky, a bit sweaty warmth in my body. These minutes felt like long hours.

I went home; it was already dark, Pedro was playing the piano as usual. He was an exceptional pianist and composer. The lightness and gentleness of his body came across in the landscape of sounds, cascades of fluid caresses. I sat on the floor near him.

I told him I was leaving. He was not surprised, and hugged me tightly. Though his body was rather slim, he held me with strength and intention. There was not much more to say. Our relating had always been one day at a time, coming closer and dancing with the music of the moment. We had no holdings on each other, and when together we enjoyed it for what it was. His passion was music. My longing was lying ahead in adventure and inner explorations. The harmony of our agreement was clear when we made love. Like his music, time did not exist and we met in the watery universe of our creativity. After making love, he often would get out of bed and play the piano, I would paint, the colors of love....

The day after, I walked up and down Via Veneto appreciating Italian fashion, the daring and elegance of store windows, choosing my last luxuries before flying off civilization. I stopped at an exquisite shoe store and bought the finest turquoise suede boots, like a glove caressing my feet. My next purchase was a pair of sunglasses. That was plenty for my journey.

I went to see Michelangelo's David for the last time, always astounded by the beauty of this sculpture. Sat there, absorbing its perfection. At the Sistine Chapel I paused for hours, letting myself be touched by its images.

At the end of the day, I walked to the theater where my friend Eliza worked. She was a lively young Spanish girl. Her curly honey hair and bright eyes made me cheerful. We danced together on a nightclub with Pedro's band. I wanted to say goodbye and give her my fur coat. We sat backstage and chatted for a bit. She wished me a good trip, dreaming to meet me soon in India. She never did.

Already into the evening, I got the bus back home and prepared for my journey. I put aside US$100 to take with me and gave the rest of my cash to Pedro as well as my Nikon. I reasoned that India was a poor country and probably ranking a high rate of crime. I was ready to explore unworried, without the need for protection or to be guarded.

I packed a small red canvas backpack that I had stitched by hand: one caftan-style dress, one wraparound sarong, a box of colored pencils, a white watercolor-paper booklet, and little more...

On my last day in Rome I went with Pedro to a recording session. His singer-musician partner lived in a large house. I sat in the room next to the studio listening to their play. Their musical partnership made my cells tingle.

Late in the evening, we had dinner together. Satyam asked if I was returning the next day. "Oh, no... I am going to India tomorrow. My time here is over!" I said. He smiled. He was a soft, beautiful looking guy from Puerto Rico, dark brown eyes, and a mellow voice. I noticed that he was wearing orange clothes, and had a photo of someone hanging on a beaded necklace. The orange color turned into just a flash, forgotten by his eyes looking straight at me. He asked if I could do him a favor. "Siccuro, cosa vuole?" He would like me to meet and give a hug to a friend he had not seen for a while. Easy! "Oh, you are flying to Bombay, that is great! You can get a train to Pune, it is about six hours. The train leaves early in the morning. As the plane usually lands in the midst of the night, you have enough time to take a taxi to Victoria Station. In Pune, you take a rickshaw." He described a rickshaw as a mini-car with three wheels, the most common transportation in India. "It is not expensive and everybody knows where the ashram is." What? "The ashram is the place where my friend lives." Ah! I wrote it down as the name of the street. Did not sound difficult. His friend's name was Veet Marco and he was Italian.

We departed with a long hug, and he wished me a good time.

Pedro and I spent our last night together in a cozy way. I remember his eyes looking at me as we made love, and our laughter in the mid of the night.

After having my usual long morning shower, I chose to travel wearing a dress I had bought at the market in Ibiza. It had long large sleeves, the area around the breasts was decorated with colored embroidery and tiny mirrors, a black long skirt attached, sewn by hand. I loved that dress! My new boots were light and comfortable. I had one ring on each finger, and several earrings on my multi-pierced ears. A neat freak/gypsy, long hair, and the confidence that this was the most meaningful decision I had ever made.

As I was ready to take the bus to the airport, Pedro asked me not to open my bag until arriving in India—there was a surprise for me. I noticed it was a bit heavier than I had packed.

I asked him to think of me if he ever truly committed to love. He hugged me, squeezing my hand with intensity. "I hope you do not come back like a *butano*!" This word means "gas" in Spanish, and in Ibiza the employees of the gas company were recognized from a distance as they used to wear a bright orange uniform and called butanos. Without understanding his comment, I quickly responded, "I am not coming back!" I waved goodbye from inside the bus.

At the airport, I called my parents to let them know I was going to India alone and intending not to return. I do not remember their reaction. I had only a few coins and not much time to waste.... Nowadays, I appreciate their endurance in that moment.

The plane was half full, but there were two other women sitting in the same row as I was. They were both wearing orange clothes. Humm... They were Swiss sisters, returning to India. A physiotherapist and a nurse, they looked rather proper and friendly. They asked me where I was going. I didn't really have any special place to go... One of them insisted that I should go to Pune, they were going to the ashram, had I heard of? Oh! The place my friend asked me to visit. Yes, I might go there, but first I wanted to stay in Bombay. Bombay!? They were shocked. No, that was not a place to stay, too crazy, you will be wasting your time, you need to come to the ashram, we have a reservation on the plane going to Pune, you can get on the same flight. No, I will stay in Bombay. One of the sisters shook her head, "If you change your mind, you can join us, the plane leaves at ten, but it is often late, you will have time to decide..."

"You are a sannyasin. You don't know it yet. See you in Pune!" I had no idea what she was talking about!

Quantum Leap

"If you had equal faith in that part of you that is fading...
As in the one that is growing...
Faith in the underground river of life that knows how to get to the ocean..."

DAVID WHYTE   *Poetry of Self-Compassion*

Water leela

In between worlds. Clouds. Voices. Sky. Earth. Spirals. Vortex. I want to remember. I want to move towards the center, until there is stillness, until I remember forever.

Landing. I walked on the airstrip to the main building. Stink of pee and sweat and incense and god knows what else. Impossible to figure out the combination of scents. Humidity in the air, unusual smells and noises elicited a rush of sensory overload. Overcast sky, hot sun. Smoke and pollution merged with the natural veil of clouds. I felt a peculiar, undeniable nonchalance.

I moved towards the passport control station and stood in line for a while until my document got stamped. My eyes turned in all directions. Familiar faces...though nobody I had ever seen before.

Strolling into the building—a bizarre scene! People chaotically moving, piles of suitcases dumped on a corner. No signs. Travelers bending over luggage heaps, trying to find their belongings. Luckily, I didn't have any! The confusion captured my attention and made me laugh. Most people upon arrival looked already exhausted and distressed. I was light and alert.

As I opened my backpack to change money, I found one of my Nikon cameras inside it, an envelope with US$100, and a note with Pedro's handwriting. "You may need it. Love."

The next step, out on the street, required my full attention. Hundreds of beggars and taxi drivers trying to grab my dress, calling, asking, anxious for attention and money. I was fascinated, innocent enough to look into their eyes and respond with a clear "No!"

It was hot and I was thirsty. I came across a shack with a guy selling coconuts. I sat in the dust sipping sweet coconut water...

In the midst of the crowd I saw a procession of about twenty people carrying a dead child on a small bamboo bed. Music and chanting, the cortege moved fast amongst people, animals and cars. Death was my first image of India.

Another drink prompted me to go on. Where? I had the address of a student lodge for a few dollars a night. I showed the address to the coconut guy. "Madam, rickshaw!" He pointed to the many black, rounded roof, little three-wheeled cars painted with yellow stripes, speeding along the road. Oh! That was a rickshaw! Desperate horns, skinny, intense-looking guys on the driver's seat, they advanced through the traffic in zigzag motions. I nodded my head. Stretching my hand I waved, and in a second one stopped and I jumped in. With the address in hand, he speeded! I had no idea where we were, or where we were going... I kept my head out the window, looking at every detail on the way. Extreme poverty entered my eyes. Metal-roof shacks, bamboo huts covered with dirty rags, bodies all over, an array of scents and colors and noises shifting at high speed, big eyes, shabby clothes, beautiful smiles, and a lucid sense of rest. No words, no judgments; resonant longing stirred by this mix of hell and paradise.

Abruptly, the rickshaw driver stopped in front of an old building and pointed to the large front door, which was half-open. We agreed on payment and I got out. I saw a huge wooden counter, full of papers on top, and an older woman sitting on a chair. She spoke broken English and I understood that I could sleep there for a small fee. She took me upstairs through a long corridor displaying several cubicles, pieces of colorful cotton hanging over the portals—there was no actual door to the "rooms." A mat on the floor and a slim mattress, I do not remember about sheets. The shower was at the end of the corridor and the bathroom was a hole on the ground, next to it a water faucet and a small bucket. I realized it should be used to clean myself. No toilet paper seemed to be needed. I paid her for one night and retired to my assigned space. Tired and ready to sleep, yet excited, I showered and went to bed with my dress on. I fell deeply asleep.

Early morning, I woke up with loud radio sounds and crispy voices. As I got out to get something to eat, someone approached me offering dope. "No!" I kept walking and the guy followed me. "I have anything you want, madam! Anything! Madam! Listen! Sex, drugs, anything!" I kept walking until he gave up.

The streets of Bombay evoked nostalgia, familiarity, relief. Spirited expressions of faces and eyes, infinite hues of colors, music coming out of primitive instruments played by street people gathered in small groups. In a state of euphoria, I followed a band of musicians, dancing in abandonment. I merged in mysterious intimacy with the landscape and people. Immersed in this state of insanity ardently welcoming my soul back home! No trace of the well-educated Brazilian girl. Past memories were dreamlike. The rhythms took over. My dress fluidly draping my body, warmth arising from my legs into my heart and throat, I danced! I cried throughout this day, washing lifetimes of separation, rejoicing in this reunion with myself. I ate snacks from road stands and drank spiced tea with milk and sugar from dirty glasses. It tasted delicious!

Closer to dark, I needed to find another place to sleep. The "hotel" of the previous night was out of question. I glanced at a lost-looking young Western couple seriously staring at a map. We took a rickshaw together and found a YMCA dormitory. The level of comfort wasn't any better, but it was safer.

I spent a week or so in Bombay, naturally stoned out. No drugs were needed in such an environment. The affect of sensorial stimulation was satisfying in itself.

Flowering jasmine, urine, rancid sweat of dirty clothes, the distinct fragrance of silk exposed outside small shops, fried meat, frankincense and sandalwood incense burning, varied bulk grains offered in large bins outside the markets, warm milk, human feces on the ground, smoke from tires burning, sick animals lost on the streets, the permeating background of humidity coming from the ocean, boa constrictors, shining gold threads, shocking magenta and turquoise dyes exposed in draped saris, echoes of the past in every dilapidated building. A myriad of unknown memories resided in the subterranea of my soul...

Aroma emanating from a diversity of spices, scrumptious foods and hot chai enraptured my olfactory hunger. I explored the universe of tastes, savoring exotic dishes. The pungency of certain foods was at times difficult to swallow. The heat of some condiments brought tears to my eyes more than once; the freshness of tropical fruits was a blessing in the warm weather. I enjoyed getting juice all over my hands while trying to eat a papaya or a mango. At twenty-seven, at the peak of health, I had no concerns about sanitary conditions. Nothing would interfere with this feast of pleasure. This celebration of the senses made me feel earthy and vibrating. At the same time, there was something intangible, invisible, like a caress, guidance, reminiscence. Uplifting waves. Old and new imprints, comparisons and references lost in the gushing of sensations.

The sounds were no less intense, nor more harmonious. Radios turned on to the max, carried under people's arms while they wandered in no hurry. Voices discussing endlessly in loud high-pitched tones, horns put to use without discrimination, stray elephants and pigs and dogs and cows communicating in their own language, music on loudspeakers coming out of restaurants and stores, invaded my ears. Children crying, mothers screaming, beggars lamenting, and the melody of rudimentary instruments like tins and homemade drums and flutes, feet banging on the ground creating the cadence for spontaneous dances, cars with voice amplifiers advertising something or another, never a second of silence. Nonetheless, I was remarkably peaceful.

My eyes were charmed with beauty and grace. They sparkled attentively, captivated by the women carrying themselves with humbling dignity. I perceived elegance that did not come from education or social rules, but from almost defiant kindness. I stared at the many hues of fabrics wrapped around slim bodies, blankets hanging out the windows, paints displayed on rather elemental advertising billboards, walls roughly brushed in fading tints...

I met deep dark eyes reflecting pain and innocence, as well as rare contentment. Nothing appeared to be impossible or surprising. The uncommon view of animals crossing the streets in between cars and people, cobras being allured by "enchanters" playing flutes, to dying cats and dogs, elephants and buffaloes...

One day I ended up in front of the Victoria train station.

Pune? Yes, the express leaves in a few hours. I bought the least expensive ticket. The controller laughed when I asked for a seat. He pointed to a cabin already packed with women and children, no place for one more person. I stood in the corridor, resigned to standing. A while later, a well-dressed Indian woman approached me speaking fluent English. She invited me to come to first class with her. I gladly accepted. She was eager to practice her English and talked nonstop. She lived in a small town, mid-way to Pune, where tambouras were manufactured. Emphasizing how interesting it would be for me to visit this village, she invited me to stay at her house overnight. Her chauffeur was coming to pick her up and it would be a pleasure to have a foreigner as a guest. Her husband was a businessman and enjoyed meeting new people, bla, bla...

When the train arrived at her station, I got out with her. She called a porter to carry her suitcases, and suddenly walked away very fast, waving goodbye! The train had already left. I was left eating dust.

Outside the station I found a line of narrow shacks forming the only "road" in town. It was evident by the looks I got that I was not safe. I was slightly scared. Nobody spoke a word of English, and there were no women around. Inside the shacks there were men and boys carving and assembling tambouras, a classical Indian musical instrument. Sounds of attuning, and lots of sawdust! Next train only next day...

At the end of the road, I found a chai shop and stopped to have a drink. The chai wallah understood I wanted a place to sleep and, with a head sign, took me to look at a space behind his shop. The floor was plain earth, the bed was a small mat, the door did not close and there was a spinning fan on the ceiling. With no other choice, I lay down feeling stupid and exhausted. The fan was so wobbly that I feared it would fall on my head. It was hot and there were flies, so I was caught in between the discomfort of the heat and buzzing flies, and the shakiness of the fan wings turning fast. I chose to keep the fan on. Awake for most of the night, promptly opening my eyes as soon as I heard a noise, I had no difficulties getting up at sunrise.

Another chai was nectar. I thanked the man for his offer. The torture of that night over, I had some time to look into the small shops and their tamboura production.

All communication happened through the expression of our eyes meeting. I appreciated the elaborate craftsmanship of these instruments, the easiness and relaxation in which such a production was conducted. This taste of rural India stayed with me, beyond the discomfort of the situation.

Later I came to know that it is a courteous gesture for educated people to invite a foreigner to their house. In fact, they do not mean it, nor expect that you accept the invitation. Well!

I jumped on the train as soon as it arrived, finding a seat in the midst of many women. By then, I had figured out that there was a compartment for women and children. They accommodated to fit me in, with shy smiles. I did not know that the dress I was wearing, that I had traveled with from Rome, was typically from Rajasthan—a region of North India, where the gypsies originated. Only poor gypsy women wear this type of outfit, mirrors sparkling and open back. I was outstanding, being a white woman dressed in this costume. I was greeted by other woman wearing similar dresses, with a namaste gesture, and soft words "Shanti, shanti, ma." "Peace, peace, mother of the divine."

The namaste is a common greeting in India. With both hands folded in front of the body, and a slight bending of the head, this gesture is graceful and silent. Its significance is "I salute the divine within you." Though I had never seen it before, my heart knew it instinctively.

I was at ease with those simple women. I was surrounded by a sense of harmony and rest within, even though I hardly slept and there was no space to move. The piercing quality of their eyes, the gentleness and softness with which they moved, the loving way they touched their babies, the innocence of their smiles, the beauty and colors of saris and jewelry…

One woman extended me her hand: she gave me a bindi, the usual small colored dot that most women glue to their third eye. It is a protection for what enters the energy field through intuitive perception, and a way to reflect others' non-well-intentioned gazes. The other women giggled as I was showed how to glue it between my eyebrows.

The poverty of the shantytowns bordering the railway lines was indescribable. Scarcity, and yet, there was a sense of festivity and peace. I could not explain from where it radiated. My body relaxed. One woman asked, "Married?" Probably the only word she knew in English… When I said no, she turned her eyes around and slapped me on the face tenderly, "Beautiful, beautiful, ma!" I smiled feeling the silkiness of her hand. Though she probably worked hard, her hands were slim and delicate.

It was hot and I was wearing my Italian suede boots. They had cost me enough money to cover a year's expenses for a whole family in India. Time to let go! I took them off and made a gesture to give them away. They looked at me puzzled. Then a very young woman held my hand and touched the boots, in a typical Indian way, meaning she was ready to accept it. I handed her the boots, and she was laughing and laughing loudly. I was barefoot.

During this train ride, I experienced tenderness, sensuality, fragility, delicacy, permeating my body. Those Indian women, unaware as they were of their beauty and sensitivity, introduced me to the world of earthy goddesses. The strength of their presence shook me up. Their grace, intrinsic rest in their bodies, divine connection with their feminine spirit and the nourishment that those qualities offered… I had never met any woman in the Western society who transmitted such refinement and grandeur, though I had lived in sophisticated cities, acquainted with cultured and wealthy artists, actresses, models, and royal gentlewomen.

A few hours later, I distributed my jewelry amongst them in acknowledgment for their innocence and grace. I had several antique gold earrings on each one of my pierced ears, and a ring on each finger, reminiscences of my Parisian years. The women giggled in incredulity. Each piece moved around until someone claimed it with a smile.

After that train ride, I gradually became more aware of my movements and gestures. From where inside my body-mind did my impulses and actions arose? Slowing down, paying attention from inside out, relaxing my eyes, enjoying my body from within, realizing the richness of information my senses convey. If I only listen… They are the source and reservoir of intelligence. My ability to observe sharpened. Delicacy and strength started to grow intertwined, rather than fighting against each other. I started noticing the instants of hesitation when I was feeling vulnerable and open.

The quality of femininity and loveliness that I observed and absorbed looking at Indian women has been a precious reminder. The delicacy of their hands moving, the subtlety of their glances, the poised swing of their bodies, sometimes exceptionally slim, sometimes fuller, but always heartfelt, lithe. The poorest women, especially, keep a female essence long lost in most civilized cultures. These qualities are inherent, transmitted directly through their beings, while merely walking, washing clothes, carrying loads of bricks or wood over their heads, squatting while chatting. Expressions, somehow banal, are yet eloquent…candid, sincerely meaningful. This train ride compelled a different awareness of my own body and movements. Their feminine essence touched mine, cell to cell, bone to bone. Many times those faces came back into focus, in a flash, reminding me to receive life with gentleness…

For so long, I had hidden softness, delicacy, and susceptibility as a woman, under strategies of protection. Afraid of being burned again, beaten up, ostracized, humiliated, I avoided reawakening sundry recollections of oppression and torture. I felt that the female aspects of my consciousness would never find balance within my actual body. How could those traces of terror be erased? However slowly, they have been washed. Through a conscious effort to stay present with feelings and mindsets, the energy locked in those memories has been recycled as resource rather than deficiency. In recognition, no matter how ancient the dwellers of my soul, prevalent imprints steadily backed off into the realm of ghosts with no power. As the inner river got to stream more intensely, the strength of receptivity became decisive. It manifests now as inner guidance and support.

I still live moments of internal split, especially in instances where rigidity and control intimidates tenderness. This process of integration is ever growing.

The smell of coconut oil shining over braided hair, the tinkling of bangles covering skinny arms, the reminiscence of smoke impregnated in saris, the swiftness of movements, all in one, made my life richer and livelier. Their resonance, as visual and kinesthetic impressions, mysteriously textures the silent and transparent background of my daily life. In just a second, this kindling memory comes back, and I am riding that train cuddled by Mamma India.

I arrived in Pune late in the night, and as instructed took a rickshaw to the ashram. The driver stopped in front of a large gate with golden letters "Shree Rajneesh Ashram." A man wearing a long red robe was sitting in front of the gate, which was closed. His beauty impressed me: long beard, blond and a look of gaiety and calmness. He sounded German as I approached him to ask for information. I asked if Veet Marco lived there, he did not know…but I should come back in the morning, the gate opened at six. I inquired about a place to sleep. He shook his head. After a pause, suggested that I walk down the street, close by there was a house with rooms for rent. It was already too late to ask for a room, it would be fine for me to find a space in the veranda.

It was a beautiful clear night. The street was full of large trees, nobody in sight. I got to the house and walked through the garden towards the veranda where I found a few people sleeping on the floor, over mats. I opened my lunghee (Indian word for sarong) acquired in Bombay, and lay on the floor. I slept soundly until the roosters started to make loud sounds.

The house was placed a bit away from the street but I could see many people walking towards the ashram, wearing long robes in shades of red and orange. I had no clue why. I was hungry and decided to find something to eat, then try again to locate Veet Marco. All men and women I met were foreigners and friendly, very friendly. The teeming of rickshaws and people increased by the second and by the time I had a shower and walked towards the ashram the gate was once more closed for "discourse." I was then informed that Bhagwan gave discourse every morning. I had no idea who Bhagwan was, but wasn't interested either. My task was to give a hug to someone and keep on my way.

Farther down the road, I enjoyed a cup of chai and a good chapati (thin Indian bread), then took a rickshaw to the market downtown to buy sandals. By the time I got back to the ashram, there were hundreds of people coming in and out of the gate, a river of red and orange robes, beautiful wild faces, intense looks, some rather serious, many laughing and seemingly having a good time. Unrelated to the surroundings, I was set on my mission to find Veet Marco.

I approached another gatekeeper. He sounded English and welcoming. I asked about Veet Marco. "I have no idea, we do not have any organization here. You have to go around and ask. Eventually you will find him somewhere." "Does he live here?" "Oh, yeaa…you will find him working during the day around the ashram, just ask." I was puzzled and stood there a bit lost, digesting his answer.

Suddenly the man asked my nationality. I said "Brazilian but…" I had no time to complete my sentence. He instantly told me he was going to call someone to help me and in a few minutes two guys walked towards me.

My "guides" were both Brazilians. Long curly hair, dark shining eyes, both slim, they looked like brothers but I found out they were not, one from Sao Paulo and the other from Rio. I was running away from my culture and conditioning, and did not want to speak Portuguese. I kept rather to myself. They were effusive and inviting. "Oh! You will feel at home here! We also came here for a short visit and never left." They asked my name and introduced themselves: Prageet and Gyaneshwar. "Xuxu, I will take you around!" I did not like the intimacy of the Brazilian slang for "sweet heart" that Gyaneshwar used so quickly with an accent from my hometown. I was reserved, insisting on speaking English, while they kept talking to me in Portuguese. He took me by the hand and we went further into the ashram's garden. There was a large meditation hall surrounded by a luscious tropical garden, lots of huge bamboo and exquisite flowers.

Gyaneshwar stopped to talk with several men and women, introducing me as we went along. The beauty and wildness of the people we crossed called my attention, but this Veet Marco was not on our path. At the end of the afternoon, we met "a" Veet Marco…but he was Swiss, not Italian. Gyaneshwar left me with wishes of good luck and let me know where to find him if I came back the next day. I would rather lose him from sight and find my way alone. Not interested in befriending a Brazilian calling me "xuxu."

The day was over. I heard that people had to go home to change for darshan, another new word. Sounded like an important event.

My black dress was heavy and not easy to wash, so I got two sets of white kurtas (a typical Indian style tunic) in the market, with a pair of sandals that left my feet stained with a dark oil used to treat the leather.

Back to the place where I had slept, I talked to an Indian lady who seemed to be the owner, and was assigned a space on a large terrace full of thin mattresses on the floor. The weather was warm, though nights were cool. I slept cozily wrapped in my wool lunghee.

I walked around the neighborhood called Koregaon Park, a quiet, residential area in the outskirts of town. Pune stands at a higher altitude than Bombay, thus has a milder climate, and was used by affluent English officers during the British Raj for summer vacations. Now, the area comprised dilapidated mansions with usually over ten servant's rooms in a row at the back. Their vast gardens were often neglected and overgrown. The crowd of Westerners and Indians wearing red and orange clothes did not fit the conservative upper-class Indian population. It was rare to see anybody out of the houses around the ashram, except beggars and sellers of all kinds of stuff, as well as magicians and gypsies.

I had breakfast at a nearby cafe called "Prem's." Funky wooden tables with old metal folding chairs, good chai, papaya, bananas, chikkus (small sweet Indian fruit) and a decent omelet. Not that I remember what I ate that specific day, but that was the only thing I ever ate there, as the menu did not offer a great selection. Oh! The fruits were so good!

My body was vibrantly open; having been so close to death had opened a new window of perception. Wide, see-through, unveiled by mind assumptions. I experienced the fragility of the physical body, the unpredictability of life's currents. I looked into the illusion of having control over decisions and choices, I was humbled by the mysterious weave of events that took me by the hand and moved me from here to there. Each moment presented itself as a wonder, and situations did not related to the past or the future. My task was simple: find that guy, just because someone that I did not even know, asked me to do so. I had no reasons to say no, so I said yes. It was not about making sense, but about listening to the subtlest resonance of truth inside. I did not know more than that. In the same way that the parachute jump had ripped shields, facilitating limpid perception, I was becoming aware of that crisp quality at each moment. Yes, a fruit salad, yes, a chapatti! My belly is content. My legs want to walk.

I could only respond to life with the silkiness that was melting the corners of my mind, my education, the expectations I carried from my family and social context. I listened to my body, to my heart, to my soul. In the loose environment of the ashram, surrounded by India's ancient reverence for the mystery of life, I moved with the fluidity that I found at the bottom of my breath.

Several people approached me. My white clothes stuck out, they wondered what I was up to. Nobody knew Veet Marco, and I thought the whole thing was bizarre. Red clothing, people's comments about "discourse" and therapy groups, neither interested me. I wished to be left in peace. I disregarded the small talk and focused on my chore.

Back to the ashram, I stopped at several departments, which seemed to be divisions of different types of work that served the commune. I visited a building called "Number Seventy," where the medical center, the kids' hut, and a restaurant were located. There was also a cheese manufacturing space cared for by a beautiful Swiss man, and a sauna next to a session room. I was led from one place to another, slowly getting acquainted with the whole place. I met another Veet Marco, but he was not Italian either. I came to know that Bhagwan was the man who gave discourses and that he was enlightened. Another word I had never heard... I did not understand why people would go to listen to this man every day. Several people told me that I was a sannyasin and it was only a question of time until I recognized it. I heard that sannyasins had to wear red and orange clothes. I did not inquire further.

Later in the afternoon, someone invited me to the "music group." Alive music and dance for an hour! I entered the large meditation hall, framed by a tropical jungle garden. There was a couple at the center of a circle of maybe two hundred people. They initiated the singing with tremendous enthusiasm. Peter was playing the guitar and Aneeta had an impassioned voice. Their fire touched my heart. My body enchanted, I got lost into the dance and songs, my voice opening. Most people seemed entranced.

On the third day I finally found the "right" Veet Marco. He was smoking a beedie (thin Indian cigarette) behind the ashram. He asked me about his friend in Rome. When was he coming for a visit? When are you taking sannyas? I am not! I gave him a hug, and walked through the ashram to take a rickshaw to the train station.

SNAKE IN PARADISE

I had heard Goa was a place with lovely beaches. I jumped into the overnight train going south. Arriving in Mapin, I was told to get a cab to Candolim.

Cruising slowly in a large old black car, absolutely outdated, I enjoyed the blurring tropical scenery, stray dogs and mud cottages alongside the road, skinny buffalos, coconut, palm, mango and banana trees, breeze suggesting the ocean close by. The driver dropped me in front of a chai shop, sand and waves down the dusty road.

A white page. Sight!

Turquoise hues at the horizon line, soft blue sky, fading moving clouds. The vastness of the ocean ate my eyes, called my legs into walking.

I ran to the seashore, and dove headfirst. I carry the spirit of the water snake. Knowing how to rest and then, suddenly, moving in no-time. Spaciousness and liquid motion invited her into paradise.

Reaching the place within where nonsense makes sense, where oil and water mix, where skins touch, where the heart is defenseless. Where no pity is useful, where rawness is essence, where the core is exposed, where no composing can make it elegant, where the surface is crowded with senseless gossip, where depth is bottomless, where the blood is alive. Making peace with it all.

Listening accurately, and responding truthfully. Trusting the synchronicity of waves and wind. Resting in aloneness, not so that I isolate my form and hold on to the crystallization of my ideals, but so that I connect with the water quality of life, bodies, spirits…

Salt in my lips, sun in my skin, wind blowing my hair, seagulls on wings, pregnant coconuts, palm trees bending. How could I have ever tried to design straight lines going to square stations? Life is curving and twisting in all directions! I was madly thrilled.

The sand beach stretched for miles in both directions and rounded at a certain point, extending further behind rocks.

As the sun was setting, I walked back to the chai shop, wet, hungry and wondering where to sleep. I ordered something. A blond, attractive woman approached me. She was on her late twenties, wrapped in an orange lunghee, wearing the same beaded necklace with the photo of a man at the center, as I had seen in Pune. We connected in a friendly way. She introduced herself as Himani Sun and explained that Bhagwan had given her this name. It meant "the meeting of the sun and the moon," male and female energies converging. Her life learning was to find this meeting inside herself. I had never thought of names having meanings; her explanation impressed and interested me. She was

American, had been living in India for a few years, had two kids born in Goa, around six and seven years old. She lived in a hut on the beach and invited me to stay with her.

We had dinner together at her home. The aya (Indian woman who cooked and cleaned the house) had prepared the food. The space was one large room with cushions and mattresses on the floor. We ate surrounded by candles, as there was no electricity. Her boys were extra-blond, long hair, big blue eyes, shiny faces, wild spirit, relaxed and caring. I slept next to them. Before saying goodnight, they taught me an evening Indian prayer. Shanti, Shanti, Om.

In the morning Himani and I went swimming and the kids went to the school nearby. She asked me if I would like to stay at her house with the children while she visited her boyfriend in Pune for a few days. The aya would take care of everything, and the kids were used to be alone. Humm… Yes. When the kids came back from school, she let them know. Each boy took one of my hands, they were happy.

Himani left, I was restful and cozy at her place. The boys were lovely, exceptionally articulate and mature for their age. They were kind, light and friendly. In the morning they went to school, and at lunch they came to meet me at the beach. In the afternoon they did homework, spent hours drawing, content. They loved to sit quietly for sunset on the beach, watching the fireball sun dissolve into the ocean.

Dinner and the day was over! They sat in silence with their eyes closed for a few minutes before going to sleep. The older boy explained that was meditation. "You just have to sit and wait until your heart opens. You will feel happy alone." Ah! My love for sitting quietly had a name.

I enjoyed this family life. The boys shared unforgettable sweetness teaching me something every day: Indian mythology, the story of Nanak and other Indian saints, songs and invocations. They talked about Bhagwan; he was their master and he was enlightened—that meant he was "happy forever." They loved going to Pune to visit him.

A week went by and Himani didn't return. These were the days when phones did not work and there were no faxes or emails. The kids were not worried; they assured me that if she was in Pune, she was fine.

While living at Himani's house, I sat quietly every day, alone on the beach in the morning, and with the children in the evening. I started doing yoga, recalling a practice initiated with my mother as a young child. I met people from different nationalities, many of them wearing orange clothes, hippies, freakies, tourists of all types. However, I was not interested in relating or social gatherings. I chose to retreat and rest.

One afternoon, I passed by a carpet dealer set inside a large tent. An Indian guy called me in. I love oriental carpets and the baba looked cool. The conversation turned into an invitation to smoke a pipe. Why not? I sat with him and a few other men at the back of the shop, relaxed against piles of carpet. Chai in one hand and the pipe passing around. Slowly my body became weightless, my visual field expanded becoming sharper and clearer, sounds had no meaning. I experienced softness and fluidity as if my flesh was merging with the objects around, like watercolors running over wet paper...

Only many hours later I came back into the world of time, realizing that we had smoked opium. Again, I pondered, "If it sensitivity inside me, it must be possible to retrieve it without drugs?

Early in the morning, I walked to a tiny stall on the beach, built with bamboo and banana leaves, where a young boy sold lassis—a typical Indian refreshment made with homemade yogurt, water and mango, beat up with ice in the blender. I loved its flavor and coolness!

By then I had shifted my wardrobe to fine white cotton lunghees, and in the evening my wool shawl gave me enough warmth. I was barefoot, had had enough of the dirty Indian sandals... My body was gaining in sensitivity and radiance. I sensed each cell regaining its own pulse, throbbing from the core, shining through my skin, gleaming almost visibly. Like an orgasm prolonged indefinitely, a tingling constantly aflame within. The contentment that this state offered was enough to keep me from one day to another without many needs.

I slowly explored nature's riches. At the end of Candolim there was a jungle area with a small hidden path leading to the next beach. Even farther, there was a secluded beach called Vagator. Set down in an amphitheatre fashion, the half-circle white sand beach configuration naturally created a protected area for swimming, where the ocean was lake-like. At the end, to the right, there was an old fort built high on a hill. When I climbed up there, the river joining the ocean was visible at a distance. I fell in love with that spot. Quite far from the main road, this area was accessible only through an open field with no outlined pathway, and further required an arduous descent through rocks and small trees, so not many people found it. I had spent a day there and was looking forward to returning.

About a month later, Himani came back. She was grateful for my caring for the kids and asked if I would like to stay longer. A few days later I decided to move on towards Vagator.

I started walking through the beach, and then took a short cut through the jungle. I was in no hurry, had no specific place to go, so kept walking and trying new pathways. Moving a bit deeper into the forest, I lost sight of the ocean. The land was flat and the trees rather dense and tall. I had an inner sense of direction, but after a certain point, no reference in the landscape assured me that I was moving towards my intended destination. Sooner than I expected, it got dark and I had no idea where I was, nor how to get to Vagator... Going back was pointless. I kept moving, occasionally meeting a few unfriendly barking dogs. No sight of lights, house, people, or the ocean. I was lost! Concerned with wild animals, I could not relax enough to lie down and sleep. The only choice was to keep walking, in the hope of finding a way out. It might have been very late when I saw a small hut hidden among the trees, and a dog ferociously howling. I stopped, and from the house an old lady opened the door... She had a candle. I could see her wrinkled face. I screamed at a distance asking for directions afraid to come too close to the yapping dog. She pointed and screamed back something I did not understand. I had the suspicion she only wanted to get rid of me. I walked into the direction she pointed but it did not take me out of the jungle. The night went by, I did not find my track. Waves of panic, heart racing, waves of peace, stopping and listening, waves of fear, walking faster, feet hurting, waves of lucidity, enjoying the beauty of the night, all speeding by while the darkness turned into light. I walked aimlessly the whole night. When the sun came up, I finally met a man who showed me the path to Vagator. I wasn't that far...

Later in life on different occasions I remembered that night, feeling lost in the same way with no choice but to keep moving, waiting for the sunlight to illuminate my path.

Arriving at the ocean, in a zombie-like state, I fell asleep on the sand with the soothing sound of the waves. The day passed in awe and wonder. Alone, nature daintily talking to my soul, I had no motivation to move any further. Late afternoon, I climbed the hill towards the ruins of the old fort. I was learning to play a bamboo flute, so I sat there inviting music through my instrument, watching the river merging with the ocean...

In this peaceful space, I sensed someone standing behind me. I turned my head and saw a radiant man with a calm facial expression. He was just there. Long blond hair, handsome body wrapped in a red lunghee, bright blue eyes directly looking into mine. He silently sat next to me. We watched the sun set. Then he held my hand and we walked down towards the beach. We did not exchange any words. I noticed that he had the same beaded necklace, as Himani and her kids.

We lay down on the sand together, and slowly started caressing each other, ever so sensitively. His innermost kindness and physical beauty touched me. We made love with the waves crashing near our bodies. Unhurried and gently we met in motionlessness. When I finally opened my eyes, I was surprised to realize that he was gone. Not a word... Who was this man?

I bathed in the ocean, evening by then... I loved the darkish waters, barely guessing the next wave, suddenly cooling my skin.

I walked towards the jungle alongside the beach, looking for a space to sleep. I found just the right spot, a small clearing with ocean view, protected by large tall trees, the sound of crows rustling over their leaves. I made a bed on the sand with my lunghees and slept still feeling my body caressed by this mysterious man.

In the following days, I made this jungle spot into my home. I went to the village and got a straw mat as a bed, bought a clay pot to cook and make tea, milk powder and herbs for chai, a basket to keep rice and flour for chapatis. After arranging rocks in a circle for a fireplace, I was set! Most fruits were picked up freely from trees. I was not concerned about what to eat anyway...

Soon I found out that crows and monkeys loved milk powder. The only way to keep them away from the Nestle tin was to tie it with a rope, hanging upside down from a branch. However, smart monkeys making funny noises often woke me up trying to untie the rope with their hands. As well, determined crows insistently called my attention by banging their beaks on the metal can.

A few days later I met the blond man again. This time we talked, barely. His name was Laya. I concluded he was English, by his accent, and that he had been in Pune, because of his red colors and the mala (the word used to refer to the necklace with the photo on).

He took me to his house up above the beach—a large one-room space surrounded by a garden, where a mat and a mosquito were set as his "bedroom."

An international wild tribe gathered at his place in the evenings to play music and sing. They worn red and the mala, and I understood that most of them transited between Pune and Goa. My connection with them was visceral and earthy. Nothing came into my mind asking for explanations.

Laya spent time with different women but seemed to be unattached to all. I was relaxed with him, appreciative of his silent way. Our friendship extended for the years to follow.

At his house, I met Ahata, a New Yorker with intense eyes and Pisces intuition. We came close at first sight. He asked me for a massage. "You are a Tantric!" What? I had never given a massage before, though had received massages my whole life from my grandmother who was a true witch and natural healer. Ahata insisted, "I will pay you, just try!" We arranged a space on the floor inside the house for my first session… My hands knew what to do, where to touch, how long to hold, how fast or how slow to move. We sat in silence for a long while afterwards.

He spread the word that I gave "amazing" massages. So, others decided to try on my hands. My knowledge of the human body from my yoga and dance background came through my hands effortlessly. The sensitivity that I had developed while making love, feeling my own body and relaxing from within, translated into empathy to others. Most of all, I enjoyed sharing the silence I experienced alone, becoming tangible through touching.

Ahata and I became good friends. We were spontaneous in a wild fashion, no mind to interfere with the power and immediacy that magnetized our meetings. Our sexual connection had no comparison or classification. We played with exquisite bites of desire, met unexpectedly, and laughed like foolish kids. He was funny and provocative in a unique way, untamed and unreasonable! I cherish his craziness and our companionship!

Besides my new "work," the days were spent on the beach, swimming and walking, sitting quietly, eating occasionally, making love whenever it happened. More than plenty!

I decided it was time to let go of trying to control anything. Life was surprising, mysterious and out of my hands. How could I possibly try to control its reproduction?

I was open to become pregnant if that was what life wanted to give me. Through this experiment I relaxed to such a degree that making love became a merging with life itself. My body opened without reserves. Each man I made love with enriched my sensitivity and ability to receive. My awareness became more and more focused inside myself. There was no future. The past was far away... Once the preconceived ideas creating anticipation and expectations on the other dissolved, there was opening and receptivity without frames. The energy used for protection, to keep the body on guard, even in the slightest way, turned into greater consciousness and observation of subtleties within.

Searching for freedom was the bottom line of the motivations we had to converge to this place. The desire to find ways to break out of Western conditioning and expectations was explicit. This unconventional gathering disowned old ideas and social rules. All was up for trial! Each day was special and full. Beyond good and bad, right or wrong, there was life happening in thousand directions, with countless invitations and lessons.

The jungle "population" was inconceivable. People from diverse walks of life gathered on this small beach, sharing a unique experiment unlikely to be available anywhere else in the planet. Mixing races and backgrounds, communing at sunset, playing music, eating and dancing... A universe in itself! I do not remember walking too far during the months I spent in this idyllic scenario.

One of the jungle's inhabitants was a Swiss banker. He worked in Zurich for six months and lived in Vagator during the other half of the year. Apparently as freaky as everybody else, he came forward in magnanimous sharing, offering food and cash to whoever might need. He built a palm leaf roof in between two trees and under it, hooked a hammock. Next to it, he had a small kitchen with a handy gas stove, excellent pots and food brought from Europe. He often went to the market to buy luxurious items such as Nescafe. A fisherman delivered fresh fish and he prepared meals daily, available to whoever wanted to partake it. I appreciated his generosity, imagining this man sitting at a bank in Switzerland!

Goa was party's paradise. Peculiar breeds of hippies-freakies-sannyasins-Indians-curious-tourists gathered for all-night-long music and dance events. Remarkable concerts, talented musicians improvising, creating an atmosphere of enchantment and stunning rhythms. The people's scenario ranged from almost naked to princess-like fashion; there was no limit to imagination and fantasy. Elephants and other animals, often adorned in colorful fabrics, were part of the picture.

One late night I was coming back from a party, walking alone through the fields that extended from the road towards the beach—a mile of open space, nobody, no houses, no lights. Used to walk alone, I feared nothing in nature. I was moving slowly when I realized someone approaching rather fast. No time to think. I was grabbed from the back, strong arms and hands restrained my chest and arms. A man's voice said, "I am going to fuck you and I will kill you!" I sensed a thin, though muscular body immobilizing mine, and the cold metal of a gun under my chin. There was nothing I could do, screaming or running would not help. There was nowhere to escape.

Strangely, I was profoundly calm. My breath went deeper into my belly. I heard my own voice, "Why would you kill someone if you want love?" The guy certainly did not expect a philosophical conversation in those circumstances. Neither did I. Still holding the gun next to my head, he moved a bit to the side, so I could see his features. He was young and dark skinned. I asked him if he could move the gun away from my face. He did so, but secured me by the wrist.

Speaking nervously in broken English, he told me he was Nepalese. As a young child, he had witnessed someone kill his mother. He was very angry. He had learned to steal and kill, to survive. I told him I had nothing to give him, and asked if he would let me go. He reacted irritably pointing the gun towards my front. "No! I want to make love with you!" There was no thinking time. My immediate response was to give, rather than fight. Somewhere inside there was lucidity. If I wanted to stay alive, I had no choice. And there was relaxation… The guy had a soft heart and I could feel it.

"Ok, but let's make it comfortable."

I unwrapped my lunghee, placed it on the ground, and let him come over me. He was light and slim. I relaxed, opening my heart and letting him move at his own pace. His energy was infantile and shortly, he was done. I asked him to escort me back to the party. He acted honored walking next to me. Ahata was surprised to see me back, and to hear my update. My body was shaky and I did not want to spend the night alone. We went to his place, and he held me for the night with loving care.

This experience showed me the way of non-resistance, beyond my conscious choice. It made me realize how the body and the mind are connected. As the circumstances did not allow for the mind to take over, the body was open and relaxed, even when encountering danger. I felt the strength of vulnerability, and the wisdom of presence. Oddly, an incident that could have turned into a violent encounter, developed into collaboration and understanding. However, I became more careful when walking alone.

Another memorable night… Vagator beach was designed like a new moon: my jungle "home" was at the extreme left and the old fort was at the extreme right. Sitting quietly at my spot, I heard the distant music of an outdoor party coming from the other side. My location was almost directly across, over the ocean, and the wind amplified the sounds. The tantalizing sounds lured me and I started walking through the beach. However, as I got to its center, the music was inaudible. The stars and the rocks were silent. The waves were gentle and I sat contemplating the waters. No desire to move further. After a while, I walked back to my place ready to go to sleep, but suddenly the music was again loud and clear. Let's go! By the time I got to the inner curve of the beach, the sound subsided. I spent the whole night walking back and forward. Early morning, the brightness of the sun impelled me to reach the party's location, in time to see an elephant roaming and drinking leftover chai from a large pot, a few musicians playing faded notes, people bathing naked in the ocean...

In those days, the characters floating around were unique and every encounter expanded my horizons and ability to receive life's nuances. A few meetings stayed with me for their eccentricity and puissance.

Rani, a Dutch girlfriend, took me to Paul's house. Welcoming and simple in his way to stand on his own feet, he was an attractive American guy in his mid-thirties. Paul spent most of the year in the Himalayas practicing yoga, learning to move beyond ordinary states of consciousness into subtler energetic realms. His master emphasized the importance of maintaining relationships rather than remain in isolation. So, after each season in the mountains, he spent a few weeks in Goa and then returned to the USA. In his home country, he had a precise routine: he would steal something small in a department store, but make sure to get caught and be put into jail for a few weeks. In this way he was forced to integrate his yogic powers with ordinary living, grounding his physical body in preparation for the next level of spiritual practice. For a few years, he had been back and forward.

He offered to initiate us in Tantric Yoga, briefly explaining what that was about—learning to merge with a sexual partner in a way that the boundaries of the body were lost, and from that experience expand into merging with the oneness of the cosmos. His voice was warm and assuring, his eyes were clear and looked straight into mine. I trusted him. The three of us spent the night together. We used no drugs. I only remember eating pieces of mango nicely cut and arranged on a clay plate. There was no body, nobody, no mind, no choice, a current of electricity uniting our bodies, spirits, the walls, the ocean, there was nothing separated within or without. The dance of the universe was happening within my body, every molecule rejoicing its vibrancy in never-ending expansion. At the same time I was conscious and alert, as if my body did not belong to me, it was life's possession. Timeless dimension, ethereal body, I rested awake, in ecstasy...

Early morning, the sunlight called my eyes to open. Gazing around, I realized Paul had smoothly left the room, and my girlfriend had also disappeared.

Out of bed, I jumped from the veranda to the ground level ignoring the stairs, agile as a cat. I started walking along the beach moving away from Vagator, just straight and determined, not knowing where I would end up. Concentrated energy in my legs moved me effortlessly. I walked the whole day feeling insubstantial, meeting nobody. As the sun was settling down, I sat to rest merging with the colors of the sky and the trees and the clouds and the waves. From a distance I sensed someone approaching. I saw a figure only comparable to a Michaelangelo's statue or a Masai tribal man. A majestic, wild, tall, strong, blond man. He sat next to me. My body had no consistency. He was earthy and warm. In a silent gesture, he took me by the hand and indicated movement towards the ocean.

I followed him, jumping over the rocks, away from the sand strip. We arrived at a cave. That was his home. He was from Czechslovakia, had traveled around the world and had been in Goa for a few years. His body and aura seemed untouched by civilization. He was building a wooden boat to travel south. I stayed with him, helped assembling his boat—a well-crafted wooden platform, held in place with natural ropes gathered from trees, and a primitive canvas sail. We did not have many words to exchange. He talked to the ants, to the birds and wild animals; we ate chapatis and fresh fish. Swimming, walking in the forest, and making love…

One day, we were watching the waves hitting the rocks and splashing over us. We were both standing at the edge of the ocean as we embraced in a hug. Suddenly he lifted me off the ground, and gracefully turned my body upside down, holding my ankles only. He twirled me in the air, my waist-long hair flowing in the wind, my naked body floating above the water. Balancing himself on top of a rock, he turned me around very fast, swinging in a circle! His hands transmitted trust and letting go! One second of him loosing his grip and I would be gone. His strength, absolutely still, afire my belly.

The days passed with rare words. Like animals, we communicated through our bodies and eyes, touch and movement.

A few weeks later, his boat was ready and he decided to sail south. Would I like to come? No, I was ready to go back to Vagator, another day walking…

Back "home" in the jungle, I met Rani. She was concerned. Paul had left, he did not like to get involved with people he had initiated, she explained. I was grateful.

The experience with Paul had a strong effect. I lost sense of physical boundaries and fears. My body was essentially permeable, as if I had liquid bones. There was no outer movement, no sense of direction, except inwards. I lay bare, motionless, over large rocks, aware of inner movements in lightness, trespassing the solidity of the stones, merging into fluidity within and without. I lost outer references. Everything seemed to be fluctuating continuously. I sensed my body, the trees, the rocks, the animals, the clouds…vibrating like energy rivers, pulsing in distinctive rhythms. Time of introspection and reflection, inner observation and wonder.

Walking on the beach one afternoon, in a flash I noticed my arrogance. I walked like a queen! I was naked, had no money, no resources, nobody that I really knew around… And yet, I was walking as if the world was at my feet. No concerns, no worries, no fear. I surprised myself in this observation. Who am I? What gives me sense of identity? Where does trust come from? Does it make any difference if I am here or there? Who lives inside this body? These questions turned into constant inquiry. I kept listening to my own replies, and could not stick to any answers. I did not know who I was, or why I was alive. I was deeply content and the anguish of my early years had been washed. I felt clean and fresh, recovering joy and innocence unveiled crystal clear through my shining eyes. I sensed their fiery beam from within.

Another burst of understanding was delivered in a quiet morning, while I was playing with the waves not so far from the shore. Suddenly, a man came running towards me. In a flash, long dreadlock hair, his flying body held mine, we both rolled around in the water and before I could have a spark of thought, he penetrated me in a wild and yet gentle way. Like two animals, spirited and playful, healthy and bustling with vigor, we enjoyed unwavering sexual pleasure for a few hours, unhindered sounds, flesh in resonance.

When we separated, I sat at the shore. No rational words, or ideas in between. Without interference of preconceptions, I dove into a state of union within that reflected the underlying bond of body and spirit. Unexpectedly. No protection, no judgment, no expectation. I observed how the mind controlled my body, restricting its potential for bliss and love. Though this isolated experience did not carry the maturity of integration, it indicated a possibility that I knew was within. With that imprint in my cells, offered by someone who dared to let go in such extreme way, I began to recall it, easier and easier. That memory lingered like a tuning fork.

This connection suggested another realm of potentiality. I realized that most human beings lived far from the inherent aliveness and pleasure that the body was able to experience. During these months in the jungle, sleeping under the stars, I felt my body intrinsically connected with the spirit of life in all forms. I noticed how social limitations had distorted my body's raw sensitivity and suffocated its expression. I understood that when life's zing was controlled by external forces it lost its original purity, and turned into mental activity. This encounter broke this pattern ruthlessly. I experienced the movement of my physical energy following its instinctive flow, disconnected from usual considerations and restrictions imposed by the mind.

I perceived the wildness of humanity's soul as a divine gift almost completely lost. What a blessing to recover it! This incident ignited my soul's love of freedom. I knew my life was only worth if I could let its fire burn, expressing love through the instrument of my body.

I met this man again and made love several times in other circumstances. Even though his style was radically uncompromising, my inner space was different, and I was not able to open up in the same way. I got lost looking into his crystal blue eyes, observing his fine features, hearing some of his story-lines...

Monsoon suddenly started and the jungle home became useless. Impossible to stay outdoors while the rain was pouring non-stop. I moved to Laya's house, where at least there was a roof, though nothing else inside it. Ahata was also living there and other friends continuously dropped by. Chapati and chai and a fire going. When the rain gave us a break, the beach was still there for a swim. Some of the people who usually came to the house left for Pune. I suddenly decided to move on. I still had my Nikon camera, too heavy to keep carrying around. I gave it to Ahata; he was a dealer of all kinds and was glad to have some merchandise on his hands. I threw my passport in the garbage, just outside Laya's house, determined to never go back to the West. Free and loose, I asked life to take me by the hand.

My feet led me to the train station. At the last minute, Rani decided to join me. Where are you going? I had no idea... Let's take a train and then get out when we like the landscape.

At the station we met an Indian man, elegantly dressed, who asked where we were going. South, I said. He asked if we had tickets already. No, we had no money. In my previous trips I realized that there was no ticket control on third class, so I was planning to just get into the train and sit there. The man confessed that he had won a large amount in the lottery. Feeling lucky, he gave us a few rupees, thank you! We kept it for food.

No ticket control, as I expected. We got out in Mysore. This village is surrounded by sandalwood trees, which are cut down for extraction of essential oils and manufacturing of objects. The whole place exuded this delectable scent. We walked around and further into the forest. Rani got scared and tried to convince me to go back to Goa. We had a fight and decided to go separate ways. I kept walking alone until I found a clear ground to sleep. The trees encouraged me to keep exploring.

I spent a few days in Kodaikanal, a mountain town where hallucinogen mushrooms grow galore. Cold nights, I slept in the veranda of an abandoned house, barefoot and wrapped in my wool shawl. An old woman offered me a mushroom tea, which I accepted. The beauty of the eucalyptus growing around, the delicacy of colors tinting the sky, the Indian babas sitting at the chai shop, watching my spirit inside a young woman's body, letting the wind blow and whisper her way.

I moved through the south of India, Kerala, being transported by an ancient spell. The train crossed unforgettable landscapes, biblical descriptions, lost days of yore... Children and women seen at a distance, like paintings evoking peace and devotion, men and bullock carts, unhurried.

I came out in the middle of nowhere. A tiny village, no "whites" around, I stood out like a duck! A woman came close and held my hand. Without asking any questions, she took me to the temple set high on a hill. Large marble stairs leading to the top, thousands of people elbow to elbow! The woman painted my face with colored powders. As most of people were likewise decorated, I guessed it meant something... I enjoyed the playfulness, like being in a town with children who had grownup bodies. It was extraordinary.

This woman kept me under her wing, moving swiftly through the crowd. She took me to look at a pond full of fishes that stood in a vertical position, with their heads coming out of the water. Later, I came to know that these were considered to be divine fishes, found nowhere else in the world. They offered me their blessings while I laughed with the absurdity of that moment.

This day at the temple taught me about trust, nonsense, superstition, love, intuition, female bonding, and about innocence. I was immersed in a collective mentally averaging three to four years old. The objects sold in the market were handmade; small tin home utensils, toys made out of pieces of trees, food exposed in large cotton bags; there was no developed mind involved in the creation of the environment.

The woman stayed with me all day. She did not speak a word of English, nor did I speak her language; just our eyes meeting, her fine hands holding mine.

Back down in the village, she pointed to a road leading out from the main agglomeration. I understood she wanted to take me somewhere. I moved my head as the Indians do, in consent. We walked for a few minutes and came to a hut, which seemed to be her house. She invited me in, some children and a man sitting at the door. She pointed to the mat on the ground inside the main room, made a gesture for me to lie down. I did. As I was only wearing a lunghee with nothing under it, she started massaging my body in an intense and rapid way, strong strokes, she flexed my limbs in all directions, like electricity running through my whole body, pulling, pushing, and stretching... I had no way to figure out what she was doing, but fell in unison with the flow of her movements. She rubbed oils and herbs over my skin, and their effects were sensible within seconds, life fire through my veins. At the end, she poured warm oil over my third eye until I lost awareness of my own body and my mind could not follow any thoughts. Timely, she delicately tapped me on the face. Strangely, I was awake promptly. She pointed to the village. I namaste and walked back alone, my feet hardly touching the ground.

Another train late in the evening. Crammed! Once inside, I was informed that it would not stop for the whole night! The only space I found was on the top "shelf" of the women's compartment, where there were six beds smashed with people. I was pulled by the hand to the top and squeezed in a corner. I was suffocating from lack of air and strong smells. My body still under the effects of the massage, in a vulnerable state, my mind went bizarre. Compulsively, I started counting people inside the compartment. I could not stop it! More than fifty women and children in this small space! Counting again and again, that was the only thing keeping me from screaming. There was no way out. I kept watching my breathing, and slowly I relaxed. Everybody else seemed fine. They were just there, sitting, sleeping, talking, eating. I could not sleep, and had to hold the need to go to the toilet as well. We traveled through the night without pause. When the train finally stopped, early morning, I got out, not having any idea where I was! As I walked on the street just outside the station, I fell and lost consciousness.

As I woke up, the sun was up as well. I was in a state of trance. Memories of war and concentration camps flooded my consciousness. I saw in detail faces of people and locations. I saw myself as a very skinny and young girl, standing inside an overcrowded train, traveling through a winter landscape. I heard voices speaking German, and I understood their fear. I was delirious. I sat on the street for hours while crowds were moving by, nobody bothering about this white woman lying on the sidewalk like any other beggar. I looked at the saris moving near my nose, appreciating the brilliance of their colors, the richness of infinite nuances in harmony, gold threads sparkling. When

I was able to move and walk, I asked for fruit at a stand and got a mango, which I ate with special pleasure. I walked through town and found out I was in Bangalore.

From there I kept moving erratically and rarely met anyone speaking English. For food, putting my two hands together was enough to get something. Sleeping, mostly on the ground, either on the streets, or outdoors in nature.

One evening in Madras, I asked a woman for a place to sleep. She pointed into the direction of an open land where I could see people sleeping on the ground. I joined them, glad to have found a less noisy spot, out of the pedestrian traffic. The morning after, as I woke up, I looked around and saw that lepers were surrounding me. I thought of my family, my friends, the boyfriend I had left, Derek and Liza, so distant... What was I searching for? I still was not sure. But inside my heart, I knew India was my guide and home. I did not miss anything, or anybody. I looked at a woman staring at me, and saw her beauty; beyond her physical distortion, I saw her soul.

At the train station, I met someone who spoke some English and discovered that I was a few hours away from a small fishermen village. Sounded idyllic. As per instructions, I ended up in a small busy town, from where I was supposed to walk on a trail leading to the beach. Most people had very dark skin, looked more primitive, and I could not find anyone to give me further directions. I stopped at a stand and got some food on a banana leaf. The first bite turned me upside down. It was so spicy! My heart jumped out of my chest! Next thing I remember, I was flat on the floor of the hut with a crowd around me, a woman throwing water on my face, fanning over me, trying to get me back! I burst into laughter!

From the crowd stood a man who could speak enough English to ask where I was going. He would be happy to take me there, assuring me that it was a beautiful place. He looked like a decent man. I accepted.

We walked on a trail for several hours, jungle and animals. I was not sure anymore that the man was trustworthy, but too late... He was behaving respectfully and we finally arrived at a conglomerate of huts in front of a magnificent ocean landscape. Striking!

We walked towards an open space where a few houses-huts converged and maybe a hundred people were idly sitting. They rushed towards us. Suddenly, my guide disappeared inside one of the houses. I was left alone, surrounded by people pushing and pulling to come closer to me. I could not breathe! Surely, they had never seen a white woman. Men and women smiled in shyness and curiosity, the children screamed and pulled my lunghee, reaching for my skin, small hands touching my body. I started shaking beyond control, I could hardly inhale, I could not move.

I feared for my life. I wanted to scream and had to refrain from reacting, not sure that I could contain such intensity. Their energy permeated my aura, invading the layers of my emotional protection. I experienced racing thoughts.

A young woman approached me with a plate of food. I expected to be able to eat privately. However, they continued to stand around. I ate with a hundred eyes watching me, people making comments in a language I did not understand, giggling. I was in panic, and could hardly swallow the food.

Another woman led me to a porch outside a house; the floor was earth and the space was covered with a palm roof. She gestured me to lie down. It was getting dark... Women and children lay next to me, not bothering if their bodies touched mine. I could not sleep nor move.

Early in the morning I stood up, wired and exhausted. A child brought me chai. I pointed to the beach, as I wanted to walk. A small group of women joined me, with lots of kids. They took me a bit further into the forest that bordered the land. We arrived at a special clearing spot where they sat in a circle and placed me at the center. They started singing and quickly I relaxed into their softness and innocence. I was bathed by a purity of heart above considerations. I was their guest. They offered me their home, their food, their protection, their blessings. I received their dark eyes into the depth of my heart. Another initiation into trust...

My escort took me back to town later in the day. I took the train in the evening. Another ride towards an unknown destination.

Late into the night, the train stopped for repair. Across from the station was a modern looking coffee shop. Time for a cup of tea. I sat at a formica table alone. Soon a rather well-dressed man asked if he could join me. The place was weird, strange vibes. I was sleepy. The guy offered to bring me a drink. He came back with a cup of chai and sat next to me. I did not like his pleasing and talkative manner, however accepted his offer. The moment I put my mouth on the edge of the cup, a sudden reaction hit my guts. I heard myself saying, "Why do you want to poison me?" I was shocked; so was he. He immediately reacted in excuses. Yes, he was trying to poison me, he was a white slave boss and I was a beautiful young woman. He was giving me a strong sedative and then would carry me to one of his places to be used as a prostitute for wealthy men. They paid good money, he was not going to hurt me. I was startled, I had never heard of such thing. In a second I stood out and left the restaurant.

As I looked outside, there was a bus parked. I read the front sign "Pune." Instantly I understood that my wandering around had only prepared my way back there. From hell to heaven! Life was magically guiding me once again. The man on the necklace was calling me. It was clear now! I got into the bus, nobody asked me for a ticket. I sat at the back, my belly was trembling. Gladly the bus started moving, shaking up and down, people snoring... I was on track!

HOME

My aimless pilgrimage guided me full circle.

Entering the ashram's front gate, I was able to perceive, see and feel anew. This wandering time had shattered my mind's logic, broadened my vision, made my senses keenly open. My heart was porous, my ears more alert. I looked at the river of people moving in all directions. Their faces were radiant, their bodies were vibrant, their eyes were unusually shiny, their smile arose from the heart and belly. Some looked busy, some walked leisurely, but I sensed relaxation and no striving.

I walked slowly, relieved to have found my way back. Suddenly I realized that the days in search of Veet Marco had given me the excuse to taste something I was unable to absorb at that time—the flavor of love in the air. Now it was bluntly visible. Flowers, features, robes, bamboos, children, harmony, birds, colors, laughter, serenity, joy, suave crossing of bodies and spirits. How could I have missed it?

On the left side was "Buddha Hall," the place where meditations happened throughout the day. Just outside it, bordering the paved pathway leading to the back of the ashram's garden, there was a low stone wall. I sat there, watching the stream of people coming in and out. In my previous visit I stood separate as a spectator, focused on my task, impermeable to what was being offered. Now, my eyes were empathetic, my mind was clear, judgments had been washed; my body was responsive, ready to embrace the aliveness of this environment. I was home!

A few minutes later, a large car slowly came out from the gate set further back at the end of the lane inside the garden. Moving towards the main entrance, it stopped next to me. A man with a long beard was sitting alone at the back seat. He turned his head and looked straight into my eyes. His glance was electrifying... I returned his gaze, my eyes glued to his. His eyes were empty and luminous. Unexpectedly, my hands came together joining in front of my face, while my body lowered to the ground ever so slowly. I moved featherlike. As I stood back, he waved his right hand unhurried in a gesture of acquiescence with an almost imperceptible smile. The kindness of his beauty, the intensity of his silent presence, the grace of his gestures, were flower-like... I was vaporous, entranced by his fragrance, refreshed by his mist.

A sharp awareness of these qualities inside myself lit up. Delicacy, lightness, radiance. His beam was poignant. My body was tingling aloud. The car moved on towards the street.

My eyes closed instinctively. I heard comments that Bhagwan was going to the hospital to visit someone. Oh! That was him...

A little later, a guy in a red robe approached me with a heavy Italian accent. "Your personality is crystallized, you are ready to take sannyas..." I was not in the mood to talk. "Go to the office and ask for it." What office? He pointed into the direction of the large building across the way. Though I had no idea what he was talking about, I walked toward the office.

Marble, pretty clean, a few women running around.

"Are you here to take sannyas?"

"Yes..."

A woman with a Dutch accent received me.

"You will need to fill in this application."

She was clearly impatient and handed me a paper with some questions. Legal name, address, education, profession...

I was naughty with my answers. No home address, trying to forget my education, professional gypsy learning to live. I knew he would understand. The Dutch lady, I wasn't sure...

"Where are you coming from? Are you ready to take sannyas?"

"I have been traveling... Yes."

"How long have you been here?"

"I arrived early this morning. I feel this is my home!"

She did not smile or look surprised. Rather abruptly, she asked "How many books have you read?"

I thought the woman was nuts!

"I went to University, I have a master's degree... I've read many books!"

She got upset, hasty in answering.

"You don't know what sannyas is about! Go to the meditation camp for a month and then come back!"

I left the office, sat back on the wall. There were more and more people coming in. What to do? I didn't even know what I was asking for, but in my heart.... How many books had I read? What nonsense! I later found out that she meant Bhagwan's books— transcripts of his daily discourses.

Hungry and confused, I walked to Prem's restaurant. Satgyan, a sweet French girlfriend from Goa, came to hug me. She was living in an apartment nearby. Unhappily she had no space for me to stay with her, as her boyfriend Fritjof had hepatitis and would be resting in bed for a month or two.

Inquiring about accommodations, I found out that most people lived in bamboo huts near the river. I was offered a place to stay, no need to pay rent, the owner was in the West for a month. Bamboo walls and palm-leaf roof, a thin cotton mattress on the floor over a few mats.

From what I had understood during my interview at the office, I was to meditate for a month. My only knowledge of meditation came from Himani's kids. I concluded that I was supposed to sit quietly for a month and then return for sannyas.

I sat all day alone undisturbed inside my little hut. Resting in bed I could watch the sky through an opening on the roof. At night, the stars were magnificent. I sat and sat and sometimes got some fruit to eat, but not much... The greatest pleasure was the well where I went to bathe once a day. Sinking inside, Bhagwan's eyes were with me. My life converged to a single point of significance: his silent invitation. If I was asked to sit for a year, I would...

Sleeping at sunset, waking up at sunrise, I kept my account of the days by attaching small pieces of string around a bamboo pillar.

Closer to the end of my retreat, darkness came by but I couldn't sleep. I was feverish, uncomfortable. Late into the night, an unbearable pain broke through my whole body, especially my head and back. I could not move, nor stay still. I crawled out on my fours, trying to find someone to help me... I knocked at a neighbor's hut, a woman woke up to talk to me. Alarmed, she kindly got a rickshaw and gave me money to go to the ashram's medical center. Crying in pain, hardly able to keep my eyes open I knocked at the emergency room. The doctor on call was a young German who possibly had never seen anyone in that state. He freaked out! Without even asking my name, he put me back alone in the rickshaw with directions to Ruby Hall Clinic in town.

Intuitively I knew that I had meningitis. I was familiar with its symptoms and effects. I was probably going to die soon.

At the hospital, I was taken on a stretcher for X-rays and blood tests; then placed on a public ward's bed, surrounded by several other people coughing, snoring and making weird throat noises. A flimsy curtain separated my bed from others. I wanted to be left alone and close my eyes. But a nurse came with an injection and a few pills... I fainted.

A while later, I jolted when someone strongly shook my body, waking me up. A doctor, a nurse and two skinny guys were standing next to my bed. Before any words were uttered, the nurse forcefully turned me onto my belly, one of the guys jumped on my legs, tightly holding them both, while the other restrained my neck, holding me down to assure no movements. In a lightning I understood that they were giving me an epidural injection to test the cerebro-spinal fluid. The pain was way beyond description. I had no extra energy to react.

The doctor in charge was kind and straight. "You have meningitis. I am sorry... You are going to die within a day or two. We will take good care of you!" He tapped me on the face, a gesture that intended to be comforting. His calm transmitted easiness with death. I was peaceful. I was ok to die there. I was twenty-seven and had lived a good life. Nurses came by and my arms soon were full of needles and drips.

A few days later, I was still alive. I guess the medicine worked because I had never taken allopathic drugs before, so my body was clean and responded well. My eyes had a hard time opening when a nurse or doctor came by to check for life signals. The pain was persistent, violently breaking my conscious connection with the physical body. I saw myself floating above it. From that distance I was able to watch its mechanism with amazing accuracy. I saw how this bacterial invasion was affecting my brain and spinal cord, how the membrane enveloping my brain was swollen, blood moving throughout, the muscles tightening as a reaction, how the medicine was affecting my vital functions and fighting the bugs. It was fascinating. From this experience I kept an unusual awareness of body mechanics and energetic anatomy. No class or book could have offered me this perspective.

Death was in my body and consciousness. Aloneness was the reality of death, no escape. I befriended it.

During my stay, several people died in the ward. I watched the families come by and stand next to the dead person in respect and silence, sometimes singing heartfelt prayers. I thought that if I died there, someone would come and sing for me. That soothed my soul.

The doctors and nurses were doing their best to care, but not trying to "save my life at any cost." Death was received as a natural part of life. This very fact was healing.

Once a week, a Christian nun visited the hospital. Coming to my bed, she asked my name and why I was there. "Oh! My daughter, you will either die or become brain damaged!" She made the sign of the cross over my forefront and followed up her routine.

Breakfast was lukewarm milk; lunch and dinner menu was over-boiled cauliflower and potatoes. The other choice was spicy Indian food, but the smell of it made me sick. I rarely ate.

One of the cleaners was a Rajasthani gypsy. She didn't speak English, but her eyes spoke of innocence. "Sister, sister..." Her only words, delivered with a sweet headshake. She looked at me intensely. As an untouchable, she was surprised that I responded with delight. She giggled... Realizing that I was not eating much, every day she brought me a few Maria biscuits, which she probably stole from somewhere. She was careful when disclosing the gift and placing it on my hands. That was heaven's cookie.

A few weeks later, I managed to get out of bed to pee. I had been using a pan in bed. To my dismay, I saw someone washing the dishes from dinner on the bathroom floor, using the water that ran out of the toilets. I wondered how I survived!

At last, I felt my legs under my body. The pain was subsiding. Weak and skinny, I got dizzy trying to stand up, but I wanted to move.

I thought of my friend Satgyan and calculated that Fritjof might still be in bed with hepatitis. How to find them? I had in mind the name of their apartment building. The windows of the wardroom opened to the parking lot of the hospital, where rickshaws waited for clients...

One evening, I jumped out of the window and asked a driver where that compound was. Nearby...he nodded. I took the risk to get in without any money, hoping that I would find my friend in bed, get some cash and let Satgyan know I was at the hospital. Luckily, the rickshaw waited. My friend, still yellow-eyed in repose, gave me some rupees and I returned with the same driver. Nobody noticed my absence. I was exhausted.

The next day, Satgyan brought me fruits, cookies and two fresh red robes, as I had been wearing one lunghee for almost a month. That was my first sannyasin dress. She mentioned that Bhagwan's enlightenment day celebration was to happen a few days later. "Cherie, you have to come!" I was not ready to leave the hospital yet, but her presence and invitation made me suddenly want to get up!

The day before the celebration, I was released from the hospital and called into the director's office to pay my bill. I had no money. The guy in his serious suit was stiff: I could not leave without paying. It took me a while, trying to convey that it would be impossible to get any money if I did not leave. Finally, I signed a document promising that I would return to pay the bill within a month. He shook my hand and said, "You are lucky to be alive!"

Walking out into the buzzing streets was a shock. I knew the owner of my hut would have returned already, so I walked towards the ashram, possibly half-hour away. Near the Mobos Hotel, a place where many transitory sannyasins lived, I met a familiar face. He asked if I would like to spend the night at his room—he could stay with a friend until I was able to find a place to live. That was a luxury, to have a room with a bathroom, even for a night! Yes, thank you… I slept as in the Garden of Eden. Next day I continued to walk towards the ashram.

Ahata was around the corner, what a nice surprise. He was sure that I would end up in Pune. He had sold my camera and had half of the money for me. After all, life was still playing its magic! I could pay the hospital and use the rest to rent a room.

There was a feverish ambience in the ashram and a long line to go into Buddha Hall for the celebration. The space was large enough to accommodate over a thousand people. The ocean of shades of orange and red now included my bright robe. I was feeling rich and glad to be walking again. I had never seen Bhagwan before, except for our brief eye contact through the car's window. His figure was small and delicate, though his presence spilled over the whole hall. I felt as if he was physically touching my body, remarkably frail at that moment. The power of his closeness, so many people squeezed all-around, loud music contrasting profound silence, all in combination made me feel that there and then, I was going to die. Meningitis was nothing. My heart was beating out of my chest, and yet I was serene and poised. I had never experienced such love and openness before. My sexual experiences had been just a preparation for this feast. No words or explanations were needed. Now I knew why I had left it all behind. His emptiness filled my longing. The silent lover… There he was, not in the way I had imagined.

As the meditation was over, I was in awe and beatitude. My body floated in between people, no sense of solidity within or without.

I spent a few more nights at Mobos, resting and waiting.

A few days later I was having breakfast with Ahata and another friend from Goa came by. She let me know that there was a message for me on the bulletin board. Curious, I went to check it. It was from the main office—Bhagwan had accepted my request for sannyas and I had a darshan appointment dated a month ago... That message had been posted the day after my first interview.

Back to the office, I met another strong Dutch woman. She immediately asked if I had been sick. The question took me by surprise. The celebration seemed to have erased some of my brain cells... I could not remember my time at the hospital. I said, No! She was puzzled.

Misunderstandings underlined my meetings with the office girls! Anyway, she gave me another date, requested that I use no scents when coming to meet Bhagwan, and explained the commitment to wear the colors she showed me on a fabric sample chart, including light orange to dark red tonalities. She asked if I would like to keep my birth name or ask Bhagwan to give me a name with a meaning that would be a reminder of my meditation. I asked for a new name.

I found out that I had enough money to buy a hut! Ahata helped me to negotiate and my Nikon was transformed into real estate! I thanked Pedro for hiding it inside my bag.

Shopping at MG Road, I bought a few meters of a light peach silk fabric, not sure if that color was "official," but I loved it. I chose a darker red lunghee to wear over my shoulders. I got a few kitchen items, a thin cotton mattress, sheets, a towel, and I was set! I took a picture, needed for the official sannyas request, which the photographer gave me for free when he heard what it was for. Bhagwan was his master!

Happy in my new hut, I sewed by hand a loose robe for darshan. I still did not know what sannyas was about. But I was ready!

There was music and dance every day at Buddha hall. I expressed my delight, dancing my heart out. In my wildest dreams, I had never imagined such a place! Hundreds of people dancing and then sitting in silence, in harmony. That was way more than I had asked for.

Bhagwan gave daily discourses in the morning, and he alternated between Hindi and English every other month. I was not interested in his words; what emanated from his presence was plenty. During these waiting days the discourses were in Hindi. I sat in his presence, drinking the sounds that came out of his mouth like melodious music. I came to know that the meditation camp I had been asked to do during my first interview referred to different meditations presented during the day at Buddha Hall in a marathon style. It didn't mean to sit alone in my hut...

Most people referred to Bhagwan as their master, a concept so far unknown to me. Titles were irrelevant for me. For so long I had been searching for the key to intentionally access the silent space of my heart, like a long lost-memory I grieved to retrieve. At once, he threw me in it! I wanted to dance for him, forever grateful. I wanted to allow his ocean-love to wash me out!

My body still needed care. Searching for a natural healing approach, I met Dr. Vasant Lad. He practiced Ayurvedic medicine in town and guided me through a cleansing program with herbs and massage. I sensed a doubtless familiarity with him and this ancient healing art. His kindness and calm presence made me understand the shift I had gone through, in body and consciousness. His loving support was fundamental for my recovery. Nowadays, I still cherish his gift and guidance.

My darshan date came up! I got ready early counting the minutes to go to the ashram. Meanwhile, I sat in a chai shop and leisurely flipped through a booklet for children. It told the story of an Indian woman called Meera. She had merged with the divine source of life through the image of Krishna, and devoted her days to the celebration of his love, dancing madly through the streets and temples. I fell in love with the story. I wished to be named Meera, considering that all I wanted was to dance for Bhagwan. I walked through the dusty road royally, wearing my peach silk robe.

At the ashram, there was a cheerful atmosphere. Appreciating the beauty of the people around me, I was blessed. Wild faces, slim bodies, bright eyes, warm hugs. There was an orderly line to enter Lao Tzu—the house where Bhagwan lived with a few helpers. Inside the garden, we were directed to the meeting room—a round space, marble floor, open to surrounding gardens, only protected by mosquito netting top to bottom. Impeccably clean, there was an empty chair at the center. When everybody settled in absolute silence, he walked in slowly in namaste, and sat motionless.

My memory of darshan is tinted by joy transformed into utter stillness and further, muteness. I had been given a seat at the back, and there may have been thirty people in the room. Someone called aloud the list of people ready to receive sannyas. One at the time, each person was guided to kneel in front of Bhagwan and wait for the new name. He would write it down on an official paper, and then explain its meaning. I observed his gestures, the sweet cadence of his voice, the twinkle of smile in his eyes, his patience with each person.

I was the last one. As I came closer, he touched my forehead over the third eye, a few seconds that resonated the memory of eternity. He pronounced my name gently with a clear intonation. Prem Komala… "Komala means the center of the lotus flower, it floats above the water, it is very soft, like velvet… Prem means love. Your meditation is to remember the softness of love." He talked about being attentive to the softness in my heart. "Never close your heart, that is your meditation. Always remember that softness…" I could no longer make sense of words. The sound of birds, the music, the abyss of his eyes into mine. I flew back to my seat and was the last person to leave the hall.

At Lao Tzu gate, I met Ahata who hugged me strongly. Komala! The courtesan's name from Siddharta—Herman Hesse's book, he said… That book! How could he have guessed? An uncontainable giggle turned into loud laughter! Walking alone to my hut, I stopped by a road stand to buy a Limca—disgusting Indian drink, imitation of Coca Cola. Sipping that sweet liquid, I walked to my hut feeling set alight.

Throughout my life, I had experienced states of empty mind and uncaused joy. My interest in sex had always been as a doorway to those moments and their aftertaste, subtle qualities unfettered from body bonding. Mysterious paradox. This innocent surrender to love was noticeably independent of specific people. During those encounters, awareness cut through the identification with my personality and I recognized the power that these outbursts carried—inner freedom.

The intensity of these experiences left imprints shouting to be acknowledged. Their light-memory, rather than erased, had been recalled again and again. It was impossible to escape from the undeniable lucidity that they provoked. Resting in my bed, after darshan, I experienced the same bliss in aloneness. Awake for most of the night, I treasured the scintillating stars…

The day after taking sannyas I was eager to start working at the ashram. I had uncontainable energy. Though I had no information about how the work was organized, I was ready to perform any task that might be useful to maintain that amazing place.

Once more at the office, I was directed to Arup, the first Dutch woman I had met. She told me it was not possible to work without first doing groups. What groups had Bhagwan recommended? He hadn't…. That did not sound right, everybody had to do groups to prepare them to work. Had I done Dynamic? What? We stumbled once more into an absurd conversation. She told me that Dynamic was a meditation offered in Buddha Hall, every day at six am. I replied that, I did not like to wake up early and if I did by chance, I loved to sit quietly by the river… She stopped engaging. "I will ask Bhagwan about you. Come back tomorrow."

Talking casually over meals, I learned that Bhagwan usually suggested a series of therapy groups to all newcomers. I had no interest in therapy. My motivation to work came out of an overwhelming joy asking to be released, a sense of flowering that needed space and time to fully bloom. I felt so bountiful! However, if he asked me to do groups, I would.

The next day, there I went again! This time I had a bit more information of how things worked in that crazy place. I was ready to agree with anything. Surprisingly, I got a message from Bhagwan saying, "Start working immediately. Your love and devotion are enough. No need to do groups." Arup seemed irritated as she delivered me the news, but arranged for someone to take me to Number Seventy, another complex of buildings on the street behind the main compound.

I met my "coordinator," an intense German guy called Deva. He took me around. Number Seventy was a large house surrounded by tropical gardens, combining a restaurant, sauna, session rooms, a medical center, a large bamboo hut for the kids whose parents lived in the ashram, a few small craft shops, as well as residential rooms for workers. The environment was lively, teeming with Italians and French.

I was given the job of cleaning the communal showers. Equipped with a big hose, I was to wash the walls and the floor, scrub the corners and the cracks in between the tiles to eliminate mildew. Deva suggested that I do it naked, more comfortable and easy. That was up my alley! I love water! No time frame, that was my day's work! He was going to be around, so if I finished early enough there would be something else...

I wasn't in any hurry, enjoying getting wet and taking time to scrape each dark spot in the grout. Before I completed my assignment, my coordinator came back. Oh! It is great! You can come with me now. I dressed and he took me around the building, to a room upstairs. It was an impeccably clean space with a large bed and a few objects. He invited me for a rest. I realized it was his room.

As we entered, he hugged me with tenderness and strength. My state of mind did not judge his approach, rather enjoyed the warmth and softness of his body. We lie in bed lazily and soon were making love. I was not so sure that was within the ethics of my job...but I relaxed in the easiness of the moment. Embracing me, he said, "Don't take work very seriously, that is not what it is about."

After a cup of tea, he took me to meet Kavisho, a beautiful French woman. My next job was to iron her robe. In a few minutes we found out that we had lived in Ibiza at the same time. There was a sweet connection between us that deepened through the years.

My cleaning career did not last long. The following day I was introduced to the coordinator of the restaurant. Anugata was an outspoken Swiss-Italian mama, with a witchy look and a witty mind, full blast into being an instrument of challenge. She moved fast and had a great laugh. My job was to coordinate the fruit salad team. I loved being outdoors, where the kitchen prep table was set up. Peeling and cutting mangos, bananas, papayas, pineapples, chikkus, and mixing it with my hands... Juicy! Our hygiene criterion wasn't high. I did not know much about parasites and other creatures that in time became familiar. My "team" was composed of five or six helpers: Italian, French, Indian and Spanish, once in a while a German. For a few months I befriended fruits and sometimes played waitress during dinner. It required an alertness and precision that I enjoyed immensely.

The ambience during working hours was buoyant and harmonious. Sometimes mischievous, others tempestuous. In this mix of cultures and different mindsets, provocations were bound to happen and reactions bound to be vented. All situations offered me an opportunity to look inside. Happiness and anger went hand to hand, tears and laughter were shared with equal acceptance. In the ocean of heartiness all emotions were washed.

The ashram was run in a collaborative way. People from all over the world spontaneously converged around Bhagwan and through their working together, amplified the potential of focused intention. This apparently chaotic environment offered the ideal opportunity to face issues related to every human emotion, and a myriad of mind designs. Provocative circumstances made me look at the ways my mind pushed me into habits rather than spontaneity and creative intelligence. Just the miscellany of races and cultures and ages was enough! I watched resistance turn into allure or wonder, and certainties turn into dripping eventualities. And sometimes, into stronger stubbornness... However, this crossroads invited merging, even when body and mind debated against irrational demands or absurd deadlines! This gift of exposure and understanding was the pay, as there was no money involved or any other kind of compensation for working.

A few days later, I was again called at the office. I was glad to receive a food pass for Number Seventy restaurant. Unaware of the unspoken policy, I had no expectations and could not understand why others expressed surprise and jealousy. In time, I came to know that a food pass was only given to workers after a few months commitment, and most often they were only valid for the cantina at the ashram, where the food was rather unattractive, Indian dhal, rice, chapati and bananas. To eat at Number Seventy was a rare privilege, as the menu was prepared with imagination and taste, European style. Absurdly, my mind compared. Wishing to be near Bhagwan, I wondered why I did not work or ate at the kitchen inside the ashram, closer to his residence. Maybe I was considered a Brazilian flake, hopeless after all... Meanwhile others complained about the military-style regime of the ashram's cantina, where most Germans worked under the coordination of a blazing Italian woman.

In addition to kitchen tasks, I was asked to give massages at the sauna, a small room next to the restaurant. Kavisho also gave sessions there. We giggled together, wrapped in lunghees—our official uniform.

Life was simple. In the morning I went to discourse. For a few months I only heard Bhagwan speak in Hindi; it was more appealing to let his voice enchant my heart, without the interference of my intellect. Months later, when I started going to discourses in English, my mind was then used to dissolving while listening to him.

Dancing was my preferred activity. Music group was an energy explosion, and I never missed it. I frequently went to Tai Chi classes and to the afternoon meditation called Kundalini, which included shaking, dancing and then relaxing.

Life at the ashram demanded rediscovering my own resources and qualities, and often provoked surprising responses. I observed how family-social-cultural education forged thick layers of protection over the fluidity of my being. While noticing different styles of personality's crystallization (yes, I did get what that meant!) the limitations created by upbringing became obvious. No matter the outlook, European, tropical, American or other, the brightness of the innermost light was veiled. No smartness was better than other. The mind was the mind, was the mind... Until the arrow turned inside, we kept chasing our own tail!

While the opinionated mind sowed fear and separation, Bhagwan's presence encouraged inspiration, sincerity, and conscious intention. Nice shift of perspective.

Sitting with Bhagwan dissolved edges often provoked to stick out during a day's work. Like bathing at the source, his waterfall-like juice energized my body, washed my repetitive thoughts and behaviors. As I walked out of Buddha Hall after discourse, my body was weightless and my soul nurtured.

This daily injection of transparency provided fuel for shifts in my body, mind, and emotions. Bhagwan's presence intimated infinite possibilities—the open sky, the unthinkable—making me dare inner territories that "I" could not have outlined beforehand. If "I" would forget, he instantaneously reminded me to go back inside. The "I" was anyway the only cause of forgetfulness. How could "I" be the instrument of remembrance when this very state dissolved the sense of identity, the definition of who "I" was?

"Taking sannyas" was an acknowledgement of this realization. Living in this paradox, existing through the "I" and yet letting it be constantly washed out, was my experience of surrender. Bhagwan's presence invited the music of life, and simultaneously cultivated the silence of emptiness. Sitting with him refined my ability to listen to life's whispers, perceive its insinuations, move with its subtle indications. Ah!

Soon it became evident that what I used to call love was romantic identification between two inconsistent "I"s further enhanced through mutual admiration. Continuous support of increasing self-definition, instead of softening their false solidity, indeed reinforced both. I noticed that, when the core identification was threatened or broken because of an event or a new element, the "love" was also challenged and "problems" arose. Sometimes other layers of identification were discovered or empowered anew, other times the relationship dissolved because there was no perceived core to hold on to. No wonder why relationships usually didn't last long... And when they did, most people did not look happy. Locked "I"s trying to reinforce their boundaries and yet continuously building steam... Difficult task!

I realized that through my relationship with Derek and Liza, the love I sensed was possible had nothing to do with living in a triangle. Instead, to awaken its latent potential and be able to share it with others required an increasing ability to embrace and expand, finding vastness inside my own heart. It was a solo job! THAT was Komala, the softness Bhagwan talked about...

The shock of my separation from Derek had broken my identification with the outer love in an irreversible way. He represented my dreams and aspirations in a complete package. The jolt of releasing it forcefully had created a gap. Inasmuch as "I" had lost control and sense of direction, the inherent forces of life took over, guiding me to what my being was sincerely seeking for. The mysterious way I found Bhagwan was in itself an unequivocal endorsement of wisdom beyond comprehension.

Yes, unpredictably I had fallen in the hands of existence. Its pointing fingers had placed me at the feet of the master. However, "existence" was rather intangible. To express my gratitude, I had to approach it through its representative on planet Earth: human beings, friends, anybody I would meet on the road, in fact, myself to start with…also plants and trees and animals, symbols of its terrestrial zest. How could love become my response to life, rather than a concept, hanging out in the world of prospects? I wanted to learn to intentionally live in love, innocence and openness.

I started experimenting day to day. Whenever I caught contraction and limitations in my body, emotions or mind, I would go dancing, and open into expansion and fluidity. Whenever I noticed myself repeating something I "knew" from the past, I would stop and listen. Sometimes in the mid of a phrase… It was absurd to try to impose old experiences while living in an environment that constantly changed, presenting new situations and opportunities at every second. My moods and impulses became increasingly unpredictable. Whenever I felt attracted to someone, I soon became aware of my identification, and asked myself… What did she/he reflect that reinforced my self-definitions? Surrounded by people of all nationalities, religions and cultures, this was an amazing terrain to observe my likes and dislikes, judgments and attractions. What was beyond this mind that constantly separated and compared? In this introspective mode, I felt aloof and calm. Nothing disturbed me. Words, actions, demands…it did not make any difference. The intensity of my search had come to a full stop! I did not want to get distracted. I was like water, moving in between it all, untouched, transcending the usual hooks of my own mind. I felt lighter and lighter, lively. In contrast with this inner etherealness, I physically gained weight, guess as a consequence of relaxing and dropping my teenager's ideal of being super-skinny. There was a different sense of femininity coming into my body, less elusive, womanly… Considering that the food in India was rather lousy, and I didn't eat much anyway, it was clear that my body was reprogramming itself as a consequence of emotional and mental shifts.

At work, I expanded my ability to withstand my mind going through fits when something was not the way it expected, which happened often. As an example… At the restaurant, I was assigned to beat the white of eggs manually in a large stainless steel bowl. It took a long time to get the eggs to foam. Suddenly, Anugata would come by and command that I drop it! I was needed for something else urgently! The eggs were left halfway through… Several times I saw someone else throwing the whole thing down the sink, as they were useless. How did she know that I had such attachment to completion and got irritated when I had to leave a task in mid-air? One day, as I was happily beating the eggs, I saw Anugata approaching and I started laughing! I stood up before she got closer and asked, "What would you like me to do to next?" That was the last day she asked me to beat eggs.

In that environment of intensity and flow beyond control, our intuition spurred with tremendous force, guiding unthinkable actions. From all sides, either at work or in personal relationships, I was constantly surprised by the synchronicity of events and communication, timely revealing perception beyond logic.

Feeling blessed by the grace of life, there was no space for expectations. My attitude was cool, as far as being emotionally reactive to anything. There was not much that ruffled me. I did not care about the food, the mosquitoes, the poverty, or the lack of Western commodities. I smiled at strong personality traits when they manifested through bad moods, reactions, melodramas, and other forms of theatrical expressions. I was able to look at my own series of "under-the-sleeve tricks," developed to get what I wanted, or to convince someone else that I was "right." In the ashram's environment, I had what I always dreamed of—freedom—nobody was trying to push me in any direction, though I was told what to do every day... Strange paradox. I was aware of my responsibility to my own intention, and the way I offered my energy to experiments and self-observation. How could I ever complain of anything, if I was there with clear intention? Any circumstance could be useful, and most valuable the ones that disturbed me. I observed my mind mechanisms slowly withdrawing and becoming useless.

I was on a ride that had no way back. I could not explain my luck to be living in Bhagwan's community. The way life brought me there...

The sannyasin "family" that I grew more intimate with, gave me a sense of connection beyond the narrow spheres of the biological family. We moved on the same steam, with a growing sense of freedom, embracing different aspects of life within ourselves, and around us. Through years of living, meditating, experimenting together, I immersed in this experience of love beyond "mine," submerging to a point where it became easier and easier to recall it alone. I found brothers and sisters, fathers and mothers disguised in long robes and radical manners. A natural acceptance and recognition of differences was integrated. Greater humor developed while looking at my outlines, my self-image being blurred at high speed! My spirit was set on fire with intimate encounters, countless and unanticipated gifts.

Bhagwan continuously invited unwavering openness. He was the mirror, the call, the excuse "not to forget it." Dissolving layers of obliviousness, piercing the crust that concealed the serenity of being without comparisons or goals. I called that love— unbounded intact spaciousness. Bhagwan made this quality visible.

Seeing my being through his light...the joy of life was soaring without hindrances. The master was my steppingstone. He spelled out my defenses, and trapped my hideaways. I saw my fullness as I looked at his. The light in his eyes was within mine. The grace I appreciated in his gestures bounced the delicacy of my heart. The peace I sensed in his essence was my longing.

The word master became meaningful. Bhagwan mastered the art of being. I wanted to learn it.

I did not know what this process entailed, or what was necessary to be freed from my mind's tricks.

Through the lightness of his presence I had perceived the solidity of my own thoughts, the momentum of ideas that veiled direct perception through my senses. I understood how my body had replaced feeling with thinking, how my mind had adopted social-cultural concepts and generated ready-made responses to situations, to create the illusion of safety. It was clear that when my mind swept over the senses, it killed the newness of the moment, smashed spontaneity, reduced unlimited potential to guidelines within narrow limitations. The situations in the ashram outsmarted preconceptions, as they changed so fast and so unexpectedly that it was impossible to compact them into thought forms. They escaped as liquid mercury out of a broken thermometer. As a child I tried to catch the silvery flow. Now it was impossible to run after my own mind. The crispness of events turned my ideas upside down, made my expectations stand as ridiculous.

What to do about stubborn thoughts? They were impossible to stop, that was obvious. However, learning to let them be, seeing their absurd assumptions disconnected from present reality was shocking and relaxing. As this mechanism slowly was loosing its controlling power, its true function became more precise. I was discovering my intelligence uncontaminated, using my mind with more focus. Interesting paradox.

Life in the ashram offered unrelenting opportunities to substitute my ideas, my desires, my dreams, my imagination...for life untamed, undefined, unexpected. There was expansion and a giggle with it.

To "make sense" had always been difficult for me. Wearing red clothes and a necklace with someone else's photo in it was nonsense. I was glad that it was so!

Bliss, sex and some

My hut was in front of the river. Early mornings, I sat on a rock looking at people bathing, washing clothes, buffaloes splashing, the sound of countless birds, and monkeys chirping on the trees. Nobody in a hurry... Leela—the play of life.

Connections were revealed beyond the mind, cracking the heart open. The gentle radiance of most men and women was astonishing. I have always appreciated beauty, either through art or nature. Now, looking at human beings with such loveliness and grace was a blessing. I sat for hours, just watching people walking around. Beauty seemed sprout out of freedom and love.

Relating was utterly spontaneous, commonly sensuous, often sexual. The easiness and respect of these meetings has matured into a depth of friendship that lasts to this day.

Sexuality was colored by my connection with the master. Something fundamentally different and unique was in that link, my personal issues and individual makeup were secondary. At the core was this commitment to myself, which consequently extended to whosoever I was relating to. When some difficulty arose, there was the clarity of the background—Bhagwan's light bathing the scenes.

One of the meetings that touched me profoundly was with a young German, Kamaal. He was fifteen, came to Pune with his parents, had recently taken sannyas. He asked me to make love with him. It would be his first time. His innocence and physical beauty was exquisite. I had never before, or later, initiated a man in this way. The softness of his skin, the integrity of his body, the tenderness and care that we both had with each other, sensuality naturally revealed by gentleness and sweetness and waiting and being present. Heavenly, boundless... Sex again was on my path of love and meditation, making me aware of extreme delicacy within.

Most men around Bhagwan had developed a feminine quality, contrasting with external wildness, long hair, long beards, naked chests, sexuality embracing strength and softness, giving and receiving, moving and resting, touching and being touched.

I remembered Chi... Male and female coming into harmony. Shiva and Shakti dancing together.

I met women with whom I melted in sensitivity, exploring self-acceptance and deep subtleties of sensuous pleasure. With these women, I experienced orgasm as a merging with myself. The exquisite silkiness of holding it beyond sex, beyond physical union... Mere fragrance suspended in time.

Looking and touching someone that mirrored myself physically and emotionally made me understand some of my defense mechanisms. The acceptance that Bhagwan imparted was softening my heart to the point where I was able to see and release old issues of anger and resentment with my mother. I could see my reactions as lack of ability to respond with love, as lack of clarity and awareness. Nothing needed to be done. Like clouds dissolving into the clear sky, old feelings came forward and became thinner, slowly vanishing... I started to see my mother as a woman, with the fears and difficulties that she might have had to find her voice in the family, relate with my father and make choices. A new sentiment of appreciation fostered, and I wrote a long letter telling her where I was, and what was happening in my life.

The ultimate lover was Bhagwan. No relationship had ever brought me such lightness and contentment. Mysterious that his silent presence could invoke so much... I had no desire or motivation to hold on to love represented by one man. If a man would come who was able to stay in the expansion that I felt through Bhagwan, yes, I could live with him forever. I could not try to fit, make myself smaller, or compromise in any way. Either it was there, or not. If a relationship was not entirely based in nourishing and enhancing my ability to be in that inner space, it was not worth my time. Each meeting carried that awareness. I was not willing to get lost in insignificant day-to-day details. I started learning to disengage from my own pettiness and become more focused.

Sex was integrated with other activities, and happened unplanned, at all times of the day or night. I have always been selective in the way I choose to share sexual energy. Even though my sexuality has been greatly open and lighthearted, I was aware of using it to deepen my ability to stay present within, refine my sensitivity, and mostly, open my heart and soul to the bigness of life. There has always been immense respect and true lovingness towards the men I have been with, no matter what their motivation was to be with me.

It became obvious that the intelligence of the being could not be experienced through the mind or concepts. It had to be ripped apart from the glue of conditioning, either through the sharpness of circumstances that shocked into alertness, or through the softness of kindness, acceptance and love. I preferred the second option, though not always had a choice.

Having some money added a new dimension to my life, and I was determined to enjoy it for as long as it lasted. My work had an unusual schedule with precious free time in between shifts. I found out there were individual sessions offered in the ashram: bodywork, shiatsu, acupuncture and the Samadhi tank—a bathtub fully enclosed with a lid, filled with salty lukewarm water. I signed for ten sessions. Having a massage and then resting in warm water inside a dark cabin facilitated an important healing. At each session, I went deeper and deeper within, relaxing in this dark hole, loosing body sensations, until left with the finest awareness fueling my spirit. Memories of being inside the womb... My mother's fears and doubts, her connection with me, her first child at the age of twenty-one, my father's absence during her pregnancy... Those memories were imprinted in the very programming of my cells. As they were merging and opening in water, the comfort of the darkness made it safe to let go... Like unweaving ancient brocade and being able to observe the quality of each thread, looking closely, touching its texture... Those sessions anchored future revelations and shifts.

My body was delighted swimming in the wells hidden inside gardens. Fresh water, the pleasure of diving and then drying out in the sun... Sometimes, a trip to the nearby lake—a luxury only available if I got an invitation from a friend with a motorbike. Ahata soon came back and we enjoyed several rides into the outskirts of Pune. That was ultimate pleasure!

A regained sense of innocence in my body was all embracing, sparkling, bubbling, unpredictable, constantly afresh, kaleidoscopic; while the mind was linear, roundabout, or skillful in pirouettes, non-existent beyond its own sight. The intelligence of being penetrated into its own depth, seeing itself inside-out, extending infinitely, losing sight of itself simultaneously. Who was there to tell the story? I was often speechless.

The rigidity of mechanical habits became strikingly obvious. My personality stuck out dramatically, I could not run away from its loudness, as much as I tried. It was like trying to hide an elephant on a sock. In the ocean of absolute possibilities, dead phrases stuck out! The broadmindedness of the environment slowly melted some aspects of my mind and behavior. The rebel, the seeker, the artist, the daughter, the wife, the lover...all started to die. Songs and dances and laughter and tears and colors and love and tolerance, insinuated flexibility.

I felt grateful to Derek, Liza, Chi, who had been indirectly instrumental for this transformation. I wrote inviting them for a visit. No interest...

Most of my friends were Dutch and Germans, but all sides of Europe were represented in the commune. Plus lots of Indians, secondarily Americans followed by other nationalities; some Israelis called attention for their straightforwardness and earthiness. Japanese tended to gather in small groups, but I came to meet a few of them.

Prageet and Gyaneshwar became close friends, and they reminded me of my first visit always with jokes and humor.

In the liveliness of this environment, relating to death was as essential as rejoicing in vivacity. A few weeks after my arrival in the ashram, a young woman died. Her body was brought into Buddha Hall and there was a celebration with music, dance and silence before her funeral. We walked together to the place where her body was to be cremated. It was the first time I saw someone in a funeral pyre. That vision stirred intense emotions, as if I could remember myself being burned. I made a point of staying there until the body was mostly gone. The ceremony was simple. The body was placed on top of a wooden pile, and some oil or ghee (purified butter) was used to start the fire. We gathered around singing and dancing. Walk into the holy fire, step into the holy flame! Ah! Ah, ah, ah, ah, ah, ah! Alleluia! Life and death merging...

Another sannyasin died within a few months. He was also a young man. Having lived a blessed life, their deaths were celebrated with concentrated joy and warmth. There was nothing to lament. Bodies transformed into smoke! We danced until the very end.

Bhagwan's father left his body within that year. When I arrived in Buddha Hall and saw his body in front of the podium, I could not understand what was happening, he looked like Bhagwan so much!

I went to the burning ground, participated in the ceremonies, sat watching the flames consume the bodies. This intimacy with death came naturally. I was fully engaged with life, and death was part of it.

Between life and death was energy darshan. Every evening, Bhagwan received people for initiation, as well as workers, group leaders and participants. Usually thirty people or so gathered in Lao Tzu house to receive his energy in a direct and mind-blowing way. Bhagwan sat at his chair and around him the mediums were organized in clusters according to his guidance. These groups of women were placed behind the sannyasins called in front to receive energy darshan, one at the time or a few people in a line. Bhagwan touched their third eye, the drums were exploding, and if you were the one receiving his touch, you were blasted out of the planet in a few seconds. His touch made every fiber of my body-pulse, there was no space to hide, to hold on to, to control, to tighten up. That was totality!

In synchronicity, all the lights in the ashram were turned off, the gate was closed, and in Buddha Hall there was simultaneously intense music enlivening dancing bodies in ecstasy.

The present became fully consuming, flashing like a million colors in phosphorescent scintillation.

Past lives

The internal shifts taking place in my body and mind began to be noticeable. My voice started to change soon after I arrived in Pune. I felt like a young boy, not knowing how my intonation would sound every time I opened my mouth. My words echoed phony, too faint, too strong, or too critical; often I was unable to say what I wanted, phrases got stuck in my throat. I noticed fear, shame, self-judgment. It was interesting and irritating to watch how I had no control over repeating old patterns, so I listened... Through this simple exercise, many unnecessary words and statements slowly vanished. I started to hear my voice fresher, livelier, and surprised myself with out-of-the-blue responses. Much laughter arose for no reason. I was plain happy.

Insights came in their own tempo. Sometimes while walking in the streets of Koregaon Park, I realized that life happened without consulting my opinion. Couldn't I live and let life take care, trusting that there was a bigger force than my tiny mind and universe of ideas? If I looked back, it was obvious that some unimaginable force had guided me. How could I possibly conceive that I had any pick in the direction my life would take in the future? Relaxing with every day as it came was more than enough. Living with people who were dancing in the same pace was an opportunity I did not want to miss.

I spent most of my free time in Buddha Hall. All day long there were meditations, and I loved the ones that involved movement and rest. "Dynamic"—an active, cathartic meditation, never caught me; though I heard that "everybody" was supposed to do it, I bypassed it. I loved to sit alone, quietly near a tree, or in front of the river.

Bhagwan never gave me any guidance, nor suggested any groups. "Doing groups" was an ongoing material for gossip at the ashram. Most new sannyasins were going from one group to the other, basically designed to shake the Western conditioning. Though I had never been a "doer" type, my mind was suspicious. Am I so hopeless that he does not even bother? I kept remembering his first message "Your love is enough!" The love I was feeling was his gift, not "mine," that was clear. Though I had longed for it, asked for it, searched for it, it was difficult to simply receive this present.

I was content with my work, going to discourses and meditations daily. I enjoyed receiving sessions, for as long as my money lasted. Besides the Samadhi tank series, I booked for some bodywork and shiatsu, as well as hypnotherapy individual sessions. During one hypnotherapy session I was amazed to realize how deep memories of the past were stored in the body. I recalled an incident with my mother when I was a young girl, and just that memory suddenly triggered an intense pain in my arm! She used to hold my arm to tell me she was upset with something I had done. The humiliation and ache was still held in my arm almost twenty years later! Those sessions served me personally but also offered a ground of observation that became useful and integrated with the work I came to develop later as a healer and teacher.

My body and mind were becoming more liquid. Observations and insights came up effortlessly. What I was learning seemed to have been stored deep in my cells and now, memories were being triggered by the focus of meditation. I walked as if I was pregnant, protecting extreme gentleness in my body.

The ocean of orange color influenced my emotional body in a startling way. Since childhood, I had disliked the color orange. My mother was especially wise in her maternal instincts, yielding with love to my emotional needs, not always fitting any logic. Her care and intelligence were expressed in different ways, including the choice of my wardrobe. She insisted that I had at least one piece of clothing of each color at all times. So, I always had a red pair of pants, an orange skirt, a yellow shirt etc... I wore what I liked, but the rainbow was inside the cupboard! Oh! That orange skirt freaked me out! I could not stand looking at that color and used to hide it out of my view...

Orange is the color that nurtures and activates the emotional body. What emotions were provoked by its inducement? I had never thought of it, nor at the time had any ideas about this correlation.

Suddenly, I was in the midst of thousands of people wearing orange. I never got a real orange robe, rather chose nuances around it, turning into red... However, the constant sight of orange affected my psyche and brought up buried memories that changed my life dramatically.

In those days, I did not talk much. My interactions at work were practical, and my intimate meetings were rather silent. Time was precious and I had already spent a lot of my life roaming around. I kept my mala with Bhagwan's photo on my neck at all times. The touch of the wooden beads instantly recalled a sense of remembrance that was physical to start with, and slowly turned into a cloud around my body pulling my attention inwards.

Bathed by a continuous sea of blood-colored flowing robes, I moved around while life was pushing me into deeper waters. The richness of color nuances united our bodies and spirits. In this self-resonant container, our differences merged. The concerns with appearance gave space to observation of internal processes.

During one of my Samadhi sessions, I was invaded by the memory of vivid scenes of a concentration camp. I was a young Jewish girl. The bed was cold metal. My soul was cold. My body was skinny. Coughing intensely was hurting my ribs. My body was weak, but I was strong in mind and heart. Someone told me my mother had died a few days before. I didn't understand suffering. I believed it was possible to live in peace. I believed there was a spirit guide. I was dying. I couldn't move. My eyes were hot. My throat was dry. I tried to understand and to forgive. I could forgive. I couldn't understand. My chest was full of pain. Coughing shook my whole body. I was sad. My head was heavy. My body fell from the cot onto the cement floor. Everything faded away. Inside the warm water tank I was sobbing intensely. I panicked in the darkness, my breath stopped.

When the woman in charge of the session knocked to open the door, I was transported somewhere else, unable to speak. I did not understand what that was about. She noticed I had had a powerful experience and offered to take me home, making sure I was ok. I did not know where I was and had a difficult time finding my way home.

Resting in bed, another window opened up. I saw a young teenager, very slim, inside a crowded train. I was that girl! I could hardly breathe, in fear and despair. Other painful scenes came alive in the screen of my field of perception. I sat in bed, and made a few drawings of those places and faces. It was a relief to look at those images. I knew those places inside my guts. I could not make much sense of it and slept in tiredness. Upon waking up very early, I walked towards the river and sat on my preferred rock. Suddenly I understood that those memories were linked to my fear of dying young and the panic attacks I used to have as a child. I was alive again! A hearty laughter burst forth, at the same time I was crying in amazement. So many corners of my life had been invaded by those veiled memories… The dislike of orange, sure… That color induced those memories and I was not ready to face them before. Now, like a birthing, they surfaced and I could move on. A visceral feeling of alleviation and lightness.

I sensed that the intelligence of the subconscious incorporates everything. This underground bank of information gathers different kinds of resources from the past. Even the tiniest tinges seem to remain available, ready to be retrieved. All rests in the mind field as "reserve funds." As events unfold, what previously remained incomplete pushes to the surface, trying to find its way out into light. The lessons we are due to learn are conveyed in their own timing, no matter how we try to avoid them. This process of integration and expansion often forces our control system into panic before it actualizes in physical, emotional and mental reality. Bhagwan's presence and India's unique energy field offered direct access to the unconscious mind and facilitated conscious transformation of its latent potential.

Clearing emotional memories released creative energy. Each further step taught me to absorb and deeper integrate life force. Looking back, I noticed that whenever there was more energy available than I knew how to handle, I would find ways to waste it. Suddenly, it became easier and easier to shift this process. Instead of looking for outlets, I was able to dive in, and utilize the resources abiding in inner emptiness.

A few days after this breakthrough, I went for the first time to a discourse in English. It was strange to listen to Bhagwan speaking a language that my mind could engage. He spoke of enlightenment and of the sangha as a gathering of seekers of truth. As he slowly expounded on a state of bliss beyond the mind, I "knew" what he was talking about. His words were irrelevant, though they were soothing and poetic. The sangha gathered naturally around the energy of a living Buddha. There was nowhere to go, but deeper inside.

I could not imagine ever leaving that place. I did not miss anything or anybody, though sometimes I wished for some of my friends to show up. There was no point to call them formally. I had been led there... I guessed it would be so for anyone else who was ready. None of my friends ever came.

Many lessons were delivered in ordinary ways. Every time I had a question, almost immediately the answer presented itself in real life.

Once I was sitting at a café... A man sobbing intensely called my attention. His whole body was shaking. He was a strong man, blond, most likely German. His beauty and nakedness touched my heart. He lifted his head and looked at me. I looked straight at him. There was despair in his swollen eyes. He was wearing a red robe but did not have a mala. He extended his hand towards mine, and held it firmly. I closed my eyes; we held hands for a while. He stopped crying, stood up, and made a head sign for me to come with him. We walked holding hands in silence to a hut, not so far from mine. It was clean and tidy and we could see the river. He asked if I could spend some time with him, and explained that he would be leaving town that evening... Yes. We lay in bed with our clothes on, embracing with gentleness. His body was weightless, though his physique was broad and full. For a few hours we remained quiet. His crying would come and go. At sunset, I left. Though we did not utter a word, a transfer of energy happened—I knew he had killed someone. That was a bizarre feeling. I just knew it.

The day after at breakfast, I heard that a German guy had been accused of killing an Indian man during a fight. It was dark and the only witness could not recognize the man that had been pointed out as guilty. Nobody was sure that he had done so, but the ashram had taken his mala away and asked him to leave Pune immediately.

This event shook me up. I sensed the quality of life-energy in its pure state. Life force was neutral. That man may have killed someone out of uncontrolled anger though his heart carried such tenderness. I became aware of my responsibility as a recipient of the gift of life. How could I make more conscious choices? How to transform life's potential into actions and creations that nurtured its flowering and expansion? I realized that many of my actions in the past lacked care for others. I had moved in my own timing, in my own way, disregarding other's feelings and limitations. I wrote a letter to my parents asking their forgiveness for the ways I had treated and related to them in the past. I understood how I might have hurt them, how they really meant the best for me even when I judged that they were not giving me what I wanted or needed. My heart relaxed and opened to them in a different way. There was softness and understanding in place of accusations and blame. Understanding dissolved the edges of my sense of identity. I saw how the duality between my parents represented my legacy, qualities ready to be unlocked. That was my challenge—to crystallize their oppositions into complementary harmony. It was time to use the opportunity to uncover much of what they had hidden, find the meeting point inside my heart. I started to become attentive to the escape routes I enjoyed taking in order to avoid feeling my inner conflicts.

It was clearly impossible to move from unconsciousness to consciousness in one jump. I would have loved it to be so! Instead, diligence, time and patience were required. The master kept sitting with us everyday.

A silly event stuck in my memory as a loud lesson. One afternoon I had finished work later than usual and was getting ready to go to music group. I had to be fast to get into the ashram in time. On my way to the shower, I noticed that my fingernails were dirty from the kitchen, and actually too long. Suddenly I got fussy about caring for my hands and… Ah! My feet needed a good pumice-stone scrub. I had been barefoot in the garden. No time to go home and get my kit. As I walked into the communal bathroom it was empty. On top of the sink counter there was a pumice stone, a nailbrush, a nail clipper and a nice Western file (the Indian ones were terrible), neatly arranged in a line. A foolish smile sat on my lips; I looked around and saw nobody. I used the items and left them as properly as I had found. "Relax and wait for what life provides…" I took it as such. Useful recollection for later times.

A strange episode made me suspicious and insecure. I was spending the night at the ashram with Gyaneshwar. Before going to bed I noticed that his room was rather empty. He had said something about it, but I did not pay much attention. "Don't be surprised!" He did not answer when I asked what did he mean. We spent the night together in a friendly way. In the morning, I woke up and he had already left! Something wasn't quite right. Instinctively I opened the door of his small cupboard. Empty! Odd… I left the room and went for breakfast. He was nowhere to be seen. I did not see him around during the following days either. I stopped by his working place and asked his coordinator about his whereabouts, an evasive answer… He might have gone to Bombay for a job… With all his clothes? And he didn't say a word to me about it? We were really close friends. I gave up asking. Soon, I noticed that a couple of other friends had also disappeared.

For a while there had been a lot of talk and excitement about a piece of land that the ashram was purchasing in Gujarat where the "new" commune was supposed to be built soon. It was thrilling to imagine a larger property, the ocean nearby. I did not engage much in gossip, so didn't know the details. While Bhagwan was in Pune, why would I bother about moving? Maybe Gyaneshwar had been sent there…

A few days later during discourse, I completely spaced out while Bhagwan was speaking. I was transported to the bottom of the sea, white sand, the water was crystalline and there were hundreds of sea stars all around. From the depth of the ocean, I perceived the rays of sun penetrating and diffusing through its turquoise color. It was magnificent. At once, but in slow-motion rhythm, the stars started to rise. Each one waved through the water at a different speed, moving vertically. As soon as they reached the surface, they would explode and ascend to the highest place in the sky, shining so brightly that I could hardly keep my eyes open. Watching this inner movie took all my attention. In a flash I opened my eyes! Bhagwan was leaving the hall, slowly walking in namaste. The transition from this vision to his presence made me aghast!

I walked as slowly as the sea stars... In overwhelm, I sat on the wall just outside the hall. I loved sitting in that spot. My body did not move, though I knew I had to go to work. To my surprise, a while later the gates of Lao Tzu opened and Bhagwan's car came out. A few people gathered, in surprise and excitement. Bhagwan was sitting in the back seat and looked at me as he passed closer. For the second time, I was sitting on the same spot when his car glided by. A few people ran behind the car, some crying, others laughing. I was dazzled.

I finally managed to go to work. Nobody noticed I was late, everybody was talking about Bhagwan going to America, may be the new commune was going to happen there. He had left for health reasons, possibly to have a back surgery. America, of all places! I loved India, I could not imagine going to live in America...

Soon it became official that Bhagwan was in New Jersey, with a few sannyasins that had been sent there earlier to care for his needs, including Gyaneshwar. I was jealous and sad. All Westerners were supposed to leave India as soon as possible. I was thrown into a gap. Where to go? I had no idea.

I continued to work, while many people decided to leave immediately. The climate in the ashram was chaotic. I chose not to engage in chatter and just wait. One evening, after my late shift, I walked home around midnight. I loved walking in the dark, with the smells from the trees and flowers, no traffic, rarely anyone else on the road. It took a while until I realized that I had missed the entrance to my conglomeration of huts. Oh! Maybe, I got distracted by a monkey... I walked a bit back and found the chai shop located at the entrance of my village, but there were no huts anywhere, the field was empty. Confused, I walked again a bit further... No, that was the chai shop. I decided to walk directly towards the river to find the large tree and the rock that stood just next to my home. In the dark, I stumbled to get to my familiar spot. Nothing computed in my brain! I had left my hut at lunchtime, and I could not find it a few hours later. Blank. I came to the tree and the rock was still there, but nothing else... The village had disappeared! A sudden panic hit me, my heart racing, I started running towards the ashram, I was going mad!

Arriving at the front gate I could hardly speak. The guard in charge hugged and held me until I calmed down. He knew what had happened. That afternoon hundreds of enraged Indians came into Koregaon Park with sticks in their hands and many bullock carts, and invaded the villages of sannyasin huts, destroying our homes, then loading all they found inside on the bullock carts. Anyone trying to interfere was met with aggression. With the movement of sannyasins leaving town, some Indians were irate. They were losing a good source of income, as well as the appeal of Western goodies circulating in many ways. The police were called but as with everything in India, there was no hurry! By the time they came my village had been destroyed. So much for having a home! I had nowhere to sleep and was left with my only robe, a lunghee and a pair of sandals. The guard took me to his room. He lived in one of the ashram's dormitories, further down the road. Riding behind him in the bicycle, my senses were super alert, the strong scent of champaca bathed my heart.

The day after, I went to work early. Anugata had heard about my situation and lovingly invited me to stay with her at the Music house, another conglomeration of huts, in the direction of town. After my morning shift I had a shower in Number Seventy and took the time to wash my only robe. I was still in shock, and had the following twenty-four hours free. I walked to the ashram, wrapped with my lunghee, holding my wet dress in my hands. In front of the office, there was a large round fountain, not always functioning as such. Often it was covered with a net, so kids would not fall inside. That was the perfect place to sit and put my dress over the net to air dry. It was hot and would not take long. I sat at the edge of the fountain wall and closed my eyes, the sun touching my skin… A few minutes later, I opened my eyes and my dress was gone! No! That was too much! I looked, asked people around… Nobody had it. There was no wind, someone had simply stolen it! I walked into the office and told my story, I needed help! I was given a few new robes and invited to move into one of the ashram's dormitories.

Sooner after that I was called into the office and told that I was to lead a group. I had never participated in a group before… "You will know what to do… Bhagwan will be with you!"

The group was called "Tantra Touch." The room was full. I didn't "know" what to do, but I tasted his presence in my heart. From that felt-sense, words and movements happened… Looking into people's eyes, listening to Bhagwan's silence. Surprisingly, I was able to transmit to others what I had received from him: trust, joy. I was able to bring my past skills into a new context, linking the threads that had led me to him like a garland of flowers.

While so many friends were leaving, a girlfriend from Goa who had gone to work in Japan for a few months came back with lots of cash and great generosity. She offered me a gift of two groups with well-known therapists in the ashram. She was amazed that I had never done a group and enjoyed the fact that I had given a group without any previous experience. I remember her saying, "You know the sound of Aum in your heart…" As many other words I heard in those days, I took it in without trying to figure out what she really meant.

My first group was a weeklong Rebirthing training with Siddha. I had no idea what to expect. The group met at one of the chambers, a room located in the basement, totally sound and lightproof. The doors were heavy and the walls upholstered with foam and vinyl, in my memory brown. It was not an uplifting environment. There may have been forty to fifty people. Siddha was an American psychiatrist, well known for his pioneer work with rebirthing. I have no recollection of details of what happened during these days… The group happened in nakedness. The very stripping of clothes set the tone for the stripping of behaviors that masked our essential nature. I have always been at ease undressed. Looking at other people's nude bodies I captured their most sincere expressions. The shape or form was irrelevant. Beyond that there was a muttering language, yearnings and aspirations, pleasure and pain signals, worth more than a million words. In nudity, it is difficult to lie, to pretend, to hide… I cherished being exposed in that way, seen without veils. And I appreciated relating to others who were willing to expose themselves likewise.

I stood naked in front of the group. Siddha asked me how old I was. "Twenty-eight." "You look like a teenager!" I saw my pride flash! "That is integrity! My body has integrity." I responded. I looked into his eyes… He was simply looking at me. He touched my nakedness, the vulnerability that carries the deepest strength. I looked at him. I was simply standing, my energy collected at the center, inward still point. I knew we were to be friends.

During this group I had the experience of losing all boundaries and yet in touch with the physical body in movement and pulsation. No fear, no thoughts, no holding back, allowing my energy to open and flow with its own intensity and throbbing. Again I was experiencing that bliss inside, learning to access it consciously.

Siddha's presence was a gift in itself. He was simple and relaxed, with a loving and supportive sense of humor. We did not exchange many words, but the twinkle in his eyes said it all. As the group finished I was taken by profound exultation. That was way beyond joy! A glimpse… I had been taken to the innermost core and did not need to hold it in stillness only, but had moved outwards as well. A staggering and new sense of balance emerged. The essence of my heart and power had merged. Ancient history erased, witches being burnt, *satis* throwing their bodies in their husband's funeral pyres, Jews being persecuted and killed, women being kept incarcerated, bodies cut into pieces… I could not justify, could not talk, feeling my belly bursting with an unexplainable, uncontrollable laughter. People came close, disconcerted, and asked what had happened. I could only giggle…

Through the years, Siddha has been a dear friend. Nowadays, we live a few miles away and still meet regularly, in the midst of our busy Californian lifestyle. I am grateful for his care and love.

My second group was with Teertha. He was a charismatic therapist, a flirter, rather aloof. I sensed his depth but had never been particularly attracted to him. He led Encounter groups, an intense process designed to release anger and break through deeper layers of conditioning. It was impossible to maintain any "proper" behavior within this group structure. This approach did not interested me…

I was invited to participate in the "last group" in Pune, only open to workers. It happened in the roof of Krishna house—a large space, holding close to two hundred people. The ambience was electric. I sat in the front row, feeling the intensity on my back, the room overcrowded with people sitting on the floor.

As Teertha came in, the silence was thick. I closed my eyes and out of the blue a question popped up. I opened my eyes as he was saying, "Who has any questions?" I stood up and heard myself speaking… I asked an ardent question about what was really love? How could I live in love? In less than a second his icy answer… "Shut up! You are a coward!" My mind was shattered instantly. I burst into tears and fell back on my seat. The inner pain that had made me move around the world, the longing that nagged me since childhood, all surfaced at once. Raw fear. I realized that I had to face the fear I had bypassed by leaving Brazil. My self-image was of a strong and courageous young woman, who had dared to leave comfort and security to search for love and freedom.

Nevertheless, I realized then that I had disregarded my vulnerability, making myself strong to follow my intuitive hunch, and finally get to Bhagwan. Through his words, I suddenly got in touch with the fear behind it. In fact, I had ran away! I ran away from an overwhelming fear of death, of being killed again, burned alive once more, having my body cut into pieces over and again. My apparent audacity was covering my raw panic. I was a coward! Yes, the apparent intrepidity to leave home, to move all over alone, to stand on my own feet since so young, that was the counterpart of this deep fear! I could not stop crying… The silence in the room was deadly. I guess it was mind-blowing for everybody else, to hear the first person standing up in front of a large group asking a question, which might have also been burning in other people's hearts, being shortly cut with an answer that sounded so absurd! He stuck the sword in my heart, and stirred it…

Teertha's voice broke the silence. He called my name and asked me to come sit on the floor, in front of him. He was sitting in a large armchair, so I was placed in between his legs, with my head resting over his belly. His hand stroking my head, one of his assistants, Premati, held my hand. I spent the rest of the morning in this position. Listening to the noises inside his belly, my flesh and bones softened, and the fear anchored in my sacrum dissolved with his touch. I was oblivious to questions and answers, emotions and mind. The gurgling of his belly focused my attention. That simple! I sat there throughout lunchtime. No impulse to move. During the afternoon session I sat next to Premati, we held each other with care. During the following years, our lives came close and this first moment of intimacy in sincere affection remained as the tone of our relating. I did not hear a word of what anybody said. At the end of the day, crying started again. Teertha proposed an exercise. Each person should find a partner to spend the night with, and I do not remember what we were supposed to do with that person… The only recommendation was to do Dynamic in the morning. That would be my first time.

I was not in the mood to meet anybody, much less spend the night together. I had cried so much that my eyes could hardly open. I stood up to leave. Everybody was moving around the room, hugging and meeting… I tried to find my way in between people when someone hugged me from the back and held me strongly. This woman's body was tremendously overweight, fluffy and soft. When I opened my eyes to look at her face, I started crying even more. She was much older and unattractive. I had no energy left to resist. I closed my eyes, sobbing even more with my head on her breasts. Unexpectedly, she let go of my body, and at the same time, someone else hugged me from the front. This time it was a man. I hugged him and relaxed. When I opened my eyes I was surprised with his beauty and beaming eyes. He asked if I wanted to spend the night with him…. Yes.

We spent the night together at my place. I had moved from the dormitory into a large room in Lakshmi Villas, a complex around a courtyard, with a lovely garden. A friend had paid for it in advance and had decided to leave sooner…

Making love with Veet was bliss and beyond. My body was open and soft. A deep release had happened during the day at the group. My pores were ultra-sensitive. Our connection was nectar made of flesh and bones and heart and mindlessness. I fell inside my own well.

During that night I understood that life is change. Even Bhagwan's presence was temporary… I was not sure I would ever see him again. Growing and flowering was happening as I learned to let go. From my own experience it had always been so. Veet reminded me of balance within. He had the intensity of my German ancestry, and the fluidity of my Brazilian upbringing. We met like liquid fire, moving into and with each other. I felt my own fire without losing my feminine softness. Bathed and embraced, alive and restful.

I had taken seriously the suggestion of Dynamic, so in the morning I mentioned that I was ready to go. Veet said, "Are you crazy… Just relax!" I did. We enjoyed resting in bed until the last minute and walked to the ashram together through the traffic, horns and people, yet so peaceful inside.

Back in the group room… A blond German woman was sobbing; she stood up and kept saying that she was afraid to go back to Germany, she could not face being away from Bhagwan. She was standing near a tall column, one of the supports for the roof. Teertha asked her if she wanted an answer. She nodded. "Put your arms around this column, hold it tight, even tighter…" he said. She did what he suggested. "Keep holding this column and at the same time walk towards me… Hold tight, keep holding!" Suddenly, she got the point! A wave of giggles spread over the room…

Another evening exercise. Instead of letting go of our emotions, Teertha suggested that we move with them, grab them, go behind them, hold on to them. We were to spend the night holding on to someone. Forget about letting go!

I realized that since my separation from Derek, I had not moved towards men with intentional clarity, exposing that I wanted to be with them. I rather stayed in a space of magnetism that made them come to me, not risking re-enacting the pain of rejection.

I was touched by Veet and wanted more of his juice. He was an exceptionally beautiful man with lots of women around him at all times. So, I decided it was time to risk and asked him for another date. He was ready to be with me, but would like to bring another woman as well. We slept in a house in town. A large living room with mattresses and pillows…and another twenty people. Heart and sensuality soaked with Indian ragas. I dared to express my desire grounded on my own strength, though aware of my vulnerability. My belly was warm, my heart was dancing and the pattern of keeping it safe was gone then and there.

Just after this group, there was a meeting for the workers and a great number was asked to leave immediately. I was asked to stay and help close the place. There would be a lot of demolition work and clearing up the offices. That made me relax. I did not even have a passport!

The restaurant at Number Seventy closed sooner after that, I was transferred to work at Mariam's, the small cantina inside the ashram. It was cozy and intimate. Nobody had much of an idea of what was to come next. The suggestion was to go back to our native countries and wait for news. I did not want to go to Brazil!

I needed to move on. I thought of asking my father for help. This time I sent a telegram and got a positive answer. He was going to wire US $300, to a bank in Bombay. We exchanged telegrams with all the details and he confirmed that the amount had been sent. Trusting that I would have the cash in my hands in a few hours, I borrowed only enough money for a one-way train ride to Bombay.

At the bank, of course I had to wait for hours. I finally got to talk to someone, gave the details of the wire transfer, waited again a long time "for verification" and when the attendant came back, he let me know that the money was not there. I requested to talk to the general manager. The transfer had gone wrongly to Delhi. Nothing they could do. My father would have to request the amount to be sent back to Brazil, and then re-wired to Bombay. Couldn't they request the money be sent directly from Delhi to Bombay? It was in my name, it was available in another agency of the same bank, and they were recognizing that it had been a mistake on their side. No, madam, not possible... The bank was ready to close, the manager was getting irritated and I was left empty-handed.

I had to find my way back to Pune with no cash. I walked to a fancy hotel nearby, hoping to meet someone. I sat in the lobby, ready to ask someone for a small loan, lots of rich tourists... Wearing a sannyasin robe and a mala was not very acceptable, though I looked clean and bright. A few hours later, I saw Prageet walking into the lobby going towards the tearoom. What are you doing here? We both asked at the same time. He was shopping for the ashram and had driven from Pune. I could go back with him... Relief!

Almost immediately after my return, Laya showed up in Pune. He had been in Goa for a while. I was always happy to meet him. He had a surprise... He handed me my passport with my expired return ticket inside it. How was that possible? I had thrown it in the garbage! Well, he saw me doing that, and being an old sailor, he expected that one day the waters were going to make me move... He had rescued it and kept it safe, and was hoping to still find me there. He gave me the address of a man nearby who could fix my expired passport and stamp it properly. He planned to return to England with his Australian girlfriend, a few days later... He gave me an address in London.

I went back to work feeling lighter and ready for a new phase. Some cows had been brought to live inside the ashram; I chuckled every time I passed by. They were placed just next to the meditation hall, which had been dismantled.

I relaxed in this waiting mode. Everyday after work, I walked to Lakshmi Villas, had a shower outdoors in the garden, and sat in my room. Every night, before going to sleep, I experimented with a meditation that consisted of sitting in front of a mirror, illuminated by a candle, looking directly into my own eyes. That was a strong confrontation with all the fantasies and projections that I had with my self-image. As I stared into my eyes, my face would change into a hundred expressions, though I had not moved. Slowly, my face disappeared and the mirror was empty, the light burning... I slept deeply afterwards. I had no desire to go anywhere.

Not many people were left at the ashram. We were moving from one task to another to close the commune. I helped with different projects: demolition, sanding wooden beads for malas, gluing hundreds of Bhagwan's photos onto the lockets, stamping thousands of envelopes for a special mailing, and regularly cleaning the kitchen after meals.

One morning, walking into the front gate, I saw a woman coming towards me, looking lost. Her face was familiar... Ah! Ana, from Ibiza! She had just arrived in Pune for the first time, disappointed that Bhagwan had left. Nevertheless, she stayed for a few days and took sannyas. We met for chai and got updated with our lives. Upon her departure she left me an envelope with some cash, which I was to use to leave India and get somewhere.

Monsoon started and the daily routine became less fun having to hassle in the rain and mud. I still did not know where to go...

One day, I was cleaning the spiral stairs that connected the sitting area at the cantina to the kitchen, upstairs... The boredom of that task and the continuous rain combined, abruptly sparked a resolution inside. I stopped in the midst of my task, went to Durga, my coordinator, and announced I had decided to go to Amsterdam. As she was Dutch, she smiled, see you there...

I went straight to the man who took care of passports and visas. It only took a few minutes and a few rupees to update mine. From there I took a rickshaw to town to get to a travel agency. Some more baksheesh and I was set, my expired ticket also suddenly valid. I got a reservation to Rome two days later.

The streets around the ashram had lost the vibrancy of the earlier days... It was quaint and unfamiliar. I was still in bewilderment, but the possibility of seeing Bhagwan again was enough to make me move.

Living in India had been like a ride on a magic carpet. Mystery. Awe. Enchantment. Dignity. An incredible gift. Resting at home inside. What I had given away had been returned to me a thousand folds. I wondered how to stay in that state of grace back in the West, surrounded by a culture that emphasized opposite values.

Bhagwan's discourses accentuated the usefulness of the mind in the right context and the need for meditation as a must for sanity and true contentment.

My challenge was to go back to the West and continue to nurture this new awareness—relaxing in the emptiness of the mind, as well as using it with precision.

The rickshaw, the train, the airplane came in a sequence ultimately dropping Komala in Rome.

European spin

Almost no money in my no-pockets long robe, wearing light bamboo sandals, I carried a maroon velvet handbag containing a few personal items, my drawings, a lunghee and another pink robe. I had lived for over two years without any security or money; as a matter of fact, all had been provided with easiness. The sensation of being still surrounded by the protective mist of India made me feel confident and relaxed.

I went to the drugstore inside the airport, and sat observing the variety and design of an infinite array of products. So absurd! The way people dressed and moved around, the visual urge of advertisement, the sound of voices in Italian. I sat for a long while.

Where to go? I had heard of a commune forming in the center of Amsterdam. Though I had no address, it would be easy to spot friends wearing red.

First step was to get to the train station. Back to the days of asking someone for a ride… I approached a young couple. They asked where I was coming from, and where did I want to go, and offered me a rice to the center of Rome.

At the train station, I checked the schedule and prices to Amsterdam. More than what I had… At the information booth I talked to a sweet old man, very Roman in his accent, he was curious about my way of dressing and the locket with the picture. I gave him a short explanation. He looked at Bhagwan's photo, looked at me and said "I work at a hotel in the evening as the night guard, I have enough money for myself and my family, if you come back tomorrow, I can help you with the ticket. He looks like a good man (pointing to the photo) and in your eyes there is sincerity… Come back tomorrow." That was a good omen. Just needed to find where to sleep for one night.

I thought of getting the subway to the center and seeing if I could find someone I knew in one of the cafes where we used to hang out. I walked down to the subway station, just below. As I was staring in front of the board trying to figure out what train to catch, a woman approached me excitedly. She saw Bhagwan's photo on my mala and immediately recognized him from a book she had read. She wanted to know more about it. I stopped to talk to her. She was touched and teary when telling me her story. His words and meditations had transformed her life. As she heard where I was coming from and my intention to leave to Amsterdam, she invited me to stay at her house. She lived alone and had an extra room. More than jetlagged by then, I was pleased to accept her invitation. We took the subway and arrived at her place—very clean, a block from the ocean. She worked during the day as the cashier at a supermarket, and she insisted that I stay as long as I wanted. She would love to hear stories of India and Bhagwan. I was not very talkative, but was glad to share with her my experiences.

I slept sound and long. Silvia was already gone to work when I woke up… I spent time in the bathtub, a luxury that I loved! Looking around the house, I was surprised to find a few books on the Jewish heritage, many photos of concentration camps and details of the Second World War. Flipping through the books I found exact pictures of the places I had drawn while in Pune. That was Bergen Belsen. I had never heard of that name, a camp alternative to Auschwitz. I started sobbing.

At dinnertime, Silvia told me her family story. Her both parents had been killed in a concentration camp. We had a strong time together. I rested and walked near the ocean for a few days until I felt ready to move on. With great generosity, Silvia presented me with the amount for the ticket and some extra. A few months later, I was able to pay her back and have never met her again.

At the train station, the old man at the counter insisted that I accept his gift, even though I let him know that I had enough for the ticket. He was persistent with his contribution for my journey!

The express train from Rome arrived at Amsterdam central station around midnight. My only acquaintance in town was Helo, my Brazilian friend who I had not seen since we were living in Paris. I found her number in the phone book, but it was too late to call.

The train station was lively with lots of people moving up and down. I had no place to sleep and a few liras in my pocket. Relaxation and patience had always worked in similar situations, so that was an opportunity to practically exercise these qualities.

I went to the newspaper stand distracting my mind with the latest European magazines. A few minutes later I saw at a distance someone wearing red. I approached this woman, who I had never seen before. She was glad to meet someone fresh from Pune and invited me to her home. A nice bed with fresh sheets. Humm… Good to rest.

We had a few common friends and she excitedly talked about the "jail," a previous government prison that had been converted into a sannyasin commune. She was considering moving there and indicated that it would be the best place for me to stay.

The day after I went to visit Helo. She lived with her Dutch husband and had her first baby. Our lives had taken different routes. I enjoyed being with her, but our priorities were quite distinct. I was looking forward to reconnect with sannyasins and the joy of sharing a more expansive lifestyle. I took the tram to check out the "jail."

The "jail" looked like a penitentiary, a tall wall surrounding the main building. Inside, it had been painted freshly and decorated in a simple, clean way. Maybe fifty people were living and working there; each person had their own cell, some were shared. All cubicles were open to large corridors converging at a central round space. The second floor was supported by metal structures, and open towards the downstairs.

The climate was busy and energetic, full of excitement and creativity. The kitchen was already organized, the food ready at a precise time for every meal, the cleaning department full on keeping the place neat, live music a few evenings a week, and meditations throughout the day. There were commune meetings scheduled regularly to sort out the details of this new experiment and lots of familiar faces from Pune. A calm and warm feeling in my belly…

I talked to the person in charge of receiving new commune members. We knew each other from Pune. I could choose to stay as a resident or commit as a worker. Residents contributed monthly rent and a small fee for maintenance while workers were waived the rent in return for taking care of the place, cooking, etc… In any case I could take a month to come up with the payments. Most people who had been in Pune for long, were now getting jobs and reorganizing their lives in town. I chose to work in the commune while I would be looking for paid work. I was given a cell and felt happy to be "home" again.

I started working as a model at the art school nearby. Good pay, pleasant people, and an environment that I enjoyed. I signed for several classes, calculating that with a few hours a day work, I would have enough money to cover for my monthly expenses and enough time to help with the commune.

The Dutch "core" was dominant. Things were organized a bit on the military side. I carried my lightness into this new situation with humor, and started to learn Dutch to be able to read the labels in the kitchen. Someone gave me a bicycle and life was anew in flow.

A few weeks later, Satgyan, my French girlfriend came for a celebration at the jail and we joyously met. She had come to Amsterdam to participate in a professional deep-tissue bodywork training called "Rebalancing." By the way, starting tomorrow! "Cherie, tu dois venir avec moi!" She was a charmer and her sweet voice convinced me to come for the introduction.

The presentation, as well as the course, was taking place at a large house in a nice area. A spacious and clean room, about thirty people sitting on the floor. I was introduced to one of the teachers, Satyarthi. We had a good click and he told me the course was fully booked, the space was not large enough to add any extra participants. The idea of being in a long-term training had never occurred to me, but now it sounded like something I would love. I had no money and the cost was high! Anyway, there were no more places, but I stayed for the talk. I got interested… At the end, one person stood up and announced that she was dropping out. Satyarthi came to talk to me. "Hum, you have no money… When do you think you could pay me?" I heard myself saying, "At the end of the course!" No thoughts in between. "So, come tomorrow." His eyes transmitted challenge and doubt that I would ever pay him anything, but he liked me and I was determined. I had three months to sort it out!

In a few hours I had to decide how to shift my situation at the commune. I was not going to have time to work there any longer, and did not have money to pay to be a resident.

Satgyan introduced me to a group of Germans who were also participating in the training. She was living with them in a squat house, and I could also join. No rent! No hesitation!

The building was in a rather good shape. It had two floors: in the first floor lived a couple, and in the attic there was a small room, and a large open space where four people slept on mattresses neatly placed on the floor. I got to be the fifth. The guys had painted the rooms and the heating was working. Nothing could better fit my needs. I engaged in the Rebalancing Training and moved to the squat house a few days later.

Rajneesh Rebalancing, as it was called then, had been developed in Pune by a few bodyworkers in the ashram, inspired by Bhagwan's vision of the body as a temple for consciousness. This training was presented by three bodyworkers: American, German, Swiss. They shared their expertise with different flavors, combining basic concepts of Rolfing with meditation and emotional release.

I enjoyed learning something new, and it was grounding to have a daily routine. Most other students had a background in massage, shiatsu, acupuncture or other healing-arts education. It was enriching to share and exchange sessions with them.

Learning to touch others in a deep and precise way amplified my ability to impart the sensitivity I had developed in prior years. It was interesting to be able to communicate my understanding of the body's inner works, and articulate my own perceptions in a lively and meditative atmosphere.

Though this was a full-time program, I still had time to model in the evenings, which gave me enough cash for food and small expenses. I had no idea how I would be able to pay for the course. I sent a letter to my father asking for his support. He answered with a flat no.

Soon I started to have requests for paid sessions. It was so natural for me to touch others, now with skills that brought more focus and intention to my hands. My new "clients" enjoyed my competence. In no time I had a steady clientele. One of the guys living at the squat built a massage table with pieces of leftover wood, covered it with foam. Funky but in solid German style. We placed it in the attic, and during the day piled our mattresses on one corner to make the space into a session room. I was booked out. I started to get referrals. There was one large commune house near the Van Gogh Museum, maybe thirty people living there. They had a common massage table, so it was easy to go there and give sessions to a few people in a row. There were many sannyasins in Amsterdam at that time and Rebalancing was a "hot" word. My cash was growing fast. I started paying Satyarthi, who was surely surprised. We became good friends.

It was fun to be with Satgyan every day. We had a sweet girlish friendship, and we were both getting stronger through this training and acquired skills. At "home" the guys were solid and warm, we cooked together, often exchanged sessions, went out for many cups of hot chocolate and cake, sometimes slept together. There was a caring friendship between us. Amsterdam was a pleasant city. Once in a while we took a trip out of town for a walk in nature...

This training called forth valuable insights and increased awareness related to the body-mind-emotional connection. The sensitivity I had developed through relaxation, meditation, illness, making love and being in nature, was focused on a precise and effective approach to healing myself, and others. My previous "real life" training enabled me to stay present, and support others to release physical and emotional pain. The silence of meditation only deepened. Without the reminder that Bhagwan's presence, I had to find it inside myself.

During one of our outings, a friend took me to a meditation with a Tibetan man, at a conference center in the outskirts of Amsterdam... I did not know much about Tibet, nor its spiritual heritage.

We arrived at a nice house surrounded by a lovely garden. It was late summer. Inside the room there were maybe fifty people, quite serious. The atmosphere was solemn. I sat in front. An Oriental man dressed in a simple robe came in with someone who seemed to be his assistant, and a translator. His presence had an unusual sweetness. He sat at a large chair and we remained in silence for a while, until a bell rang... Time for questions! The audience asked rather sophisticated and intellectual questions about meditation and other issues. The man listened with unwavering attention, though he did not seem to understand English. The translator would talk, he would reply and the translator would again return his words in English. In between this coming and going of words, he made amazing sounds, and often laughed loudly, which did not seem to be connected with the questions at all. The audience kept silent. That went on all morning. I felt touched by his presence, but the talking was boring and incomprehensible to me. I was not interested in philosophy, and the questions were too theoretical... As the morning meeting was over, people made a line to come closer to him. I was sitting in front, so was called to move into the queue. As each person approached him, the man briefly touched their forehead giving them a small scarf. I did not know what that was about... I received his touch and gift and walked towards the garden. I had decided to stay outdoors for the afternoon.

I sat on the grass. In an instant, I could not think nor name anything. I was transported to a deeper level of being while my mind was echoing far away. My eyes stared at the trees, at a child playing with the earth... My ears resonated with silence. The colors were jumping at me. Shimmering light coming off the plants. I spent the afternoon resting against a large tree. When my friend came out, I did not recognize her. She talked to me, but I could not understand the meaning of the words. We walked to the car together, and drove back to Amsterdam. I went straight to bed. I had been once more thrown to the darkest and lightest spot within, where nothing held together in logic or linearity. I sensed Bhagwan's presence with me during the night. The day after, my mind slowly came back to regular mode. I had been drunk with being... Later I came to know that I had met the Karmapa and that it was a privilege to receive his blessings. Truly.

Another meeting with a remarkable man happened in an auditorium in Amsterdam. I went along with friends without asking much about it. Krishnamurti had a totally different quality. His clean, severe presence conveyed crystal clarity. Like a diamond, he shone in simplicity and precision. His dark blue suit and shining shoes... I noticed how properly he was dressed. So different from Bhagwan, and yet the same essence. His words were adamant: there is no teacher, go inside.

The Rebalancing training was the heart of my life. The intimacy we shared during the course underlined other activities. As a consequence of exposing emotions and letting go of body restraints, my connection with friends was more honest and direct. We developed communication and basic counseling skills during the training, integrated with energy and bodywork. I continued to give private sessions and making an excellent income. Additionally, I got a regular job at a spa. It was fascinating to express my understanding of the inner works of the body in a professional setting. And joyful to feel myself more earthy and receptive... My intuitive touch was becoming firmer and focused.

The training included a two-day Encounter group, a style of therapy well known in Pune, both feared and sought after as a powerful way to discharge deeper layers of built up energy. This process allowed for "letting hell get loose" with no limits of emotional and physical expression. In an enclosed room we were encouraged to look at aggression as raw life force, that once released could be integrated in loving and creative ways! But until then...

While in Pune, I wasn't interested into digging out my anger. I chose to nurture easiness and softness, relaxing with being vulnerable and gentle. Seems that I first needed that foundation of trust and mellowness to be able to acknowledge the fire underneath, let it erupt and have enough distance to watch it burn my defenses. As this Encounter group was an integral part of the Rebalancing training, the opportunity was unavoidable.

We gathered in a boat-workshop space, rather dark, set especially for groups with insulated walls and covered windows. It was a gorgeous day, sunny, blue sky, rare in Amsterdam, and I could see the birds flying around through a small window. The guest therapist leading this section was a fiery go-for-it type of woman. The group was silent and there was certainly anger in the air... Naively, I stood up and said, "I do not understand why we are constantly talking about living in the moment, and now it is a beautiful day and we are sitting here trying to get out anger from the past... Can't we go for a walk?" That wasn't the appropriate comment for the occasion. I was surrounded by at least twenty Germans and the group leader was eager! She asked if I really wanted an answer. I said, yes! She asked me to undress. The group participants were sitting in a circle, so I stood naked at the center and she banded my eyes. I heard her voice instructing the group to outpour their anger on me and let me know why they could not enjoy going for a walk on a beautiful day. She instigated each person to push and hit me, expressing feelings they had kept inside for a long time.

At first, I was being pushed from all sides and my dancer body was floating in flexibility, I was actually enjoying it. Rather fast, the intensity increased and I could no longer relax with the course of action. Added to the movements, people were making loud sounds, and getting fiercer with their assertion of rage. My body started to get hurt, scratched and punched and my long hair was pulled violently, to the point where it was not possible to keep cool and flowing. Suddenly the wave reversed, and I connected with ancient rage, seeing myself being hurt and abused in different circumstances. The heat of reaction had been ignited, and my body started hitting back in full strength, my hands pulling any hair I could grab. I lost sense of physical boundaries. I fell on the floor with the heaviness of many people over my body. I felt that I was getting killed. Nobody was backing off, rather charging at full force. My screams were beyond control out of a state of panic. Memories of being stoned to death as a woman alone in India came into sight vividly. Experiencing the merging in annihilation where the anger and the pain that causes it become one. Recognizing the need to be strong and transcend horror and violence, and all the mechanisms of defense that took place in reaction to being forced to deal with fright beyond imagination. The attacker and the victim feeding each other in the cycle of perpetuation... I was terrified, hardly able to breathe. Hours later, I was left lying on the carpet crying like a baby. From far away I heard people talking about taking me to the hospital, as I had several bleeding wounds. The group leader asked me, "What are you feeling?" I heard my voice deep and sore, "I do not need to fight against others to be strong. I can be gentle and survive." Those words echoed in a strange way. I was taken home and given a bath. I was depressed and sad for several days afterwards. I definitely learned to recognize anger and understand its dynamics. Not sure if that was the best way to get this lesson... Nevertheless, in a few days I was over it. My body was stronger and my work more effective. A new connection with people became available, into another bottom line.

The play of lovers was more brotherly than romantic, as we spent the days together. Veet's memory was still fresh and I did not want to settle for less. There was nobody around that touched me in his way. There was warm friendliness between most of the students, which often turned into sexual play. We were more like kids fooling around than adults trying to reach nirvana, or an orgasm...

A few months into the training, we were invited for a surprising celebration at the jail. With music and great joy, it was announced that the commune had bought a ranch in Oregon, USA. Large enough to accommodate thousands... Some selected people had already moved there, preparing for Bhagwan's arrival soon. Updates would be passed on to us regularly.

It was exciting to imagine reuniting with friends and being with Bhagwan again. Having a place only for us, that was wondrous! We had to wait anyway. It would probably be a while until we would be invited for a visit, or to live there?!! There was great excitement in the air.

As the training ended, I had paid my tuition in full and had some extra cash. It was the beginning of December and Bhagwan was already at the ranch. There was going to be a small celebration for his birthday, he would give satsang for a few lucky ranch residents. We were asked to wait for a personal invitation. There was no time frame, but

I wanted to be alert and ready. To be able to reach America, I would have to go back to Brazil to renew my passport and get a visa. I couldn't quite figure out the logistics of this next move.

There was a new commune starting in the English countryside, near Devon, open to new residents. I had Laya's address, but no phone number, so I risked taking the train and the ferry to cross the Channel.

Arriving in London I went directly to Laya's address. The door opened, a lady responded… They had left to Australia just a few days before… Subway to Kalptaru, the sannyasin center in town; there I would get information about the commune and check for a place to stay.

Friday afternoon… At the center, I found a buzz of people getting ready to go to Medina, the new commune. There was going to be a group and celebration with Teertha, and a few other Pune therapists. I did not have enough to pay for it. I wanted to go! I sat at the reception room the whole afternoon. More and more people arrived. Nobody I knew… Excitement and hugs and kisses and laughter, people dragging suitcases. I realized it was colder than I had imagined, I still did not have a proper winter jacket, but too late to think about it. I was sad and resigned not to go.

A very straight man sat next to me and asked my name. I wasn't in the mood for conversation, and he was too uptight. He insisted in engaging in conversation, I relaxed. He was a pharmacist from Belgium, and this was going to be his first group, he was a bit anxious. "You are not going for lack of money? That is a pity…" he commented. "Would you be able to pay me back if I lend you the money?" I was honest… I wanted to go to the ranch as soon as possible, I had nowhere to live, and no work, but I would do my best to pay him back. We agreed on the amount I would return to him in pounds. He gave me his address and phone number in Belgium. I managed to repay him a few months later.

I got into the bus at the last minute. We arrived at Medina late and I was unprepared to be in the countryside—no proper shoes, no warm jacket and no bedding. A deep breath, a bit more magic, and I got set! The organizers were adorable. In the best-hostess-English style they provided me with all I needed. I had a cozy bed and was ready for another ride of questioning, dancing, and my first Dynamic meditation ever. I did jump up and down until my lungs and legs could not take it anymore. And was glad to have postponed it for that long!

During one session with Teertha, I said, "I do not know what to do next…" He answered again mercilessly, "Yes, you do! Don't waste my time!" I suspected he did not like me… I didn't like his arrogance either. However his promptness shook me up and I saw the way ahead clearly. Yes, I knew what was next and had to keep moving.

On the bus ride back to London, I sat next to an English guy who invited me to stay at his place in Kensington. His house was full of windows, clean and spacious. We spent a few days together as if we had been married forever. He would go to work and I would go for a walk, buy food, and cook a good meal; later, we would eat, meditate and make love with sweetness. His name was Prem Kavyam, which means love and poetry, and that was what he offered me. We never met again.

A few days later I went to check prices of tickets to Brazil. In the airline queue, I met a Brazilian woman who had a ticket that was going to expire in a few days, she could not get any reimbursement for it, would I like to use it? She was willing to go to the airport with me and make sure that all was ok. I had nothing to lose, so I booked my departure for two days later.

I called my brother to let him know of my arrival date. I planned to visit my parents in Rio and wait to be called to the ranch.

I had been living in Europe with ease, but now I was a bit shaky to go back to my own country. I had been so far away from my earlier conditioning and lifestyle that it was difficult to imagine going "home." I was looking forward to reconnect with my family and friends, and yet was not sure how they were going to receive me. I was cautious and wondering if it was possible to bridge these two realities, inside my self and with others.

On the Way

"You feel incomplete within, but this is because you are a seed.

The seed is groping in the dark, trying to push its way through the earth.

The seed breaks through stones, passes through layers of soil and surmounts all obstacles in its upward path towards the sun. But it has no knowledge of what it is doing.

If you ask it, "What are you doing? Where are you going?" It will not be able to give you an answer. There is some instinct within it that directs its course.

It must reach the sun; it has to touch the sky. There is no other goal.

Unless it sees the sun it will never bear flowers; there will never be any celebration in its life.

First the seed becomes the tree and then the tree becomes the seed. You are born, then you die, and then you are born again. It is a circle.

The world is a wheel, it keeps on revolving and revolving. But you never seem to arrive anywhere.

Man must awaken; he must make this journey with full awareness.

Nature brings you to the human state and now you will have to continue on your own. This is a tremendous responsibility and it worries you. That is why man is always so worried.

The animals and the birds and the trees and the stones and the streams are not so worried. They have no cause for anxiety; they are unconscious of what is happening. Man is anxious because he sees clearly that, no matter what happens, it is inadequate. You feel that whatsoever you are it is not enough, that something is lacking. This feeling disturbs you, stabs you like a thorn, and unless you become conscious, unless you become aware, it will harass you your whole life.

Your journey with nature is over, nature has brought you as far as it can—and it has been a very, very long journey. It has not been an insignificant thing; it has taken a very long time. This evolution to the human stage is the highest flowering in nature. The journey through the darkness of nature is over. Man has reached to the frontier; he has come to the crossroads.

If you go back to nature now you will be repeating the cycle of births and deaths all over again—this is what humans generally do."

OSHO   *The Great Secret*

Brazil for a break

My brother picked me up at the airport, I was glad to see him. On the way home we stopped at a bookstore. Obviously displayed at the entry was the Portuguese translation of a series of Bhagwan's discourses *"The Mustard Seed."* I smiled!

My family was happy to see me after a few years. My hair was down to the waist and I was wearing a maroon Indian robe, quite different from my stylish teenager and European sleek look. I was not concerned with my physical image, no makeup, no jewelry. My body had become more womanly, rounder, no longer as bony and slim as it had always been. My mother's only comment was, "If you are looking like this and happy, something good must have happened." My father looked at my mala, "I know this guy, I have some of his books! Did you meet him in person?" It was true... He had a few books translated into Portuguese next to his bed, but asked no further questions.

They made comments on how horrible India was, though they had never been there, but asked nothing about my experience and life in that country. As they realized I had plans to leave again soon, there was an air of upset and no support to be expected.

I connected with a Brazilian couple I knew from Amsterdam. They had moved back to Brazil and were setting up therapy and meditation workshops in Rio. They were glad to organize a bodywork group for me. Perfect timing, good income, and the opportunity to share my life with Bhagwan with friends.

"Groups," in the sannyasin world, were an invitation for sharing the joy of our inner discoveries, relaxing, becoming more aware of the attachments of the mind, opening to Bhagwan's presence as a tuning fork for these qualities.

While in Rio I got some new clothes. My mom made sure to keep me on track for good looks. Although she did not like the idea of only one color, we went shopping together and she gifted me with some nice things. I found out that there was a large sannyasin commune being built in the countryside near Sao Paulo, connected with a meditation center in town. I dug into what was left of my grandmother's jewelry, transforming it into cash to buy an overnight bus ticket to Sao Paulo, and cover basic needs. I was yearning so much to be with Bhagwan again, that my only focus was to gather the practical needs and leave. There was not enough integration in my being to remain as relaxed as I had been in India and in Europe.

Grateful for the care that my family had with me, though we only met briefly, I said goodbye, ready for a new adventure.

I went directly to the address I had for the center—a simple house in a suburb. I was received by Vardan, a delightful Brazilian woman who I had met in Pune. Her remarkable smile and gazing eyes welcomed me in a comforting way, but… I should know that there was a waiting list of over forty people. She suggested that I come back three days later to talk to Somesh, the commune leader, who was away in the countryside.

I sat in the veranda, what to do? I asked if I could stay in one of the commune houses until he got back. "There is no space, we are four to five people in each room… It is really tight."

Besides Vardan, I knew just another couple from Pune. There were about seventy residents, most of them living in the countryside. I was glad to hear that Prageet was there and would come back with Somesh. I decided to wait for Kundalini time, shake up my body, and let things settle inside. After the meditation someone offered me a place to stay—a garage set up as a guest bedroom, five minutes walk from the center.

I sat for three days in silence. No need for food. I had nowhere else to go, nothing else to do. The owner of the house listened to ethereal music continuously and kept incense burning… I kept breathing and waiting.

When I walked back to the center, though I had never seen Somesh, I knew I was going to stay in Sao Paulo. I was called into his office. He was a deeply calm man, in his late thirties, serene, a softness that was transparent in his body and voice. Just looking at each other, I unexpectedly said, "I am here!" He responded, "You stay! Go see Vardan for a room." That was the length of our first conversation.

As I came out of the office, Vardan was giggling, surprised that I had been invited to stay. I was given a room at Somesh's large house, two blocks away from the center. It had three bedrooms; he had his, I had mine and the third one was empty. There was no furniture anywhere, except for mattresses on the floor. I enjoyed the "Zen" look of the space, wooden floors and large windows. As all the other commune houses were packed, I felt shy and blessed with this invitation, accepting it gracefully. I hardly met Somesh in the house, as he spent most of the time at Bodhisatva, the commune quarters in the countryside. Sangita, his assistant, and her young son also moved into the house. However, most of the time I was alone.

My communication with Somesh did not require many words. Sense of humor, yes! Again behind the lines, through an exchange of gazes, or a smile on the corner of the mouth. I loved to be with him, cherishing his restfulness and heart. His kindness and understanding was reflected in his excellent skills as a therapist and commune leader. Soon he asked me to be his assistant in workshops offered regularly in the countryside location, as well as to offer Rebalancing sessions at the center. In addition, I got the job of translating one of Bhagwan's books, together with Bia. My routine became established: during the week I was in town and during the weekends I drove with Somesh to the countryside, a couple of hours away.

While in Sao Paulo, Rebalancing sessions were booked in a package of ten in a sequence, so I moved with each client through the whole series. We took photos at the first and last sessions, and impressive changes were visible in the physical structure and facial features—more relaxation, openness, and alignment. I enjoyed supporting others to find more balance and grace in their lives, setting the ground for the mind to rest in neutral gear, and meditation to happen.

Usually there were seven to eight sessions booked during one day, each lasting one and a half hour. My days were full! To complete, I was in charge of the afternoon meditation, either Kundalini or Nataraj, alternatively. Dinner time...and ready to go to bed. I was satisfied with this simple and demanding routine.

Through this rigorous schedule, I learned to rest within and stay present with each stroke. In that intensity, I started to understand and be able to see subtle energy patterns, as clearly as the physical traits. It was impossible to space out, or let the mind take over. It was imperative to respond to the situations in the moment. My capacity for receptivity expanded as well as my ability to be penetrating, both through touch and communication. A life training, still useful today.

Soon there was a waiting list for my sessions. The income from sessions and groups went to the center. I received accommodation and food.

During the weekends, at the countryside, the groups took all day and into the evening. The commune was set on a large property belonging to Somesh, with horses and other animals, a vegetable garden, a beautiful pond, and walking trails in the forest. I was content in that waiting mode. Houses were being built at a fast pace and I loved to be part of another creative endeavor. There was a similarity between this piece of land and the house we had when I was a child. I rejoiced in a childlike way, wearing muddy boots and helping outdoors whenever I had a break from the groups...

Prageet was around for a couple of months and then got invited to go to the ranch. I was jealous, but lovingly helped him to pack his suitcase and sent him off wishing to meet him soon in Oregon.

Curiously, most of the men and women in the commune at that time were experimenting with having sexual relationships with the same sex. Nik, my assistant in sessions and groups, was an excellent bodyworker and dancer, and we often exchanged sessions. His sense of humor, intelligence and playfulness, made it natural for us to "hang out" during the day and once in a while, extend our sharing to a night together. He was in between men and women, and I was one of the women he enjoyed. I was glad to have a friend to play with no romantic agenda. Bodily joy, mindless and spontaneous.

My other playmate was a woman, with whom I had a sisterly and sensuous connection. I esteemed her earthy love. The delicacy and heartfulness of merging with a woman's body enhanced awareness of my own needs and sensitivity.

This was a healing time for me: it linked events and landscapes of my past with the newness of Bhagwan in my life.

While I was there, Somesh started to give energy darshans once a week, set up like Bhagwan had it in Pune. A few mediums and the best of Brazilian drummers! On Saturdays the center was usually packed for this event and I was one of his mediums. A good mind blowing blast! In my perception, he played it with a fine sense of humor and the women he chose had the same quality. We moved wildly, shaking the body and the mind. Bhagwan's presence was tangible. We were drunk with the wine of life.

Finally, the announcement arrived: we were invited for the first celebration at the ranch to happen in July 1982. We were in April… I needed cash and soon!

In a few days, with Somesh's support, I set up a series of weekend groups outside the commune, reduced my sessions at the center and added a few out-call clients. I went to Rio for a few days, offered another group, and once more, said goodbye to my family and friends.

Inside the small airplane on the way back to Sao Paulo, I closed my eyes in relief. A man sat next to me. I immediately recognized him—he was a popular illustrator in Brazil and we had met several times in Milano, as he was a friend of Derek. I doubted he would recognize me. My presentation had changed radically; from a sophisticated young married girl, in the best of Italian style, to a long-haired, plain-looking woman, dressed in a red cotton robe, almost ten years later.

He was a seducer by nature, so I was not surprised when he approached me. He had been watching me at the airport and commented on the way I moved, the grace of my body and gestures. Where was I coming from? I asked if he remembered me. Yes, I was familiar, but he could not remember that we had met before… I let him know my previous name, and my new name. We chatted during the trip, getting updated on our lives. He was going to a presentation of his latest book and asked me to come to his hotel for the night. No, I had work waiting for me. He was not used to receive no as an answer, especially from women. As we both relaxed into this coincidence, I decided to spend the night with him. I was curious to come close to a man who was living in such a different world and values. He was a charming man and there was an old friendliness from our prior connection. His intelligence was sharp and he questioned my choices in a probing way. What was that about? I used this opportunity to share without justifying or defending, responding to his questions about Bhagwan, meditation and the significant changes I had gone through. We spent the night together, he was tender and caring and I enjoyed our physical intimacy. Next morning, it was clear—my focus was to go back to the center and move on with my work. This night offered me an opportunity to open up without judgments, recognize our different paths and choices, and yet find a meeting point with tenderness and respect. I left the hotel while he was still asleep, leaving a thank-you note. We never met again…

I focused on offering groups and sessions to gather enough money to travel. Within less than two months I was ready to leave Brazil. I sent a letter to the ranch asking if I could come earlier, the response was, "Yes, be prepared to work hard!"

Muddy boots

I flew directly to New York and then to Portland, thrilled to arrive two months before the official beginning of the "First Festival." More time to go around the land, meet friends, and see Bhagwan before thousands would arrive.

I was greeted at the airport by a man with shiny eyes, wearing red jeans and a cowboy hat. He was the driver assigned to take us to the ranch, a long ride ahead, about seven hours or so... Together with a few other visitors I boarded an old yellow school bus belonging to our baby commune. My belly relaxed even after twenty-four hours no sleep.

Arriving at the ranch equaled landing in paradise! The vastness of the space, familiar faces rushing to receive us, now more groomed-looking than in Pune, with red jeans and shorter haircuts, warm temperature, and lots of dust, all merged as a welcoming hug from the universe. The enthusiasm of our meetings went up another octave. Having our "own" land was a dream coming true.

We were invited into the reception area, where Bhagwato welcomed us. I stood in silence while she described the different settings: accommodations, restaurant, Bhagwan's house, meditation tent etc... Ever-extending bare land, with sparse pine trees as far as the eyes could see. Six hundred fifty thousand square acres!

As we were driven to our accommodations, friends from Pune showed up planting trees along the road, driving old pickup trucks, like mirages appearing in front of my exhausted eyes, hugs and surprised waving hands. I was given a tent on my own, bliss for that moment, and fell asleep in the midst of a warm afternoon. Dreams within a dream...

In the next days, we surely got busy. Medical exams, filling up forms with this and that practical information. My expectation in coming to the ranch was to work outdoors, farming or planting flowers—a wish for many years. Surprise! I was asked to work at the boutique, a large circus tent, almost the only enclosed location in this vast property. I was disappointed and yet overjoyed to be on the land.

As the festival started, thousands of people from around the world showered in. More circus-like tents were placed around the property with different functions: groups, individual sessions of all types, restaurants, and more... A city of small tents placed on wooden platforms extended over the fields. Separate mobile shower and toilet units served the nomad population. Often we had to wait long minutes in front of these trailers until it was possible to squeeze in between a crowd to get a shower. The great art was to keep the towel clean! Even in those challenging circumstances we related with ease and laughter.

The teeming activity and people gathering for the realization of this project was beyond imagination. The organization and intelligence that it required was wondrous. I felt fortunate to be part of it.

At the boutique, I helped Kumud and Kendra to organize and sell piles of orange-red tee shirts with various images and slogans about the ranch. This simple job taught me about being centered in a practical and interactive way. We had all kinds of designs, but it did not make much difference, this or that, the color was red anyway! The whole thing was a joke, the intention being more frisky and monetary than high fashion. But…most people asked for this design with that neck, don't you have it? Well, that particular combination was not available. Don't you have these sleeves with that picture on the front? And so on… It was hard for most people to take what was available, even in that environment of relaxation and jest. I had to say no recurrently. No, we do not have that. No, we do not have that. No, we do not have that. I repeated this same phrase a thousand times. Interesting to watch how the mind is always looking for something that is not there.

During that summer, I became intensely aware of my own "looking for something that is not available," and observed this mechanism happening almost compulsively with small details. It seems to be a lifelong learning: to recognize what is available and receive it, instead of feeding my desire-body reaching for something else.

Reuniting with dear friends and sharing the excitement of this adventure was fully engaging. I was happy alone and eventually spent some nights with a man who worked at the boutique, in the book section. He was a businessman from New Orleans, handsome, and very different than my usual friends. As his background was rather conservative, and he had never been in India, our meetings were centered in the present moment and mutual appreciation of our hearts and bodies. I was not looking for a romantic relationship; I was more interested in being part of Bhagwan's vision for building a city centered in meditation, love and creativity, all the qualities that I had held precious coming together in one place.

At the end of the summer, hot days and warm nights, I volunteered to pick up veggies at the truck farm. I woke up around five and waited for the bus in the dawn. The freshness of the early morning was invigorating, earthy joy, sunlight and zest.

Once in a while I managed to go to the river that bordered our land. It was wild and delightful to soothe the heat by dipping naked in the water. The snake inside had a chance to come out and play again. The freshness of the river was cleansing and energizing.

I also loved to go for walks in the wilderness. The immensity of the land was majestic. The fact that it was "ours" brought another twist. I often sat alone in the hills, enchanted in silence.

Building a city dedicated to the light of awareness, to the joy of being alive, with Bhagwan's presence as an inspiration, was absolute motivation. And that was just the scenario, an excuse and support for my own process of unfolding and learning. Sharing with friends was an added bonus. No consideration would take me away from that place. I was ready to offer unlimited energy, conscious that my contribution was insignificant in the context of such a large enterprise and in face of the generosity of many people who had already donated large amounts to make this project possible. I was grateful for this good fortune in my life.

Six months went by in a wink… I was invited to work in Vancouver for a few weeks. During this Canadian time, I was feeling seasick almost every day.

The money grew fast in my pocket, and I was ready to go back to the ranch. While packing, I heard myself saying, "I am pregnant!" For the last seven years or so, I had not used any birth control, had made love unconcerned, with different men, and had never got pregnant… I was sure to be sterile and glad with this idea. My periods were irregular; sometimes I missed one or two months, I did not worry.

I went to the pharmacy: in a second the test showed positive. I was shocked! A few hours later, I was in the car driving back to Oregon. I listened to my belly, talked to my heart, reflected on the situation. I was sure that I did not want to have a baby.

Back at the ranch, I asked to work in the farm. I was sent to the greenhouse, but informed that I would be needed at the office soon. Office? I was so happy to be outdoors! I learned to produce sprouts in large quantities and enjoyed this job while it lasted, wishing that the idea of placing me in an enclosed room would be forgotten. Sometimes I had to drive for a delivery at the truck farm, sneaking for a swim in the river…

I decided to stay at the ranch as long as possible and then go to San Francisco for an abortion. Taking time to tune in and be in touch with my body, I knew my fetus was a boy and I sensed the connection with the man who had made me pregnant—my friend at the bookstore. He was physically beautiful, with intense eyes and a warm, well-built body, maybe fifteen years older than I. He had discovered Bhagwan through his books, and came to the ranch at the very beginning. He was constantly complaining about the work and other arrangements at the commune. His approach to sannyas was very analytical and goal-oriented. He was with Bhagwan to "get enlightened"; he asked a million questions whenever his mind got entangled with something he had a hard time to logically understand. Of course, that happened very often, as nothing around Bhagwan was ever logical… I took him lightly and his personality was rather fascinating to me, as I did not know anybody from his background, so "American." His language was far away from mine. I appreciated our friendship. I loved his warmth, care, and beauty. There was always a sense of rest and realness when we spent time together. I enjoyed him as a friend and lover but not as a man whom I would like to have a relationship with, much less a child.

As we met upon my return, he invited me to his trailer for dinner. We were pleased to meet again and lay in bed watching the magnificence of the stars… I told him I was pregnant and had decided to have an abortion. As I completed my phrase, his hand, holding mine, got instantaneously icy. He did not say much. I explained that I did not count on him being a father, nor needed anything from him. He asked me to stay for the night but his energy was somewhere else... From that day on, he ran away as soon as he would see me at a distance. His attitude surprised me, as I expected some more maturity from a man who already had a seventeen-year-old son. I took his attitude as a reflection of fear, since I had no claims or demands. I cherished our intimacy as lovers, but was not emotionally attached to him.

As our emotional tie was not deep enough, I did not feel I was carrying "his" baby. This fact made it obvious to me that it was not "my" baby either. The fetus growing inside my belly had come in his own right, had his own intention and related to me as an independent being. That was evident.

My belly was getting fuller fast, my breasts larger. I was indubitably pregnant. Relaxed and self-content, resolute about having an abortion, I used this opportunity for all it could bring and teach me. I knew it was going to be once in this lifetime, therefore I was determined to experience what it had to offer. Even while working and relating to others, my attention was focused in the connection with this being.

The first level of awareness was of the body, its transformation in form and sensibility. I took care in noticing the minimum changes, my belly enlarging visibly, my skin stretching, my breasts becoming tender and soft, my eyes shining in a particular way, my legs aware of slightly increasing weight, greater intensity in moments of hunger. Every detail expanded my awareness through this distinct physical reality. I delighted in being quiet, sensing this metamorphosis. Each day a new sensation called my attention, like an intangible sound within.

I gave my feelings and emotional responses a lot of space and time for reflection. The presence of another energy field inseparable from mine, and yet noticeable as unique and independent, made me walk, talk, move, eat, and sleep with special alertness. It was comforting to be assured that life was to be trusted. What other possible proof would ever be greater than this experience? This sense of ease was beyond any logic or evaluation of the circumstances in a practical level. It arose from deep inside my body and took my heart for a ride. I was joyful for no reason, the spring of new life bursting at the core, reminding me of what was meaningful moment to moment.

Mostly alone, I was not in a flirting or mating mood. The only man I spent time with was a dear friend from Number Seventy. I cherished his "Californian" ease. He was candid, sincere, blond with big blue eyes, my age or a bit younger. His simplicity and beauty attracted me. He stood out among many of the guys who held on to a "spiritual" look and behavior. He was straightforward and innocent, appreciating the changes in my body, caring for the feeling of this new moment, touching me with delightful sensitivity. We spent hours together in the evening, forgetting that our schedules started early the next day, but I always slept well afterwards, refreshed and loved. I had no desire to be in love or in a relationship, embracing the fullness of being on my own and carrying a beloved inside. Receiving and enjoying this gift was plenty.

My mind had an insignificant role during this phase. My heart took the lead without hesitation, embracing my own life and the new one inside as one. This communion was not threatened by the idea of interrupting this pregnancy. I was grateful for this "visit," for this spirit that came to share with me the beauty of these days. He offered me insights into my own choices. He enlivened my body, pushing me into the mystery of life with intensified trust. Sitting alone, looking at the hills at a distance, in the openness of the desert I would talk to my friend… That is how I related to this being—as a friend, a sweet friend, invisible, though caressing my soul with gentleness and amazing love.

I realized that for most people, having a baby was a natural extension of their lives. However, having spent the last years freeing myself of the limitations I had taken in as a child, I could not bear the idea of choosing to do the same to another being. I was not ready to care for someone else. In earlier years, when considering having a child, I realized the extensive responsibility of being the guardian of a life. Recognizing that motherhood required immense sensibility, love and intelligence, besides time and dedication, I did not feel qualified for this role. I was not able to offer what I considered indispensable: stability, maturity, wealth, harmony and true love in a relationship of parenthood, and most of all, clarity of my own purpose in life. Yes, I knew I had innumerable qualities to nurture a newborn and mother a child; nevertheless, they were not enough.

I was not conscious enough to relate to another human being with the respect he/she deserved from day one. I was not capable of offering the understanding I would like to have been bathed with as a child. It was obvious that much of my daily movements and actions were still steered by unconscious patterns, repetitions that I was unable to avoid or transform into choices of freedom. Yes, I could also see a baby as an opportunity for growth, for more responsibility towards myself; however it seemed like a gigantic task, a difficult challenge and way too risky. I did not want to use someone else's life to enhance mine. Living in an environment where collaboration was fundamental, I did not want to isolate myself taking care of one person. The decision for an abortion was doubt-free. Maybe I had high expectations towards myself. But I could not do it halfway.

As this was such a deep exploration, I trusted the timing of my own body and waited for the right moment to leave the ranch.

In preparation for my abortion, I booked a session with Siddha, who I loved and trusted. We met in the late afternoon, the colors of the sun setting in the background. Looking into his eyes naturally opened my heart. His warm presence and clarity has inspired me through the years. The contents of the session did not matter, but the completion that it sealed was soulful and meaningful. I said goodbye to this being, and he was ready to leave my body. There was gratitude filling up the space inside and around me. I lightly walked out the door feeling blessed. I sat with the stars and sang aloud.

I was almost four months pregnant when I got a ride to San Francisco. Early in the morning, I rolled out of the ranch in a large car with four others. Sitting next to me in the back seat was a tall, strong, intense, friendly Israeli guy called Pari. As I did not have a place to stay, he invited me to come to his house, shared with a few others. I felt comfortable and cared for. We spent the night together. He embraced me as if we had been together for years.

The day after, I went to a women's health care clinic in Berkeley. The nurse in charge was adamant—I could not wait one more day! The clinic had a waiting list, so she referred me to a private gynecologist, booked an appointment for the next day and arranged for the payment. I was surprised, and thankful.

Pari offered to drive me and accompany the procedure. The nurse explained the method used for the removal of the fetus: a suction device vibrates the uterus until the growing embryo loosens its grip and moves out, that is how I understood it. I was so calm that I decided not to have any anesthesia. The doctor hesitated. I insisted. Pari was holding my hand while the machine was shaking the walls of my belly with intensity and force. His strong presence as a man supported my body to relax and feel the delicacy of that moment. I was softly talking to this being. I could feel the fight of life trying to hold on, and then letting go! A burst of laughter happened at the same time. Pari joined me with a deep belly chuckle. The doctor and the nurse made comments about how loving we were with each other. How long had we been married? "A while…" Pari said.

While resting for a few days, I had a strong sense of bonding with my mother. I recognized her care as a mother. We had not connected for a few months, so I phoned. To my surprise, she was leaving the day after for a trip that included San Francisco. A week later we met in town. I shared what was happening in my life, the time at the ranch, the experience of the abortion. It was difficult for her to accept my choices, but another layer of affection between us opened up. This brief preview of motherhood gave me insights still valuable.

During this time-out, visions of other times visited me randomly as vivid as the memories of the ranch just a few weeks ago… Buried memories became available at the foreground of my conscious mind. I remembered being pregnant in other circumstances, having had three babies who died at tender ages, the pain, the despair and fear, the guilt of feeling responsible, split between having to care for my children and being pulled to the art I was dedicated to. Both were meaningful, I had to make a choice. The conflict was heartbreaking. Allowing those memories to surface, and the emotions sealed with them, brought healing and a clearer sense of purpose for this life. I did not want to have children. I wanted to dedicate my life to the crystallization of consciousness in my being. I needed time and that did not seem to be a task for just a few months. My full strength and focus was needed for the inner journey. I decided to get sterilized as soon as possible.

Back on my feet, I had to make money again. It was costly to be at the ranch and I had run out of cash. A few friends were doing striptease in one of the theaters in San

Francisco. I decided to try it. A trip to a second-hand sexy shop to choose some garments that suited the role, high heels, black dress, some flashing jewelry, I was ready! My long hair tied up, I passed the test and got the job.

Another interesting experiment was ahead. The environment was solid greed, sexual perversion, lack of refinement, sadness and pain in many eyes. I used this time to stay centered and maintain my body and spirit untouched in the midst of it all. I danced feeling the love in my heart, offering the beauty I knew inside, touching the silence of the moments I had been with Bhagwan, sharing the joyous memories of making love with dear friends... I did not engage with the men who were watching me but offered what was at the core, grateful that they were facilitating my way back to the ranch. After the shows, the girls would go inside a booth and receive phone calls from the men who were in the audience, mostly sleazy sexual comments, or request for some acting on the next show. Once a man surprised me with what he said. "You must be doing this out of love for someone. You do not care about the men watching you, you dance for someone else..." I was amazed to hear this comment from someone I would have judged insensitive and gross by his looks. Once more, I saw how my judgments clouded deeper layers of perception. I learned to stay centered when confronted with strong sexual energy. I focused on letting my heart shine light into my sexuality, and felt that the connection between both was a choice of awareness, no matter the circumstances.

I collected the cash I needed, and went back to the ranch for a few more months. I helped build a fence around Bhagwan's house and again it was time to leave. The winter was approaching... On my last day I was having lunch, eyes down, a bit sad, wondering when I would be able to come back. Suddenly, I heard a voice calling my name. Someone sitting just in front of me... That was Veet! What a delightful surprise! I had not heard from him since our time together in Pune. He had gone to the mountains in India, and then to Europe. We were happy to meet again and spent the rest of the day and night together. I was upset about having to leave, but he planned to meet me in California on his way back to Germany.

I was invited to live at the commune in Berkeley. There were about fifty people living as commune members, spread over ten houses or so, around Berkeley and Oakland. The main house had a beautiful garden and a comfortable kitchen where we cooked every evening. The commune also included a meditation center where daily meditations, groups and sessions happened. We worked outside the commune to make a living, contributed equally for rent and food, and sent a monthly donation to the ranch. We shared cleaning, cooking and shopping tasks to maintain our houses, and kept the meditation center active with a full-time program. Life was full seven days a week. And fun!

Veet came by for a week. I borrowed a car to pick him up at the airport. From our first meeting in ancient India to this modern American urban environment there was no difference at the heart. With his visit, my work schedule went out the window! I could not get it together. I did not want to miss spending time with him. We enjoyed having picnics at the park in San Francisco, going for walks, eating out, and long mornings in bed... He invited me to go to Germany with him. Though I was in love with him, with my heart aching, I said, no... My priority was to go to the ranch and I did not want to get distracted. It took me a few days to resettle inside.

Back to my working routine, it was an extreme shift of viewpoint. In the commitment of using the work as an opportunity to watch my actions and motivations, there was no time or space for resistance. I flew with the challenges of this situation. I was in a new country, having to find my way and cover high expenses every month. I guess, my determination was enough to facilitate the opening of opportunities. My willingness, or natural inclination to take risks, made it lighter and easy.

At the center, I presented some of the daily meditations, offered Rebalancing sessions and small evening groups. All the income from this work was donated to the commune. To bring in personal earnings, I cleaned houses, and offered private bodywork sessions.

I put some ads around in visible places, offering my services as "the cleaning witch" with European standards. My first call was from a man who needed approximately six hours of cleaning; he gave me the address and we booked a time. I got out of the bus as instructed, landing in a strange neighborhood in Oakland. Map in hand, just learning to move around, I walked into a dead-end street passing a few dilapidated houses. I was considering going back when I saw a man sitting outside the last house. "Are you the cleaner? I am waiting. Come in!" I doubted that it was a smart move to go in, but too late... I entered the living room... Old food stuck on the walls, dirty dishes, half-full coffee cups, beer cans, clothes, newspapers, tools, games, cards, shoes, you name it! The guy was rough, clearly drunk. I had to think fast! My instinct to leave bounced against the fear of being hurt. I spoke in a professional way, explaining my plan of action. I asked him to leave the house while I was cleaning, it would be easier for me to move around... He took a chair and sat on the porch, once in a while he would roam in, "Do you need anything?" "No, thank you!" I cleaned and cleaned and cleaned until the house was arranged neatly. The guy behaved well, even had gone out to get a pizza for lunch. The day was over. I wasn't sure that he was going to pay me, but he did as agreed.

Determined not to repeat this experience, I placed more specific ads offering weekly services. When answering calls, I requested an appointment for an interview before taking on the job. That was a good move! Most homeowners were surprised, but my request motivated respect. I dressed in red clothes, but elegantly. I got jobs in beautiful houses, with families who were appreciative of what I had to offer. This gave me a basic income, added to weekly shifts at a spa in San Francisco. Coming home for dinner at the commune was delightful!

I had to wait to go to the ranch as a full-time resident. Part of this process included a few months in New York. A testing metaphysical "training." I hated New York. I wanted to go back to the ranch! And there I was, stranded in this obnoxious city, working nonstop and it was winter!!! I experienced for the first time the consequences and the intrinsic quality of desire. I had never really desired anything before. At every step what I wished for had come to me. Unwavering intention had been enough. Not then!

Reality was distorted by my craving. I got exhausted cleaning elegant apartments on Park Avenue, giving sessions at a spa in Brooklyn Heights, and working as an evening waitress in an elegant café in Greenwich Village.

There was no time to rest, except in the taxi back home around two in the morning. I would close my eyes and relax until he stopped. Only then I looked to find out where I was—glad I had indeed been brought to the right address. I was living with a friend and her child in a tiny one-bedroom apartment in Brooklyn Heights; at least it was quiet and I could go for a walk in a rare while.

The "castle" in New Jersey where Bhagwan stayed before going to the ranch was empty, except for the caretakers: Vasant, my dearest Norwegian friend-brother; Krishna, an American man, and a couple of women, Susheela and Homa. Once in a while there were meditations and celebrations for the community of New Yorkers. It was lovely to get out of Manhattan, enjoy the view of trees... I started to spend time with Krishna, and occasionally stayed overnight whenever I managed to move around my schedule. A lover and a close friend made New York more acceptable. Within a few months, Krishna left the castle and moved to an apartment. To my surprise, the first time I slept there, a sign over the door called my attention: "This house was Henry Miller's residence from...to..." I remember his words, "Live with passion!"

I had used my material resources to move with my inner guidance. I still had my wedding gift... That piece of jewelry symbolized the quintessence of beauty and love, and was worth a large amount. It had been in a safe, taken care by my mother. I asked her to sell it at an auction, and what I received was enough to cover a year's living expenses. However, I sent it to the ranch as an anonymous donation. Breaking up a significant bond with my past, I was declaring my totality in willing to be part of the ranch's creation, asking life to take me without reservations. Nowadays, I would love to have it back.

My emotional body was stretched thousands of miles away. I had only enough energy to work and sleep. Suddenly, I decided to drop my desire and sink into New York. I could not fight it anymore. There I was, I had no idea for how long more. I had to wait, I better enjoy! That seemed inconceivable but should be possible.

First I relaxed about gathering money and started spending beyond the rent and basic food. I went shopping for a few nice clothes, having fun with the choices and variety. Even if I could not afford to buy what I was used to when living in Milan or Paris, I appreciated simply looking at good-quality design and refined craftsmanship. I took time to go around and admire urban beauty and creativity. This leisure gave me a different perspective of the city. Yes, it was a big city, there were no forests, no wild animals, no silence, but that was what it was... Crazy people rushing for money, artists trying to become someone, foreigners from all corners looking to live a decent life, the city of ambition and opportunities. I perceived all forms around as particles of the mind frozen in solid colors, each recalling infinite possibilities! In this letting go, the essence inside became again tangible. I could sit in silence in the midst of chaotic traffic, or in the crowded subway. I still had my preferences. Yet, I was fine being just where I was. I suddenly acknowledged the crystal quality of this multidimensional human concentration. The unique amalgam of energies reflected the light of different cultures, splitting the spectrum of the human rainbow into millions of sparkling nuances. This vital prism generated intense creative power. I could use it for my advantage as a tool for meditation, or fight it as the "enemy." Tough luck! There was no way to win on that try! So, I let myself be bathed instead of trying to run away.

I started smoking cigarettes! At the café there was so much cigarette smoke that my clothes and hair picked up its smell. I really disliked it. The idea of smoking blew my mind at first, but made me feel more relaxed and in tune with the city. At the café, all personnel had a drink at the end of the shift. I regularly refused it, sticking to my clean diet. Time to get loose! A whisky, after all, would not kill me. In a few days, New York became a more pleasant place to be. I was falling into its rhythm, aware that all was temporary.

A few weeks later, I dropped the waitress job with the cigarettes and the whisky and started to model at an art school. Being in the artistic environment was inspiring. At the same time, I continued offering individual bodywork sessions.

During these months in New York, I received a few postcards from friends at the ranch. The place was growing... Siddha regularly sent me loving notes of encouragement. A simple image and his few words had a magical effect, reminding me of love and joy, and that the ranch was real. Just a question of time...

When I finally relaxed in the city, I got a phone call from the commune in Berkeley. I could go back! The winter was over! Sunny California was like a mirage!

Ahata picked me up at the airport and I was welcomed in a new room in a lovely house, so quiet! In a few hours, I got sick! More like homesick for the noise and stimulation. I celebrated my birthday in bed with fever, letting the buzz out of my body, and the smoke and alcohol...

We lived simply, bringing care, love and meditation into our daily tasks.

I gave sessions at a spa and at the center. I managed to go to the ranch for the weekends. It was a twelve-hour ride, and we would drive through the night on Friday, arrive early Saturday morning, work all day, sleep, work all day on Sunday, leave in the evening, arrive in Berkeley Monday morning and go to work... A couple of times I was lucky to fly in a small airplane with a friend who was a pilot.

Finally, I was called to the ranch as a resident—I could stay there with no time frame. I was in seventh heaven...

Veet had moved to the ranch and, per the rules, residents could not make love with visitors for health-care reasons. It was still very cold. The new residents were placed to live in tents! In the morning, still freezing, it was hard to wake up and go to work! However, uncontainable bliss made me jump out of bed and face the ice outside. That is to say a lot! I was alone in a tent, and Veet was living a few yards up the canyon.

Upon arrival, all newcomers were tested for venereal diseases and only after the test results came back from the lab we were allowed intimacy with another resident. In this way, we were surely safe with the partners we chose. So I had to be celibate. However, Veet came to sleep with me every night. We bundled in bed together with clothes on and all the blankets we could gather, our noses froze and we laughed a lot during the night. At the last day of my abstinence period, we had a special date to meet for dinner. He did not show up. I was expecting to meet him at my tent. He did not show up either... I went to his tent, not there. Possible job change or working late, often happened...

The next morning he woke me up with a hug and announced that he had a job change, had met another woman at work and they had spent the night together. He wanted to see her again. I was once more taken by life's surprises. I was in love with him! Our schedules were now very different and our working sites quite far away.

I was so happy to be at the ranch that this shift did not affect me noticeably. Only a few weeks later, a bit more settled, I suddenly felt sad. I missed the beauty of our connection, yet knew I could not hold on to him or anything... A few days later, when Bhagwan passed in his car, I realized that I did not want to miss a second of that opportunity to receive his love and silence. He had opened my heart, no silly guy would close it. I danced wildly when he approached me.

From the tent, I moved to a trailer, behind Magdalena, our commune restaurant. Great to have breakfast a few steps down from my room... We shared minuscule rooms with a roommate, and mine was an Indian woman who regularly woke me up, in the midst of the night, singing loudly a traditional prayer to the master. The first time it took me by surprise, then I got used to this ritual. Whenever I had a guest, she would gracefully go to sleep in the living room... We were definitely learning tolerance.

A strange incident happened sooner after I moved there. One night I woke up with shivers, not caused by my roommate chanting, but my body could not stop quivering. I did not know what to do, so did nothing until it subsided. The morning after I felt disturbed and sick. Looking at the tiny table placed in between our beds, I noticed that the small vase with miniature cactus I had as my only "garden" had collapsed and dried. The shivers came back and I was concerned. I went to work thinking I might need to go to the medical center for a check. At lunchtime, a click! I had not talked to my family for months, and I was sure something had happened. From the public phone I called my mother, and heard that my grandmother had died the day before. She loved me fondly and had woken me up to say goodbye...

While living at this trailer, once a week I was part of a security team who stayed alert during the night, equipped with Motorolas receiving and passing on information in case of emergency. In those days, we were already facing threats against the community and a network of security had been devised to protect the residents. Between my roommate and the Motorola at my bedside table, I was getting trained to wake up at any time!

The work at the ranch was precisely and intuitively distributed between the residents. Most of the population at the ranch had at least a bachelor's degree, and many had PHD and further titles. However, jobs were not distributed according to educational or professional skills, but assigned according to more intangible qualifications; sometimes just at the whim of the moment, if you happened to pass by when a plumber or an electrician was needed. Perhaps karma had its play, and the mood of the coordinator at the jobs department, called Ramakrishna, might also have influenced outcomes. In any case, surprise usually coincided with new job notifications. And there was no other answer than yes! Considering that we were moving with the same focus, no matter where your placement was in the mandala of that creation, the center was magnetic and the only priority.

The woman who played the role of Bhagwan's secretary also overviewed this extensive enterprise, as the head coordinator of all departments. Sheela was an Indian woman, educated in the United States, who was not shy with words. She had persuasive flair, a broad perspective, and a liquid mind. All other coordinators referred to her. Though this intricate and high-speed crisscross of functions worked in an awesome way, there was no precise guidance or rules to follow. Different people were given different responsibilities, and most often asked to perform tasks unfamiliar to their previous training. And yet, the complexity of building a city from scratch called for a greater force than our individual determination, though it engaged all that we had to offer, and more... Beyond the surprise of finding a top lawyer serving you pizza at the restaurant, a weaver calculating orders for the construction materials with perfect confidence, a doctor driving a backhoe with good posture, or a therapist trained as a fireman, every detail was taken care with accuracy and new talents were revealed with each undertaking.

My first work assignment was to give bodywork sessions. I voiced my preference for an outdoors job, hoping the coordinator would realize that I was born in Brazil and loved being in nature. Instead I was designated to install a fluffy burgundy carpet in the main room in Jesus Grove, the house where the ranch coordinators lived. I was to work with two other women and one guy. None of us had previous experience laying carpets. We were given a book that should be self-explanatory, a few instruments that we did not know how to use, and a huge roll of carpet, so heavy that it had been delivered with a forklift. On the side, a few carpet knives and foam molds to protect our knees. It was amusing! Four highly skilled professionals with university degrees sitting in this empty room, gathering brains and bodies to focus on this task. Before the day was over the carpet was in place. That was the beginning of the carpet crew. From there, as we were "experienced," we got to install many other carpets in the trailers that had been brought in for the new residents.

The physical requirement for this task brought me back to an early age. I was crawling most of the day. The combination of the formaldehyde coming off the carpets and this forced position often made us giggle, uncontrolled. When an accident happened, instead of making it dramatic, a good laugh called for a creative solution. When something was not right, that was just as it was... Let's keep moving.

A few months later, I was invited to a friend's birthday party at one of the restaurants. Arriving at the party, I realized that my mental age had regressed to a point where I did not manage to even understand what others were talking about... I had been crawling for too long! It amused me to feel like a baby in the midst of adults discussing meaningful things. I perceived myself small and it was difficult to stand on my legs. A few minutes later, I went home with a funny sensation, and the recognition that I was recovering a sense of grounding I had missed at an earlier age. In the following days I noticed that my awareness while standing up had shifted dramatically. I felt taller, supported by my legs. The earth was under my feet!

Building sites sprouted at the speed of light, a colorful ocean of people kept arriving to partake of this creation. During my carpet crew career we started to build townhouses to accommodate the rapidly increasing number of residents. Construction crews were set twenty-four hours a day. I loved to work through the night, and regularly volunteered to be on night shifts. It was enchantingly quiet, though hundreds were working concentrated in one building site. In the morning, it was a pleasure to go for a walk, sometimes visit my friend Varsha at the truck farm, sit a bit further in the hills, nobody around. Best of all was to have a bath without any control on time or water usage! In case of being with a lover, after the bath, the bed and the room for ourselves! The greatest luxury...

I spent nine months in my fours, devising new techniques for stretching, mending, cutting, and gluing pieces of cheap carpet. Always within a deadline because everything at the ranch had a deadline, and always impossible. I did not take anybody or any demand too seriously, rather focused on what was in front of my hands and eyes. The ambience of playfulness and lightness shared by most residents was contagious and carried others who did not have such an easy time.

After more than a year without going out of the ranch, I was sent to Portland. The commune ran a commercial hotel in town and someone had placed a bomb in one of the rooms, making front-page news in the local paper. The whole top floor's carpet needed to be replaced, of course immediately! Two tall strong guys were added to our regular team and in record time we completed this job, while the guests were waiting in the lobby for their rooms to be ready. The only day I went for a walk around the block, I was hit on the head with a tomato. There was enormous prejudice against Bhagwan and his people. That incident made me understand the blindness of intolerance. It was shocking to feel hatred expressed randomly. I was thrilled to go back "home" after a few days in Portland.

We worked seven days a week, varying schedules according to imminent needs, usually between ten to fourteen hours a day. Our timetable included an interlude at lunchtime, animated by Bhagwan's drive-by. He made a loop around the ranch, and we waited for him in line along the roads, playing music and dancing. In the evenings, I often shook up my legs at Omar Khayam, our disco. There was nothing else I wished for.

This opportunity to pour my life into such an enormous project was extraordinary. Feeling plugged into infinite energy, my strength and vigor were endless. I easily worked non-stop, stretching myself without limitations, accomplishing tasks, introducing new ideas and solutions, overcoming lack of sleep, lack of food, nothing was difficult. I was the luckiest person in the planet! Relating became less meaningful in a strictly personal level, but took another dimension in collaboration.

One morning I walked into one of the townhouses we were building, and the carpets for the whole house (there were nine bedrooms and a living room), were rolled up at the entry in the living room. I vividly remember stepping past the door-line and sensing that I had not a drop of energy left to lift my leg for the next step. I passed out then and there. The voices rushing to me were faded. A few people moved my inert body into a car and dropped it at our medical center. I remember nothing else... A few days later I opened my eyes and asked what had happened. I had been sleeping for a week, with a drip needled onto my arm. A soft voice said, "You can stay as long as you need to rest..." There were other excited voices in the background. It was drive-by time, but there was nothing in the world that would make me move. I turned over and slept some more. A few days later I suddenly stood up and asked for the drip to be removed. I was ready to go to work! It was a beautiful day. I walked a long way to the site of the townhouses, and joined the carpet crew as if nothing.

We built houses, hundreds of A-frames, a large hotel, restaurants, a shopping mall, a meditation hall for thousands of people, more houses, several offices, a large space for sessions and groups, a garage for an expanding fleet of cars and buses. We built a large lake, and another lake, and developed a self-sufficient truck farm, and an animal farm along with buildings to accommodate visitors, festival participants and residents, and later a program called "Share A Home." It was exciting to see focused creativity translating love in a visible way.

The residents' working schedule often had no time limits. I remember spending three-four nights without sleeping, working almost nonstop to complete a project before some building inspector would come by... I noticed my own mind settings as if they were uncontrollable self-commands, solid in their fixed form and interconnection with the body. Certain phrases would get out of my mouth before I had any choice to stop them, or a body movement would reflect a thought as a mimic, beyond my conscious choice. I realized even more clearly that my life was led by unconscious choices most of the time. I was crudely shown my lack of discernment. I watched the movie of my repetitive internal process. Interesting! Observing Bhagwan, was directly at the other side of the spectrum! His movements were poised, intentional, holding consciousness in the background, visible through his grace, calm, alertness and embracing vastness.

Regularly, I woke up between four and five thirty to sit in meditation for an hour. I had to be at work sometimes as early as six am. This quiet time was sacred. Looking back, it is hard to imagine that I managed to create this gap-space in the midst of all the other demands and still go for breakfast—delicious porridge with lots of cinnamon and banana on the top. But it happened naturally... If I had been on a night shift, it was not as easy to wake up in the late afternoon and get going, but often I found time to watch the sunset...

One morning Neera, my coordinator and dear friend, came to our construction site to let me know I was getting a job change. I took off my knee-pads and drove with her to the main office. There were three other guys also waiting to hear their fate, looking quite serious. We were asked to take Tarot cards. Mine was "Trust in Allah but tether the camel." Pratima, whose job was to distribute and organize the workers around the whole ranch, nodded her head. "You got to be practical!" Then she let us know that we had been chosen to be car mechanics. I burst into laughter! I knew nothing about cars, nor had any interest in learning. I could not stop laughing. The guys were pissed. One of them was a very elegant and proud man. "Ok, if that is to be so, when do I start?" Pratima said, "I will check..." She went into another room and a minute later came back with the news. "Komala, you will not be a mechanic yet... You will be the support coordinator of the welding shop. You guys can start with the car mechanic training immediately at RBG." RBG was the shortcut for Rajneesh Buddhafield Garage. I laughed again. Not that I knew anything more about welding...

I walked to the welding shop to meet Leela, a vivacious South African woman. She introduced me to the welders, getting into the details of what I was supposed to do: straighten up the paperwork, organize files, create new systems for information and job requests, overview and manage the office. On the side, it would be good if I could spend some time cheering up anyone who got serious or uptight. There were only two women at the welding department and the men included Prasad, one of the main therapists in Pune. I appreciated his beauty, and he was on the list of people who I enjoyed being around. Soon the office was organized and I started to have idle time. A few more tasks were added to my responsibility, including ordering all the parts for the cars, buses and trucks of our ranch fleet (probably over two hundred vehicles.) I did not know the difference between a brake and a carburetor but had to learn it quickly. For a few months, I spent my days between the welding shop and the garage.

During my RBG training, I was a go-between the car mechanics and Su, the main coordinator of transportation. She was an Englishwoman, intense like few. I loved working with her. She provoked my alertness and ability to focus, fast cutting through bullshit or lack of clarity. I had to be quick, timely, and know what I was talking about. From the mechanics I received information on what needed to be ordered, why, how urgently. I followed up by gathering information on prices from the research department. No computers yet in those days.

Every day I met Su, usually for three minutes max, or over the Motorola, if it was something extremely urgent. I reported to her all costs and deadlines, in order to obtain her approval. Then I passed on the request to the ordering department, and tracked it until the delivery was confirmed. The absurdity of this job put me in a playful mood. I had to talk to many different people, mostly guys who were not happy having to justify their needs, report an accident they had been responsible for, or explain nifty details to someone who had no clue of what they were talking about, often asking basic questions. Spending most of my days talking about car parts definitely challenged my Scorpio moon nature, always in search of meaning and depth.

I started to enjoy listening to my voice absolutely disconnected from contents, more concerned with the quality of care and interest directed to whom I was speaking to, rather than what I was talking about. That was a significant shift in my communication skills, later useful in my work with sessions and groups.

Renuka was one of RBG's coordinators, and we became close friends. We giggled for no reason, just the sweetness of that play. I was asked to spend some time at the bus garage, to cheer up their crew. It was an open space, quite cold, where four or five guys and one girl repaired our fleet of out-of-date yellow school buses, the main transportation at the ranch. They froze in that place and enjoyed when I came by for a chat, and a warm cup of tea. One of the guys was a young Englishman who had been a professional Formula One racer, now humbling trying to fix nuts and bolts on old buses. His sense of humor usually cheered me up!

The welding shop, the RBG and the bus repair terminal were next to each other and very close to Rajneesh University. There professional training in the healing arts and various therapeutic approaches were offered, in a more organized way than in Pune. Veet worked there and we sometimes met for afternoon tea.

Our working spaces were called "temples" as a reminder of our intention to be part of this experiment in a sacred way—that is how I considered it. The temples were named after different mystics, or people who had brought some beauty or poetry into the world in their unique way, such as Allan Watts, Lao Tzu, Gorakh, Jesus, Mirdad, etc... As we were fiercely engaged in building this new commune, meditation moved from Buddha Hall to all places and at all times. Whatever work I was assigned to do offered a doorway to meditation, a path of inward observation and increasing awareness, a means to share my love. The various challenges I certainly encountered turned into opportunities for reflection and understanding. Work was a reminder to keep going back to the source.

In the mornings before we started, and at the end of the day, we spent a few minutes together singing a traditional Buddhist prayer, "Buddham Sharanam Gachchami... Sangham Sharanam Gachchami... Dhamman Sharanam Gachchami..." That was translated as "I bow to the feet of the enlightened one, I bow to the commune of the enlightened one, I bow to the ultimate truth of the enlightened one." Then someone would come forward and say aloud what we called "reminders." A spontaneous expression of what was his/her intention in being at the ranch, at work, what they were there to be reminded of. It was often a few phrases, different for each person and at each day. Just the acknowledgment and freshness that came with it touched my heart. In my turn, there was always a moment of gap before I would utter any words. That instant represented the delicacy of my connection with Bhagwan, as if he was sitting there, waiting to listen to what I had to say. Buddham Sharanam Gachchami... Sangham Sharanam Gachchami... Dhamman Sharanam Gachchami... My soul understood this prayer.

Bhagwan had been in silence since his arrival at the ranch. We only saw him once a day during drive-by and four times a year for celebrations when thousands of visitors sat in silence interwoven with intense music and dancing. As the ranch was located in a rural area, our meditation hall had officially been built as a greenhouse. I guess we meant a human greenhouse...

As Bhagwan's physical presence was not as available as in Pune, our connection with him was now less personal, and had to be found inside at all cost. And we worked a lot for that! For me, working and being part of this majestic creation was priority. The work was my link to his love and stillness, so I offered all I had. It was like digging an infinite hole inside, and the joy of touching that bottomless space was more than I could imagine earning for an entire life. So, when I am asked, "Did you work without getting paid for twenty hours a day, seven days a week?" Yes, I did and more. What money could buy that combination of people, Bhagwan's presence, the expansiveness and beauty of the land, the intelligent amalgam of thousands of well-educated artists, poets, scientists, from all corners of the world, coming together with such focus and commitment?

I was grateful for the ones who were financing this experiment, which absorbed millions of dollars. I felt lucky to be there even when I had not contributed much in a material way. I was aware of the mathematics and grandiosity of it all. It was amazing to walk around and see the houses I helped to build, to look at the growing flowers that I planted a few months before, to eat the sprouts that I learned to germinate... And it was bliss to go back home and find my laundry washed by a caring friend, to notice my room impeccably clean every night when I went to bed, to eat delicious meals timely ready at the restaurant... Or to meet a friend driving a funky yellow school bus when I needed to move around.

My next job was at Baal Shem temple, coordinating and organizing transportation for the purchases of everything we needed at the ranch. At that point, there were about two thousand residents, and during the festivals maybe up to six thousand visitors. From dry food to toilet paper, from car brakes to Bhagwan's personal trivia, and whatever else in between. I received phone calls from more than twenty purchasers assigned for each department, organized this information in a sensible way, scheduled freight to our warehouse in Portland and followed it up until it was finally delivered to the temple that had ordered the item. We had a fleet of semi trucks and five drivers going back and forward from the ranch to Portland, so I planned the transportation of items from the warehouse to the ranch, and later from our dock to each temple. This required wide overview, as well as meticulous care for details.

I worked with PH, an Australian man with an unwavering character, strong and dependable, with a sharp sense of humor. His intense green eyes were always alert and he held to the ground with a Bodhidharma-like character. He took care of the practicality related to the trucks: maintenance, loading and unloading, calculations with weight and time, and driver's schedules. He also drove to Portland and sometimes to other locations to pick up construction materials, and backed me up when I was squeezed or overwhelmed with my tasks. We worked well together! I enjoyed his strength and decisiveness in movement and he appreciated my clarity and ability to take on a lot of work without fuss. We both moved fast, without much talk. He had a non-nonsense approach to all that was going on at the ranch, his criticism was merciless and funny. I really enjoyed our collaboration.

It is amazing to think that not so long ago, this entire operation happened without computers, faxes or cell phones. The complexity of flying parcels generated a mess of miscommunication. I realized that we needed a fluid system in harmony with the fluidity of the way things moved anyway. Control would not work.

We were busy all day and often into the night. When a truck full of merchandise arrived, we unloaded it together, sometimes for a few hours. We checked that the contents were in fact what it had been ordered; if not, returns had to be prepared with their related paperwork. We arranged packages into large shelves with labels, then called taxi drivers from RBG to pick up and distribute them. Finally we called the related departments to let them know the delivering schedule. No time to space out!

I became a truck driver companion, once in a while going up and down to Portland with the guys, driving somewhere a few hours away to pick up a load of apples or just hanging out together at dinner time, after long hours of unloading never-ending boxes. The drivers came from different backgrounds. PH had been a professional hairdresser; the other drivers were an American University professor, an English hypnotherapist, an English business consultant, and an English builder and landscaper. Wearing oversized overalls, I played with them, moving intensely and often being thrown into situations that had no logical solutions.

We received usually two or three truckloads a week, totally packed. Everybody needed something urgently. I learnt not to take them seriously, to listen and respond from a realistic point of view. Truth is, more than often the so-called reality was bent in unimaginable ways.

I was on the phone all day long. Another level of opening happened in my heart and throat with this exercise. I became more sociable at dinner time, forced to let go of my attachment to "silence" as such, now feeling the silence that was there anyway whether

I uttered words or not. At the same time, the awareness of my mind-comments, happening even when I was "silent" became more obvious. At drive-by I sang and sang and danced looser than ever…

The working situation reinforced a constant willingness (or unwillingness…) to break through barriers, veils of personality, forcing the courage to scratch the veneer of self-image and social rules. The intensity of creativity and relationships imposed spontaneity, unexpected behaviors, startling sincerity. I have always enjoyed situations that stretched my resources, stirring surprising solutions out of the blue. That was a full plate!

One incident that taught me a good lesson happened when I was dealing with an outside delivery. Sometimes merchandise was transported to the ranch directly by the source company, usually when the order was large enough to fill up a truck—sometimes construction materials, once a week special food, and occasionally odd orders. Either PH or I was expected to go to the reception area, a few miles away from our warehouse, and welcome the driver. Our security department used well-trained German shepherd dogs to sniff the truck and the driver for detection of bombs and drugs, neither allowed nor desired at the ranch. As the news about the ranch always talked about how horrible and dangerous we were, the truck drivers were often scared by this kind of reception. Besides the practical aspect of this greeting, there was the emotional comforting and convincing the guy that he would be ok driving in, and it would not take long.

I was notified that a truck full of paint was arriving. I went to receive it. I greeted a rather angry driver. He insisted into dropping the merchandise then and there. Not an easy one… Finally I managed to convince him to come to our warehouse where there was a proper delivery dock, with a forklift and all we needed to unload. I had learned to move the forklift and arrange things around, mostly boxes, from one shelf to the other. But for bigger jobs I always called one of the guys.

That day, nobody was available and the driver was impatient. I asked if he could use the forklift to unload; his response was absolutely no. Well, I had to do it! I got into the forklift and moved it out of the warehouse into the dock. I had placed a large sheet of plywood to bridge the dock to the truck, now with the back doors opened. I proceeded to hook the forklift onto the first wooden pallet piled up quite high with paint buckets and wrapped with commercial shrink plastic. That was easy… Then I started to back up as slowly as I could, to take the pallet out of the truck. The whole thing was a bit wobbly… As the rear of the forklift hit the wood, the difference between the dock level and the plywood thickness made the forklift jump and with this slight abrupt movement, the paint buckets fell onto the dock and burst open, spilling colors all over… The truck driver started screaming at me, and I started laughing. God! That was a major fuck up! How am I going to get out of this mess?

I took my Motorola trying to find PH and he was nowhere. I walked to the bus garage adjacent to our warehouse and got the mechanics to help clean up the paint and the guy's truck. In the midst of this emergency, PH appears and looks at me with a smile.

He could not stop laughing. Why didn't you call me? Well, I did... The truck driver was trying hard to keep his bad mood, with crossed arms in a corner. PH jumped into the forklift and took out the rest of the pallets and this chapter was over.

For every accident that happened at the ranch involving loss of money, the person responsible had to write a concise report explaining how the accident had happened, and if there was any way it could have been avoided. I sat to write my report, recognizing that sometimes I just do things out of an impulse and "learn on the go" idea. I could have avoided this disaster if I had better evaluated my limitations. Then I had to go to one of the coordinators and read my report. I sat in front of a woman who I knew well, and read my lines, estimating the damage and recognizing that sometimes I better be more cautious, and yet the situation was as it was. No comments, no excuses, just awareness.

During my time at Baal Shem, a major event transformed our daily routine. Sheela made an announcement during a general meeting at Buddha Hall. The commune had grown enough and we had created overflowing beauty and comfort; now it was time to share Bhagwan's love with less fortunate people. We were going to invite street people from all over America to come and live with us. I do not remember the specific contents of this message, nor do I want to get analytical about the political motivations that may have been at the source of this experimentation.

Working at the hub of transport and communication, I got acquainted with further information about what was happening. Several people were sent to different towns in the USA, with the mission to invite homeless people to come to the ranch. Suddenly, we were opening the doors of our paradise to hundreds of drunkards, drug addicts, criminals, and dropouts that somehow ended up on the streets. A variety of colors, accents, ethnic backgrounds... I enjoyed seeing this wave of craziness invading this controlled environment. At least, that was how it started. Some of my friends were sent to Chicago, Boston, New York, Miami, and other large metropolises, to collect new residents.

PH was immediately sent somewhere. The comments of returning recruiters were outrageous. Some of them shepherded a busload of homeless people across country having to part fights, deal with medical emergencies, and the dilemmas between people who were not used to socialize.

One mid afternoon, I got an urgent call. I was asked to be ready in half an hour to meet Jerome at the reception. He was going to drive a bus to Portland airport to receive a group of homeless guests arriving from Puerto Rico. "You speak Spanish fluently, don't you?" I wished I didn't, but, yes, I do... I wasn't sure what to expect, and I did not like to go out of the ranch. At the airport I was expected to greet about sixty people or so. That was a journey! Jerome did not speak any Spanish and was only interested in getting back home as soon as possible. After managing to convince everybody to get into the bus, we started driving, hoping to make it back in record time. We called the ranch to communicate that we were on our way. The person at the reception let us know that they wouldn't be ready to receive these people until seven am, we should find a way to make the trip longer...

Oh, no! We stopped at a forest, there was a waterfall nearby and I thought it would be good entertainment. Most people were tired and angry, complaining it was taking too long. Screams, confusion, people running all over; I decided to let go of control. It was like a madhouse. What if we lost some of these people? I was exhausted having worked during the day, and stayed awake inside a bus during the night.

We arrived early in the morning and I started to have doubts about this great idea. The ranch was getting more populated and the usual restful vibe was taken over by people fighting, things being stolen, a mess in the restaurants and more noise around. Most residents started to retreat and rarely go to eat; that was my choice.

The days were long and usually full of unexpected situations. Besides working from seven to seven, I got an extra job in the Security department. From eight in the evening to two in the morning, I drove around the area where the "Share-A-Home" people lived keeping an eye on people. Often, I had to go inside the A-frames to appease quarrels between housemates. Usually I was accompanied by a male partner who stayed in the car, in touch with the central Security office through the Motorola. There were about six people in one room, enough for plenty of disagreements. Even though, all guests were checked for weapons and drugs, some of the guys were street-smart beyond belief. I found "weapons" built with bent forks where the tines were crushed together into an arrow point, and spoons made into sharp knives by filing them against a rock. Indeed, ingenious and creative people.

Though my slim body type did not convey physical strength, I went into their houses alone and fearless. Born and raised in Brazil, I was used to relate with different types of people, poverty and violence being a common denominator. These people were extremely sensitive, intuitively understanding my role and intention, they often responded with warmth and humor. This job forced me to reach out in unusual ways. Suddenly, something would come out of my mouth... A suggestion, a question, a request, and the initial aggression turned into apologies, laughter, or a sharp comment, surprising both of us. Each challenging situation offered a chance to recall a quality of heart untouched, behind the craziness. Sometimes it was absolute madness. I wondered how did they get there? Was there any chance to recall and nurture the purity of heart in people who had been hurt, mistreated and ostracized so drastically?

Those were intense times. I hardly slept and PH was also stretched. The amount of purchases had increased, so did the trips between Portland and the ranch with trucks full of stuff. Our warehouse had no doors. When it snowed, wind blew into the space and snowflakes sprayed over our desks...

I had no sense of solidity. Everything around and inside was unbound; thoughts, emotions, restrictions. At any moment a simple phone call could turn my schedule upside down, with an emergency that needed to be taken care of, no matter what. The immediacy of action was the only response. My body was a current of energy that could take any shape and move as the sirocco. And there were storms continuously, and tornadoes and hurricanes! It was pleasant and scary. I experienced the source of life without form, the very animation before crystallization. In the same way, destruction was as easy. There was a new sense of responsibility towards my life and towards others, understanding the power of awareness and the suffering of unawareness—the razor's edge.

As time passed by, layers of judgments became evident in the volatility of the situation. In that intensity, awareness penetrated deeper breaking down my defense mechanisms. I noticed arrogance in myself and in sannyasins as a group. We were identified with being privileged, living with a master, building the city that will never die, being "better," more intelligent, more this or that. At an individual level this attitude had been cultivated by our protected environment; at a communal level, through Sheela's political actions, in those days reaching peak performance. The falseness of any concept of separation became self-evident. There were no true justifications for prejudice.

Suddenly, I wasn't sure anymore what made me different than anyone else. The social madness that surrounded us was as evident as the madness of my own choices if seen absolutely. They could only stand as unquestionable if seen in reference to a fixed context. The Share-a Home experience thawed the coherence of our sannyasin universe. It was ironic to realize that even if Bhagwan embodied absolute emptiness and fluidity, we had built a group image around him, based in achievements and concepts of righteousness. As the Californian kids say, "Go figure!"

I decided to face what disturbed me. This decision coincided with a new assignment for all residents: we had an obligatory schedule to go for dinner at the Cafeteria that served the Share-A-Home people. As we had a cantina style with shared tables for meals, there was no way to stay isolated. Also, most people were eager to talk to us and ask questions. I sat at dinner listening to bizarre stories and relaxing in the prevalent chaos. I heard of men who grew up sharing their beds with bears in an Indian reservation, of musicians living in the streets of New York because they did not want to compromise and just get a job, of women who had been beat up almost to death, of criminals who had evaded their jail sentences, of professional killers paid by the government to exterminate prominent politicians in far away countries and more... I listened in amazement. How did we all meet at the feet of the master? I let myself get wet with the rain, so to speak...

Noticing that I used "silence" as a refuge from the noise out there, I experimented with letting the noise break through, reach the defended spaces inside. Could I preserve integrity and feel safe without the need to push away? What would happen if I disregarded my comfort zone? Sometimes I felt like screaming, invaded, disrespected. But more and more often, I touched a deeper peace beyond my ideas of meditation, respect, and what I needed to feel genuinely content.

Little things suddenly became immensely significant. For example, one day I went to get socks at the residents' boutique, a large warehouse full of mostly secondhand clothes. I do not remember how that system worked, but whenever a resident was in need of clothing, that was the place to go. Once in a rare while, there were new items. I found pure cotton socks and was able to get three pairs, one of each color in tones of red and orange, of course. The joy of this simple gift was way beyond what I can describe. Like a child, innocence bathed my heart. Just a pair of socks… I was overwhelmed with the realization of how I had taken for granted most of material things I had possessed in the past. Suddenly a pair of socks was a treasure.

It may have been at that time that Bhagwan started to give discourses at his house to small groups. These evening gatherings were by invitation only. I was privileged to be invited a few times. The coziness of the room, his presence showering serenity, as well as vehemently suggesting a new quality of inquiry, made me feel protective about what I was being given. For weeks, I could hardly talk to anyone. I was afraid to lose him before having come to a point of true balance and clarity within. I was afraid to lose the gentleness I had found inside my heart, and to be hurt in the delicacy of my body. Unexpectedly, I became aware of the extreme fragility of his body and that there was no guarantee that he would be around for too long. I experienced panic, and for the first time, I wrote him a letter asking for guidance. I also asked to be present at his death.

A few days later I was called again to the evening meeting at Lao Tzu, and I was invited to sit exactly in front of Bhagwan. Usually that spot was allocated to Teertha, who was then placed behind me. In this sandwich of energy, I listened to Bhagwan talking and looking straight into my eyes. Closing or opening my eyes were both options nearly unbearable. He talked about listening to my own nature, spending time in nature; it was not necessary to hold on to his words, he was giving us silence, the inner space from where all the answers would come. Listen to the birds, sit next to beautiful trees…

Coming out of the house, there was snow on the ground and the peacocks were dancing in the light of sparkling snowflakes. The stars were bright and I felt he would always be with me no matter what. Siddha was driving the van out of Lao Tzu house, once more his presence was significant. We went to the cafeteria. Already late in the night, there was warm food put aside for us…

I recognized the sangha as a charged field of consciousness. The convergence of people around a living master generates an electrical current of intention and intensity, which in turn self-recharges in its very movement—continuous circuitry. At the core, there was the emptiness of a man who had come to understand the flow of life beyond control, and lived in an absolute state of receptivity. At one end, space and porosity, at the other, excess and need for discharge. In other words, consciousness of life realized as ever expanding creation, met by unconsciousness of mind trying to define, direct and control what is bigger than itself.

Literally, the torrential energy of the sangha made it obvious that I was trying to do an impossible job. Trying to protect personal circumstances, genetic, karmic, and/or evolutionary preconditions was like bottling the ocean… In those circumstances, resistance was met by indestructible plasticity. Sooner or later, the water washed the rocks, rounding their corners and sharp angles.

We worked long hours, sometimes up to twenty hours a day, sometimes more than that... This rhythm was cleansing, as no pain, emotion or thought had the ability to stick for too long. At the end of the day there was essence revealed in creativity. With added stamina and challenges, we kept building our dream city.

After nights awake, I had glimpses of abandon... I could call it love, overflowing joy undiscriminating about the potential receiver, arising from so deep inside that I was not able to trace its source, absolutely ineffable. Just like Bhagwan's presence walking in to sit with us. Yes, he was there, we could see him. And yet, he was translucent. Through his transparency, I could see my solidity, my clumsiness. Sitting in his presence, I was recovering visceral knowing. Nothing to do with his words, which I rarely remembered. A refreshing sense of individuality was transmitted, not as an ego distinction and affirmation American style, but as a sense of navigation in life that did not compare, did not separate good and bad, me and others.

As I had the privilege of having a car at my disposal, sometimes I would take the job of the taxi driver, and go around the ranch delivering parcels. It gave me a break from the phone and time to have a cup of tea at the truck farm, sit under a tree, say hello to a few friends...

Digambar came into my life, out of the freezer! One afternoon I decided to drive around and do some deliveries, ending my day at the main storage space for the kitchen where he worked. We had been talking on the phone about pallets for months, but I did not know whom he was. There I met a curly-hair, bright blue eyes, vivacious guy, a face I remembered from Pune. Numerous adventures resulted from our friendship and a sweet brotherhood that we share to this date.

As a supplement to my daily job, I was on Security shifts once a week overnight. Rajneeshpuram had been incorporated as a legitimate city, federal law required a police force. Some residents were trained as regular police officers and were on duty "in town" as the Rajneesh Peace Force, wearing uniforms and guns. The Security team was a support for the Peace Force and mostly composed of once-a-week members who had a twelve-hour shift added to their regular jobs, as in my case. We were placed in pairs inside small booths situated in strategic locations around the property. I loved the nights awake in those booths, or driving down the bee house near the river, or up to the top of the ranch in a snowy night, dark and stillness. The focused time we spent in the security booth forged sweet friendships. I could not stand wearing uniforms made of polyester for such long hours, but enjoyed listening to coyotes howling, in between reporting cars' license plate numbers to the next booth down the road, big skies and awe.

The ranch comprised hundreds of square miles; crossing our private property, there was a state road. Considering that we were not welcomed in the neighborhood, mainly populated by Christian farmers and cowboys, sometimes we had to respond to intimidation from people displaying guns, not always easy or pleasant to deal with. As a security member, I was called into those situations with a male partner to resolve conflicts, often late into the night. My role was to play the feminine energy support, just standing there, while my male partner dealt with the person and issue. In this position I witnessed weird and abusive situations, reflecting the boredom and fear many people lived in. So much so, that they needed to get out of their homes in the mid of the night to disturb a group of people who were peacefully trying to create an environment of harmony and collaboration. It was bizarre and sad.

As the Share-A-Home program settled down, with many of the participants leaving and others getting integrated in the daily life of the ranch, things at Baal Shem got more relaxed. Suddenly PH got very sick, and was confined at the medical center. He was taciturn and upset, not knowing what had hit him. During his absence I took over responsibility for the whole operation, with the support of the truck drivers. Again, there was just spin… I was more involved with the coordinators of RBG, and was invited to go for dinner at Jesus Grove for a coordinator's meeting. I told Sheela I was busy, and did not go. I had no interest in discussing anything about work at dinnertime. A second invitation came by a few days later, I also did not make it. Nowadays, I see that power was not my issue. It must have been clear that I would be useless, as I never got invited again.

Soon after PH came back, I was called to Ramakrishna, and sent to the accounting department. Renuka was one of the coordinators of the Currency Card office, a debit card service within the commune. Accounting! Well, I studied abstract mathematics for a few years at University, inspired by my interest in the mathematical formulation of the Moebus ring and laws of symmetry, but that was long ago… However, balancing my own bank account never interested me.

Computers had just been introduced as a real novelty! A few people knew enough about them to teach and set up systems. I was sent to a computer programming class in the evenings. During the day, I did full-time accounting and managing about ten people at the Currency Card office. Renuka and Sabah came to meet me and pass on the basics. Sadhvi, whose job I was substituting, taught me how to read the daily computer balancing sheets for the business in the commune. It was a report with so many sheets printed in large format that we needed an empty room to spread them open on the floor.

I was sent to Portland for a proper accounting training, and my life was about counting money. A few days a week, in the evening, I was at the cash register of our "casino" and disco, ringing payments for gambling chips, beer and snacks, dancing in between clients, and balancing it at closing time, usually around midnight.

One day I received a phone call from the reception. My mother had arrived at our hotel in Portland and was getting into the bus to the ranch in a few hours! I was informed that she had sent me a message a few weeks earlier, but I had not received it. That was a surprise! Pratima let me know that she would be a guest of the commune and that I could take a few days off to be with her.

We met at the Welcome Center, at the entry of the ranch property. Her first comment was about my "uniform"—the Currency Card workers wore a horrible maroon polyester dress, the worst of American cheap taste. Used to my independent elegant-wild taste, she did not know what to make of my new look.

I was glad she had made the effort to come by to meet me in unique circumstances. The ranch represented my expression of love and life choices. However, she was critical about most of what her eyes could catch, and my choices. I did not want to justify myself or try to convince her of anything. Our conversations did not extend very far....

Her visit lasted three days. I had just received my ten-dollar card monthly allowance that residents were granted to spend at one of the ranch businesses. So, I invited her for pizza... We had a few meals together at our communal restaurant, went for a walk, she slept a lot and decided to leave.

My father sent me a cash gift that I immediately transformed into a bicycle. Like a kid with a new toy, I was delighted to ride around! Specially coming home late in the night after my computer lessons...

Working at the Currency Card made me inquiry into the power and meaning of money. I was dealing with people's issues around payments, loans, donations, and consequently fear, greed, generosity, control and more. I started to look at my relationship with money, realizing that it had been almost nonexistent. Having grown up in a wealth environment I had soon realized that money did not bring happiness. I saw no reason to go after it. I had left it behind as I had left home. In a magical way, I had always been able to do whatever I wanted and move at my own whim, with or without money. I had a healthy impulse to work hard when needed; from my father's attitude I got that work was joy and passion, so it was easy to focus into anything if I was motivated by love, creative burst or idealism. Nothing else seemed to be a good reason for work, and making money had always been a consequence of my totality. At the ranch I became aware of the immense creative potential of money. I was grateful to the people who had offered large amounts to make the realization of that project possible. I came to understand the dynamism of earth and fire resulting from cash flow, the genesis of form and instigation of motion. Yes, a curse or a blessing, it was up to me. Denying its power would not take me much further. I kept watching the traps of identifications with having it or not, an array of attached emotions, and looking at my own restrictions, either by judging or avoiding relating to it.

For a year or so I counted money every day. Talking to thousands of people about their accounts, and solving various problems caused by our lack of professionalism as an official "bank." As I had to deal with large financial institutions around the country, I realized that the monetary structure of the ranch was a bag of tricks. It considered many perspectives and focused on one: as fast as possible, and before it crumbled! There was circulation instead of accumulation, and its very speed was keeping it all rolling. A different game than the usual "amassing and holding on to it as tight as possible." Like the magic theater that the Indian babas performed on the streets in Pune—if you would really look, it was easy to see that we were riding on a wave of mirage and material illusion. We generated an energy waterfall, transforming the sun into thousand of rainbows. After all we had built a real city, nevertheless serving a purpose independent of its physical reality. The stiffness of money was being transformed into the plasticity of wealth. I was learning more than just counting money.

Simple events took me out of routine, presenting amazement and mind-blankness. I had to go from the Currency Card office to the main accounting office a few times a day, maybe a kilometer away. My bicycle was a delight! One day I came out of the office and it had disappeared. I looked all over the area where I had parked but no signs of it. I was upset and determined to find it. How? I had no idea from where to start. A bus was coming by and I jumped into it without thinking. It was not going where I was supposed to go; instead it went towards the truck farm, just the opposite direction. Before its final stop, I asked the driver to let me out, in a spot away from any buildings. For a few minutes, I walked with determination up the hill, towards the desert. Suddenly I sat on a large rock and cried. I was sad that I had lost my bike. I was sobbing like a child. Suddenly, I looked ahead and in a glimpse I saw the wheels of a bicycle hidden behind a tree. I walked towards it and there was my bicycle! Nobody was around! I picked it up and dragged it with me a good fifteen minutes' walk down to the road. This ordinary experience recalled my ability to open to presence and knowing beyond the mind, not necessarily "esoteric" or "spiritual" but simply earthbound.

Beyond male–female

Sometime in 1983... General meeting this afternoon! What could it be about? We were already working sixteen hours a day. Anyway, it was pleasant to come together in the midst of the day.

General meetings usually conveyed announcements related to work, updates on how our projects were developing, or information about political affairs. Sheela was the master of ceremonies and our only direct connection with Bhagwan. As his secretary, she met him regularly and passed on to the commune members his practical guidance.

I was going to spend the evening with a guy who I had been dating for a few weeks. He had a quality of innocence and beauty that touched me since the first I saw him walking in the snow carrying a toilet! We were in the midst of a construction "crunch" and the place was crowded. He worked at the plumbing department and his unassuming elegance called my attention. His features reflected a delicacy I sensed in his heart. That was confirmed when we first got together. I appreciated his European sensitivity. So, we met at Buddha Hall and sat together waiting for the latest news.

Sheela announced that we were moving into a new phase in anticipation of an epidemic disease called AIDS, which had recently been detected and was spreading fast. As there was not yet much research about it, and it seemed to be transmitted through sexual contact, Bhagwan had requested that we absolutely follow some rules of precaution. She then described our future sexual behavior. With the exception of a couple who had been together for over thirty years in a monogamous relationship, everyone living or visiting the ranch was to comply with these instructions, otherwise they should leave.

The fine points were described either during this meeting or later on by one of our main doctors. I vaguely remember the details. First choice was to be celibate; if that was not possible, we were to make love with condoms, gloves and a spermicidal cream used in a precise way; then we should wash our hands and body immediately. Ah, no French kissing whatsoever! All we needed would be provided in our houses and there was no excuse for disrespecting this code. Residents and visitors would be tested for the disease within the next days and would be regularly checked every six months thereafter. There was silence and "oh, no!" echoing in the hall... I looked at my friend and we were rather disappointed that our sweet romance was going to be regulated by plastic gloves. We gave it a try, but after the first night I decided that I was ready to let go of this pleasure...

The press came out with hard criticism and sarcastic comments about this announcement. In time, we realized that Bhagwan's guidance saved many lives. Our communal life-style was truly intimate and a few people were already HIV positive. The awareness forcefully imposed at that early stage prevailed throughout the years to follow. These measurements were adjusted as more information about the disease became available.

Staying celibate led me to different experiences relating to men and sex. For more than a year I did not make love. However, I spent nights with male friends cuddling and resting together. Once in a while someone would freak out, leaving me in the middle of the night. I was not interested in plastic gloves and condoms. Most friends in fact appreciated this new way to connect in love, recognizing the sweetness and innocence of our meetings. These moments of rest were precious and unique. My heart was opening wider, finding renewed quietude and carefulness. I soon forgot the physical play of sex, becoming more attuned to the subtleties of a finer quality of touch and presence, relaxing together with no expectations.

One afternoon I was working at the dock at Baal Shem, dressed in my baggy orange overalls, waiting for a flatbed truck to pick up something. It was cold and the driver came out to talk to me, ready to collect his load. His eyes and face were of an old friend.

His job was to drive a funky truck, picking up and delivering all over, and to pilot one of the ranch's property small airplanes, flying between Portland and Rajneeshpuram. Anand's bright white hair and shiny blue eyes conveyed a heartfelt joy that he nowadays expresses through his art. He asked if we could meet in the evening. Yea...

Our rooms had only enough space for two twin foam mattresses on the floor, hardly any space to walk in between. The rule between roommates was to alternate places, if we had ongoing relationships. My roommate had a steady girlfriend, and that was his night out with her. I was alone in my room!

Anand came by with some food from the deli, always a luxury, and we enjoyed a nice dinner, naked in bed, with candlelight. I let him know that I was not making love with anybody, but would enjoy spending the night resting with him. He stormed in a vehement reaction that made me laugh! He was feverish in his speech, convincing me that I was missing an opportunity, making love was a gift and meeting someone in that space was precious. He wanted to make love with me and we were going to get the gloves and condoms immediately! His determination broke through my vows of celibacy and, more than a year after our first AIDS meeting, we made love with all that it entangled. I realized that this time gap had deepened my ability to stay centered and to merge from an even quieter space inside. Making love became further ecstatic as it did not have any longer the element of desire, but a different awareness and sense of choice beyond biological chemistry. The gloves and condoms forced clear intent and deliberate connection not necessarily linked to physical sensations.

Anand let me know that he had a girlfriend who was away for a few weeks, to whom he was sincerely committed. Premati was a dear friend, someone I respected and loved since our first meeting in Pune. Through the following years we related as lovers and friends, embracing challenges in the process of learning to share our love. I am now writing, almost twenty years later, sitting at Anand's living room in Sedona.

The currents of life at the ranch were stronger than the little fish trying to swim left or right. Our working schedule forced spontaneity, or misery... Our choice!

Through the years, my meetings with Veet continued to have a quality of totality with no holdings. We would meet by chance, or intentionally visit each other in the evening. He moved through several relationships, and yet we always met as dear friends.

I was content alone. I was not looking to engage in a relationship, and yet, when someone touched my heart, I had no doubts...

For a few months, I spent time with a few older men. Strange that concurrently I connected with four men who were in their late forties. Being in my early thirties, they were really old. Now, realizing that I will be fifty in a month, I smile...

I alternated spending time with them, the rhythms of our work facilitating our closeness or pushing us away. We gracefully danced together. Once in a while, I would be in bed with one of them and another would stop by for a visit. However, there was easiness and friendliness in these situations.

I appreciated their maturity. The fact that they had been married at some point and lived a stable life taught me to appreciate the conscious remembrance of love in the continuity of relating, even when moving through rocky times. One of these friends shared with me... "Being with one woman for many years made me realize that all my moods and preferences are always my own interpretation of reality. It is not possible to fall off love, once you have tasted it. You just need to make a priority to remember it, especially when you feel it is not there anymore, when you are clouded by the mind... There is always a way to remember the openness and be in love again and again with the same person." This observation made me aware of my own intention from then on. I listened to him. I could feel that love was always his first priority when we were together. A warm Scottish man, ex-advertisement consultant in London, he spoke with the same elegance I imagined he dressed in his business days. His sensitivity and solidity was healing, as well as preparing me to embrace a new phase.

Another of my older friends was a tall, handsome English man, who embraced me in fullness. I could only say "Yes." His observations made me stop and reflect. Often, his demands made me review some of my set behaviors just because they were so doubtlessly coming from his heart. I had no other choice than to soften mine. He was firm and steady and straight in his words. A different style than most of my younger friends who had been more inclined to rest in silence, letting life take the lead in a loose way... He confessed to be sad that I was not willing to be with him in a continuous relationship. He had a strong sense of commitment and used to say, "You do not care, that is why you want to be free and floating..." Then, I really did not grasp what he meant. Now, his words resonate in understanding—care and commitment go together. Only later, I came to experience that the recognition of the preciousness of love naturally evolves into awareness that supports conscious bonding. That did not mean social marriage, but the marriage of alchemy, transmutation in remembrance. As my heart and soul matured, I long for the commitment that penetrates nuances, that continuously enlightens the essence, dissolving the illusion of freedom as open-ended choices.

My third friend was a lawyer from New York, Jewish, extremely funny looking. His physical presence did not attract me at all. But we happened to work together and something about him instantaneously called my attention. I hesitated in accepting his first invitation for an evening date. His sincerity, merging with contrasting naivete and brilliance, was fascinating. I could not imagine making love with him, and in fact we never did. Our connection had a unique tone. I clicked with his intelligence and humor. I learned with him to see the universe of the ranch with judgments, until then that option had not occurred to me... But he had lots, and piercing ones! Being a lawyer he was engaged with issues that involved knowledge of maneuvers and political choices that most commune members were not aware of. I listened to him, appreciating his acutely sharp mind. He was especially bright, almost picturesque. When we walked together I felt like walking on air. His body was awkward, slightly out of shape, and his movements were clumsy. I had to watch my judgments again and again. That was a strong exercise.

During the time we were working together, Bhagwan declared that a number of sannyasins were enlightened and my friend was one of them. Already in those days, the concept of enlightenment did not mean much to me. In Pune, that seemed to be an experience I was sure to relate to, a sense of direction that had been set with no way back. I "knew" what that was and I was sure to be either already there, or very close to this state of unwavering bliss described in different ways by various mystics. At the ranch, life was more down to earth. Enlightenment became more like a joke, something that belonged to the past of India and did not quite fit with cowboys and muddy boots.

My friend received this announcement with a great laughter saying, "Bhagwan is crazy!" I cherished this guy, enlightenment or not. He did not seem to be stroked by the wind of recognition, on the opposite, he was clown-like and simple. Many people started approaching him with questions. It was interesting to be close to him and observe how projections were built on hot air. A few months later, he was considering leaving the ranch. "What do you think?" Though for my life that would be an absurd idea, I felt for him it might be good, so I said, "I guess you can never walk backwards. If you leave, you can always come back later..." He left a few weeks later, I suspected mainly due to his assessment of the political situation. A few months later, he returned. I was glad to see him dancing at drive-by! He remarked, "Yes, you were right, we cannot go backwards, but there is a lot of sideways... I am back!"

The fourth man was someone I would never even talk to if we had met elsewhere. Too straight for my taste. He used to be a professional photographer in Northern California. Coming out of a long-term marriage with grownup children, he met Bhagwan at the first annual celebration and since then had been living at the ranch. We communicated on the phone daily due to my work. He had a resonant, deep voice I enjoyed listening to. The phones at the ranch were only used for business and were controlled for gossip or any other use besides strictly practical communication. So, it was artful to insert a one-second reference to a meeting place and time in the midst of a business call. He was discreet enough to manage to arrange for a date with me. Coincidentally, at that day and time the commune unexpectedly gathered for our first funeral. So, we met on the bus to the crematorium. That was a major event. We stayed together through the cremation, and walked back to our houses, already dark. I loved walking in the evenings! Through this unusual meeting we became friends. We spent nights together but making love with him was dry; his body was uptight, though his heart was sincerely kind. I watched my reaction to his lack of aliveness, and my mind holding onto judgments. I purposely focused on meeting him in my heart. Suddenly in the midst of lovemaking, I stopped, sat up in bed and said, "I can feel your heart, but sex with you is boring... Let's drop it and hang out as friends." He was shocked. "I never heard that before..." I could not say anything different. We laughed. "Ok, I enjoy being with you, we can drop the sex part of it..." This abrupt honesty brought more relaxation between us. We kept spending nights together, content to rest and embrace each other.

Throughout the years at the ranch I was clear that nobody was worth my energy and time, if that meant losing the connection with the vastness that Bhagwan offered. The usual relationship entanglements such as demands, upsets, expectations, jealousy seemed to be a waste of time. I did not want to miss what I considered a wondrous opportunity to learn to relate in true love, beyond the limitations I had encountered before and saw many others struggling with. Bhagwan showered us with steady and constant grace. I really wanted to learn that! I recognized that I had no idea of what love really was in a down-to-earth, consistent, day-to-day way. I realized that the first step was to choose people or situations that reminded me as much as possible of his love and presence, so that it would become my own experience. In this way, a natural selection happened for romantic meetings and sex. I paid attention on how someone's presence made me feel in my connection with Bhagwan—expansive and open, or not. If a man would join me in receiving his blessings, I was welcoming. Instead, if he imposed conditions or demands that pushed me into becoming narrower and more contained, then, forget it!

The intensity of our work and schedules created a distinct rhythm, difficult to push or pull at my own will. No choice but to relax. Trying to go against anything was a torture.

One of the most wanted privileges at the ranch was the fire tower, a small cabin located in isolation on top of a hill, from where fires could be detected. There was twenty-four-hour vigil at the tower, occupied by couples that usually stayed there for two or three days at a time. That was the bliss-job—having time to do nothing with a lover in a beautiful spot. Sure, I was invited four times and for one reason or another, I was never able to go. That was a difficult one to let go of. Every time I got a request, something would be in the way...

During July 1984, we had our third summer festival. What we had accomplished in merely three years was remarkable.

Koan

The account of the next events may not be factually and timely precise. For historical details, other descriptions are more accurate.

I guess just after the 1984 summer festival, after a few years in silence, Bhagwan resumed giving public discourses every morning at Buddha Hall. In the evenings, he would meet journalists from all over the world, especially invited to the ranch. They would ask him questions. A few residents were invited for those meetings held in Jesus Grove.

The morning discourses often involved political issues. That was not interesting to me, though it was delightful to sit with him again.

I was invited to Jesus Grove in the evening for two weeks every day and then several other times sparsely. Bhagwan was extremely vivacious, humorous and charming. His answers were poignant. It was strong to sit a few meters from him in a small room, during these intimate and powerful gatherings. At home, I sat quietly to digest his energy.

There was a sniff of change in the air, but nothing that I could pinpoint. During the festival in 1985, I was at the Currency Card department, coordinating the work of over twenty people squeezed in a room that originally held about ten desks. This increased crew was attending to thousands of visitors, while trying to improve our computer system. Consequently, there were mistakes and confusion.

On a hot afternoon, Sheela came in for a visit, as usual flashy and full of zest. "Hey, guys! How are we doing with the money?" She moved around, asked me questions, played with some of the guys that looked serious or upset, and within minutes there was a climate of animation that was typical of her enticing personality. She could hardly move around the desks tightly arranged against each other.

Taken by surprise, I felt a hand caressing my head. Hummm... I purred like a cat, the gentleness and yet firmness of this touch gave me goose bumps. I turned around and saw Dhyan, a beautiful man who used to be at the Berkeley commune while I lived there. He was the quiet type. His physical beauty and elegant posture had always called my attention. He was tall, had penetrating dark eyes and exquisite hands. There he was, in a second waking me up from a longtime sleep. He invited me for lunch.

There were about five thousand people at the ranch at that time. A large, outdoor area had been arranged for meals, wooden tables and benches spread all over. It was not easy to have a date and find the person in the midst of the crowd, but we did meet. We were to be together, I knew from the first moment. I was ready to move again in a relationship and stay with him throughout whatever issues might be coming up. I had been nurtured by seven years on my own and a new phase was ahead.

We connected through the silence of our hearts. We took time to go for walks, and in the nights held each other for long hours, simply resting. In a few weeks I proposed that we ask to move into the same room—a request that was not always granted by the accommodations office, but ours was, immediately. We carried his mattress to the house I lived.

Dhyan was kind and gentle, yet strong and firm, sometimes stubborn and determined. We matched in those qualities. He grew up in Minnesota, and I guess this fact had an effect on him as far as being able to stand long winters, both weather-wise and emotion-wise. We both worked at the accounting department, and I learned a lot from him. I appreciated his focus and precision. He helped me to stand with more grounding and clarity. I knew I could count on him no matter what. Even when he was upset, he was still present, straight and honest. It was a puzzling paradox to feel him angry and yet meeting me with an open heart. The background of our connection was undoubtedly meditation, and respect for our journeys. I am deeply grateful for the years we spent together, and for what I still receive from our friendship and love, from his dedication and sincerity all along.

A few weeks later, working as a manager at the Currency Card, I was called by one of the main coordinators. She asked me to check the amounts in the accounts of two people and if they had withdrawn any cash. I checked their accounts as requested—it was my job to do so, though it was a strange inquiry. These two people had left the ranch in the middle of the night; their reasons were unknown, but they were not to be allowed back nor talked to if they would call. I was told to maintain that information confidential, as many of the issues I had to deal with in that position. I had a personal connection with both of them, and was very surprised with their sudden departure. However, I trusted their decision without knowing their motivations. This fact stuck as unusual and I wondered what happened. Different versions came up a few days later, but none seemed to be plausible.

A while after that incident, I got another call from the same coordinator. She asked me to prepare envelopes with the money available in the accounts of the main coordinators working directly with Sheela. She would personally come by to collect them. That was bizarre, especially because there was not more than one hundred dollars in any of those accounts. Why would they need petty cash at the same time? I prepared it, but she did not come by. A few hours later it was announced that Sheela and a few other people had left the ranch.

I do not recall the many details—just the bubbling of gossips, practical rearrangements, uncertainty, and Bhagwan's discourses coming down harshly on Sheela and her assistants. I listened to Bhagwan's remarks, without getting personally involved or having an opinion about facts that were not concerning my life directly.

One day I was called to go to the airport urgently! There was a surprise! Bhagwan was leaving in a small jet with a few of his close assistants, and his destination was unknown. I waved goodbye, wondering if I would ever see him again.

A few days later, he was arrested and put in jail by the American government. We gathered at Buddha Hall to watch the news on a big screen. It was pathetic to see such a man in prison clothes. His responses at an interview were piercing and unforgiving, and the diamond quality of his presence was as clear as ever. He expressed anger, though as calm as always. Finally he returned to the ranch for a while, and we sat again in Buddha Hall drinking of his silence. Not for too long, as he was forced to leave the country a few weeks later. That was the final goodbye! From the Portland courthouse he flew to India.

The following months were tumultuous, as the events precipitated the commune dissolving and being invaded by government authorities.

Many friends left and the climate was chaotic; blame, disappointment, mistrust, anger, greed, the hell was definitely loose! A general announcement organized by a new group of coordinators made it clear that we were to leave the ranch as soon as possible.

My working days hit the peak when thousands of people started to come to the Currency Card to close their accounts and request their deposited money back. There was no money to be given back. We never kept any of the cash deposited, the flow of cash was constantly being reinvested and used for the many projects in process. We were caught in mid-air! The information that I received from my new coordinator was that we would receive a daily quota (again coming from generous donations) to be distributed equally between people—US$100, per person, no matter how much they had in their accounts. I should also let them know that, as soon as possible, they would receive the rest of the money they might have deposited in their account. Not an easy job! I interviewed hundreds of people a day, dealing with a variety of emotional outbursts. Money provoked them all! This training was useful personally and professionally, as I better understood the ties between money issues, emotional behaviors, fear and attachment.

Parallel to the disbursement at the Currency Card was the allocation of airline tickets to people who did not have one, mostly long term residents. Dhyan held legal responsibility for several of the businesses in the commune, including the travel agency. According to federal laws, the regulation was quite strict and did not allow for tickets to be issued without cash backup. This was considered fraud, and the signatory was legally responsible, facing court and possible imprisonment. He was in a state of panic, as every day hundreds of thousands of dollars were signed on tickets without any monetary back up. Miraculously, a few generous people facilitated the closure of the ranch with grace beyond what would be imaginable.

I was asked frequently, "Where are you going?" I had not a clue. To avoid engaging in long answers, I decided to choose a place and say it aloud, just for easiness sake. My brother had lived in Cambridge, Massachusetts, and had enjoyed the local art community and multicultural events. I had heard from other people that Boston was the fastest-growing city in the USA, easy to get well-paid jobs and teeming with opportunities. I asked Dhyan if he would like to move there with me and we agreed upon it. So, whenever I was asked, "I am going to Boston." I was firm and decisive. "That is a good idea!" Soon, a few friends had decided to move to Boston. They left earlier, and sent messages of encouragement. Dhyan got his ticket to Boston from his brother. I was so busy with my work that I did not think of arranging for mine. When I decided to request it, the travel agency had closed. I did not have a cent. I tried my father once more, and heard another no for an answer. I waited for someone more generous.

I could see that the emptiness of Bhagwan's being had allowed for our "fullness" to overflow, in as many ways as there were people involved at the ranch. I was calm and trusting, sometimes excited about the future, sometimes sad for the disbanding of my loving family. The practical demands of my involvement with work, taking care of what was needed to close all the businesses and the infinite details that needed to be sorted out, kept my mind busy. In the evenings, lying down with Dhyan, we wondered what would be next.

I was still spending time with one of my "older" lovers. Dhyan respected my choices without reacting, though sometimes shaky. Several times he drove me to my friend's house for the night, embracing me back in the morning with caring warmth.

My friend was going to San Thomas, in the Caribbean and invited me to come along. That was tempting... But as I reflected, I realized the need to bring what I had cultivated inside to an outer expression, interfacing with a culture and challenges that I tended to avoid. I decided to dive headfirst and bypass what I usually would choose—sun, beach, relaxation, magic and mellowness. Not that I desired snow, asphalt, tension, logic and difficulties... I wanted to focus on making money fast and get ready to meet Bhagwan again, if that would ever be possible. In any case, I would have to bring his presence into my life, no matter where I landed. I chose to leave with Dhyan.

There was balance and integrity in the way I stood next to Dhyan. No more dreams of romance. We had been bathed for years in an ocean of love and were now emerging, still soaked with its color and taste. There was rest in my body and heart, and my spirit was light and unfettered. We were companions in a mystifying journey.

We decided to stay a little longer, part of the "last crew," dismantling and dispersing what had been left of the commune.

End of December, the snow was coming down, and our crew got reduced to less than a hundred people. It was fun to spread out on this large property, no set schedule, meeting in the evenings for a glass of wine. We condensed our living, eating and working quarters and there was joy beyond the state of affairs, rather unsteady. In fact, it had always been so... However, while the speed of events surpassed our personal control, unsteadiness had been disguised by grandiose projects, carnival-like masks representing our illusions and projections. While the invisible current running at the core was stronger than each individual, we were unable to recognize the undercurrents building up underneath the surface. The king was naked!

I worked with Sabah, my dear friend, accounting and writing letters, walking in the snow, eating leftover coffee beans covered with dark chocolate, laughing, wondering when and where we would meet again.

There will be as many different versions of "life at the ranch" as there were people living and visiting it. As a genuine mystery school, the multidimensionality of that experiment will never be expounded in words, no matter how rich or alluring a specific account might be.

I sat in silence for a few weeks before I could write anything about the ranch. Like being inside a dark cave with phosphorescent walls. I saw a myriad of sparkles, where to start? It was impossible to convey the intensity of thousands of people intentionally aligned and the power generated by that configuration. Like sun rays converging towards magnifying lenses... Life had prepared me for that venture, and in delight, I burnt with it.

Whether we had signed on for that or not, the pressure and power of the setting did not allow for half-hearted engagement. That was a marriage of totality, passion, and commitment. A no-way-back affair. Almost twenty years later, the ripples of this era still rebound...

Situations constantly generated breakdowns in our control mechanisms, exposing what we mostly tried to cover up with personality adornments. This naked perception and its consequential quality of sharing and creativity are way beyond description.

Most people live within the confinements of familiar, social and cultural settings that are hardly ever discussed, much less questioned or challenged. To adventure beyond these preset boundaries, even if only at a physical level, already requires an unusual perception and clear intention. Even though these conventional structures apparently seem to offer security and comfort, ultimately they insulate our consciousness from our own life's potential, hardening our ability to sway with the winds of change; they engage our energy in protection rather than intelligence to respond, suffocating the essence of being, the courage to discover, in the name of values that usually do not bring happiness much less bliss.

At first, the commune in Pune, and then the ranch offered a terrain of experimentation, a space where boundaries were not established nor reinforced. On the contrary, they were constantly pushed a bit further, for good or bad... Absolute trust in the greater force that keeps creating and destroying seems to call for absolute lack of control. At the ranch, we had the opportunity to break our own self-image a thousand times in a day...and to comply with our illusions and dreams, a thousand times in a day...and to face our hesitations, fear, ambitions, a thousand times in a day... Our personalities had a chance to be inflated, get stronger and stage countless dreams. The essence of being had a chance to be polished, and resurface from deception, illusion, politics, and expand.

Suddenly the alarm clock exploded, making a sound loud enough to shake us up! Some of us bounced in diverging directions, trying to collect the pieces of our consciousness scattered, trying to glue the bits together... Some of us sat quietly, watching in marvel the broken mirror, realizing that the images did not live inside it—there was nothing to paste or fix.

I feel blessed for having had a taste of a rare flavor of earthbound consciousness. Even if interweaved with murky undercurrents... The stirring of the waters made the mud come to the surface. In my perception, this time of cleansing was necessary to crystallize a new level of integration and intentional alignment. Whether you were located, there was no escape from the reflections that the mirrors offered—a thousand of them in your face!

This bridge of aloneness-togetherness sealed a certainty—nowhere to go but inside. So many mirages reflected the flame of watchfulness again and again. Even the chaos of nonstop action was incandescent with remembrance. The ranch cycle forged longtime friendships, revealing the sweetness and recognition of love expressed in impermanence, swirling with different paces and songs.

During these years, I did not inquire or get involved in politics. From my experience in Brazil as a teenager, political action didn't have any impact on individual consciousness. Political systems did not seem to nurture love or awareness, even when established with good intentions. I did not bother to follow the media or try to understand what Sheela was doing or saying. I assumed she was with Bhagwan for her own reasons. She had a role within the commune, useful in the context of our collective intent. Her capacity was instrumental for the creation of that experiment. Strange as it may be, her actions pushed the commune into another level of inquiry and liability. I kept my sense of integrity throughout that time. I did not see her as an authority or as someone that I relied upon to decide about my life. I saw Bhagwan's allowance and instigation of her outspoken outrageousness as a call to her, none of my business. He did suggest, engage, invite... And we were free to bite the bait at our own convenience. I kept my interested centered in personal relationships, time alone, and work.

Could we have learned the same lesson with care and gentleness, with subtlety and kindness? Would a less radical approach have purged the layers of unconsciousness that we carried relating to power, its use and misuse?

Looking at that group of people as collective consciousness, events proved that we were not mature enough to sustain a project of that magnitude relying on individual responsibility and co-creation. Sheela's role was pivotal in holding us together in a focused way, as we lacked the maturity to stand up to her, and to Bhagwan, in order to maintain integrity as a community and as individuals. As much as we may have wished it differently, we were baby-stepping.

Sheela knew how to appeal to our dreams and to our projections of the man we called our master. Her role gave her permission to use her intelligence and creative power, as well as her manipulative mind and unconsciousness in ways that we were not able to perceive, or counteract. Collectively, we got caught in reacting to her and to the events as personalities that felt betrayed or abused. As I see it, we were not able to respond as individuals and assert ourselves centered in the clarity of our discernment. Her no-nonsense approach bordered the edge of pure folly, and was a key to further invoke our sanity, in a paradoxical way. What each one of us was able to receive and utilize, remains our individual responsibility.

I did not define myself as part of a "group," even though we were seen as such by outsiders. Our only bond was the intention to find our own uniqueness and to use our master's presence as a catalyst for expanding awareness. Our common ground was the love of a man who was launching us into deep waters. Apparently "guiding" us, he was simply pushing us closer to the abyss of our own self-responsibility. How could we be fabricating another group identity around him, unless we misunderstood the very core of what he was pointing towards?

The protection of the so-called group identity labeled around us, served as a double-gun: it offered the isolation and safety needed to dare dissolve into a bigger picture, while containing the energy needed to find our own strength and individuality. Not without birth pains...

We were against the wall: forced to let go of past conditioning secured to cultural, ethnical, moral, religious or any other definition; forced to respond to each situation using only the elements that it involved, foreign and unexpected as they might have been. Our spiritual ideals were smashed, our dreams were reduced to dust and intrigues. In the midst of deception, we were forced to wake up to our own discrimination without outer reference points.

The outer settings, such as the incorporation of the city of Rajneeshpuram, the institution of Rajneeshism as an official religion and other similar silly acts, were a cover for the underground messages that conveyed the "real" thing. These practical and inevitable setups created a façade that facilitated our human unfolding. These political arrangements allowed us to live in a country where freedom and individuality are loudly professed, however coated with hypocrisy and lies. Bhagwan's presence and the development of the ranch, supported by Sheela's public apparitions, uncovered pretense and dishonesty—ours and others, provoking and irritating the status quo of American politicians and local citizens. Was aggression and intimidation justified for any reason? Probably not... Was the ranch setup the only way for us to learn to take more responsibility for our lives? Probably not... Was the inevitable destruction of our city the only way for us to wake up to the dream of Shangri-la that we may have carried as an escape-route from our pain and contraction, fear and anger, which in fact surfaced for many as a result of this experiment? Probably not...

The fact that we were called by a collective name forced me to reflect as an individual. Could I have acted any different or have been an agent for a different outcome?

Is consciousness the ability to change and expand in the recognition of a hidden potential, like a sculpture is hidden in a piece of marble? Or is it the ability to simply acknowledge the isness of whatever? Or both, simultaneously?

The pace at the ranch offered me daily opportunities to allow the flow of life to wash my ideas and a superficial sense of direction. It urged intangible sentience, presence without container. Surrender did not mean unconditional acceptance of unexamined beliefs or ideas, or anything else imposed by an outer source. It translated the purity of essence becoming visible through the non-essential. It also meant "minding my own business" rather than referring to someone else for approval or orientation. It meant recognizing the empty center as the only aim.

When I experienced unconditional opening to what life was bringing me, there was a response arising out of insight, spontaneous intelligence beyond self-judgment.

My choice to be at the ranch was focused on my interest to learn to live in freedom from the mind, to express love in visible and earthy ways. The communal framework provoked particular directions and stirred me out of usual gears. The outer experiment was over.

A kind friend offered me a ticket to Boston. We booked our flight a few days later.

Now what?

January. Leaving the ranch, coming down the hills towards Portland, nose glued to the window, snow falling. Dhyan next to me, both quiet.

It was freezing when we arrived in Boston. Our first night was spent in a veranda enclosed by glass windows, no heating. We were six bodies warming up by sleeping close together. I was not enthusiastic in face of a heavy winter, but there we were...

Together with fourteen other friends we rented an old ten-bedroom Victorian house in Brookline. We cleaned, painted, repaired it and moved in record time. As none of us had bank accounts, we paid our first rent with cash.

The next step was to find work. We were excited and moved by necessity. We soon found a good place to buy designer discount clothes and furniture. We were minimalists and in a few days set up a home with simplicity and beauty.

My room with Dhyan was one of the living rooms, next to the entry door. It was large with two great windows to the garden. We had a fight while trying to buy a mattress. He suggested that we buy two single mattresses instead of a queen-size one, just in case we would decide to separate, so we didn't waste money... I was upset! How could he possibly think so? We got a queen-size mattress. Our closet was the coat cupboard, big enough to hold about ten hangers. We did not have more than that... A nice plant, a piece of round glass found in the basement supported by a pottery bowl became our bedside table, a Japanese paper lamp on the corner, fresh flowers, nice bedding, a white wool carpet next to the bed, and we had a lovely room.

I started to model at the art school. Dhyan got an accounting job. It was fun to see him dressed up in a suit going to work. I looked for ads in the newspaper trying to decide what else to do. Accounting and management skills were well paid; I wanted to make money fast.

I had an interview at a temp agency, just to try a "straight" job. I was immediately hired by the Sinai Hospital, a large medical facility with an accounting department of over thirty people sitting in two rows of desks in a long, dark room. On a Monday I started working as the supervisor of a group of six people. Accustomed to true efficiency I figure out in a few minutes how to improve the filing and organizational system. My new colleagues did not seem to be very enthusiastic, but the manager appreciated my suggestions and followed up. By Wednesday I had been offered the job of supervisor for the whole accounting department. The radio in the room was kept on all day long, just low enough to make it impossible to hear anything distinctively, and just high enough to irritate ears. The place was doom, repetitive work, and horrible food at the restaurant. By Friday I gave notice to leave. A good experience.

I applied for a high paid job as a human resources manager of a large marketing company, wondering if I could get such a position. After a few selective interviews, I passed the tests and was called for a final meeting with the company's director. He received me in an enormous thick-carpeted office. Sitting behind a mahogany desk, he was full of himself. With my resume in his hands, he looked at me with appreciation. He let me know that I had been selected as their best candidate for the position and explained that I was going to be sent for training in Chigago, and then in Los Angeles, where they had other branches. He had the employment papers ready for me to sign. The conditions and salary were tempting... As I was listening to him, I realized that I did not want to work in that environment. It was good to feel that I was able to get the job; coming out of the ranch was like landing from another planet, not knowing how to relate to people whose lives were centered on such different values. This man looked at me politely and said, "My last question... I see that you had an excellent position in Oregon, why did you leave the company you worked for?" I responded, "The Company went bankrupt..." "Oh! I am sorry to hear... Why did you leave this town?" "The town went bankrupt..." He looked puzzled. I knew that he had not remarked that I was coming from Rajneeshpuram—the ranch had been incorporated as an official city under that name. The media had been cruel to Bhagwan and the events around him. I was sure that he wouldn't have hired me if he had noticed my association. However, to act upon religious prejudice is unlawful, so it was too late for him to change his mind. I said, "I am sure that if you had noticed that I had been associated with the Rajneesh commune in Oregon, you would not have interviewed me. Anyway, I am not interested in this position. I appreciate your time and offer." I stood up, shook his hand and left.

Reading the newspaper, a small ad called my attention: an interior design company needed an accountant, with design and computer experience. I called for an interview. The owner, an elegant lady, liked me and my skills fit her needs. The office was in a penthouse, next door to her apartment, in a central location with views to the river. That was a part-time position, four days a week. It suited me well.

In the extra three days, I offered Rebalancing sessions at a medical center. If there were any gaps in my schedule, I accepted house-cleaning and modeling jobs. Dhyan worked as much; however we found time to go for walks in the park, and were glad to be making money fast.

Bhagwan had dismissed our wearing red clothes, phase for the rainbow to take over... Dinnertime at home, we were usually twenty people sharing a good meal, time to gossip and relax. A couple of Russian musician friends, often joined us for lively violin evenings.

Digambar came for a visit and decided to stay. A few days later, Renuka joined him. They found a house with another couple, a few minutes away. Sabah visited us on her way to Europe. Life was still moving fast and there was no sense of loss, rather enrichment.

Meanwhile, Bhagwan had been traveling around the world. I was eager to be with him again and this intention brought everything I did to a focus point.

We had decided to stay in Boston, just for as long as it was necessary, but not longer. Not knowing where we would land next, we took advantage of being in a large city. Dhyan and I went to jewelry classes in the evening, and I enrolled in advanced bodywork trainings.

In six months, we had saved enough and decided to move to Hawaii. We indulged resting on Kauai, at a friend's place. The island was beautiful, we had a lovely time hiking and enjoying the warmth of the tropical forest and the Na Pali coast, but there was not enough economical vitality to support us financially. It would be too hard to make a living there. We moved to Maui, where there were friends from the ranch, work was easier and more rewarding.

We rented a lovely three-bedroom house on a quiet street high in Kula. I rented an office in town to give sessions a few days a week, and managed a jewelry store part-time. Cleaning houses added to my income.

Digambar and Renuka moved into our house a few months later. Life was joyful and playful, though we worked hard. Our house was cozy and comfortable enhanced by a vegetable garden that Dhyan cared for. We followed up Bhagwan's traveling schedule and I relaxed with the idea that I might never see him again.

Our six-month lease was expiring... Bhagwan had landed in Bombay, and soon was moving to Pune. I was ready to go to India. Dhyan did not want to leave America. We went back and forward trying to find a common ground. I realized our life together was bringing Bhagwan's love into my everyday movements. I was enjoying having a home, and valuing more and more the delicacy of our love. Through our relating I was learning to connect with Bhagwan's essence. So, I decided to stay with Dhyan and relax.

I ordered a few thousand dollars of tools and supplies to start making jewelry, only to receive the shipments in the mail in the same day that Dhyan came home announcing, "I am ready to go to Pune!" We sat in powwow, and decided to drop our house lease, sell our car, and fly to India as soon as possible.

Anticipating that I might stay in India longer, I decided to visit my family. During my stay in Rio, I had a sense of completion with my father, letting go of resentment, seeing him within his limitations and love for me. Nothing special I needed to say or do, just forgiveness.

Mama india

Maui-Honolulu-Bangkok-Bombay!

Dhyan had never been in India, thus asked if we could take the train to Pune, instead of flying. I tried to dissuade him, but he got upset.

Upon arrival, due to misleading information about train schedules, we sat at Dadar station all night. Hungry and sleepless, we watched a procession of beggars, mothers and children sleeping on the floor, vendors screaming out their merchandise...

At dawn we got the train. Tuck-tuck-tuck... The slums were at first sight, Bombay had not got any better. However, the immediate familiarity with the landscape, people's faces, even the offensive smells in the air, soothed my heart.

At the commune we were received with hugs and excitement. There might have been two hundred people already there, and new arrivals pouring every day.

Bhagwan's presence was in the air. Through his energy I was suddenly laughing at myself... I knew this unbounded expanse was neither his nor mine, it was life itself. He was a reminder of life's limitlessness.

We spent a few nights in a nearby hotel, and soon found an apartment to rent. The configuration of Koregaon Park had been updated. No more huts, instead, construction sites. We took the first brand-new apartment in a complex called Popular Heights. A true luxury! As we were inspecting our new residence, maybe on the sixth floor, Dhyan opened a window to look out to the funeral grounds, just next to it. Unexpectedly, its thick glass fell out and splashed down the street. Nobody was passing by...

Dhyan was getting quieter... I was at home! We shared our new dwelling with three friends, and set our home with a few items: a good kettle for tea, an electric hotpot, a cotton mattress, straw mats, new sheets, and some fabric for decoration. We were proud to have an electric shower! A few days later, one of our housemates turned on the water and the whole apparatus went up in flames! We rushed to smoother the fire with towels. First-class apartment!

At the commune, I was asked to join the accounting team. Dhyan was a guard at Bhagwan's house. He alternated between day and night shift, therefore I spent a few nights a week on my own. In addition, he was asked to set up the computer system for the entire commune, starting with the accounting department, so our works overlapped. His genius was absorbed by this heroic task, not without some headaches...

Bhagwan was giving discourses twice a day. Once more, we gathered in the same room where energy darshans used to happen. In the morning, we were invited into relaxation, the birds singing and his voice merging with it all. In the evenings, he

189

showered intensity and love, encouraging the musicians to go crazy and the rest of us to dance wildly.

There was wholeness in this reunion, the previous innocence and looseness from Pune One had been enriched by the years at the ranch. Most of my close friends were back there within a few months.

One of my immediate decisions was to get sterilized, a minor surgery commonly practiced in India. I had a few sessions as a preparation for body and spirit, and asked Renuka to come with me.

Arriving at the clinic, I saw a few women sitting on the floor at the waiting room, entertained in talk. Coming closer...I saw that they had a small mountain of sterilized gauze directly placed on the floor (where everybody stepped, and...spit often) and with bare hands they picked up each piece and cut them with rusty scissors! The small pieces were placed inside a large glass jar, ready for the surgery room! I decided to relax for the ride.

Dr. Saraswati, who performed the surgery, was a kind man. I looked at Renuka smiling. The nurse gave me an injection, and a second before passing out I stared at the blood spots on her apron. Coming back a bit groggy, Dr. Saraswati was talking to me in a low voice. "Komala, this is a good name for you my dear... Gentle, you are very gentle, like the lotus flower." I was in paradise, though the room did not look like so. This decision strengthened my sense of focus in meditation and my life path. I was relieved and never doubted it since.

My accounting career was soon concluded. I was asked to give individual sessions and be part of the Rebalancing Training teaching team, now a professional three-month intensive taught by six different people. It was the most popular course at the commune, booked with about sixty participants per trimester.

During the following years, I was further trained in several therapeutic approaches to body-mind and emotional awareness. I worked full time giving sessions and groups. This steady focus rebounded inside with great impact. Being present with others' difficulties in the light of meditation compelled me to look at my own issues with more clarity.

The easiness of India, my work, friends and life with Dhyan resulted in absolute contentment.

Being in Bhagwan's presence was stronger and meaningful. I listened to him every day. Now, his words touched my own experiences and continuously pointed the arrow inwards. A series of discourses on Zen masters laid bare an illogical familiarity with those stories. I had heard them a thousand times! They sank deeper and deeper as a transmission of understanding beyond the mind.

Six months passed by in a flash and it was time to renew our visas. Dhyan was delighted to get out of India; his love for the country had not increased and his complaints were constant. We flew to Bangkok and then took a bus to reach Koh Samui and Koh Panghan, two beautiful islands in the south. Beaches and palm trees, coconut water and delicious fresh food, small cabanas in front of pee-temperature, ocean waters... Dreamland! Nevertheless, I wanted to go back to Pune as soon as possible. My desire body was caught in the magic of the master's presence. Every second was precious, as if I knew it was not going to last much longer. I made an effort to relax into these holidays and "drag" myself to the ocean, swim, walk in nature, and rest while waiting for our visas. We did have a good time and a few moody days...

A shopping spree in Bangkok and in less than two weeks, we were back to India. Relief! I loved this mystery-home-land.

My relationship with Dhyan had been supportive and loving; however I missed more sex than we had. Our genuine link was through meditation and we spent long hours together in silence... We slept in an embrace, even when we were upset with each other. The undercurrent of our connection was undoubted love centered in the heart. However, our impulse to make love was not strong—that was the naturalness of our meeting. Following my own needs and attractions, I spent nights with other friends with whom I shared sensuous and sexual energy. This caused a few ruffles and happened more than often...

Anand was also in Pune. I loved how he communicated in a straight, honest way, sometimes pushing me into corners and provoking reflections about my choices and behavior. We still enjoyed making love and spending time together. Our closeness was difficult for Dhyan and for Premati. Oftentimes we were placed to sit in discourse next to each other, in front of Bhagwan. In those moments, we forgot about our relationship issues and met through the love of the master. I made choices that supported my liveliness and sense of expansion but felt like walking on a tight rope!

What inner dynamic generated such a situation? What was I learning from it? What was my blind spot that caused pain to others?

I wrote a letter to Bhagwan... "Whenever I follow the impulses of my body and heart that make me feel alive, restful, silent, my actions often cause pain and reactions. If I offer my fullness while relating with Dhyan, he is not able to receive it. If I close down...I feel contracted and shut off from loving Dhyan as much as anyone else. I do not seem to find balance within. It is obvious that the outer difficulties reflect my inner difficulties, but I do not understand how."

A few days later, he answered, "When you are alone, be alone; when you are together, be together." That simple! Not that I understood immediately what that meant, but the directness of the words stopped my mind chat. There was nothing to solve or change. Staying present, through the difficulties, through the love...

A few weeks later, my relationship with Anand as a lover was complete. We were to be friends from then on. Our relating had provoked meaningful insights. The commitment to stand in the love we shared and not avoid difficulties increased the intimacy and trust between the four of us. I honored Anand's and Premati's sincerity and deep affection. Our friendship stayed as the essence of love. We went to the bottom line, and in that broken-open space we found integrity.

Though my work was full on and I loved it, my motivation in life sprung from relating in love. From an early age, other human beings brought to the surface my worst nightmares as well as revealed joy in oneness. I keep responding to those calls of love and revelation, challenges and bliss. They invite the full moon inside my heart.

WHAT TO SAY?

Another year had gone by...

I had been invited to offer trainings in Germany, Switzerland and Finland. We flew to Koln, where I worked for a week and we took a train to Basel, where I had a few groups planned. We enjoyed some shopping, chocolate and beautiful walks in the woods.

During our stay in Switzerland, I received a special invitation to go to Spain to give sessions to a woman who had chronic back pain. She had been to several specialists with no apparent improvement and a mutual friend recommended my sessions. Gioia, who lived in Basel and was spending a few months near Barcelona, called me and I agreed to meet her at the seaside upon my return from Finland. I would give her daily sessions for a couple of weeks and return to Pune at the end of the summer. It would also be a timely opportunity to visit Derek. I called him, and we were both looking forward to meeting after several years.

Dhyan returned to Koln to start working. I went to Finland, and to my surprise, my two-week training was fully booked with about forty people! How did that happen, I still wonder! It had been organized by one of my clients in Pune, who owned a bookstore and meditation center in Helsinki. We drove to a large conference center/residential facility in the countryside. Surrounded by professional dancers, business managers and psychotherapists, I enjoyed summertime with midnight sun and wonderful, soft light. Alone in my room, overlooking a peaceful lake, I pondered the miracles of life. I sensed a surprising familiarity with the people and the landscape, so different from my tropical background.

The financial results were excellent and I called Gioia to let her know that I had decided to return to Pune earlier. She was disappointed. I was clear—being with Bhagwan was first priority. I wished her good luck...

I met Dhyan back in Koln for a week or so... The community was a homey place with dear friends. He had rented a nice room, and decided to stay in Germany. I agreed to visit within six months, sad to be away from him, but had no doubts that my place was near Bhagwan. We were not splitting up, but honoring our needs.

Dhyan was generous and caring. He expressed his love with attention to earthy details. The day I left, he took me into his room with eyes closed. Surprise! On the floor there were many parcels, beautifully packed, collecting everything I might need in India: from the best toothpaste to beautiful gold earrings, from vitamins to a poetry book. I was melancholic leaving him. During our last evening together, I could not stop crying. He took me by the hand and let me know we were going for an initiation into Koln's beer gardens. We walked around town, going in and out of pubs. Just time to order a beer, sip it fast enough to feel the buzz, walk out and into the next place, the same routine. A few hours later I was utterly drunk, and we were both laughing. In bed he held me for the night with immense tenderness and strength. We were such dear friends. What was to come next, we did not know… One day at a time, truthfully as we went along.

With a suitcase filled with minerals, miso, and other precious German goodies, I flew back with puffed-red eyes!

Arriving early morning in Pune, I dropped my luggage at home and went directly to work at the counseling desk at the ashram. Intending to place my passport and recently-earned money in the safety deposit, I was holding my purse between my feet under the table to protect its valuable contents. I had German marks for the next year! When I stood up to go for lunch, the bag had disappeared. Not possible! I had not moved away from the place… I looked all over with no luck. My work's worth was gone in a second! I was left with zero cash! I related the event to the main office. Nothing more I could do. Two days later my bag was found in the garden, far away from the place I had been sitting then. I opened it, and half of the cash was inside. What to say…

I moved into a large room in a shared house on the street just behind the commune. It was one of the typical homes in Koregaon Park, with a fenced garden, a few stray barking dogs, a couple of cows, loose chickens and a family of caretakers living in the back yard. I decorated it in style. A few trips to MG road to get a thick carpet, plants, a nice mirror, silk bed coverlet, a comfortable wicker chair… Great pleasure to have a spacious place to live! The owner, an older lady, had her residence upstairs, and I shared the downstairs with Sajeela and Renuka. Indeed, a lovely combination. We even had a small kitchen with a refrigerator!

Bhagwan's discourses were longer and longer, sometimes passing three hours! He was pouring his intensity on us, and I was ready to receive it.

Life was simple. Work was interesting. I continued to teach at the Rebalancing training and had been asked to give a few groups on my own. I was constantly around people, starting at seven am with a private session, then the training or a group during the day. Late afternoon was discourse, so by dinner time, I preferred to sit quietly and go to bed early.

I had more free time alone, as Dhyan was not around. I missed him. It was interesting to have his love and support from a distance and yet be free to move on my own. I spent time with a few other lovers eventually. Besides discourse, work and meals, hanging out with friends at lunch or dinner, there was nothing much to be fancied.

My work happened out of love and expansion; long hours passed by in pleasure and relaxation, though I was working about ten hours or more a day, seven days a week. In the commune, everything I ever did arose out of this inner space. No matter what direction I would take, whatever was my role. I had no other desires… Simple tasks filled my heart, took my full attention.

One afternoon, just after the monsoon season, the smell of mold in the air was slowly fading with the warmth of a sunny day... I sat on the steps of the metal stairs outside my room, holding a plastic bucket filled with detergent and a brush. I was ready to clean my German tennis shoes. No hurry, glimpsing the cows moving nearby. After long storms, each bird seemed to be more precise in his chirping. I moved my hands scrubbing and scrubbing, looking at the dirt vanishing. In an instant, no action, no body, nobody. The universe stopped in peacefulness. Just washing my tennis shoes! The shoes and the cows and the sounds and the clouds were suddenly floating in space. I sat motionless until dark. I lay in bed and slept in no time.

The following days, I kept moving speechless, yet my voice responded to others' questions. And then laughter broke out! Yes, suddenly, washing tennis shoes with a few cows for witnesses!

In this place of inner relaxation I met Prem. We had known each other for many years. He had just returned from Europe, having healed from cancer a few months before. Bhagwan had spoken about his impending death, how lucky he was to know in advance that he was going to leave his body. He could use this time to prepare himself and let go... Nevertheless, he was back!

He was vibrant, in integration of heart and body. We came together in a magnetic way. There was nothing to hold on, we were resting in eternity, nowhere to hide. He offered all without defenses, his body merging with mine, and our eyes singing a song without words... During the following months and years, we spent nights together, as he would come and go from Europe, not able to stay in India for too long. At every meeting I was left in gratefulness, gentleness caressing the core, stillness with open hands. He would come and go, spend time with other women; however every time we met I was visited by the same delicacy of the beloved. Like being under a waterfall, my hands let the water run in between my fingers. Abundance did not evoke greed. Wholeness and completion at each time, overflow did not ask for more.

I let it be fluid, open, free of decision. Though his love was inspiring and bursting my heart open, at a crossroad I chose challenge. I was not ready yet to stand under the shower of vulnerability and strength delivered in one bundle.

Dhyan kept asking me to return to Germany. I was not ready to shorten my stay in Pune and planned to leave at the date previously agreed. I sensed something needed to ripen in order for us to continue to live together.

As part of my ongoing training as a therapist, I participated in a seven-day course, which addressed childhood issues as the root of ego structure.

Curiously, the day before the training started I met Dharma, the man I had gotten pregnant by and had not seen for a few years... Our "baby" would have been seven years old. He had been away from the commune and was in Pune for a short visit. We chatted over a cup of tea—a pleasant and mature conversation. He had been back into the business world for a few years and sensed he was missing something. We talked about my pregnancy, and I acknowledged that by having had an abortion then, I gave birth to myself. There was a sense of completion and respect from both of us as we said goodbye.

During the group process, indescribable single-mindedness, inconceivable physical and emotional exertion are used to carve inner emptiness. No escape from crystal silence and innocent freshness. I looked at the energy dynamic between my parents and its effect on my own psychic and constitutional structure. I saw more clearly how their play molded specific aspects of my personality, masking the purity of spontaneous responses.

In this light, I expanded my ability to recognize and embrace my true nature. The next step was to integrate this understanding into my relationships, and work. Sure enough, old knots inside manifested most clearly in intimate relationships, when I was most vulnerable, therefore less on guard. Quite simple, and yet a challenging task to take on.

I realized that my relationship with Dhyan needed to be reviewed. The time we had been apart made me look at my emotional patterns and face my inner splits. I relived memories of another time, when he was my son and died at an early age, possibly as a consequence of my negligence, leaving me in guilt and anxiety. I carried an unwavering need to be forgiven. I realized that when spending time with other lovers, I often felt guilty for causing him pain. My asking for forgiveness was always part of our dynamic in reconnecting. I understood that I needed to forgive myself, to accept my own learning process and my limitations, thus honoring that we were both in the same boat, learning to love and be honest. That realization deepened our connection. I sensed that I needed to be in his skin to experience his difficulties with me, and he needed to move with another woman to understand my attraction to other men. I voiced that at the last day of the group.

I was due to fly to Koln a few days later. The day I finished the group, which had been in isolation, I received a fax from Dhyan letting me know that he had been extremely sick for a week. During these days, a girlfriend took care of him and he felt very close to her. He was ready to spend time with her as a lover, and wanted to let me know before the fact. Something in her had touched his heart in an unusual way. He was asking me to come as planned, but he might still want to spend time with her. He had rented a room in his apartment for me, but if I preferred, I had the choice of staying somewhere else. He was looking forward to meet me again. I was amazed by the synchronicity of events and the universe's immediate response to my requests.

Fax in hand, I went to meet Zi. We had been close friends and lovers for a while. I sat in his lap crying. He embraced me tenderly and laughed… I felt lucky to live in an environment where we shared such intimacy, where it was possible to explore our inner world in raw honesty.

I was invited to staff the next training, scheduled a week later. I chose to stay and take this extra time to reflect. I decided to stay at Dhyan's apartment and discover what jealousy was about. I had never felt jealous before and guessed that would be a good lesson.

I arrived in Koln a bit shaky, Dhyan came to pick me up happy to see me. Our silent way of recognizing each other was untouched, and his embrace was wholehearted. He took me for a Haagen Dasz ice-cream, a ritual I appreciated every time I arrived in Germany, and I moved into his apartment. He was then working as an accountant in the afternoon and as a DJ at the commune's disco, in the evening. His girlfriend worked at the disco, so I was never sure if he would come home alone or with her…

I started watching my reactions and fears, bodily sensations and thoughts, trying not to get distracted or avoid pain. I observed my own needs and feelings, sometimes relaxing deeply and sleeping long before Dhyan arrived home. Often he would come and sleep with me, other times, he would stay with his friend at his room, at the end of the corridor… I could hear when they were talking or making love. Sometimes I was able to embrace him and understand his love for her. I could see his beauty, maturity and joy strengthening inside. Sometimes I would cry in a panic-like way, not knowing what-why that emotion was so uncontrollable and compulsive. Uncertainty touched my belly button.

He was undivided when we were together and in fact, his body was more solid, more loving, and we were more silent than ever. His attention and care with me had always been precious, and this new circumstance only enhanced it.

One of our housemates had leukemia and was on the verge of dying. Her passion and clarity through this process added another dimension to my emotions. It was difficult to hold on to the attachments of my body, as I looked at her lightly living her last days, reminding me how short and uncertain life was. In her late thirties, she was a vibrant, beautiful woman. Her presence helped me to stay centered.

I left alone for Finland for a month of groups and sessions. I offered a counseling training in the countryside and a movement awareness course at the Dance University in Helsinki. Bathed by the midnight sunlight, the softness of the landscape opened my heart wider.

At the end of working periods, I usually choose a special gift for myself. This time I dreamed of an emerald, its light caressing the soft skin in between my breasts.

Back in Koln, I noticed how the mind's job is to hold on and fix… It was easy to tune into the rightness of each moment if my mind was clear and silent, and yet, as soon as expectations gained terrain, emotional pain surfaced.

I was determined to touch the core of jealousy, like catching the bull by the horns… I did not back off, I did not lie to myself, I did not indulge in suffering, but allowed the emotions to run freely. Contraction, control, comparison, denial, fear, uncertainty, need for recognition, betrayal, hurt, demands, irritation…

Usually, in the mornings when Dhyan was with his girlfriend, I would wake up sad and wait for her to leave, so we could have breakfast together. This was an intense time for Dhyan as well, as he was as honest and courageous as he knew how to be. One morning, his girlfriend came to wake me up alarmed, asking me to come to his room. He was in excruciating pain, his lower back had been injured and he could not move. He asked me for an adjustment, and after hesitating and trying to call someone else without luck, I adjusted his spine back into place, not without a strong commotion between the three of us. Somehow, after this incident, I relaxed with the situation, feeling our connection as friends and lovers for life. It did not matter with who he decided to sleep with, I loved this man for who he was, and that would always be so... Maybe life would bring us apart, but the beauty of our love would be untouched. He went to work and I did not see him all day. I went to bed early in the evening feeling restful.

The following morning I woke up simply happy! I went to the park for a walk. The sun was shining and the air was fresh... Suddenly, tingling disturbances were washed out, I felt free and in love, independent of whom would be ready to receive it. I sat in the grass, delighted in the soft sun, walked along the river and spent the rest of the day on my own. Late afternoon Dhyan came home eager to talk to me—he felt complete with his girlfriend and grateful that I had been open for this experiment. We celebrated with a long walk near the lake and a lovely dinner, then lay in bed together for the longest time.

Two months had passed...a long stay for me away from Pune. My groups in Koln were financially excellent and I had enough to go back to India for another year. In this rhythm I lived luxuriously, getting my nest more settled with a nice silk comforter, a wonderful handmade ceramic teapot and other small details that made a difference in my daily life. A day shopping at Ehrenstrasse provided for my needs. I looked everywhere for an emerald ring to remind me of the jewel quality of acceptance inside my heart and the learning I had gone through. I did not find anything I liked, so I gave up...

This experiment with Dhyan forced me to face vulnerability, and to be more honest in asking for what I needed emotionally and physically. I valued the beauty of our union in love. At the same time, I recognized my need for sexual communion.

Our connection had never been primarily sexual, rather the silence of our hearts united our souls and bodies. Then, sex might happen or not. It did not make much difference... Meditation was our grounding, and yet... My body enjoyed sensuous meetings, delighting in the paradox of disappearing into the other. The steadiness of his love had allowed me to recognize and follow my own impulses. The solidity of our friendship offered me rest and earthy ground. At the same time, my bond with other lovers offered me bliss in a loose and ethereal way. During these last years I had developed both extremes in a strong way: absolute commitment as I contained my energy in my relationship with Dhyan, and absolute letting go, as I moved with other lovers in sensuous and sexual ecstasy. Through my relationship with Dhyan and other lovers I expressed different energetic qualities, however they were fragmented into outer manifestations. A phase of expansion was completed. I was ready to learn commitment and convergence in totality, Tantric threshold. Could we respect our paths and still be together? Could I embrace my multifaceted sparks within and hold the offer without budging, even if there was no one to receive it?

I was ready to move into another gear. I decided to face my difficulties in staying faithful to him, looking at the motivations that pulled me towards other men. Where was the line between escapism and simply honoring the language of my body-soul? We talked about it, and I agreed to be with him in a monogamous way. If, at some point it became clear to me that I wanted or needed to be with someone else, we would then split up. Dhyan decided to give India another trial.

We flew to Bombay once more, and this time took a plane to Goa for a two-week vacation. I was eager to get back to Pune but yielded to Dhyan's desire to relax in the ocean. My body betrayed my willingness to please him, and I got sick even before we landed in Goa. Pure hell. Fever, shivering, bodily pains, headaches and no desire to move or do anything.

Fear held my stomach as I came close to the ocean. Seeing the waves, feeling the incoming tide in my belly, knowing that I would not be able to pretend, but had to go into another level of inner diving lesson.

We took a bus to Pune, unforgettable trip, but arrived safely. Huummm... Back home!

This time we had separate rooms, so more space and play visiting each other. I kept to my promise to be with Dhyan. The fact that our master was at the center of our lives made the relationship between us secondary, and yet, bathed with tremendous lovingness. I estimated that we were there to learn and grow in consciousness. Every day I found a way to express gratefulness for that opportunity, dancing in reverence for the master's grace.

Dhyan relaxed with my choice and we spent a beautiful time together. India was not his place. The noise, dirt, food, poverty, all disturbed him. We were both working again, Bhagwan had become Osho, many shifts had occurred in the commune while we were away, I was more and more at home, while he was more and more uncomfortable.

I enjoyed my work immensely, however came to a point where I wished for a change. I had been giving sessions and presenting therapy groups for several years, and was thirsty for a different kind of interaction. I sent a letter to Osho asking about it. I was called into his room a few days later. He was sitting in his bed, and waved me to come closer. His stillness touched my aura as I entered the room—it was strong to move within his space. As I sat next to him, he took his hand and placed it over my heart, then placed my hand over his and his second hand over mine. My heart was exploding! He said, "You go and touch people with my love." I namaste and almost lost the door!

THE SEED

During these years, Bhagwan was fiery, gentle, intense, compassionate, playful, harsh, keen, boring, encouraging, extremely talkative, strikingly silent, a myriad of nuances shining through his presence. He answered questions with infinite patience and rare brilliance, he expounded on Zen masters with the delicacy of a skilled painter, he told jokes and talked politics. He urged us to go to the hara! Rush! Rush to the core of your being! You are not this, you are not that! You are the witness that watches it all! Daily discourses ignited a new alignment. My belly radiated lightness while giving bodywork sessions and dancing every day, his energy soaked my cells. I was aflame with unexplainable inner explosions.

One day, Bhagwan announced that he was to be called by a different name. After a few experiments, he settled for Osho, meaning oceanic... His body seemed fragile, as he moved slowly across the podium. And yet, his vigor mystified thousands of people sitting with him every night. His gestures in invitation to wild dance made us giggle and whirl in delight. His intense eyes did not allow forgetfulness, and even when mine were closed, I could perceive his gaze over my head.

Osho devised new meditation techniques and set grounding for experiments with a few residents and therapists. One of them was the Mystic Rose. Sequentially, we spent seven days, three hours a day for each stage, first laughing, then crying, then watching the mind in silence. As difficult as it is to imagine that you are able to laugh for that long period of time, or cry, once the intention was set, and the group met in synchronicity, there was an extraordinary release of energy, like electric discharges refilling our souls. Cleansing ancient sorrow, enlivening innocent looseness, we witnessed all movements and none.

His presence absorbed my being. I soared in his grace and delight, accepting it as a privilege that I could not say that I deserved—gratitude.

Looking at the events that composed my life, a question came up. Was I living in the surface by coping and choosing so many changes, rather than staying in one place, with one man, one job? Was I misunderstanding Osho's words about living in the moment, following my heart? Osho suggested that I look inside for the rightness of each choice, and never compare or try to decide ahead. Some people's karmic path was to move slow, initiate and ground; others were ready to move fast as they were completing karma in this life. For an outsider they might look inconsequent or superficial, but they were responding from their intrinsic essence. I started to pay even more attention to the motivations of my actions and choices, and to ascertain their rightness within before each move.

My work was an outlet to share his love and presence. My days started at six in the morning and concluded by ten or so...depending on how long evening discourses lasted. I had no desire to go anywhere.

At the end of 1989, Osho started to miss discourses. His body movements were more gracious than ever, his energy potent each day hammering our heads with intensity, but his health was visibly deteriorating. It had been proved by then that he had been poisoned while in jail in the USA, and the effects of that act were becoming evident.

One night he ended the evening discourse with the word Sammasati! Buddha's last word, which means "remembering truth." A sound I had not heard before. Its resonance brought me back to the bottom of the ocean, recalling the image I had seen years before at his last satsang in Pune One.

I was sitting on the first row, to the side where he came in and out of the hall. Exiting, he moved ever so slowly, merciless gesturing over my head, imparting power and vigor in unbearable way. His eyes were wide open. He kept moving his hands with force, looking into my eyes. I danced with him, not sure of how much more I could take. Sammasati! That word echoed over and over. Suddenly, the podium was empty, his car rolled out in the driveway behind the hall. I was glued to my seat, stoned out.

The next day, Osho did not come out for discourse and we sat in silence in his absence/presence. A day later, I was visiting Anand, just before going to discourse. We were lying on his bed, he was crying. He felt Osho was not going to live much longer. We talked about the possibility of him dying soon. It felt unreal and yet, closer than we would wish it to happen. Anand did not want to go to discourse. I left his house alone and walked towards the back gate.

As I came into the commune, I had a strong feeling that I was going to be traveling a lot. It was a strange sensation, like a deja-vu. I saw myself moving around the world. I did not understand. I had no desire to go anywhere. I wrote a letter to Osho, asking if I was resisting his gifts, imagining ways to avoid being more open. Why would I want to leave? I expressed my gratefulness for these years with him. I walked towards the front entrance and dropped my letter at the appropriate box. I walked back towards Lao Tzu gate and sat at the wall with Laya. A few minutes later, a friend came out to secretively let us know that Osho had left his body. He asked Laya to come and help with the preparations for the cremation, as the body was going to be brought to Buddha Hall at discourse time. I was startled.

People started to enter Buddha Hall for discourse. I had not talked to anyone since hearing the news. I walked as if my feet were stuck in mud, heavy with each step. I sat and closed my eyes, burst into tears. The answer to my letter had come quicker than expected.

An announcement was made and his body was brought into the hall. It was like a mirage. He was peacefully lying in a bamboo cot. Waves of emotions moved my body, sobbing, dancing, laughing, looking around, silence and vague thoughts rushing through. Dhyan had not come for discourse. I wanted to let him know what had happened and go to the cremation with him. I left the hall and rushed home with my motorbike. He was not there either... As I returned, the body was being carried out to the burning site, hundreds of people wearing white robes walking in procession. As I approached the gate, I met Veet. He was coming out of a rickshaw with suitcases, arriving from the airport just returning from Europe. We walked together and stayed near Osho's body at the cremation for several hours.

THROUGH THE FIRE

Sammasati.

Fire. An Indian night, mid January 1990. My skin is cold. The fire is burning brightly. His face is disappearing behind the high flames. Inside my chest, heat I can't contain. Awesome calm and yet the scream. My heart is bursting with the cracking of the wood. The beauty of his body is becoming a dense cloud of smoke.

My eyes are staring at the light. His light in my eyes... Tears coming and going.

I am here, and not here. My body is transparent, inconsistent. The fullness of this moment, I will never be able to describe. Simple. Absurd.

As I look around... my closest friends. I feel the depth of our bond, lifetime friends. Constant changes, surprises, moves, love, awe, silence, dance, songs, the richness of life around Osho, the fire in the heart that brought us together. Through this rare sharing, aloneness was highlighted as the meeting point. Loosing the boundaries of definitions, coming to find the essence, without long-lasting meaning.

The night is long and slowly the curious crowd leaves. His body is becoming smaller under the large logs. I can't think. My eyes feel like they will never be able to close again. Even when I do close them, it is as if they are open.

Having offered all I thought I had, having opened all doors, I am faced with empty hands. He is gone. I have to find my way in, without excuses, without his magnificent excuse...

His finger pointed to the moon. I have to lie under its shine.

Nothing can be held. Nothing can be offered, there are no doors to being... I laugh.

Having tasted his empty cup instilled the perfume of mine. Just don't go anywhere... Be here! Komala means the center of the lotus flower. Can I stay in the center and let the water surround me? Can I touch the beauty of simply being Komala? Can I trust existence as a flower does? Can I live just for the joy of nature? Slowly becoming attuned to this space of clarity that contains nothing, I am not anywhere and yet I am fully present. Soon the mind rushes back as fast as possible when it perceives the trick! Learning at each moment to come back to this open space where nothing is happening and yet the universe is incessantly dancing, turning. There is no job for me! Unless I learn how to dance... Then there is no me.

The fire is inside my body, even though my skin is chilly. It is consuming my bark, burning my masks. This flame will always be within.

Only a mad endless dance could express my gratitude, consuming my body in the same fire he burnt with. Maybe one day the silence will melt my bones and shine through my skin. Until then, I can only wait.

Almost morning, I spotted Dhyan. We hugged silently. I was cold and shivering, still wearing my thin white robe. We drove home on my motorbike. Nothing to say. We held each other to sleep.

THE WIND IS BLOWING

Wind blowing. Water running. Waves. Excitement. Relaxation. Floating. Expansion. Fear of what I can't hold. My hands have to open.

I want to stay here a bit longer. It's too soon. It's overdue!

Keep moving! Surf, go down the river, find the ocean! Don't stop, let me go, faster!

Another view. Endless links. I keep watching... Trees shaking. I don't know who I am. I am at each moment someone else. It is scary to have boundless faces, infinite bodies. My bones know I am not the form. My heart hesitates. Changes come again, and again, another wave, another storm, another turn, it's fast, it's slow, it is unexpected! I want to stop life's pulse. I am dizzy. I am not. Take me back in time!

Openness can take me anywhere. I have no choice. Changes. Always bring freshness, and sometimes pain. I am still looking back, and I hit my nose on a tree! Laughing when I realize what is ahead. The gift of the unknown. Stay with the movement, look straight, keep your eyes open, let the body loose, enjoy the wind and the waves! Not-understanding, precious shifts, these gaps in time and space.

Expansion. The trees are growing, the birds are gone, the kids have long legs, faces are older. Inside something is always the same. It doesn't change with the changes. Stillness in movement. At the same time. The magic of alertness, the alchemy of darkness, the enchantment of light. There is where I want to live.

Stones and streams, rest meshed with dance, silence undistinguished from noise. This flow is joy. I can sit here forever. The place where nothing ever happens... Sometimes I can't handle the awareness of the flow. I want security, I want to rest, I want to hold on! Helpless.

Looking at myself from height and distance. A body floating, it can be seen from all perspectives. Changes again. Flying again. An airplane is taking me from here to there. I shift my observation point and yet remain the center.

In the house between tall trees, the birds are singing, the stream is sweetly roaring its way. Greenery and sky, clouds designing whitely.

I look at friends. There is sadness. Complicity. Love that does not fit descriptions, is not displayed in family albums, stays intimate, protected, transmitted through eyes and soft gestures and embrace. We cannot talk about it, vastness cannot be constrained by a few words. And we sense loss and gain.

I need to touch the earth, my feet on the ground, my hands getting dirt, self images melting into aloneness, diving into the center of my belly. Becoming a tree, with roots.

Let's say, liquid roots! However… The flowers are not abundant, the leaves are sprouting bit by bit, but the trunk is strong.

It is spring! Inside-out!

Dhyan was ready to leave India. I needed to stay, I knew it inside. I had decided to stop working, and had cancelled my commitments with sessions and groups. A few days later, Shanti, one of the therapists at the commune, invited me to assist one of his groups a few weeks later. I accepted sensing that I "had to." I was not ready to let go of Pune yet. My soul's home, my only ever nest. Dhyan decided to fly to Koln, and a month later I planned on meeting him there. During my last month in Pune, I received several invitations to offer groups and trainings around the world. He agreed to come with me.

I took Dhyan to the train station. We hugged goodbye and I knew we had completed a cycle, though we had plans for the future. During the rickshaw ride back I cried. Sadness, relief, not-knowing, spiraling.

Reentering the commune's gate, I was clear and refreshed. Immediately someone came towards me—it was Prem. We had not spent intimate time together since my agreement with Dhyan. He was leaving the day after. Spontaneously we stayed together for the rest of the day and into the night. Time dissolved while we were cooking, eating at my room, making love, sleeping in a restful embrace. That was our goodbye for a while. I was sure we would hug again soon. Even though I was planning to leave for a few months, Pune was still "home."

The next evening, Shanti asked if I would like to spend the night with him. He had tears in his eyes, which surprised and touched me. I said yes.

Our first night together revealed that we were intimate friends and yet strangers, in an unquestionable way. From then on, we often spent time together and made love ever so gently. My heart was stirred, and my body was nurtured to its essence. One morning, Shanti said, "I would like that our making love always be an opportunity for me to be present within myself and with you. I want to remember the depth of our meeting every time we make love. If I ever forget this, remind me. When I space out, you can call my attention…" My chest expanded, I nodded. I knew then that our lives were intertwined. I had no idea how our play would unfold. We both had plans a year ahead in different places around the world. He had been in a relationship for a few years. Though his girlfriend was in vacation with someone else, they planned to reunite in Europe a few weeks later. Dhyan was waiting for me in Koln…

During the last years, I had participated in various trainings and meditative therapies. These processes had stimulated vibrancy in my subtle bodies, and made me aware of different past life imprints. I recalled having been trained in Tantric schools where I had learned to use sexual energy as a doorway to divine bliss, as a path of integration between body and spirit. Dissolving into the other had taught me to dissolve into life, had showed me the integrity of being that is doubtless, shameless, timeless. As a consequence of these associations, I had been burnt alive a few times, ostracized and killed in different ways. As a woman, it had been difficult to maintain vulnerability and strength in balance.

Those experiences were still pulsing in my body, as bright diamonds illuminating my way home. I was ready to resume that avenue again in consciousness, understanding that my previous experiences with different lovers had opened my body and revealed the potential of my own energy range, preparing me for a long term relationship with a man that would able to receive the delicacy I had to offer. I was ready to embrace Shanti as my lover with the power of that consciousness. I was ready for relating committed to that awareness, continuously opening…continuously falling back inside, holding my partner as the doorkeeper of the palace of love.

After Osho's death, the connection between friends was stronger than ever. We hang out lazily, not much to say, the latest events had been overwhelming. Now we only had each other. Our eyes conveying unspeakable words.

Osho said, "I leave you my dreams. My salt will be tasted in the presence of my people…" I was left with a sense of infinite richness. Missing the grace of his presence, absorbing the awesome magnitude of his absence.

Earth and Sky

"The engagement, the coming together… Is as with the lion.
His penis stays erect all through it, and it does not scatter semen feebly.
The beautiful one is amazed at his virility.
Immediately, with great energy she joins with his energy,
and their two spirits go out from them as one.
Whenever two are linked in this way, there comes another from the unseen world. It
may be through birth, if nothing prevents conception,
But a third does come, when two unite in love, or in hate.
The intense qualities born of such joining appear in the spiritual world.
You will recognize when you go there. Your associations bear progeny.
Be careful, therefore wait, and be conscious before you meet anyone.
Remember there are children to consider!
Children must live with you and tend to, born of your emotions with another,
Entities with a form, and speech, and a place to live.
They are crying to you even now. You have forgotten us. Come back.
Be aware of this. A man and a woman together always have a spiritual result."

RUMI   *The Essential Rumi*

GYPSIES IN LOVE

Mid-April 1990. I was ready to leave Pune. Shanti came to say goodbye with a beautiful pink tourmaline as a gift. We had no idea where/when we would meet again. That stone was to be our messenger.

I left my room intact, unable to calculate when I would return, and packed a suitcase with the basics for another "not-knowing-where-I-will-land" time.

I was flying to Germany to meet Dhyan, and from there we had tickets to go to Brazil for six months. He had decided to leave his job in Germany and travel with me. I was in between lives.

I took the train to Bombay, and the images floating through the window blurred with tears. What else was different? The spinning kept pushing me forward, broadening horizons. My ability to watch and trust was enhanced.

Arriving in Koln, Dhyan was happy to see me, but not for too long... I told him I had been with Prem and Shanti, and had realized our relationship needed to be completed. Sincerely, I told him how important it was for me to embrace my sexuality as a meditation of integration. I wanted to bridge my inner splits with awareness, and for that I needed to be with someone willing to experiment through the merging of the body and heart. I was unable to disregard my affections and attractions, and did not want to cause him further distress. I no longer could hold our relationship beyond my physical and emotional needs. I loved him deeply, and in this recognition I had to let go.

My choice was motivated by the "bigger than I" perception. Our relationship was established in meditation and the vastness that engulfed our personalities. That would never change. And to this day, we relate as dearest friends.

I recognized without personal involvement or resentment, that his spiritual and emotional requirements were different than mine. Our paths were veering into distinct directions. I had tried to hold on to our togetherness, and honor my way. However, my awareness and ability to embrace did not stretch as much as it would be necessary for us to stay together. I could not see how to conciliate our lives as a couple, if we were to respect our essential needs. A situation that initially offered expansion and growth had become restricting and uptight. The maturity of my meditation was not enough to contain and nurture our love in consciousness.

His heart was hurting. Mine too. We had a couple of days to review our plans, but he decided to come with me to Brazil anyway. I was glad to be with him during this visit to birth-land, always bringing unconscious elements to the surface. We landed in Sao Paulo and started working together with large groups.

In a few days, our relating mellowed out, though the new environment and culture was foreign and difficult for him. We had a few fights over trivial decisions, struggling to be present with each other while knowing that our days were counted. I was juggling the responsibility of my work, my emotional connection with Dhyan, the longing to be with Shanti again, and practical details ahead.

A few weeks later, I cancelled other groups planned in Brazil and went to Rio to visit my family. I decided to go back to Europe and meet Shanti, though we had not made any arrangements and I didn't know where he was... Another jump in the dark!

I decided to go to Koln, a central place where I could work. We were both in shock when I finally booked my flight. Dhyan had dropped his work in Germany to follow me, still hoping that I would change my mind. He had no perspective, nor clarity about what to do next.

We had an absurd fight! I regressed to my teenies, screaming at him, throwing shoes at the wall. I was totally involved and yet, detached. Our battle ended with laughter, and left us with aching hearts. Ah! I am not this, I am not that! What a way to find out!

A few days later we went to the airport together. Dhyan was flying to the USA, his birth country, and I was flying to Frankfurt.

We passed the passport control together. While waiting to be called for our different destinations, I sat in Dhyan's lap weeping. I was attached to him, scared to be making a stupid move; at the same time, I was firm in my intention. He cleared my tears with gentleness, "Komala, do not forget... We are in a journey, be courageous! I love you and always will..." I cried even more, our flights were called and we separated.

Arriving in Koln, Pramod received me kindly in his apartment. I lay down in bed, exhausted. Waking up late afternoon, I received a message: Shanti had called a few hours before asking if anyone knew where I was... He had left a phone number somewhere in Germany. I called immediately. Could I come and meet him that same day? No, I needed a few days to feel my feet on the ground.

We met in a train station in Switzerland, on the way to Geneva, where he had a business meeting. At a hotel we made love, oblivious of the squeaking bed. Pune was a long way ago and we were ready for each other! He was presenting a week group in a retreat/hotel in the mountains nearby, and invited me over. I was quiet, allowing healing from my separation with Dhyan, letting the new be revealed. We took the days with ease, getting acquainted with each other in this new landscape. No more robes and sandals, no friends around, no candid Indian faces. Cars and trains, noise and jeans and good boots!

After the group ended we visited a friend in Locarno, enjoyed waterfalls and lovely walks in the mountains. Shanti had rented a cottage for the season in Ticino and his girlfriend was coming to meet him there. I went to Basel to visit my friend Sahdvi and work. Two weeks later, his girlfriend left; he let me know that they had completed their relationship. He wanted to be with me, and invited me to come by.

The cottage was located in a tiny village called Arceno, sitting at the top of a magic mountain, viewing Mount Verita. Shanti received me joyously and had arranged everything with extreme care—even his socks were aligned nicely inside the cupboard. I took it as a sign of attentiveness and consideration. Wishing to bring an extra touch to the space, I bought a bucket of paint, and as soon as Shanti left for a few hours, I started painting the bedroom. He was astounded, returning and finding me naked on top of a ladder! "Do you always do that when you move into a place? We are only here for six weeks…" I laughed. Time did not matter. That was to be our first home.

Bliss visited us for that summer… The forests nearby were enchanted and we walked every day for hours, often stopping to bathe under a waterfall. The birds, the trees, the wild animals talked to us. We walked hand in hand and meditated at the top of the rocks, delighting in the magnificent view over the lake. A local friend introduced us to hidden spots in nature, and to the Verzasca river, a beautiful stream of clean water forming several pools rimmed by large white boulders. There were plums and strawberries in the garden; Swiss chocolate, creamy ice-cream and yummy freshly-baked bread in the store nearby. We had breakfast outdoors on the veranda and sat in front of the fireplace in the evenings. The coziness and relaxation we shared was fulfilling. Shanti was tender, sensitive, caring, and his intelligence and willingness to communicate with sincerity was nurturing. Thunderstorms shook our bed in the night making us laugh and hug tightly, then make love with the same intensity. I was content.

Six weeks were over and we talked about the future. We both had work booked in different locations around the world. Shanti had groups planned in Sweden, Denmark and Holland; while mine were set in Germany, Switzerland and the USA. There was no way we could be together if we were to follow our plans. Shanti expressed his intention to be with me in a committed relationship and asked if I would like to travel and work with him. I was deeply in love with him, and ready to say yes. My independence had always been important for me, however I decided to cancel my work, and went to Basel for my last group. Shanti left for Sweden, and we agreed to meet near Stockholm a few weeks later.

I enjoyed a train ride through the Swedish countryside, arriving there just before Shanti's birthday. Shyly, I gifted him with a silk shirt, grayish-green, the color of his eyes. We stayed in a cottage, part of a retreat center, in front of the ocean. Honeymoon, time to rest and cuddle, go for walks and savor each other.

A few days later we drove with Solvei and Digant (the organizers of his work) to their home, north of Stockholm. In front of a large lake, bucolic countryside landscape, we were warmly welcomed. We indulged in Swedish summer, digging fresh potatoes from the garden, eating wild strawberries, enjoying the softness of the northern sun, swimming in the cold lake. We were closer in intimacy and relaxed in a new path. I was captivated by the depth and silence of our connection, the tranquility that his presence enhanced in my heart. Our sexuality was luscious, and we met in spirit and conscious care. I was certain that I had to stay present with this new freshness inside myself, either with him or alone. There was vulnerability and delicacy in the way I related to him, willing to be respectful of our timing and connection. Shanti was sometimes distant and vague with me. I was ready to relate with a new maturity, using our differences to come closer, rather than move away. I spent a few nights awake, letting the emotions run through.

We took a train to Gottenburg, on the coast of Sweden, and a ferry to Denmark. We started to work together, slowly finding our ways into partnership. We had different styles of presentation, and I was happy to stand by his side. The beauty of summertime recalled subtlety in contemplation. I relaxed into being a woman, next to the man I loved.

While we were there, his girlfriend started to call insistently. At the end of our stay, Shanti had decided to go meet her near Munich for a few days. I was sad but wishing for clarity. I went to visit Digambar who was living with his German girlfriend, north of Koln. Shanti was due to meet me within a week.

Shanti did not call or came by. I was puzzled. Almost two weeks later, I went to Basel to work. Shanti called me soon after I arrived. Lying in bed, happy to hear his voice, I gasped when he let me know that he had decided to live again with his girlfriend.

We had spent long hours talking about our commitment to be together and he had been explicit and firm in his intent to be with me. Just a few days had passed! I had zero cash, no work, and was in love with him…

I demanded that he come to Basel to meet me personally and say goodbye. He hesitated but finally set for a date.

SEPARATION

His decision shook me up and provoked strong emotions. However, I needed to be practical.

I was staying with my friend Sadhvi, but she was due to move to the USA. First step was to reorganize my work, get my feet on the ground on a financial level to be able to take further decisions.

I flipped through my address book and found Gioia's phone number. Hum...I called... She was at home and pleased to hear my voice two years later. She would love to meet me but was leaving the country in a couple of days. Could I come that same afternoon?

I went to her house and the door opened promptly, a lovely blond woman saluted me. Our first meeting was the beginning of a meaningful friendship. I was fragile and surprised by her warm manner. She welcomed me as an old friend. We had lunch together and I gave her a session the day after. Briefly we shared our moments. She was going to Madagascar for a few months, and generously invited me to stay at her house during her absence.

Her apartment was very beautiful, spacious, and centrally located. I could also offer sessions and small groups there. I moved in as she left.

Shanti arrived for a visit a few days later, early in the morning. I remember crying and making love, going for walks and burning a pot of rice on the stove while we soaked in the bathtub... He was determined to be with his girlfriend, and was going to follow up with his groups, traveling with her. I had no defenses or desires. I was really in love with him. He left anyway.

As I went to bed that night, I found a gift under my pillow with a note "I am looking forward to our next dance together, soon!" I was upset with this dubious intention. I called to let him know that I did not want to be on a hook; if he was leaving, I did not want to hear from him or expect his return. I rather stay with the rawness of letting go, than hold onto an illusion of future. I wished him well.

I decided not to run away from the grief nor find distractions to avoid it. When I finally had let down my defenses, and decided to be with a man in an undivided and committed way, he left! I did not understand this turn.

My work addressed primarily subtle body healing, using Color Light Therapy and touch, as well as movement awareness. In a flash, I was fully booked out with daily individual sessions.

More than often, I opened the door with red eyes, and could not stop crying during sessions. However, people kept referring my work to others, and coming back regularly.

Surprising, specially considering that I was in Switzerland! Soon I started working with groups in the evenings to be able to respond to all requests. Cash was flowing in abundantly and gracefully, though there was a hole in my heart and often a sense of despair and perplexity.

Premati was living in Geneve, and had also separated from Anand. We met and shared our new phase while walking in public parks. What is love about?

I had no idea where Shanti was. More like an abortion than a birth, our connection seemed to have been interrupted abruptly. It was difficult to let go of a half-cooked possibility, especially when my heart had been deeply touched. Our merging together was total and spacious simultaneously, precious and rare, silent and alive. However, I did not want to hang on to hope. I was not interested in spending time with other men either. That was also new!

A whirlpool of conflicting emotions stirred me up. Sitting in silence for a few hours every day gave me the only support to open my heart in softness and let go of whatever my mind-body attached to. Shanti represented the core of my attachment. I missed him immensely, or maybe I missed the prospect that he represented of my own potential. It was hard to have been blown apart, when I had "just" started to sense a quality of union within myself, still tender and fresh.

Besides seeing clients, I spent my free time alone. Life was simple: work, meditation, going for walks along the Rhine.

One afternoon, a friend dropped by with a few Osho videos, discourses from Pune or the ranch. In the evening I sat in front of the TV, and as I remember, I heard him saying… "Between birth and death most people live mechanically, just to survive. Whenever love visits you, even for a minute, be grateful. Love is a gift in between birth and death. Most people die without ever feeling love. If someone loved you for a second, be grateful for this gift. Nobody needs to love you. When someone leaves you after a love affair, be grateful. It is a misunderstanding to be sad and upset. Love is a luxury." An arrow of understanding hit my heart. I sat crying for a long time feeling deeply grateful for Shanti's love, for the brief time we had been together.

At the end of my stay, I had accumulated a large amount of cash. In fact, I had never made so much money in such short period of time. I had enough to live for at least a year in a nice way. What to do? Surprisingly, I did not want to go back to India. Most of my friends were still in Pune, but once life had kicked me out of the nest, I better take the opportunity and learn to fly.

I didn't need to work for a while. What next? I kept looking at the possibilities, until I read an ad for a resort in Tulum, Mexico, and found out that Sajeela was managing the place. That was the place to go!

Gioia was due to arrive a few days later. Her place had been wonderfully cozy and supportive of my journey and I greatly appreciated her kindness. I cleaned the house with care, went shopping for gifts for her, and enjoyed wrapping them with colorful paper.

Stopping in Koln for my last group and then flying from Amsterdam to Cancun, direct! A long thirteen-plus hours.

A friend gave me a tarot reading before leaving: be aware of your cash, something may happen...you will be with a man who negotiates with farm products, you will be together for many years... I listened. Did not make much sense, but I watched my handbag while traveling.

Arriving in Cancun quite tired, Sajeela picked me up excited. We were happy to meet again. She was managing a lovely resort/retreat place, with three other friends. She took me by the hand to one of the cabanas saying, "I will give you the best one! Shanti and his girlfriend stayed here, they just left yesterday! You will love it!" She did not know that we had been together and was surprised when I told her of our connection. I chose to stay in a more isolated location.

That night I fell asleep rather exhausted. Late in the night, I woke up listening to an unusual noise close to my body. Instinctively I reached for my money-belt, which I had attached to the side of the bed. In the dark, I found a hand over it and heard strong breathing! Not knowing what to expect, my mind raced to figure out how to move. No light to see who was inside the room. Very loud, I started to speak in English, trying at the same time to roll the sheet around my naked body, getting ready to get up and look for a flashlight! I reached for the door and finally saw the face of my thief—a young guy, looking scared with my screaming. I spoke then in Spanish, asking him to leave. He ran like a rabbit, and I stayed awaken for the rest of the night. I walked near the ocean as the first morning light was insinuating in the sky. Bathing my feet in the ocean, ready to start fresh.

These days in Tulum were magic healing. My body rejoiced in the warm ocean and my soul expanded with the white sand beaches. Sajeela invited me to stay but it was not the right choice for me. Instead I decided to return to the USA and visit Dhyan, who was now living in Boulder with a new girlfriend.

I stopped in San Diego, then flew to Santa Fe to visit friends and check out the town as a possible place to settle. I wanted earth, ordinariness, simply go to the bakery and buy bread in a language I was able to speak and be understood.

SYNCHRONICITY

Visiting Santa Fe. The snow made me stay cozy inside the cottage.

Within, millions of shiny particles flying in all directions. Broken sounds, broken images, broken sensations, spinning at high speed. Flashy thoughts, reviewing my life, all times at once, intense and fragmented, impulses moving in bursts. Random comments paraded in my mind. Self-judgment, self-inquiry, self-doubt, relentless questioning all decisions I had ever made. At one given moment, I was sure to have wasted my life, and it was too late to restart or repair it... The next moment, blessings were showering... Pieces hanging loose in the air, with no thread, no link, nothing that could justify my way, my path, my choices. I was shattered. I had talents, I had money, I had youth, I had beauty, I had charm, I had magnetism, I had easiness and I threw it all up in the air. What for? Momentarily, there was fullness and gratitude. Unquestionable, simple, fulfilling joy. And unexpectedly, emptiness. I kept watching the snow falling.

I saw no future, I had no preferences. I saw no chance of holding on to my likings. Hell was getting loose, ghosts dancing and shouting, keeping me awake and making me cry. Yet, I did not want to make it different. Trusting that the inner noise might subside, and bare another layer of sight/insight.

I prayed for a bed and nice fluffy covers! And when I was in bed, I couldn't sleep...

I wanted to live in the fullness of the potential I sensed within, had desperately looked for, had deliciously encountered and seemingly had lost again. Conversations were meaningless, esoteric junk-talk. Moments of balance were fleeting. I was lagging behind myself, especially on a practical level. I had learnt nothing. My mind compared my life with others who had made different choices, and were able to hold firm on the ground. I wobbled. I was exhausted.

Emotional pain came from the perception of what was still unlived, hidden, controlled, dismissed, contorted. I could sense it so, because I had tasted what was possible, and knew it to be powerfully alive within. I had sipped the sumptuousness inside. I knew its elation, nourishment, pleasure. It was easy to detect the other side of the coin when I wasn't living it, when I was not daring to break through my protective layers, when there was no outlet for that sparkle to circulate in its orbit. Randomly, it came and went on its own accord. I did not understand it or had any control of how or why.

Around Osho, I had experienced years of feeling no webs. Since he was not available, the manifestation and expression of that exquisite quality had to grow in strength and duration with no outer support... His energy-memory was in my cells undoubtedly.

However, another learning was taking place. Sammasati. Flickering consciousness. Remembrance, forgetfulness…

During the years living in the commune, "doing" was irrelevant. My actions expressed fullness. Stillness and movements converged, both soaked with the profundity of silence and restfulness. There was no difference. Even when I worked long days, overnights, no sleep. I sensed my life resonating with the universe and returning to me expanded ten-thousand folds, vibrating, with each breath. I was ready to die, there was nothing to be accomplished or completed.

During these days in Santa Fe, I experienced incompleteness, inner pressure to know something uncompromising and to fulfill desires that had no form, like blurred grayish ghosts hanging inside. I was jammed.

I knew how to offer my fullness to a lover. I knew how to share it through the communal work. I knew how to burst into creativity. I knew how to delight in the meeting with friends, idle times. And there I was! The lover did not want to receive what I had to offer, I had no motivation to work, no inspiration to create, my friends were spread around the world. Short of these polarizations, life was dull.

I stopped and took time to rest. Long walks, being quiet, waiting.

I left Santa Fe at five in the morning, out of an urgent impulse. A thank you note to my host still asleep, and the first Greyhound bus out of town. The airport was closed due to snowstorms.

Arriving in Boulder late in the night, a few days before Christmas, Dhyan and his girlfriend were waiting for me at the station. Cold noses, warm hearts, comforting hugs, and we drove to their house.

I had no agenda. Connecting with Dhyan and seeing him in alignment with a new lifestyle, a lovely home, a good job, and a sense of creative freshness, was healing. I was fragile meeting him again, grateful for his kindness to invite me to his home. We shared meals, went for walks, talked about the shifts we had gone through. The core was the love unscratched, the care always present, the understanding of the undercurrents, even when there was no logic to explain it, and we both had endured heartbreaking times. I slept well, bought a cozy feather comforter and a great fluffy pillow, and started to look at the possibility of settling into an ordinary daily life.

I looked into working possibilities, and my basic needs. There were several friends in Boulder and I liked the town, easy to move around, eclectic enough, though cold! But, I was willing to handle it. A good jacket, gloves and a charming hat, I was ready for the winter.

Buying a car was an adventure. With the help of a good friend, I bought a pale blue Volkswagen Rabbit. We both liked the color. As neither of us knew much about cars, that was enough of a sign. I was set to start afresh!

I enjoyed being in America again, this time around in a different scenario and with a different purpose.

I held Shanti in my heart, but did not want to connect with him, nor even know where he was. I had been alone since he had left, not wanting to invite someone else in my life to cover my sense of loss. I chose to let it throb until it would naturally wash out.

I met Di at a gathering, in a snowy night. We exchanged phone numbers at the parking lot and went for a walk a few days later. During the years at the ranch, I had enjoyed his presence and flirted at a distance. He had recently moved to Boulder, and were glad to reconnect. We started to hang out together exploring nature and town. Our friendship was protected by our common intention of keeping it simple. We had different reasons to avoid a romantic relationship, so we relaxed into a sweet companionship.

I appreciated Di's plain sense of humor and directness in life. His sincerity and straightforwardness was tenderly touching me. As he was Dhyan's closest friend, the four of us also met for meals. Yes, we were on a journey!

I woke up one day sensing freshness inside. A cycle had been completed. I was ready to let go of Shanti and the hope that we might meet again. I decided to rent my own place and stay in Boulder.

I walked to town and bought a card with a photo of a joyful dolphin, wrote a two-line message to Shanti grateful for his love in my life. I had not idea where he was. I had his brother's phone number, so I called. "No ma'am, I have no idea... You can send mail to my address and when he shows up, I will give it to him." That was good enough. I went to the post office, mailed the card and walked through the forest, relieved and restful. A few minutes after closing the door back home, the phone rang and Dhyan passed it to me.

Shanti's voice was soft, he had traced me after a few phone calls around the world. We both remained silent for a while, our natural space of recognition. He was in Los Angeles, going soon to Maui, working and having a difficult time with his relationship. I listened and said little. I caressed again the pure essence of our union, but I was detached. He insinuated that he would separate from his girlfriend at the end of a working trip, and would like to meet me again. I was not interested in future plans.

I rented a small cottage and started working, dancing regularly, cooking good meals, enjoying the outdoors, spending time with friends, often with Di.

One night, I surprisingly grasped the harmony of our meetings. It was obvious we were bathing in the kindness of love: down-to-earth, undemanding, caring, wholehearted. There was genuine intimacy, and an easy flow in the way we started to spend nights together at each other's places. As we were not engaged in future fantasies, or romantic dreams, nor had "fallen in love", but rather realized that love was falling on us, it was relaxing to allow our hearts to come closer and our bodies to merge.

Shanti called again during the first night I spent with Di. I was not home. He insisted, calling me the next day. I let him know that I was spending time with Di. He affirmed that his relationship was over and he was getting ready to meet me again. I was not! He asked me to come and meet him in Maui. No...

After several phone calls, Shanti flew to Australia, his previous place of residency, where he had a car and furniture to liquidate. He called a few hours after his arrival, asking me to come and meet him in Europe a few weeks later. We had a strong encounter. I did not want to leave. I was finding my way in Boulder and with Di, content to be simple, experimenting with a new lifestyle. He had been in the US for a few months, and could have visited me then. I was not going to Europe. A few hours later, another phone call announcing his determination to take the next-day flight to Los Angeles, to come and meet me, instead of flying East to reach Europe, as per his ticket already booked. I was surprised, and certainly confused. He was coming no matter how I would react. He gave me his arrival flight and let me know that if I would not go to the airport to pick him up, he would get a cab to my home. I was then living in a beautiful house in the mountains, just outside of Boulder. Glass windows surrounded my bedroom and framed the landscape with deer and pine trees.

Resting in bed staring at the night, I did not know what to do. My heart was soft and open, my work was being established with classes and sessions. I was willing to stay in Boulder and allow life to teach me how to relax in simplicity. Di was supportive and caring. I slept quietly.

I went to the airport. Embracing Shanti filled my heart with tenderness. A long, silent hug, and I had no doubts. He was exhausted after two long flights in a couple of days. At home, we made love and he slept for long hours. I only knew I had to wait and respond to the situation with sincerity and openness.

Di was profoundly kind, retreating, and at the same time present. His response made me feel even closer to him, and appreciate his noble heart. I was confused: I could choose to stay with him, as much as I could leave with Shanti.

Shanti and I took time to go for long walks in the snowy mountains, talk about the last months we had been apart, recognize how we still connected with each other, foretaste future possibilities at a practical and personal level, share the feelings that our separation had stirred, and allow time and space to show us the way. He was clear with the end of his previous relationship and ready to embrace our lives together, now in a doubtless way. He was going to work in Sweden for the next six months. He invited me to join him. I listened.

One afternoon we drove to Estes park, a lovely location north of Boulder. At the end of March, the sun was soft, the snow melting in patches. I was carefully driving my little Rabbit. Mid-way, Shanti suggested that we stop to walk in the forest bordering the highway. I insisted on going further. A few miles up the road, the car skidded on an icy curve and spun, without control. In a split second we were faced with an abyss on the right and a rock wall on the left. We hit the rock wall and luckily no other vehicle was coming on the opposite direction. During the spin, I heard loud and clear: This is your man, stay with him!

The car stopped against the rocky mountain, I had no sense of time. The front was so smashed that we had to get out through the back door. Neither of us had a scratch!

Police, insurance, the vehicle had to be towed, not worth repairing, a total wreck. We rested a few days at home. I decided to meet Shanti in Stockholm a month later.

He left and I went to Aspen to give a few courses that had been planned beforehand.

My belongings were packed and stored at Dhyan's house in large garbage bins. I had no idea when I would be back.

Di continued to relate to me with affection and friendship through these last days, though I felt he was touched and sad. We spent my last night in Boulder together. His honesty and sensitivity stayed with me. There is gratefulness for his presence in my life and some grief that I was not able to honor his love with my presence. The road seemed to split at that crossroad and I had to choose left or right. However, my choice rose out of no comparison, so I could not justify it. That was simply so!

I flew to Sweden April 17th, 1991, my eleventh sannyasin birthday.

Shanti met me at the airport. Our hostesses, Solvei and Digant, drove us to Fonebo, located a few hours north of Stockholm.

Northern lights

Let the lover be...a phrase from Rumi. As I hear it, the first meaning bypasses words. It translates a sense of presence through the heart that I cherish as guidance throughout life. Further, as I connect with my body, it means to allow vulnerability and sensitivity to be exposed in any form it may take. In the way I move, create, work, communicate or relate. It means to stay present in the porous quality of lovingness, not addressed to anyone in particular, not expecting to get back anything, though carrying strength and aliveness just for the sake of its intrinsic joy! It comes with the perception that everything that I hold back will die unlived, and, if I am here, occupying a body, I better live it with all I have.

Let the lover be... I had decided and there was no way back.

Springtime, the lake was still frozen. We had a lovely apartment and the place we were to work and live was like a fairy tale. A large property surrounded by magic forests, small creeks and enchanting pathways through the moist vegetation. Our room had a view to the twenty kilometers wide lake, and a small mountain in the background. Fonebo was a village with a few sparse houses, and the closest town was half-hour away. This idyllic retreat had impeccable guest space and a beautiful group room—a remodeled barn with stylish details. Wonderful to have such a space to work! Solvei and Digant had just finished the remodeling of the property. They had a fresh enthusiasm for this new project, combined with many years of pioneering work with business consultancy and coaching in Swedish corporations. They were welcoming us in their home with loving care and Northern politeness. We were their first long term guests, and they were grateful for our supportive and active role in establishing the center.

Shanti had planned a series of courses and we created an extensive program together. We offered various trainings, including a one-month-long counseling course for business managers and healing arts professionals. Our skills combined represented a rich array of expression and merged with the love that was flowering between us.

Work for me had always been an expression of love. Again, I was invited to share it with others, through the skills I had acquired during the last ten years. Outside of the commune's context, we both had to find new ways to communicate our experiences.

We were together twenty-four hours a day. I loved that intensity, especially when the lover was combined with creative work.

Shanti was undoubtedly in love with me, no more wavering. We dove into commitment, sweetness, wonder, caring for each other, discovering how to live away from the commune's nest, while preserving and sharing the qualities we had learned to cultivate. We also faced difficulties in finding new ways in a foreign country, rather isolated, without intimate friends nearby, relating with clients and our hostesses, trying to find balance and satisfaction in the way we worked together, adapting to a different lifestyle and cultural habits.

The transition to Swedish definitions and scenarios was not an easy one. I was used to the international flavor of the commune, had always appreciated diversity, the vibrancy of many languages and cultures fused into a larger pot, the tangible consequences of that richness, the awareness that it brought to my own conditioning and upbringing, the constant reminder of my uniqueness as well as my commonality... Being immersed in one culture was boring. Especially a culture set on traditional values. Working, I realized that my inclination was to invite expression, to release self-judgment and feelings of shamefulness, open the body and heart to the dance of life unconstrained. Recognizing that I was feeling constrained and limited, I used that situation to expand inside myself, bringing a yet deeper layer of my joy out into the light. It was an effort though...

Summertime arrived swiftly. We followed up with a one-month training, fully booked with over 30 people from different backgrounds. We had invited a team of assistants for this project, and it was delightful to have a few more friends and fun around us. I decided to do Dynamic meditation daily, and woke up early to jump vigorously and let my lungs release built up energy. Coming from Switzerland, Germany, England and the USA, our collaborators brought vivacity to our routine. I laughed again with Mayoori, my dearest German sister, with whom I had shared much time in Pune, as well as played with Ahado and Sneha, who had joined us from Switzerland as professional cooks. We had colorful meals Italian or French style, and buoyancy that lit up the settled Swedish standard rules. Kumud brought new technology for the colortherapy section of our work, and Pankaj added the dimension of humor with his theater skills. The training was enriching for all of us.

At the end of the summer we took a vacation up north. It was snowing in august! Beyond the awesome prehistoric quality of the environment with wild bison, moose and musk ox running in the open fields, I was not enthusiastic about this outing. We drove to Norway and spent cozy nights in "stugas" (tiny cottages), cuddling in front of the fireplace and making love in narrow beds.

Back at Fonebo, Shanti and I spent as much time as possible outdoors, enjoying the fairy-like purity of the surroundings.

Silence was in the background, strongly resonant in nature. We walked daily picking berries, had rare swimming moments in the cold lake, went for bicycle rides on the small road alongside the lakeshore, climbed a mountain nearby, and enjoyed silent spells watching the creek, and the delicate vegetation nearby. Nature infused us with freshness, beauty and ancient contemplation. It also compensated for the lack of Indian colorfulness and the commune's liveliness. The trees, certainly inhabited by gnomes, sent messages of patience and humbleness to my rebellious spirit. Meanwhile our work was very successful and our bank account was growing plentifully.

I enjoyed the intimacy and spaciousness between us. Shanti was focused on the work and the fact that we were attracting more and more people for our programs. We had issues around establishing our own needs and energetic spaces while working in collaboration, but mostly I yielded to his sense of direction, sometimes reacted with intense resistance to his perception of things or ways to present our courses, but my priority was unquestionably to let the lover be...

We were invited to stay in Fonebo indefinitely and keep working with Solvei and Digant. The winter was approaching and I was not anticipating spending a few months in the dark and cold weather. Considering that "summer" on my terms had lasted a few days, that did not sound enticing...

At the end of autumn we had to make a decision: stay or leave. I was tired of mono-cultural behavior, I missed India, and yet I knew there was no way back. Many of my close friends were still living in Pune or spending time with other masters in the East. Shanti did not want to return to India. I did not want to go alone. Our relationship was genuinely satisfying and the silent spaces we touched together fulfilled my needs for nourishment. Making love was our meditation and place of meeting with more and more awareness. Where to go?

I wanted to have my own home.

One morning I woke up in a radical mode. I had enough! Let's leave today! Shanti was more reasonable reminding me that we had a few more weeks of work scheduled. So, we decided to leave as soon as our groups were over. In the beginning of December we flew to Singapore, and then to Australia, where Shanti owned a beautiful property. We considered the possibility of living there long-term.

Aussie land

While in Sweden I had a dream... I was a Japanese woman sewing an intricate silk kimono. The details of this procedure were precisely experienced as I put together each piece of the pattern. I woke up with the vivid image of this unusual dream-kimono. A few days passed and I could not forget it. I mentioned it to Shanti and he encouraged me to actually make it real.

I specially ordered silk from the fabric store in the nearest town. One evening after a day's work, I sewed my first kimono. I knew exactly how to do it, with a precision of skills I had never exercised before. It came out perfectly crafted and delicately beautiful. I was taken aback feeling like someone else had guided my hands into each movement.

Solvei loved it and asked me to make one kimono for her. Soon I started having more orders.

As we flew to Singapore, I enjoyed shopping for silk and complementary materials. Free time was ahead and I was looking forward to being alone with Shanti and playing with a creative project.

Landing in Perth, we were welcomed by an American friend who had been living there for a few years. To start with, Australian culture and aesthetics did not talk to my soul. But I was willing to give it a try.

Dhyana, my dear friend for years, was also living there with her man. I rejoiced in the sweetness of our sisterhood.

A few days later we drove south to a small town called Denmark, on the southwestern tip of the continent. Hippyish style, magnificent eucalyptus forests, a dark-green-water river surrounded by tea trees, clear water ocean, huge boulders on the beach shore, kangaroos all over. Shanti's land was about one hundred acres, mostly of untouched forest. The house was charming and had been recently remodeled and freshly painted. Several glass walls, one bedroom, a large living room, open kitchen space and a delightful bathroom with a large bathtub. What a delight to have our own space to rest and live.

There were two horses, leisurely hanging out in a pasture, the kangaroos moved around freely and especially loved to stand in front of the window in the living room while we sat in meditation. Hump, hump, hump, they came closer and stood outside staring at us. I could not resist opening my eyes to peek.

We were not concerned about earning an income, as we had plenty for a while. The man who cared for the property had cultivated an organic vegetable garden and food was abundant. Time unlimited. Shanti started writing a book. I bought a sewing machine and had a pile of silk to play with. Loose pieces of fabric started turning into beautiful artwear.

We had no acquaintances; time for retreat.

I started to learn pottery, going to a private class every day. I loved to have my hands on the clay, watching the process of form being created, and the colors of glazes playing different designs.

We lived for a few months drinking from the freshness of nature, walking in the forest, sitting and gazing at the waves crashing on the rocks along the beach, meeting kangaroos unexpectedly behind a bush and laughing, cooking good meals, giving carrots to the horses, picking fruits from the trees, getting my hands stained with fresh mulberries, sitting silently everyday, making love unhurriedly, watching the bamboo growing in our living room corner, being surprised by poisonous snakes on our pathway, observing a beehive work madly for their honey. Being simple and in love suited me.

I wanted to have a home, to settle somewhere for a while. I wanted to learn how to live in the world, be involved with what it takes to keep a body alive and healthy, provide for the material needs that this job involves and, at the same time, stay focused in the growing awareness of presence, love and meditation. The commune days were over. I could not go back, and wasn't sure how to move forward. We took our time...

As much as we wished to settle there, practically, it did not work. As we looked at the possibilities of working and making a living, the perspectives were not exciting. We decided to leave and sell the property.

Going back to the USA opened up as our best route. We flew to Sidney for a few monsoon days and booked our flight to Los Angeles.

TANTRIC SENSITIVITY

The spirit is untamed, indefinable, permeating form, instilling grace to body and heart, revealing beauty from within. Suddenly, as it shines unbound, we recognize the beloved in someone's eyes. Do we dare?

Relating has been my path to encounter the mystery, to make it visible, tangible. Sensuality and sexuality have opened the doors of my heart and guided my soul through this life's learning. The light of intimacy has helped me to dissolve dualities. In the merging, neither I, nor thou. It has forced me to face fear, comparison, jealousy, mistakes, vulnerability, insecurity, sadness, and more.

In aloneness, what I have called trust was spirited fear. Easy to hide, retreat, dissociate, stay aloof and detached. Letting go has disguised unawareness and inability to face the other as a mirror. Until I find maturity and poise through relationships, my aloneness will remain lopsided. In relationships, trust is the unknown, the merging without boundaries. Letting go becomes the unpeeling of my own skin, sometimes terribly thin and delicate. The challenge of allowing the under-layers to be revealed, has offered me the very opportunity for self-compassion, if I only let it burn through the over-layers of protection. Not easy.

As I follow the track of memory, it is clear that "I" did not choose. "I" had no choice! Either moving here or there, "I" was moved here or there. Only very recently do I have a sense of true choice: I can actually see the options, and choose right or left, up or down. There is a different sense of fine-tuning, and the perception of movement coming from a space inside that is stable, resonant with earth rather than with wind.

Letting it be so, and yet taking a step, the paradox of freedom that I sip here and there. A fine line! That ray of attention that distinguishes the difference and shines through the mid-point...

Years of relating with lovers and clients have made me realize again and again the silliness of what I believe I might know. Yea, and I still get caught! The grip of the mind is strong! But the next opportunity comes soon. The mind keeps trying to relate to what it knows, the freshness of the other keeps breaking through relentlessly.

During the first years in Pune, we bowed down to the master. Buddham Sharanam Gachchami... It was time to surrender to the inner guidance in the form of the outer master. While opening to the master, my own fullness started to be revealed. He abided in emptiness, and carried me there.

Recognizing that most lives are invaded, rather early, by forceful demands and directives that are substantial and consequential if not respected, is painful. So, either we fight it or contract. The master demanded surrender. "Let go! Release the grip on everything you have known! Truth is freshness, is this moment anew!" No selection, no separation, no analysis, no sorting out. His all-pervasive and unsubstantial presence became the device and substitute for all other "invasions." He offered himself as the abyss to fall into, no holding on would help...

This learning in surrender seems to represent the first stage of meditation: getting acquainted with the awareness that comes from an outer source, paying attention to the surrounding objects; be it the master, our own breath, heart, emotions, sensations. However, it is appealing to hold on to the sweetness of that first taste. It is easy to get attached to the object of awareness, and lose awareness itself. Or, negatively, deny the doorway, and retreat to the knowing self.

At the ranch, Sangham Sharanam Gachchami... The commune took the role of recalling personal responsibility, and sharing in truth. The hierarchic structure and the creativity of our projects took us into expansion. It was time to bring attention to the exchange of energy, to the circle that arose out of focusing on emptiness at the center. Choiceless awareness. Recognizing the other as yourself, and yourself as the other. There was no difference. Anyone could do anything, my skills were not more valuable than anybody else's. This growing in presence required more accountability, a deeper understanding of co-creation and collaboration. It did not seem to be possible to embody this stage without having passed through the fire of surrender to the inner thirst, to the inner lover. That initial acknowledgment seems to be what magically guides each being to find the pathway, no matter how the outer may manifest. Maybe a stone, maybe a child, or a master, or a song. Suddenly, the outer object opens the door to the infinite. Within a split second, lifetimes, a few years. Time is indifferent.

Long hours of work and concentrated focus only increased my ability to be present to my own abilities and resources. Especially because our activities did not bring any personal or monetary reward, it was evident that there was no other reason to be there, except learning how to become a bit more present in my body, heart and mind.

Leaving Pune, immersing in the collective of Western culture once more. Dhamman Sharanam Gachchami... Now, having to find the truth no matter what, inside, deeper and deeper. The love that opens my heart has been the thread through these phases. That same innocence had to find its way without references, without outer guidance or devices. Awareness permeated the background, inner and outer, here and there, yesterday and tomorrow. Finally settling with what is now. Spaciousness and silence. Resistance and seeking gradually receding.

Slowly, I came to understand how in the Western cultures, the mind has been used as an instrument of perception, twisting its nature as a mechanism of organization, regulation and discrimination.

The natural instruments of perception are the senses. It is through the senses that we receive life-bites. The function of the mind follows the acuity and refinement of the senses. When the senses are reduced in capacity and quality of perception, we have less material for intelligence to develop and manifest. Sensorial perception is the food of intelligence. Any action that results in diminishing their acuteness has consequences in the transformation and manifestation of intelligence. Alive sexuality recalls for great sensitivity, as all senses are involved in the act of meeting in orgasmic bliss. Even if it lasts for one second, in that second all sensorial doors open up to heightened keenness. This does not mean that all human beings who engage in sex will have this perception and use this experience for higher consciousness. Nevertheless, sexuality offers an avenue of integration and opening into divine love.

Working as a therapist with the background of meditation has made me inquire into the nature of receptivity and energy transformation. In Western cultures, the concept of protection is widely accepted as necessary. Instead, I played with the opposite: openness, permeability, vulnerability. I experienced the porosity of freedom, expansive, however conveying integrity of intention.

The difference between getting and receiving became important. It is easy to "get" something but not truly receive it; it is difficult to allow a gift, feeling, or comment, to be transformed into flesh.

Making love has continuously enhanced my receptivity. I used it as an opportunity to observe my body and heart, to recognize inner spaces where there were clouds, tensions, ideas, intentions, manipulation, or unknown feelings that surprise me when I let them loosen. I kept choosing disclosure, revelation, fragility, permeability. The ability to receive requires space: physical, emotional and mental. And space only exists in bareness, obliviousness of past and future. Learning to hang in there longer and longer has been my learning. In the open space there is no receiving or giving, flow simply happens. This experience is healing. As the causes of deviation cease to be imposed to the body, emotions or mind, the flow of life returns to its natural course. The skills I have learned through these years are only valuable as part of my being, in the background of open space, meditation, silence. When my body-mind-emotions are open as passage for life, there is no separation between giving and receiving; only the awareness of different forms of life energy constantly moving, shifting in play. When there is holding on to giving or receiving, energy seems to implode, to get rancid. That is what I call disease. As soon as circulation starts to be recalled, obstacles melt on a cellular, emotional, mental or physical level. Life returns to its pulsing.

I have learned to relax and fill up my life-juice reservoir. Trusting and experiencing! Breathing and daring! One more step!

As I explored connecting and merging with different people, it became obvious that there are as many choices available as we dare to go for them. Recognizing the ways I had learned to hold back, tricking myself and others, avoiding going deeper into my physical body's energy, I begin to experience the body as the temple of the spirit, and honoring it as such. Each "other" reflects the richness of my potential, if I am only willing to live it! Each intimate meeting made it evident that there is infinite source of joy and possibilities with each life. The art of revealing it is a gift to be shared, rather than a possession to be kept. Sex becoming an invitation for aliveness in body and spirit. The roots of life nourishment digging into the ground.

My work, friends and lovers through these years collaborated into transforming mental and emotional understanding into existential experience, into insights that became enmeshed into skin and bones. I experienced presence as the ability to permeate and be permeated by whatever is bigger than "I," allowing the flow of life to wash the moment with its myriad of rhythms and colors. Simply not interfering. In intimate occasions, I sensed the opportunity to learn to stay in the gentleness of not knowing, because the other is fresh, uncontrollable, unexpected, and will always be so. I keep coming close, exposing myself to find out how the flow of life will sweep me this time! At each time, new nuances and subtleties are insinuated. Even when there was pain, the certainty of the richness has always been there. I keep offering it all, even when I do lose what looked like mine. Yielding to dissolution of forms and experiences without defenses is a challenge. My emotional body suggests letting go before crystallization, before the potential moment of attachment; pain might be avoided. Not possible! I can't let go of what I don't have. Crystallization has to happen. The speed of this process seems to be highly variable, and increasingly fast as time goes by.

In Time

"Keep walking, though there's no place to get to.
Don't try to see through the distances.
That is not for human beings.
Move within, but don't move the way fear makes you move.
Today, like every other day,
We wake up empty and frightened.
Don't open the door to the study and begin reading.
Take down a musical instrument.
Let the beauty we love be what we do.
There are hundreds of ways to kneel and kiss the ground."

RUMI *The Illuminated Rumi*

COMPUTERS AND HIGHWAYS

With two suitcases, we landed in Los Angeles.

Taken aback by America's flashing "you can buy it all" world, we explored the universe of health food stores and car dealers—our most urgent needs.

After a good rest, we visited Neharika. She had been Shanti's friend from many years. At first sight, she and I recognized each other from ancient times. She was about fifty. Her petite body, vibrant presence and strong voice transmitted depth and a no-nonsense approach to life. She came with us to a car dealer and helped in the negotiation of our first Toyota.

A few days later, we went to her apartment to say goodbye. She gave me a large electric wok, and hugged me saying, "Honey, you will need this!"

I bought a pair of purple ballerina shoes and Shanti got equipped with good hiking boots. Super-quality bedding, road maps and we were ready to find a place to live.

Shanti and I alternated between piloting and co-piloting, navigating through the swarming traffic. I was shivering, scared to drive in the fast lanes, especially next to big trucks. We decided to take the scenic road through the coast up north, a more relaxed option.

We stopped in Big Sur for lunch overlooking the ocean. Our intention was to visit Anand and Premati, who were living in San Rafael. However, as we approached the Bay Area, the traffic jam freaked us out! We drove into the mountains, direction Arizona. Closer to nature and open spaces, we mellowed out. Finding a bed-and-breakfast in a mountain village was enchanting. We gave each other a massage and enjoyed the hot tub. All I wanted was to find a place to create a home.

We spent a week in Sedona. The red mountains were astounding, but I did not want to live on a highway! So we drove north to Santa Fe to meet Rhea and Gawain, Shanti's friends. They offered us an annex cottage to their house, in the outskirts of town. It was sweet and cozy. We landed there, getting acquainted with the town, exploring the hot springs with fresh snow on the ground. I turned thirty-eight a few days later.

Santa Fe was an attractive town, so we decided to stay. We rented a cozy house, three bedrooms and a living room absolutely empty! After spending a few nights on a camping mattress on the floor, we were faced with the need to go shopping!

Our new station wagon got to be useful! Everyday we headed out into a shopping spree, gathering what we needed to create a simple home. The day the first truck arrived with furniture, Shanti went to bed in a state of shock! My gypsy soul choked, looking at the deliverymen carrying two large oak desks into our office.

Finally we had a beautiful home, and I started to enjoy this adventure. It was a new dance and we were stepping with uncertainty. I got exhausted driving to town, often getting lost on the highway.

We had enough cash to relax. I bought a Mac and plunged into computer self-education. Soon I started producing flyers and brochures for bodywork sessions and dance classes.

I spent hours digging a garden in our courtyard. The earth was hard and the rabbits loved the herbs and flowers. However, I diligently watered them to a successful result! A few cactus and local plants composed a sweet patch of vegetation that we could see from our desks. In spite of hungry rabbits, my first garden grew strongly!

One year later, we moved to an adobe house bordering a national forest, on top of a hill teeming with rose quartz crystals on the ground. There I created another garden decorated with lively pink rocks.

Our time in Santa Fe was underlined by a sense of inner rebalancing, retreat, reconsideration, wondering, camping trips, daily walks into the hills, rarely seeing or spending time with others. Our relating and the need to find inner-outer directions was priority. Our intimacy grew in a more practical way. We had a lot of free time and loved being in nature. We talked about our possible choices, desires, and dreams, while learning to relate to the newness of the situation.

Fourteen years had passed since I had a home with Derek, and I was again in a "small family" situation with a different awareness. I loved living with Shanti. Our collaboration was sweet and affectionate, sincere, with bumps here and there, mostly caused by our insecurity, not knowing what way to go, how to direct our boat in high seas.

Sometimes I missed our sannyasin family, but occasionally friends came for a visit from Europe and India.

Our time in Sweden had been an intermediate phase, where the connection with others was still based in collaboration. Now we were alone, and not yet grounded in a pragmatic setting. Was our love and mutual support enough to sustain our continuous expanding and unfolding? Did it happen anyway, beyond places and people? It was not easy to shift gears from the fulltime assistance and encouragement that we had for many years, both from the sangha as well as from Osho, to the desert of America rush-rush dream. How to find balance and nurturing in the midst of it?

We sat silently every day, and our time in nature reminded me of communion and beauty.

Making love was my deepest meditation, where my limitation and fears were bathed with the reminder of softness, expansion and trust. I continuously related to sex as a sacred pathway to the innermost core. We were both dedicated to use this avenue with awareness to express our love and nurture our bodies. Receiving Shanti's energy inside my body was a conscious opportunity to remember the space of merging and silence where issues naturally dissolved. I am sure we had divergent viewpoints and difficulties.

However, there is nothing that stayed in my memory, rather the growing consciousness of coming back to what was the most meaningful—the essence of love.

Santa Fe forced me to bow down to naked truth. The commune was gone and the master had dissolved into existence, nothing to look for out there. Either I would find silence and joy inside, or not at all.

A few new facets of Shanti's character came up by being in his home country, some pleasant, others not. I enjoyed meeting his family on a trip to Missouri, where he grew up. I observed how some of his qualities branched out of his parents, and learned to appreciate his beauty and intelligence in a different way. I could also better understand some of his difficulties and reactions. From being two nomads, with no–history to be remembered, we started to integrate our past in a fresh way. Sometimes it was scary and confusing, others exciting and fun.

My mother came for a visit and the simplicity of our life opened another way for us to connect. We walked and cooked together, went shopping and spent time in front of the fireplace… She made a comment that touched me, as Dhyan and his girlfriend also stayed with us at the same time, and we had a loving time together. "I do not understand your choices, but it is clear that you live with friends who sincerely know how to love and be together. It is rare to find this!" I agreed.

Besides that, I was not sure of what else I had learned, after all! I felt like a cripple in a land of fast runners who often pushed me out of the way.

We decided to buy a house and learn the ins-and-outs of real estate. Neither of us had previous experience in purchasing houses. I had my father's sense for good business opportunities, and soon spotted a few possibilities, but I did not have the courage or the clarity to stand by my intuition. It was senseless to live in a small suburban house with my lover, and have to work to pay a mortgage for the next thirty years. I had experienced the fire of life in a spectacular way and could not settle for less! Shanti was not clear either, more inclined to move into the countryside and create a retreat center with gardens and space for other friends to join us. We placed bids for a few houses and lost them all for different reasons. We were not ready for that chapter.

A year later, my money came to an end and the need to deal with financial issues in a different way was emotionally demanding. My work was valued within a context of meditation, healing and interest in individual inquiry. I was used to 100% commitment and totality. The collective in America had a different approach to spirituality and personal growth. I started offering weekly groups in movement awareness, as a gentle way to introduce myself to the community. While there were discussions and talks, there was interest… However, as soon as we dove into experiencing, the interest vanished!

I dropped the groups, and kept offering individual sessions in a private practice and at Ten Thousand Waves Spa. I had bought a Wrangler Jeep and felt more like a modern cowboy in wonderland, plowing through a foot of snow to go to work! As Shanti still had means to relax at home, I found it difficult to have to work while he was enjoying a nice walk!

Home was the place where our intimacy got nourished, where a few friends would come to share a meal, where we would cuddle in stormy nights, where we relaxed, content with each other.

We kept some work commitments in Europe, a few weeks a year in Sweden and Switzerland. In the winter, we spent a few months at Sajeela's resort near Tulum. Our European clients loved coming to a sunny spot during the winter. Vasant and Sumati, who were still living in and out of India, joined us for a program we called "Inner Holidays."

INNER HOLIDAYS

Today is the day to play with my friends, lovers, brothers, sisters, the ones who feed the fire of my heart. Cloudy and deliciously cozy, I hang out inside my cabana. Hasty wind and wild ocean...

I close my eyes.

My fish nature is joyful snorkeling. My body enjoys the waters. Time to let the sky enter through the top of my head, allow the ocean to invade my eyes and the immense space around dissolve the lines of my self-image. Deep rest.

Past experiences and ideas have been blasted, stabbed. Just the sun and the ocean are enough! In this simplicity, the mind still interferes. I don't try to stop it. It talks its languages, it is boring and it is there.

I look at his photo smiling, playing an instrument. Osho's presence is in the air, in the waves, in the blue sky, in my body.

The heart doesn't understand all the changes and movements. It knows being simple. It doesn't need to learn any better. I listen to the heart. It asks me for explanations, but I can't explain. I ask it to be more patient, I don't have an answer. I have an impatient heart, and sometimes it complains. Why don't you just stay with no-questions, in the stillness of the empty space, the love that you know is within. I don't know. I forget. And sometimes, I cry.

Being in the Caribbean washes my soul, feeds my body with joy and tingling pleasure. I have no ambition. What else do I need? Nothing I want more than being in this pastel turquoise motion. Shanti does not rest as I do. He searches how to express.

KEEP WALKING

Sometimes I doubt the movement is necessary. Sometimes I see through the movement and know that I am only acknowledging what is already happening and letting the sway move me. The fine line is to realize the difference between desire and the ability to flow with the flow. To discern between determination that arises out of attraction and impulse that responds to the zephyr. To determine if I am trying to move a mountain, or if a cloud is carrying me across the sky.

Suddenly, there is no mountain.

Resting in trust of no-comparison. Perhaps the design of my life has a richness of its own, if I only wait to see the whole picture...

When I fully allow the movement to take me into the swirls of life, there is immense joy in my heart, ecstatic ballet of freedom, appreciation and grace. My body is uplifted by my heartbeat. Alone and together, no-one.

There is no ending to the journey. The storm may strike again and once more, another home. If I only leave the windows of my soul wide open.

Inside the womb... My body feels bigger than the body that is containing it. I may be a fetus of three or four months. My mother is anxious facing the possibility of a miscarriage.

I have no anchorage to the womb, to the earthiness of the body. I do not belong anywhere. I have no roots. I have to be stronger than my mother to stay alive. There is solid intention in my consciousness. It is important to be born through this woman. Relaxation means death. Tension is held in my cells with the spirit's determination to manifest in this body. I have to use my will power. I have to be as quiet as possible to retain the force of life, so tenuous...

I have carried this need to endure in order to survive since I can remember. The striving to complete, to understand, relationships, daily tasks, or creative projects, has been a theme in my life. I have found it difficult to express thoughts before embracing their full meaning.

A breakthrough: consciously letting the words come out, before having the full picture of what I wanted to say, no sense of a priori completion, letting sounds open the way, paving understanding. Profound relief.

The search for home; constant theme. It brings me inside, on and on. My heart-home is my compass. When love anchors my body to life, then I can share. I rest, as I may never find a place outside. The heart may be my only home, my connection with planet Earth.

I sense power coming from integrity, independent of whoever is around, overflow. It has no against attached. It simply is. I rest in the hammock singing quietly. Remembering my strength comes with softness, Komala.

I look at the tourmaline Shanti gave me a few years ago. It talks to my heart. "Listen to me... I will tell you everything you need to know. No matter how crazy others think you are. Keep moving in trust."

We spent two years in Santa Fe, learning to live between computers and highways, desires and true fulfillment, shopping malls and the wilderness.

Shanti and I moved into another level of partnership. From my side, a deeper understanding of his personality grew out of understanding his original conditioning and culture. And with that perception, the difference between our connection in personality and our connection in being became sharper. Whenever I realized that I was getting entangled or identified with issues of the surface personality, I moved to the depth, finding our meeting at essence. Sometimes that meant to drop arguing about some practical issue, or a decision we needed to make, or a detail of our work together. Others, it meant to simply look at him, be silent, penetrating the love in his eyes, allowing his being to explore what was needed in the moment, beyond my reactions and emotions. I started nurturing that awareness and making it stronger in my every day life with Shanti, and consequently with others.

Events, travels, relationships were reduced to my ability to stay present in alertness. Missing the point a hundred times and getting back on the horse as soon as I realized I have fallen... And again... And again...

LAND OF DREAMS

Living in America was challenging. It was difficult to work just for money, without the resonance of people who appreciated my fundamental nature, independent of my skills. I longed to go back to India. Shanti did not need to work for a living.

A few years passed and our landlord decided to sell the house we had been calling home. We felt the need to go into a formal retreat, using meditation to guide us further.

Considering different options, we booked for one-month silent *datun* at the Naropa Institute residential center, up in the mountains of Colorado. The place was set in the lineage of Chogyan Trungpa Rinpoche's teachings.

The location was magnificent, Tibetan-like in its extreme cold weather and extensive views of a mountain range covered with snow. We were lucky to have the only separate room, next to the large dormitory assigned for the other forty participants, set in a funky cottage that shrieked with the hard winds. We were delighted to have a door to close and be in the intimacy of our own space, and down comforter!

One month of silent sitting, with eyes open, shifted my understanding of meditation. Initially, having used meditation as an experience of recollection and refuge, I was forced to move onto the sharpness of awareness that came with staring at a wall for twelve hours a day. No possibility to withdraw or separate. Instead, this state of focused contemplation pushed my consciousness into the deeper nature of presence beyond inner and outer. The key quality of those days was acceptance: people coughing, dirty floors, judgments, ice-cold days and nights, reminiscences, ancient rituals incorporated into the daily schedule, all contributed to steady the mind trying hard to find a job, while the body, supported by a small pillow, remained still.

Having had previous specific training in accessing inner energy states that instantaneously transformed turmoil into bliss, I had certainly become attached to those pathways: the master, the sangha, silence. While experiencing new avenues leading to the same end-result, my mind was fighting by all means. However, time brings patience and patience brings letting go and letting go brings relaxation. I immersed myself in the adventure of watching no matter what, and suddenly the days flew with great sweetness. I fell in love with Chogyan's presence. Though he was no longer living in a physical form, I honored the resonance of his wisdom and compassion.

I valued even more the richness of the years with Osho, and the blessings of the commune life. At the same time, I was appreciative of this new perspective and graceful gathering.

By understanding yet another nuance of the works of the mind, my body and emotions relaxed into a lower gear, allowing the gaps to permeate the spaces in between thoughts, more and more often.

Upon our return to Santa Fe, we were ready to move to North Carolina, where we had been visiting a dear friend a few months before. Shanti had spent many summers there as a young adult and loved the land. I had appreciated the vastness of the Blue Mountains, but was not so sure about living in such a remote and conservative area.

Following Shanti's dream to create a space for our work in a beautiful environment, we packed our house and moved fast! My Jeep was sold the day before leaving and we caravanned a U-Haul truck and our red Toyota, arriving in Charlotte with the spring flowers.

FREEDOM

Returning to the USA had made it obvious that our journey was now solely inwards. We had each other to relate to, but our relationship with others was reduced to a minimum.

Our friendship and love were precious, more so in this circumstance of isolation. Facts, events, emotions, and ideas had less and less meaningfulness. The constant exercise in awareness and letting go was my priority. It was difficult for me to work and relate with people who had divergent core values. I constantly questioned my choice to be in America, though I was doubtless about being with Shanti. The stretch to accommodate both was intense. I ached for India. He had no intentions to ever go back. I tried my best to relax and learn new ways.

Following Shanti's dream to recreate a community of friends in a natural setting, we moved to Asheville in full blast springtime!

Our connection with nature had always been strong, and we set about exploring the forests, smelling rhododendrons, river rafting and camping as often as possible.

We organized our work in the format of a healing school. I remodeled a Victorian house in the center of Asheville, offered to us in a magical way by a friend. The place attracted other healing arts practitioners and soon our space was hosting a full program of individual sessions, events, classes and professional trainings.

Slowly I integrated what I had previously learned, with a new way to express and relate. Not exactly having fun, but at least, being less feisty when things were not exactly "my way."

Lani moved to Sedona a short while after we settled in Asheville. I still missed India. Many dear friends came to visit, and left...

During our first Color Therapy class, a stylish, rather gentle woman was present. We heard the day after that she had gone to the hospital after the class, in acute pain. She was diagnosed with terminal colon cancer, spread so widely that the doctor decided not to complete the surgery, giving her a few weeks to live. A mutual friend let us know that she had decided to go to the Bahamas to die and had sent us love.

A few months later I received a call from Julie. She was back from the Bahamas and alive! She had sensed us close in spirit during this time out, and wanted to reconnect. I was surprised and pleased.

For the next two years she came regularly for sessions and our friendship was dear. Having recently moved to town, she had no other friends, neither did I... Our time together was treasured for the uncertainty of her life, as well as for the reflections that it provoked. She chose not to have any medical treatments and simply enjoy her days with awareness and kindness. She did a good job!

I learned to just be with someone knowing that my skills could not possibly help her health situation, and yet healing was happening for both of us at a deeper and subtler level than the physical body. Regularly, we spent time together. Once in a while she would call and ask me to come to her house. She was feeling ready to leave her body and would like my company. I would drive to meet her, not sure that she would still be waiting for me. There she was! Delicate and joyful, fragile and strong, and we would talk or be in silence, sometimes have a meal together, as she suddenly got hungry!

Julie's sensitivity nurtured my soul. Her ability to stay present with pain and the issues that her debilitated health were forcing her to deal with was remarkable. Her grace was untouched by difficulties. Within one year, she bought a house and remodeled it, always kept a humorous and gentle approach to life, managed to go to India to visit her meditation master, and passed through acute phases of body weakness. One day I would see her ready to die, the next day she would walk into my office, smiling.

I questioned the value of my work and its directive. Shanti and I had created a comprehensive educational program for healing arts practitioners and we started to have students flying in from different parts of the country. That was more his dream than mine. It was difficult for me to relate to the American collective and the lack of commitment that most people I met had towards their inner life. In the struggle to find an interfacing language, I turned arrogant to compensate for my aloneness and to define my own space. Healing for me was only possible in the context of meditation, so I regularly sat quietly. I longed for meaningful meetings, truthful sharing. I only found it in the naked silence of the heart. I nurtured mine as I sat still.

With Shanti's encouragement I wrote my first book, a difficult task for a mind that used self-judgment relentlessly. But I followed through to its completion. It helped me to exercise my ability to interface and coordinate intention with communication.

I missed recognition without words, conveyed through sincerity in the eyes. I was impatient and sad, longing again for communion. Shanti was getting sick very often, and still traveling to Europe to work. My longing for mama India, made me book a flight and decide to follow my call to Pune once more.

Just before, we visited Sedona to participate in a meditation retreat with old friends. A taste of the unnamed rekindled my heart. Sweet taste in my tongue…

LIVING THE RAINBOW

The Lufthansa flight is crowded.

Traveling to India had always been beatitude in anticipation. This time I am coughing, anxiously. Disquiet, I am sad to leave Shanti.

Reliving the *sati* burning in the funeral pyre. The pain of separation strokes me in real flesh. Past lives of sublimation are converted in bodily sensations. Successive images stroll through my inner vision.

Reaching my side, an Indian woman with her children. Her hands, such softness. Ah! I remember… I suddenly lie back, and slept as soon as the plane took off.

Bombay airport, the same the same… A long line, stink of old pee on the walls, red-eyed travelers, two am. HOME! How can that be! I am so fussy while living in America, tightness and cleanliness above all, no spots on my clothes! Here I don't bother, disgusting garbage, chaos. In a few minutes my pants are stained. Who knows from what! Who cares anyway?

The man at the computer receives each newcomer without lifting his eyes from the desk. Tcheebum! Stamp! Tcheebum! Stamp! Endless-monotonous-sound-of-bureaucracy. Maybe fifty people before my turn. I watch. To my surprise, this Indian officer suddenly stretches his neck to look at me. "Welcome sister! You have been here many times… Welcome!" He nods his head in a typical fashion. I have a new passport with no stamps from anywhere in it! How did he guess?

Taxi to Pune, Puja is waiting for me at her apartment. Joy in meeting a dear friend, no time in between.

Crickets, still dark, early morning, jetlag and the deliciousness of being a bit groggy as I hear the sounds of life waking up, voices, birds, wind on the trees…

I write with a candle by my side. Reflection and reconsideration. How to expose the subtleties of my sensitivity and intelligence? Can I risk making mistakes, not knowing if there is a direction at all, but simply envisioning and opening?

I hear Puja saying to her beloved: I have money in the bank, my work for the next year is booked out, come with me, I will take care of you for the rest of our lives. Woman's way—total.

I am surprised, as her words touch me… I wish to hear this assurance from Shanti. I am tired of having to provide for my needs. And I am ashamed to recognize that I would like to receive support! The vulnerability of asking for help, and the fear of not getting it, is in my body. I feel the human need for cooperation, and appreciate the quality of love becoming earthy. I become gentler with myself and with Shanti, sensing his needs as real as mine.

Once more I look at the male-female balance, within myself and between us. I miss being more feminine. The American lifestyle pushes for action, decisions, speed, goals. Difficult for me to follow its pace, I have no interest in achievements. The ambition, greed, and violence in the collective constantly stir my reactions, making me cry. I am uneasy, my body retracts, and my creativity withdraws. I have been beat up trying to get it together. I needed to escape and hide to reevaluate.

I write daily to undress the mind, and sit in silence to recharge the heart.

I look at my relationship to work and money. I cannot separate work from love. I work when I am in love. My life force expresses itself and crystallizes around it.

I can see my suffering in comparison. I have not mastered this dance yet. Fear, fight, anger, resentment spin inside. I catch myself thinking, "If someone would take care of me, then I would not need to feel this pain and fight inside..." Interesting! It is difficult to recognize my own expectations, needs, and feelings. Instead, the easy way out is to judge, demand or resent. The greatest challenge move through density without getting heavy or knocked down.

India embraces, soothes, forgives. It is important for me to bring this back home—self-acceptance.

I am crying... I want to be loved with no conditions, no limitations, no control.

Looking at my fear of dependency, reacting against my mother's choices, I acknowledge the vulnerability necessary to receive love. I am often cautious, reassuring myself that there are no strings attached to what is given to me, no demands. Senseless, when I do have constant demands on myself. Deep breath!

Unwinding and unfolding...

Money represents flowering and gifting, as well as control and a way to set values. From one hand comes heartfelt generosity, and from the other comes restraint and manipulation. This double message is broadcasted in the collective and I am provoked by its duality. In trust, I relax; in demand, I feel imprisoned and under pressure. Can I step out of this painful game?

While here, taking advantage of rest and meditation, I can allow this layer of conditioning to dissolve into consciousness of receptivity, so that when the challenges are again in my face, new responses may surface.

I love early mornings in India, flavor of sweetness and pale colors. The parrots are singing loudly. Light is coming behind the trees and I can see the river at a distance... I remember my first hut here.

A Kinetic Honda makes my comings and goings easier. Fun!

Balance is the constant challenge, the learning. India brings the moon shining in my heart, cooling and refreshing.

Life is plain and full in this simplicity. No doing, no schedule.

Time spent in the sauna, swimming in the pool, receiving massages, watsu, silent sittings at Osho's samadhi, walking through the park in between tall bamboos and tropical flowers. Water running, Osho's presence in the air, peaceful stone Buddhas placed here and there, alive Buddhas moving around.

When I do eventually go to discourse, I hear Osho in a fresh way, as if for the first time. I savor each word. I have received his being through my heart and soul, now I appreciate his intelligence. Penetrating like an intravenous injection, his love circulates through my brain.

Nothing I have to do, sort out, change, or look at. The lightness of being is knocking at my door. Come in! Welcome!

Though I do not "fit" in the lifestyle of the commune as years before, I am at home. I see some friends shining and others holding on. I see myself in the same light of contradictions. Even in the midst of the extreme pollution, aggravating poverty, unimaginable busyness and noise, the atmosphere inside the commune is clean and light. I walk around feeling rich and unconfined, genuinely relaxed. At the same time it is easy to be outside, deal with Indian life, order a jacket, talk with a tailor, buy food and ride my bike in between lots of new cars, rickshaws and buffaloes crossing the roads.

Puja shared with me a letter from her father. I was touched by his sincerity, care, responsibility and love. And I was jealous, wishing to have had the same from my father, knowing that I may never have it. I felt how Puja's relationship to work and grounding reflects her father's energy and earthiness, and how my life choices were still tinted by my father's personality and lack of care. I learned to compensate for his emotional absence with self-sufficiency. Knowing that I might not be given, why bother asking? Knowing that I might get disappointed, why bother expecting? Knowing that the outer source did not offer support, or provide for my needs, I learned to create for myself, dig into my inner resources. This process gave me great confidence and ability to use my qualities with enormous flexibility and courage, and at the same time has made it difficult for me to receive support from others, and even more difficult to ask for it. The years living with Osho in the commune provided deep healing and merging of this emotional pattern. I was showered with love and encouragement and care, beyond my ability to hold back from it.

Here, I connect again with the restfulness of total surrender, however with a different sense of discrimination and direction. The mind compares and prefers, the awareness that has been growing inside leaves it loose. I do not know. My mind says... If I decide to return to the USA, I will be missing again an opportunity to dedicate my life to the bliss of the inner. Who cares about creating and doing anything? I identify these voices as the mind's bits and pieces, and consider the choice of integrity as choicelessness. I wait for movements to arise spontaneously.

I observe the flow between old friends still living here, how easy it is to relate beyond the details of personalities, focusing on the bigger picture, leaving the trivialities in the background, or to be faced with in groups and meditation. Living in America, I am on the other shore; dealing with others in an individualistic way, relating to details and personalities, including my own…

India's timelessness settles in.

I met my dear Indian friend Jyoti for chai and cookies at her room. A bed and a table next to it, more than enough… I look into her eyes and we both have tears. The purity of this love has no need for words. I delight in her soft voice, in her simplicity, her devotion, warmth that comes from her body as we hug for long minutes. Eternity in a cup of chai. What a blessing to touch this tenderness. The spirit of India is the mystery of love. I know it deep inside, with pain, with bliss, with longing, with contentment, in silence, in song, in dance… This mutual recognition is priceless and only tears speak for. How can this ineffable sweetness be perceived by minds that want to grab, to grasp? No way!

I write to Shanti… Sweet love, tonight I danced with you in Buddha hall. My feet were light and my head loose, my hair flowing with the music. Innocence and pleasure… Surprised to open my eyes and look at strangers. Where are you? So close and far away…

More spaciousness inside Komala. I look at the lotus flowers floating in the small pond in the garden. I have no sense of how long I have been here. I love you.

Dreams of being pregnant. Yes, I am pregnant. Letting my belly expand… Followed by a dream of marriage.

As I wake up I sense that the part of me that fights with Shanti and with living in America, suddenly relaxed. Accepting limitations, his and mine and others, as a way to move inwards. Projections melting within, returning to the source. Self-contained life force brings integrity and roundness. I have used Shanti's love to avoid being with my own difficulties. My appreciation for him increases.

Nothing can be done about the past. I may have missed the point, learning, waking up… Now I review in response and awareness.

Sedona resonates as the foundation for the next step, as a platform for a new level of integration and creativity. Yet there is a sense of cautiousness, not to dream, not to expect.

I connect with Shanti sitting alone everyday. The significance of continuity jolts my mind. In my heart rests the prospect of maturity, the awareness of continual renewal. When the outer is used as aim, or direction, the potential of love is dispersed. When the outer becomes conscious container, the richness of our well becomes heart-felt. I have longed for that and now I perceive the fear… Fear of no-excuses, fear of responsibility. I remember my father, constantly looking for fulfillment outside, missing the dimension of contentment within.

During the last years living with Shanti, this sense of inner renewal became clearer. I have anchored in my love for him to allow the changes sweep through my personality, crystallizing what never changes. My dedication to him is a commitment to myself. I keep rekindling aliveness of heart, disregarding what I may want to cling to, noticing hesitation, and letting freshness gush in. He is my beloved. Not always easy, but the determination of soul intention gets more compelling and resilient.

We are very different, and through these differences I learn to respect our uniqueness sustaining each other to move with our individual needs, even when it means to be apart.

Our energies dance in constant rearrangement of forms and balance, one way or another challenging both of us to find our own movements and guidance. As we separate and come together, we establish trust and coziness, allow for daring and breaking through...

I wonder if what I call love is a neurotic hankering for the latent potential I perceive, nothing but a ghost of intuitive hunch that cannot be grasped or realized. As I get attached to its enchanting vaporous quality projected into the future, I escape present time, and keep missing what is real in the moment. Can I stumble back and accept the imperfection of life as love itself?

Relating certainly involves distortion of reality, as needs, desires, and projections jump into actions before I can notice their grip. Exactly thus, they offer a wondrous opportunity to discern, disengage, expose, break through.

I observe my hopes and fears disguising what is in front of my eyes. I watch my mind justifying my inability to take responsibility for my life. Sometimes I do know "nothing happens" from the very beginning. Sometimes I get lost, entangled in the appearances of happenings. Slowly I learn to discriminate and use both perceptions.

My body answers with sensuality, passion, and stillness. My pores are open and light shines through my eyes and skin. The water-like quality of the commune erases questions in the air.

Self-forgiveness, self-acceptance. I sit alone. Money and work. Pretty basic! I focus on asking for what I want with clarity and yet, staying open to what may come my way. I acknowledge needs that arise out of integrity, rather than desire, dreams and expectations. My misunderstandings are painful.

I wake up quiet, in a vague state. My daily writing digs into the dormant aspects of my being.

No sense of protection, no energy to direct or interfere. Bliss is substituted by a soft sparkle of presence within, invisible.

Outside my window the monkeys run up and down the trees.

On the streets I walk with grace. Absurd combination of poverty and wealth. Faces that shine innocence, beyond the hunger of their bodies, need for shed and amenities. The poverty I encounter in America is far more haunting than what I perceive here. It is the distress of buried souls, bodies barely alive...

"Beloved Shanti, your fax brings me your love and care. I read it several times, distilling subtle nuances. I notice the differences of our styles. I get caught in the expectation of "meaningful," intimate comments and you respond with the basics of life. My romantic Scorpio gets provoked. I notice this mechanism and stay with your love, noticing the differences in form, connecting with the essence.

My intimacy with no-references becomes absurdly obvious in this Indian context. The vibe in the air is enough nourishment. I eat little and feel full. My emotions have space to come and go without pressures. In the West the mystery is denied so vehemently that my reactions are stronger, trying to break through.

As I relax, I cherish our differences for the insights they offer. Thank you for being my partner in this learning love."

"I am not this or that enough... I missed here... I could have done better..." Exhausting inner voices... I listen without engaging. The essence matters, the form is irrelevant.

I am content doing nothing. Refreshing spontaneity. Can I nurture this inner space in the West where appreciation and appraisal, as well as financial reward, are related to form and results?

I am invited to drive to Manali with friends. Tempting. However, my call is to learn unconditional freedom of spirit, beyond circumstances that naturally attune my heart in meditation... It is not time to escape to the mountains. I want rest in silence in the midst of America's buzz. I decided to return to North Carolina for Shanti's birthday.

I wonder how can I "ever" forget this easiness? It is absolute when it is there, and evasive when clouded by the mind.

The enchantment of India cannot be described. It can only be experienced, sniffed, touched, tasted from within. My spirit is wild and the doors to magic are wide open.

Did I come all the way here just to sleep late and hang out listening to the birds? I keep it simple, just because I do not know any better. Letting go of the expectation that something great should/needs to happen. A meaningful insight, a great decision, or a wondrous creative act! That would then justify my trip here... Nothing to be justified.

I have expressed my male side through the female, and recently this seems to be reversing, coming to find a balance from the other side. Letting the female express through the male is difficult.

Yesterday reading about Rajasthan and warrior rajputs. When there was no more hope of winning a war, the rajputs (princes of Rajasthan) made an agreement with the enemy and prepared for their last battle. They were sure to lose and get killed. So, it was decided that all the women and children would be sacrificed together by walking into an enormous funeral pyre. Princess Padmini led the walk into the fire as her warrior prince left to war. In 1303 the greatest battle was lost. I remember my body burning for love and dignity.

I let the flames burn this memory within. Interesting to find out that the houses in Rajasthan were made out of adobe, a type of construction so familiar to me. I went to sleep with these colors and images dancing inside.

"I do not belong…" a familiar feeling. Pune, the only place I ever belonged. Now I am a guest, a stranger. India, mama land… Soft night, gentle rain, sweet smell of flowers and earth and musk…

No special moments. I could easily take another year off. Simply listening to the body, letting it do what it wants to do, cooking, eating, walking, hanging out in this funky apartment.

I look at myself in the mirror and recognize my eyes when I first arrived here in 1979. Light shining through…coolness…peace rekindled.

Connecting with Shanti evokes sweetness and freshness.

The day before leaving. Bowing down in Buddha Hall after evening discourse. The music in my ears… There is so much magnificence near the ocean…waves are coming in…waves are coming in… My heart is silent. There is no completion. Life seems to be revealed in waves.

Nowadays, people ask: Are you still a sannyasin?

How could I drop my commitment to life? Osho was a link to the infinity inside. As I am able to merge with it, he also disappears within.

I do not like to use the word "sannyas," or any other expression that defines, therefore creates separation, establishes status, or binds life into outlines. Useful as it was at the right time, its meaning is lost when it becomes a hindrance. A human being seems to be a canvas that keeps perpetually being sprayed with colors and impulses. Our infinitude is invariably surprising if we do not establish limitations through dogmas, names, classifications, or roles.

I returned to Bombay with Greek Mukta. We hired a Maruti van to take us to the airport. Ironically, the driver moved the back seat on the opposite direction to give us more leg space; this meant going to Bombay "backwards!" We both gagged, but there was no time to change it. A lunghee over the back window blinded the view of the traffic coming towards us at high speed, over the curvy road down the mountain. We arrived safely in Bombay.

Shanti picked me up at the airport and we went straight to a camping site near a beautiful waterfall. Earlier in the day, he had set up our tent with nice bedding, food and what we might need for a few days. His love and care welcomed me. Being outdoors in this gorgeous spot was delightful. The weather shift, however, provoked body reactions and I got sick. Days lying in the sun, listening to the water running…

Julie was still alive and happy to see me again.

Following a series of coincidences, we were offered a large estate to live further from the center of Asheville, in a small town called Black Mountain. I loved that area, wilder, quite remote and populated by magnificent forests.

Our new home was interestingly designed by an inventive architect, with pyramid ceilings, lots of glass and several cottages for possible guests, sitting on a few hundred acres, surrounded by six hundred acres of national forest. Bears were seen in cold nights, many wild animals and the two of us in retreat.

I planted tulips, we walked in the wilderness regularly, received a few friends as guests for days or months, continued to teach courses and work in our healing center in town. We hardly spent time with anybody else, and I forgot about India... Driving in the highway, sometimes I was surprised to feel content in the midst of traffic!

Just after New Year, we prepared to leave for working commitments in Sweden and Holland. Prior to our departure, we had dinner at Julie's. She was vibrant and active, having prepared a gourmet meal for about twelve people. Her house had been completely remodeled. As we hugged to leave, she said, "I am ready to make a shift. Either my body heals, or I will leave it soon. I love you!"

Two years had passed since we first met.

We flew to Sweden, and I got sick. Delirious with high fever and intense pain, I could hardly open my eyes; no clue of time, day and night being grey anyway. Shanti kindly took care of my needs, sometimes food at four in the morning! I connected with Julie, sensing her readiness to leave her body through my own body's struggle. Two weeks later, weak and delicate, I stood up to present my course not sure of the boundaries of my body and mind.

Our days weaved between the group room, warm meals, and long walks over the frozen lake or the snowy forest surrounding the property. The majesty of the silence and purity of air made me connect with the Northern spirit in a new way. Such fineness of perception facilitated inspiration for writing, and in the darkness of my free hours I completed a book on Color Light Therapy. My sensitivity to the subtle bodies was intensified and tingling with insubstantial sensitivity.

At the end of our season, we flew to Holland for shopping and friends. From there I took a train to Koln to visit Digambar. The day before we were due to leave, I got sick again, nothing that I could define, but sharp pain in my belly. I curled in bed for a day. My mind was off, I was quiet and waited until the pain subsided.

As we entered our home in Black Mountain, the phone was ringing. A friend announced that Julie had left her body a few days before, in the midst of a strong snowstorm. She was alone at home with a friend and sat in meditation until the last breath.

An outburst of tears, and yet sunlit. Light as Julie's presence was, her kindness dancing around me. I knew then that my time in North Carolina was related to our connection.

During our last session, I had asked her why she was still hanging on to the body, so sick then. She looked at me softly and said, "I am still learning to love. I know well what spiritual love is, but to love one human being totally requires much more than letting go in meditation. I do not fully understand the ways of human love and acceptance. I will stay around until I learn this..." We followed up by talking about our meeting as sisters in Rajasthan, lifetimes ago. The familiarity with which we both described precise details was both natural and unexpected. We kept talking as if time had not passed since then.

My sister was dead. Shanti's father was also on the verge of dying. Another cycle seemed to be rounding out.

We visited Sedona together for a few weeks. Lani and Kavyo hosted us in their lovely home. More friends were settling there. The environment of collaboration in meditation talked to my soul. The power of the red rocks talked to me seductively.

While Shanti visited his father in Missouri, I returned home.

Julie's husband came for a visit and gifted me with some of her clothes. I preferred to make a ceremonial fire rather than use them. Alone on our property, I gathered large logs and lit a fire to dance with her. I was saying goodbye to my dear friend, as well as to the forests and the rivers and the land that had offered us grounding.

Our decision to move to Sedona became clear. Within a few days I found someone to take over our lease, passed on the management of our Sammasati Healing Center, and hired a moving company to gather our belongings, now filling up a forty-foot truck!

Shanti's father died that spring and we drove to Sedona, via Florida and the southern states.

The landscape shifting outside, and our connection more stable inside. I wanted to settle and stop traveling. I wanted to have my own home and rest in a different way.

Isness

Pressure to create "something." I need quietness.

Flowers grow out of my inner music. I need time to listen. I am invaded by blazing energies that burn what is essential. Simplicity.

Ready to move. Internal push and pull does not allow a step in any direction. Waiting for the harmony that comes when the wheel of life is moving me. "I" cannot choose.

Experiences of emptiness have left nothing to comment upon. What is without words, nobody there to grasp it, these moments have faded away. I starve for them. My body aches. I am impatient.

I hide in my protection cave laughing and crying with the ghosts. Touching silence where the heart dances, where light always shine. I want to go back to doubtless.

A dream... Osho is sitting on a rock in front of the ocean. He invites me closer. I ask him to dissolve my fears and doubts. He giggles. Slowly, he catches a fisherman's net and gives it to me. I bring my hands together, as if dropping something inside it. He knots the net at the top and magically picks up some balloons from nowhere, many colors, and attaches them to the net. He looses the grip and the wind takes it away over the ocean. We both smile.

He gives me a pebble from the beach. It is a round white pebble. I open both hands to receive it. He dips both of his hands into the water and splashes me with salty water. I laugh, raw in my belly!

He says, "Remember the ocean." I bow down.

GROUNDING ON THE ROCKS

The red rocks welcomed us.

Anand moved into town at the same time. It was joyful to have such a dear friend in my life again. Together we found a lovely house to rent, spacious enough for the three of us. Anand transformed the garage into a pottery studio, his main activity. The house was full of light, tastefully done, wondrous views. I was ready to settle.

There were about twenty friends living in Sedona and gathering for evening meditations at Av's house. I was comfortable in an environment geared by the commitment to growing awareness and inner reflection. Creativity, expansion and relaxation were keys.

These evenings carried the seeds of Osho Academy. Kaveesha grounded its creation with the loving support of Av, Yogi, Wadud and Waduda. She had been with Osho since the early days in Pune One and Osho Academy expressed her particular vision of his light and presence. Her devotion for the master transmitted his teachings in an experiential, down-to-earth way.

This account only translates my perceptions and in no way intends to convey or explain Osho Academy activities and guidelines. It describes how I benefited and learned during my participation in its evolvement.

During the following years, we were involved in the activities of the Academy from various angles: daily meditations, working in different businesses that were being created such as a vegetarian restaurant, a gift store, and a health food store; as well as participating in classes and trainings. Within the context of work and relating, Kaveesha proposed several experiments with the intention to bring Osho's teachings visible in matter-of-fact ways. Meditation was used as a bridge between inner and outer aspects of life on planet Earth. Synchronicity at heart was the link between us. The master was the magician, showering fairy dust over Highway 89 A. As "students" of Osho Academy, we were learning to translate his light into matter, American style.

Each of our experiments, some lasting for over a month of focused awareness on one subject or aspect of our inner world, had a profound impact in my life. Any attempt to go into details would take away their significance. Their impact resulted from the dedication and totality of the participants, and the love that underlined our connection.

I plunged into this new phase without reservations and transformation of consciousness became obvious in my daily life and choices. Kaveeha's heart, joy, passion, and straight-to-the-point remarks were unique and constantly inspiring. My experiences and understanding of previous years in India and at the ranch, suddenly crystallized beyond duality. Geographical location lost meaning as awareness turned meditation into action. East and West merged inside.

Shanti had reservations about the structure and demands of the Academy, and continued to go to Europe regularly for his work. I took a break from traveling, and stayed in Sedona. I was content.

We moved through different phases. I focused on investigating the layers of emotional projections, and love as a path of meditation. Julie's comments on human love had left a profound impression and influenced small decisions in my daily life. Cutting through trivia became easier and faster. The wealth of intelligence and love shared in the context of meetings, silent sittings, intimate sharing, subtle energy trainings and working as a team, provoked irreversible shifts.

I kept writing as an exercise of self-observation, recognizing that I had a bright mind and it needed to be used as much as any other muscle. I remembered several past lives sitting in monasteries learning to tame thought forms, strengthening the idea that the mind was the enemy of spirituality. I had been trained to practice meditation as a skill to destroy the mind, believing that its use would make a human being less prone to achieve freedom. I had developed a sword-like ability to kill thoughts as fast as I wanted to avoid them and protect "silence."

During a meditation retreat where we focused on watching the conditioning we carried about meditation itself, my warrior approach suddenly was blown away. I experienced that the appropriate use of the mind actually made me free of it faster. Its misuse, yes, perpetuated stubbornness and repetition, enchaining the spirit within its false limitations.

Letting go of that strong belief freed energy for other creative projects, as well as invited me to use my intelligence with more discrimination. Another separation dissolving, and less desire to go anywhere.

Relaxing in Sedona, I faced the relentless challenges of life in America, and yet was learning not to get disturbed by them.

Shanti and I continued to spend time outdoors often; camping trips and long walks were still our preferred activities.

The richness of life was independent of facts and events, becoming more delicate, in the moment, subtler, and sweeter.

Shanti was traveling. I had a vision. Keops. Egypt.

A vast open field, a strong light. It was not very hot. Greenery and a pyramid far away.

I was learning to use my voice to transform sound frequencies into light. This was a secret teaching that could only be transmitted through psyche power. I fell into absolute stillness. My body lost solidity. I had no sense of matter connecting with it or anything else around.

I rested on the ground and everything within my field of perception was spinning. It was ecstatic to feel this convergence into magnetic force. I could see 360 degrees around and far away without moving at all. My body and my eyes were transfixed. I was dizzy but fully awake. Colors and lights speeded in a sequence of random nuances.

I knew I would be called back. Suddenly someone touched my shoulder. I realize I was in another time. It was a friend, a quiet man, dressed elegantly with a hat and a long cape, grey suit. He gave me his hand and we walked side by side. We were in Milan, medieval. The town was still spacious. We were inside a gallery or a church. It was square and large. We walked around looking at a sequence of paintings on the walls, they told the story of Jesus from birth to death. Impressive images, real, invoking strong feelings, sensuous. We walked out of this gallery and arrived at a huge garden. Suddenly I was alone again.

The experience in Egypt was with me as a secret that I couldn't share. I understood that I had learned to shift my consciousness in time, using sound and colors as a vehicle.

I was looking forward to meet Shanti. We traveled in time through so many landscapes…

THE UNEXPECTED

Neharika had visited us a few times in Santa Fe and Black Mountain. Now we were living closer and met more often. It was not a surprise when the phone rang and I heard her voice. Strong news! She had felt a malaise and had difficulty moving her arms, so she went for a checkup, finding a large tumor in her brain. A renowned brain surgeon had given her a few weeks to live, or as an alternative a surgery that was not sure to be successful. She opted for a trial and was going to the hospital the next day. She was calling to say goodbye, in case she did not make it. She was calm, confident and always firm in her love for us. "Don't worry, honey! I would like you to be present when I am ready to graduate. I will be back."

She did. But in the months to follow we visited her several times at her home in Los Angeles between surgeries and treatments. Our meetings were even more treasured, as the urgency and frailty of her body were evident. Nothing less than the fullness of love was important. My awareness sharpened for all interactions with her and everybody else. I constantly asked myself, how can I allow more gentleness and care to flow through my actions and expressions? Another step into disregarding banalities and sticking to what mattered, learning to respect and love other human beings. My intention sharpened. It was no longer important to understand the issues, but in a flash, remember!

Our meditation hall was next to a brewery and yet set with pristine Zen esthetic. It served as our community meeting point at the end of the day, where we sat in silence, listened to Osho's discourses on video, and danced wildly. One evening, just before the formal meditation started, we came to know that one of our friends had had an accident. His car hit a young couple on a motorbike coming at high speed from the opposite direction. They hit head to head, and the couple died instantaneously. Our friend was in shock and resting for the evening. We would celebrate the lives of this two unknown people with a dance at the end of the meditation. A strange sensation ran through my body... I saw the face of a woman, blond, lively, calling my name. She was about my age and her face was familiar. Suddenly I understood that she was dead—she was the woman in the accident! I danced with her, my body could not stop swirling, my eyes closed, her hands holding mine.

As I drove home, I shared this perception with Shanti. He listened quietly, and we went to bed early.

In the midst of the night I woke up abruptly. Himani Sun! The woman I saw earlier! I could not sleep any more.

259

The next day I was set to find out the identity of these two people. After inquiring, I met someone who had been close to her. Yes, it was Himani. She had been living in Sedona for a few years, and was ready to move to Australia to join her two sons, now young adults residing in Byron Bay. She left her body before meeting them again.

I walked to the top of a mountain and sat with her spirit. The unexpected was confirming its power, reminding me of life's mystery.

A few days later I talked to Kaveesha about this episode. We sat quietly in the wonder of its synchronicity.

Love

Sometimes the need to "say" something comes up, but there is not much I can put into words. All moves fast and fluidly. When the mind tries to hold-format, the boat is already somewhere else. It is more fun to ride with it.

Life is joyful, unpretentious, effortless. When Shanti is away, I enjoy my own rhythm; when he is home, we share a graceful, harmonious flow. Sometimes the mind whispers something "should" and I see myself behaving in a totally different way. Surprising! I laugh alone. My work is secondary, as usual, and is determined by the needs of the community and my willingness to be available. I am involved with several projects, each inviting creativity and skills in a different way. My liquid quality contrasts with the desert, arid landscape. Sometimes the dryness and extreme heat draw the juice of my emotional body. However, the ocean of friends compensates the environment.

Long-term internal wires seem to have been disconnected. Occasionally I am confused because preferences, priorities, opinions, even feelings don't make any sense. What I used to call love as a force motivating my movements, choices, and reactions, isn't there now. I cannot say I love anyone. I am open, vulnerable, able to listen, receptive to Shanti's presence and care. What I call love now is more like a breeze, a gift I am learning to receive, nothing I can hold or catch, give or define. Deeper there is softness and strength coming together, and such expansion! It is relaxing, dangerously gentle.

What I call love nowadays is rather an embracing that keeps extending and expanding boundaries, as it has none. It is inner awareness of my own life force; a presence that, like a huge swallowing mouth, absorbs pleasure and pain. Calm and intensity, passion and boredom, thoughts and feelings, today and yesterday, union and separation, logic and absurdity, beauty and ugliness, sincerity and lies. There is no difference. This love releases the other of all responsibility, irritates the mind with no doubts, makes the heart loose its emotional content, bursting its space, infinite, bringing a bottomless sense of freedom. Not comfortable, not romantic, not all pink. Yes, sometimes I want the illusion again, I want the beautiful images with no blur, and I want the words of understanding. Useless to want now... There is no way back.

No matter how the mind might want to justify or get a grip, it escapes and lets me stand alone, sometimes smiling, content in gratefulness, sometimes crying, painfully in gratefulness. That is what I call love these days.

Shifts in my sexuality occurred as I settled more truthfully into my feelings and body sensitivity. I recognized my ability to invite Shanti into ecstatic energetic spaces that sustained my soul's journey, but not necessarily his. It had been so since we first met, and with almost every man I had been with. I had observed this pattern as a deviation of true presence, respect, and receptivity. Yes, I was hooked into its enchantment. If that foundation was not there, then making love might be insensible, not so enlivening, or not so moving… Suddenly, this subtle manipulation dissolved. I was able to stay with what was happening between us, at each given moment, not enticing or creating a specific climate. This shift was strong for both of us. And yet, after a period of awkwardness and slight irritability, we moved into another layer of harmonization, honoring our bodies and hearts with more sincerity. The wild and the gentle, the playful and the silent, the silly and the profound, the young and the ancient, the intense and the subtle, the movement and the stillness, fused as we touched and merged with each other in realness.

THE UNESCAPABLE

January 1998. The phone rang past midnight. We were quietly hugging in bed. I knew it was Neharika. Katrina was on the phone, the doctor had just been at the house… Her voice was shaky, "Come, I don't know if you will make it on time. Can you leave now?" Neharika picked up the phone, "Hey honey! I will wait for you. Come soon!"

A few phone calls to the airlines, best was to drive… A call to Lani, who was promptly available to care for things in Sedona. We packed a small suitcase, not much brain to think about what we would need…

On the highway, eyes sleepy but focused. We counted on ten to twelve hours on the road, depending on traffic. Early morning, as the sun was coming up, our eyes were closing… We called Katrina, and Neharika was sleeping. We had a nap in a motel, and drove the last bit.

Arriving in Los Angeles in the morning, I heard Neharika's voice from the entrance. I was glad to find her still alive and conscious. I loved her in a truly special way.

She was sitting in bed, a big smile as soon as she looked at us. She resembled an old Tibetan monk, almost no hair, prominent cheekbones; her eyes were firmly shiny, kind and intense… Her presence was full and expanded. I sat on her bed, touching her fragile hands. My beloved friend was ready for farewell!

Neharika's apartment was impeccable, spacious, bright, quiet, surrounded by large trees, elegantly decorated. She had upholstered her dining room chairs with iridescent pastel green silk, a gorgeous touch! A few objects, plants, and a sense of peace enhanced by two magnificent cats. A friend had sent her a jasmine tree in blossom; its delicate perfume exuded, especially when the breeze came in stronger.

Katrina was her caretaker. Five or six friends were alternatively fulltime around her. Others, coming and going… Neharika did not seem to be concerned with the buzz around. She still had energy to discuss practical details. For a few days we sat together most of the time. At night she would request everybody to leave the house, and ask us to stay in her bedroom. Katrina shared this invitation. We helped her when needed, cooked food for guests and laughed together, saying goodbye in unconventional ways.

I do not remember eating much, but sipping tea all day long. Sleep was also forgotten. Maybe on the third night, she said, "I am not quite ready yet…. Why don't you take a rest, go to sleep with Julianne, where you can rest comfortably…" Considering that we were both extremely tired, good idea! We drove to our friend's house, and fell into bed after a long shower. In seconds, the phone rang! Neharika was asking us to go back, she was ready to go!

We were eight friends sitting around her. Neharika was wide-awake. She took time to look into each one's eyes while we sat in silence. Different emotions… She focused with each person, a special goodbye, sometimes solemn, sometimes funny, overwhelming love. She looked into my eyes and spoke slowly. "Honey… I love you soooo much! It is ridiculous!" We both laughed and cried. Neharika was fearless in her love, bold in her generosity, no holding back. No push and pull, no give and take. She embodied the spaciousness of flow in both directions.

A few hours passed, and we were waiting. Suddenly she sat upright, "I guess it is not happening, I am not going anywhere yet. You can go home!" We drove back and slept soundly.

Each day, she was getting physically weaker. Her spirit was soaring in freshness and time had no meaning. The following days, I slept on a chair next to her bed, switching with Shanti who was resting on a large pillow on the floor.

The last night was obvious. Subtle signs were noticeable. Her body was ready to be released.

As we settled in her bedroom for the night, Lani called me from Sedona. Kaveesha had been diagnosed with cancer and was flying to Los Angeles the next morning to follow up with treatments at a local hospital. I was in awe. In the background of my mind, I expected my life to return to an uneventful pace as soon as Neharika would leave. The last year with her had been full of surprises, mostly not pleasant. I was looking forward to take a break from intensity and fragility. However, Lani's call set the tone for another round.

As I returned to the room, Neharika asked me to inform the doctor that she did not want to take morphine—she wanted to die consciously. Her bones were breaking with any slight movement, and it was difficult to turn her around in bed without hearing the cracking. She might have been feeling absurd pain, however she did not complain even when she could hardly breath. She was serene, still funny in her comments. I approached her daughter with her request, as she was her official caretaker. I was taken aback hearing that she was not willing to respect her mother's wish.

The doctor came in and turned the morphine drip on, without announcing his intention to Neharika. I was shocked, and in a split second had to make a decision: either to engage in judgments and actively react, or be with my friend, not matter where she would be going! I stayed with her.

She was brusquely confused, as the morphine hit hard and quickly. She closed her eyes in obliviousness. Her friends and family had left. Katrina, Shanti and I stayed in her room. I sat next to her for the whole night, listening to her gasping breath, not sure if the next one would still force space into her weak lungs. And one more… The expansiveness of our meeting during that night was something I had never experienced before. No backing off. I did not know if I would be there either, for the next in-breath. She carried me with her. It stretched my ability to stay alert, conscious of each minute sparkle of life in her body, as much as in mine. We were free floating in consciousness with no strings attached. She had asked me to be there for her graduation, and she had managed that! Katrina slept next to her in bed. Shanti was resting on the floor next to me.

At each breath we merged and became lighter, my awareness was moving into subtler layers, rarefied.

I had been visited many times by states of non-mind, bliss, empty-fullness. However, these fleeting moments had a vaporous quality. They left traces in my cells and sensorial memory. Neharika was etching my soul with luminosity. There was no forgetfulness during that night. She offered me her last gift—brilliance in freedom, multicolored layers of perception, brimming with remembrance.

At dawn, Shanti exchanged places with me. I lay on the floor as if floating. In a flash, I opened my eyes and sat straight up in one movement. Shanti was standing next to her using a color torch over her head with pink light. She gave her last breath...

We sat in silence until the morning light came into the room. I sat with her body for many hours alone, friends coming in and out. Stillness in mind and heart.

I understood that her desire to die consciously was attached to the idea of consciousness as physical-emotional-mental presence. Until then, I related to the same concept. This incident with the morphine forced me to move with her into another realm, beyond the body, beyond the heart, beyond the soul. Indescribable, unbounded joy of no-reference... I cried, laughed, grateful for this wondrous present.

A few days later we drove to Palm Springs. Staying at a simple bed and breakfast, we soaked in the hot springs under the moonlight. Shanti and I shared tears, and kindness with each other. My body was out of tune. I ate large meals without feeling satisfied, or forgot about food completely. I had no sense of physical boundaries...

The quality of my connection with Shanti shifted into further nuances. I valued even more the preciousness of our love, beyond the differences of personal likes and dislikes, compatibilities and issues. The silence that embraced our divergences became absurdly obvious, reinforcing our connection of heart and soul.

Though I was not able to live in this clarity twenty-four hours a day, it became easier to catch myself when off-track. I noticed my reactions glued to our interactions and often stopped a sentence to rewind and review, starting fresh from a different perspective. Delicacy in my heart started to find its voice in strength rather than in helplessness.

There might be one thousand roads leading to the same place... My nature delights in the lover. Shanti's presence invited me into the sacredness of my heart; allowing my defenses to soften, I let his love touch recoiled sentiments, hidden corners. Sharing in love adds a unique dimension to my life. That recognition was with me, as I looked at him in bed in the evening, and waking up in the morning.

WATER RUNNING THROUGH MY FINGERS

We drove to Sedona with the intensity of the latest days echoing inside, reminding me not to waste time.

I had recently created a business, was giving sessions regularly, and working at Osho Academy with different projects.

The months to follow were tinted by Kaveesha's frail health, a trip to Brazil to work for a month, and Shanti coming to meet me in Rio for the first time. I had a sense of completion and forgiveness meeting my father, a few days of sun and ocean, and sharing my past with Shanti was significant. Our life together had been far removed from the source elements of my personality. For a month, I had the opportunity to face the keys of my conditioning and watch old tendencies being challenged. Shanti's presence magnified my ability to respond freshly.

At the end of the year, Kaveesha was ready to leave her body. We celebrated her transition in a graceful, all-night-long ceremony. Her body rested on a wooden support, while we gently danced bathed by waves of live music. I sat near her body, quietly receiving her last gesture of love. Such a departure!

The day after her funeral, I called Derek. We had maintained a loving connection for over twenty-five years. Whenever we talked, time disappeared. With two close friends dying a short time apart, the impermanence of life had been emphasized. So well did I know that edge! It was important to express warmth and appreciation for friends and lovers who shared bits and pieces, or long stretches of my living-and-learning. I re-stated my gratitude for our time together and our friendship. We joked about getting old; my white hair was growing visibly, he was proud of having none! I was coming to Europe in the summer and we made plans to meet then. He invited me to stay at his home in the countryside near Barcelona. I was looking forward...

Living in a small town like Sedona posed practical limitations. My experience with Neharika had given me a taste of unlimited expansion. With that savor lingering in my heart, the narrowness of circumstances became prominent. Yes, the limitations were external, but I still needed to live in an environment where I could continue to explore and learn the balance of inner and outer. Osho Academy had become formal and structured in a way that no longer appealed to me. At that point there were about sixty-seventy friends living in Sedona as part of the Academy, many of them I had been close for over twenty years. It was difficult to let go of that support and comfort.

An internal sense of urgency pushed its way through my physical body, as a new plant pushes through the earth to sprout. The first step was to disengage from my involvement with Osho Academy. To live continue living in Sedona without being part of the Academy did not make sense. I could not see our lives expanding in that environment.

Shanti had never been content in Sedona, though had a successful healing practice, and traveled to Europe once or twice a year. It seemed that we both needed a more diverse playground. I would rather choose ocean and forest, than red rocks and desert.

The years at the ranch had given me enough opportunities to learn to contain, focus and build up my essential energy. I was ready to move into balance, allowing expansion and grounding to converge, hopefully with a centered quality that I sensed had matured.

Different issues came to the surface, and made me face new decisions, some of them challenging my financial situation. Another level of trust was demanded, and I had to respond with caution and precision. I had started an aromatherapy business that was evolving and going through shifts, from a small enterprise to a possible larger distribution and more complex development. I had to cope with choices that would support the next step, and was not sure how to proceed. Long working hours have always been easy and natural for me. It was challenging and pleasurable to see a different manifestation of my creativity taking form. But I was realizing the need to be more practical and learn to gather the fruits of my work, rather than constantly start anew.

Time to dare another step. I kept questioning my choices through life, especially my decisions to move and start fresh. In retrospective, they seemed to have been inevitable, and yet, my mind compared, judged. And every day, one more spark would wake me up with the need to move on.

I had no desires to go anywhere, nor idealized any other place just for the sake of it. The movement, as always, had to arise from the inside and "move me." Nothing to do but wait.

In spring 1999, Shanti invited me to come with him for a business trip to Northern California. We flew to San Francisco and stayed with a friend in Mill Valley. Meeting this man was surprising, as I recognized him as someone I knew, though that was our first meeting. I watched my response to that astounding familiarity. I realized that he reflected much of my essential nature. Years before I would have been caught in the desire to come closer to him, unaware of the underlying dynamic. However, I took the opportunity to come closer to myself, while expressing appreciation for his mirroring image. I noticed that we both had a broad range of inner bounce; his ability to express was strong and vibrating, and his ability to hold space in stillness and silence was as well compelling and profound. He moved very fast from one extreme to the other, and his swiftness rang a bell for me. I realized that I had been feeling jammed in my movements, trying to fit on a narrow band of energy that constricted my pace and pulse. The red rocks seemed to have burned my tears, as well as rigidified my flexibility. I needed to find again an undulating motion as wide as the rainbow.

I shared with Shanti my insights. He was receptive and caring. As a man, he was definitely touched. There was clarity on my side that this attraction was not to be followed as sexuality, but taken in as understanding. My relationship with Shanti was indubitable but it was important for me to recognize and use the awareness that this meeting evoked. Shanti said, "The worst that can happen is that you will leave me. If that ever happens, I would like to have spent the best of our time together." He opened up his body and heart even more, drawing me closer to him.

I shared with this friend my perceptions, however he did not to understand where I was placing myself. His emotional sensitivity was immature, and he withdrew with caution. Through this interaction, I realized that in many instances we are gifted with messages or opportunities coming from people who are not aware of what they are offering. They may be instrumental for significant insights, even major life changes, and yet oblivious of their roles. I also noticed that it is difficult to receive without holding on to the giver, therefore we repeatedly miss amazing opportunities and treasures of understanding that are seeded along the away, just because the mailman has run away before we opened the package. Nobody to thank for... I decided to pick this one up with both hands. I would have enjoyed meeting and honoring our spirited connection, however we never met again.

Mill Valley and the eucalyptus refreshed my spirit. I loved being around trees again! And the water! The dryness of the desert was overheating my body, and provoking fevers that lasted for days in a row.

Soon after returning to Sedona, the house we were renting got sold and we had to move one more time. Out of our lovely nest, we found another house that was not particularly cozy, nor beautiful, simply served us as in-between spaces.

I was due to go to Europe and teach a course in England, then fly to France to meet Gioia for a week-vacation in Saint Tropez, and end my time in Barcelona with Derek. Just before leaving I tried to call him several times to arrange our dates but got no answer. Finally someone answered the phone, a woman came to the phone and burst out crying. Derek had died the day after our last phone call. He had a brain aneurism, quietly passing away during the night. He was fifty-three and had always been healthy. I was in shock. Death was pushing me further. His wife described his last days, asked me if I would like to visit her, and let me know that he had kept objects, photos and letters from me. She would mail them to me soon.

I went for a walk and sat with his absence. His companionship had been part of my auric field since our marriage. I sensed a hole near the back of my heart. He had represented protection, purity of love, innocence, freshness, courage, trust, and much beyond words. This layer of unspoken complicity was had always been present through the years. My intuitive impulse to call him at the right time...

I flew to Paris for a couple of days strolling through the streets I had wandered with Derek in enchantment. I sat at my preferred café near the Seine, and sipped a glass of *kir*.

I walked by Rue de Bac, and visited Rodin's house. In this simple way, I said goodbye to the one who initiated me into the mysteries of love. In the South of France, the smell of rosemary and the Mediterranean whispered sweet acceptance and letting go.

Derek's death made me feel very attached to Shanti. I missed him during this trip. Our dance was embracing our different needs, meaning we spent more time apart as we traveled alone for work. There was nothing as valuable as the subtlety and richness of the love I shared with him. The moments of simplicity going for walks in the night around our house, the vastness of the desert's sky showering over our heads, laying in bed chatting about the day, allowing more nuances of tenderness to visit our bodies, inviting more sincerity and vulnerability to permeate our conversations, making love with delicate sensitivity. It was difficult for me to recognize my attachment, but it was becoming increasingly difficult to let him go when it was his time to travel. In the way our work was established in America, it was not financially rewarding for us to work together any longer. Our styles were becoming more defined, and our courses were shorter than in Europe. Practically, we created programs in coordination, but were teaching separately.

The year 2000 started at home. Angela my Brazilian friend came for a visit. The snow was falling and we kept it simple with a nice meal and champagne. Our friendship had rekindled a few years before when we reconnected during one of my visits to Rio. I was glad to have her and her daughter as part of my life again. I danced for her and Shanti at midnight, dressed in a sophisticated Indian costume that I had designed and sewn.

A year of work mostly in Sedona, a new business partner, a few business trips to New York, another European tour for courses. The instability of home was evident again, as the contract of our temporary house was expiring and the owners were due to move back in a few months.

During the last ten years, I had met several beings who shared silence, light and love in different styles, however imparting the same essence of fullness-emptiness. Though each meeting was meaningful, they left me with the reminder to listen, trust and dare. No references. Rather than looking for the guidance of another teacher, I dwelled in my inner well, facing the darkness of its cracks.

Keep walking...

Beyond Time

"Stillness is to abide totally free from thinking.
And occurrence is when mind roams about through the ten directions without
staying still.
Awareness here is to notice whatever takes place, be it stillness or occurrence.
Although these show themselves in different ways,
they are of but a single essence.
There is no difference in quality between stillness and occurrence.
So don't make differences, just be with whatever happens.
Just as there is no difference between water and its wave...
Like an ordinary person who is free from thoughts of this and that,
there will come a time when besides just remaining totally ordinary,
all aims and deeds whatsoever will have been exhausted.
You will even be free from the previous experiences of bliss,
clarity and non-thought.
Someone with little learning will think: 'My meditation is lost!'
trying to get back to your former state.
It doesn't happen and you despair. This is called seeing the essence.
It is the realization of naked, ordinary mind."

KARMA CHAGMEY RINPOCHE   *The Union of Mahamudra and Dzogchen*

GATHERING OF FRIENDS

We met at Ghost Ranch in Abiquiu, New Mexico.

Brian's focused intention gathered about seventy friends.

As the invitation for a gathering of friends from Pune One arrived by email, I had no interest in going. So far away... No appeal to dwell in the past. But we kept getting updates. A growing list of friends confirmed their space. I saw Siddha's name on the list, I had not seen him for over ten years... I would love to express my gratitude for his presence in my life. I realized that at least thirty people in the list were close friends, and as they lived in different locations, we only met occasionally. The idea of spending a few days together was appealing. In the midst of several travels, we decided to say yes.

We drove to Santa Fe and spent the night with Waduda, my first girlfriend in Pune, and Bikkhu. Then continued to the Ghost Ranch, the place where Georgia O'Keefe had lived, which had been transformed into a bed-and-breakfast/retreat center.

Questions cooking before our meeting... How can we be together without indulging in past tense? We have aged, gone different ways, how will we meet in truth? A series of impossibilities.

In the last years, I had finally relaxed in "having to be alone," "there will never be a gathering of friends again," "just find your way anyway-anywhere." I had lived trying to find my integrity with each person I related to, learning to see the "isness" of each situation without dreams, enjoying simple moments... Not always easy, not always pleasant, not always joyful. And yet, ok. I lost the arrogance of considering my life "special." I often felt foolish in the midst of people who had lived a "normal" life. I did not see "what did I really have that justified all I'd gone through." Sometimes I envied others for their down-to-earth choices. Others, I compared and judged. However, I was finding contentment in life just the way it was. I wondered if I was falling unconscious or finally getting the point.

Suddenly I was in the midst of the ocean! Dancing with friends! The impossible was shattered...replaced with creative inspiration! And in a flash it was gone!

I drank the wine of our sharing. Well aged! My heart was round with melodies, not many words. Each sharing weaving the richness of these days together, touched me in a different way. The longing dissolved into life here-now. I had nothing to offer. At the same time my belly was bursting...

The pleasure of being amongst friends/lovers/beloveds had always been a blessing, plus the intelligence and maturity we had come to cultivate was diamond light.

Yet I had no desire to live in a group situation, could not see real possibilities to nurture this precious space in togetherness, did not want to put it into a form, or wished to hold on to it. I let it sink freely.

How to keep this quality crystal-like, yet fluid?

In the last years, as my friends died, I stepped with them into the threshold. The final letting go...the gain and the loss...the preciousness of each moment became stronger.

Kindly holding inside the hermit and the lover, I embraced both, alone-together.

Komala means the center of the lotus flower, the soft core, velvet-like, floating above the water, gently moved by the wind...

Since I came back to the West the meaning of my name sounded like a curse rather than a reminder. Often the tenderness in my heart was a drag, a quality not needed nor appreciated, but rather smashed and hurt. My main learning through these years had been to find the strength and the gentleness as one, an open heart and a clear mind, the lotus and the sword within, developing discernment that embraced both. I still lose balance. I wish to maintain the strength of gentleness without wobbling.

Space, space, space, space... I am a space freak. The space was filled with each one of us, though nobody "occupied" it. The room remained vacant as potentiality.

As each person expanded and was received by all around, stories vanished into the pool of presence. The only clock in the room was broken...

FREE FALLING

My chest is wide open. No choice or control. Intensity is running through my body and senses. Urgency to expand and inhabit spaces that have been dormant, or passive. I cannot plan, but allow movement to take over, receiving the possibilities as presented. It is uncomfortable.

Resistance has no chance to win over the power of this wave. I am forced to let it pass through without interference, sensing where the easiness is, following its course. My mind fights the unpredictable. Yet there is intimacy with the ocean... Rest within entangled with fear. No grasping or concluding.

I notice my tendency to superimpose "awareness" onto situations that would be otherwise painful or challenging—an effective way to bypass them. It recalls real experiences and wisdom, but betrays their value and authenticity. I perceive awareness as the guardian of pure space, allowing letting go and letting be without conclusions. Not attached to preferences of meditative spaces, bliss, relaxation, or clarity. Not choosing what passes through the screen of emotions, mind, and dispositions of spirit. I do not know what I need. I do not know what I want, nor what is "real."

I bow down to the gods playing above my head.

Mystery road

The difference between this-and-that is fading. My routine recalls unframed presence. Not even my feelings are essentially meaningful, more like sonorous emissions that will soon transmute and wipe out their own signals… I recognize simplicity as maturity.

The mind affirms there is a difference between going in and acting out. Living in America, the lesson has been integration.

I have always perceived my work as pure energy recycling. When the motivation of love was not visible in my life then…give me a hammock! I do not want to get out of bed… In times when I needed to earn a living, like in Santa Fe, that was a struggle. My creative impulse has been related to loving someone—a source outside of myself that resonated my heartbeat, so it was enticed to play its music. The next step is to let creativity spring out of contentment, uncaused.

The meeting in Santa Fe refilled remembrance of limitless love, neither inside nor outside, but reflected through the grace between us.

I am in Fairfax, California, in a studio located on top of the mountain, beautiful walking trails nearby, and the ocean far away. I need the green, the water…

It was strong to leave Sedona, stay away from Shanti for a while, recognizing our different needs at this point, though maintaining our relating and finding our love in a different setting. No frames, no schedules, no demands, I am like a wild horse letting my soul run freely, without a home. I miss him immensely, at the same time I moved with his encouragement. As I throw myself in the ocean once more, something inside gets polished and renewed. I look forward to be with him again, our relating has always brought me closer to my own heart.

The possibility of having a home and a garden seems out of reach for the moment.

ON THE WAY TO NOWHERE

December 2000.

Time to reset, relax, review, and wait for inner guidance. Rainy days, long walks in the forest, and the beginning of this book. Derek's death inspired me to paint and draw again. I bought a large watercolor pad to play with forms and colors. The cycle in Sedona seemed to be complete. As much as I resisted accepting this shift, it was manifesting in my body through fevers and reactions.

Shanti encouraged me to experiment and take these holidays. He felt that it was time for me to be in a more spacious and mature space, and he would come and join me soon.

Work came to me in an easy way. I missed Shanti and felt that Marin would be an excellent place for him to develop his work with the possibility to learn and offer his skills as a healer and teacher. I appreciated the eclectic ambience, the creative intelligence, the international flair, and the coziness of Mill Valley. Its small European village vibe, as well as the awareness around healthy living and nature, were nourishing elements for me.

We agreed that I would go back to Sedona for a few weeks, and return to Marin for a longer period. I was sad and disturbed while back home, feeling hesitant. Shanti encouraged me to trust.

Just be with no frills. No agendas, no further "getting better," "getting more," or "getting deeper." Finally, not even "getting more meaningful," one of my Scorpio-moon attachments.

I moved to a tiny room in a shared house in Mill Valley, just a few days before Shanti arrived for a visit. I was happy to have him around. The flowers were sprinkling colors and scents, and the weather was warming up. We walked daily and cooked together once more, disregarding the funkiness of the house. I loved being with him, and so much appreciated our care for each other. We planned to close our house in Sedona by June, when the owners had finally decided to return, and find a new place together in Mill Valley.

We talked about our relating. We sensed that our karmic patterns had been completed and we were ready to be with each other with a fresher sense of presence, honoring love beyond needs and demands. I had waited for that for so long.

When Shanti left, my heart was empty and impatient. There was gentleness. I was grounding my work, looking for possibilities of rentals, counting the days.

Less than two weeks after he left, I was in front of a nursery trying to decide what flowers to buy for my balcony, intending to create a colorful patch outside my bedroom. Suddenly, I fell down for no reason. My ankle swelled within a few seconds. Painful and impractical, as I had a session appointment a few minutes later… Instead, I drove home and put my foot up in bed wrapped with essential oils.

In this neutral gear, I phoned my father, as we had not talked for a few months. His maid told me that he had gone to the hospital in an emergency. After a few phone calls, I found out that he had broken a rib while swimming, and was going to have a surgery in the following days. It was clear to me that he was going to die and that I needed to fly to Rio as soon as possible. Considering that he was extremely vital and had never been sick, this was an intuitive hint that had no foundation on facts. I phoned Shanti and he arranged for my ticket within forty-eight hours. I cancelled my commitments in Mill Valley and packed a small suitcase.

Like being thrown into a washing machine. Angela picked me up at the airport and took me directly to the hospital. The following days were of no sleep, emotional meetings with my brother and mother, conversations with doctors, scanty food, as I was my father's main caretaker. My brother was in the midst of a work assignment and had to be away for a few days. My parents were divorced for over twenty years, they had a friendly relationship but my mother could not stay at the hospital.

My father died in less than a week. During his last conscious night I played his favorite Frank Sinatra and Nat King Cole songs, and we talked in a metaphoric way. He loved playing poker and he referred to this game as his last one. He was not sure that he had the best cards. I told him that he had always been lucky…this time was not going to be an exception. He laughed, and agreed. We talked about his cherished moments in life, and the music that had been one of his main passions. He smiled. He was attached to life and was not prepared to die. It was a painful to see a man who had lived so intensely, pushed into this greatest moment with no inner rest.

He was unconscious and in pain, in fear and hesitation—both to live or die. While monitoring the equipment in a special room where he was hooked to several drips and life support, I talked to him softly. I offered my presence for whatever he might need, and suggested that he decided which way to go: either to live and be prepared to make some shifts, or to let go and relax. He had lived fully. Either way would be fine.

In a few seconds his breathing rhythm shifted dramatically, I called the doctor and from that moment on, no return.

He fought until the last minute. He died alone in the intensive care room, as the doctors did not allowed anyone to stay with him for his last night. We were called at five in the morning to come and take care of the body.

Angela once more showed up as a caring friend in this difficult moment. My school friends came to the funeral with a few hours' notice, sharing their love and care for me and my family. I prepared my father's coffin with rose petals and he looked so lively that I was not sure that he had really made a choice.

The following months were of no-thinking-resolute-action. My brother and I embarked in a journey of practical, legal and emotional decisions, stepping into unknown territories without a guidebook. I returned to California two months later, exhausted and elated to take a break. Shanti had been at my side from a distance, however I missed his physical presence.

Upon my return, a new marathon was waiting around the corner. It was time to close our house in Sedona, store our belongings and go back to Brazil, to follow up with legal procedures.

As it was impossible to predict how long I would need to stay there, I also stored everything in California, and we flew together to Rio a few days before September 11. Though the repercussions of this event in the USA were of course huge, in Brazil they were blown out of proportion. Nevertheless, I could not wait to return home.

Digambar and another friend joined us for a few weeks, and we went for vacation to a remote part of the country, near Brasilia. Wonderful waterfalls, wild nature, vast spaces, silence, and the bliss of being immersed in a world of innocence.

The wondrous quality of nature in that region was healing and soothing. I bathed under the waterfalls letting go of much tension and built up pressure of the latest events.

My father's death was emotionally painless for me, in fact more of a relief. We never had a meaningful emotional connection, though he loved me on his own way, he was quite extrovert and superficial. I had spent many years looking at our relationship, my needs and karmic patterns with him, and had come to understand his limitations and intentions, finally accepting his choices and mine with its consequences. I was glad to have followed my intuition.

At the same time, it implied tremendous stress at a physical, practical and financial level, extending to this day, almost three years later. I stretched my physical health and endurance to resolve issues placed in my responsibility. Suddenly, thirty years after I had left Brazil, I had to go back and be immersed in a lifestyle and culture that were foreign to me. This situation brought me closer to my brother and mother, though not in the best way.

Also interesting to feel the power of genetic inheritance, almost tangible in the way it was passed from his ethereal body to mine. Suddenly his prominent qualities became loud and clear in my movements and expressions, with more vehemence and force than ever. In fact, the mechanics of his unconscious behaviors "jumped" on me from a day to another. Awesome! It took clarity of intention and piercing determination to bring awareness and relaxation to the way I decide to use these qualities in my life. Holding the bull by the horns, so to speak!

We returned to the USA in the midst of heightened airport security and virus alert. I wanted to rest away from the violence and craziness of my hometown, as well as the obligations I had to face. We went to Sedona together and Shanti left to work in Europe a few days later. I had a strong reaction to his leaving me at that moment. Having been always independent in my movements, I was tired, fragile and in need of being taken care with love. And my closest friend was leaving me to go to work! I wanted a home, and I had nowhere to live.

I got sick for a month after he left, grateful to Karmen who invited me to stay in her beautiful house in Sedona. I let the fever burn for days, got many acupuncture sessions as well as lovely massages, waiting for my body to recover so I could drive back to California. I felt like dying and had no sense of what was next. I was upset with Shanti in a way that was new and strong. I had asked for his support in a moment when I was feeling weak and in need, both states that I rarely experienced, much less expressed. He was firm in his movement and not available to care for me.

I drove to California with a smiling Ganesha statue in the passenger's seat. I rented a studio, not really comfortable but the only place I could find where Shanti could stay with me for the month of January, when he was returning from Europe.

This time it was not easy for either of us to meet in my small place. I was pressured with financial obligations, living in an unpleasant space though I had made it the best I could with new furniture and nice bedding. I was looking forward to be with him, though resentful that his traveling was adding more difficulty and stress to my life. Every separation brought tears. My body and heart needed rest and healing.

In my perception, I had been the grounding principle in our relationship relating to housing, creating beautiful and supportive spaces for us to live. At that point, I was not able to play that part, I needed him to jump in and be the man in charge. I had never wanted to have support from a man, nor had ever asked for it before. I sensed my hesitation in doing so…

While Shanti was away, an old friend was visiting and we went for walks often together. His presence was earthy, and he offered his friendship in that moment with grace and gentleness. It was nurturing to be next to a man I trusted, who could hold my vulnerability and give me his stable hand. No wobbling, no demanding, restful and strong. I relaxed as a woman, sensing the man's solidity. My body relaxed realizing that I wanted that quality of support and strength from Shanti. It was difficult to accept that I was not able to provide what we needed at a material level, and that I was rather susceptible and tired after dealing with my father's death and its consequences. All I wished was to stop working and be taken care of, and I was ashamed and afraid to admit, or much less, ask for that.

Again, it would have been easy to misread the situation and use the opportunity to distract myself from the difficulty I was facing, rather than penetrate its source. I was walking a fine line between understanding my own needs, and respecting Shanti's feelings and moods. Especially when we both seem to be demanding from each other, and not having our needs met.

My connection and commitment with him were unquestionable. I kept looking for ways to find our common ground on a practical basis, but I had no doubts about our being together. It seemed natural that a distressful situation demanded more awareness as it brought to the surface new challenges and aspects of our personalities.

Shanti came back for one month in between his European trainings. Feeling stretched and tired, I asked for his presence and strength. I could not handle his coming and going so often, and was ready to create a home for us as soon as possible. I was frail and shaky, exhausted and overstretched. I wanted to be the woman, to be taken into his arms without having to hold on to the walls of the house around me.

Making love was still my way to continuously choose letting go and love over contracting and separating. During this time I experienced immense fragility, perceiving my body made of crystalline liquid particles vibrating ever so subtly... Every gentle movement spread waves of daintiness throughout. My sexuality became surrendering to life with its difficulties and challenges. I opened my body in sensitivity, exposing the nakedness of my heart and soul. How bare can I be? How much more can I offer? What is this moment bringing? I was not sure...

Shanti was in a difficult time with all the shifts that we had moved through added to his inner reality. I was working regularly, while he was writing and preparing for his trainings without a fixed schedule. He was kind and loving during this time, though there was irritation and inner restlessness with his own direction. I asked him to stop traveling for a while, but he reacted to that request as a restriction to his career. How could love be less than work? It was painful for me to accept his choice, but we agreed that we would rent a house upon his return, due a month later. He left for another month in Holland and Switzerland.

I chose to spend my birthday week at Sajeela's place in Mexico, and we would meet again in Mill Valley just after that.

Here now

Today is my forty-ninth birthday. I wake up with the sound of the ocean and birds. My body is deliciously restful, my skin touched by soft wind. The morning sun calls for gentleness.

I am at the land where my friend Sajeela lives, near Sayulita, Mexico. My small cabana is placed on top of a hill, on a plateau where two other cabanas have been built, creating a little plaza with a fireplace at the center. We are surrounded by twelve acres of untouched land. The vegetation is not-so-dense, forest/jungle, where trees and flowers mingle together, mild weather and the Pacific ocean for the views. My eyes move around appreciating the design of the palm weave which makes up the roof, and the texture of the wood woven in the wall's construction.

Sajeela and I connect in sisterhood. I have no sense of age as I look into her eyes, or look at myself in the mirror.

Traditionally in India, at forty-nine it is time to withdraw from mundane activities and retreat. The duties of raising a family, creating a business, and making money should have been completed, and the season is ripe for meditation, finding comfort in aloneness. Though I have never raised a family, or built a fortune, I wish this new cycle will bring acceptance in aloneness and integrity.

Shanti is in Europe. I miss him. He did not want to be with me for this date, but decided to extend his trip to visit a friend. Recognizing our differences beyond our daily choices, time and space, invites a bigger embrace, the defiance of true love. Can the openness of my heart tame the mind to a still point? There is fear, sometimes doubt, resistance, wishes, ideas. And yet, they seem to fade in this moment as the waves dissolving down the beach. Coming and going... Opening my hands, letting my heart soften, I look at a magenta flower outside my window.

I am ready to create a new home. It has been hard to wait and be apart. It has been difficult to handle so much, and try to be supportive to him at the same time. I am looking forward to resting in his arms, to be his woman.

NOWHERE

Sometimes life is perfect. Warm breeze, trees sparkling in soft light, the body is dancing, pleasure tingles in every cell.

Sometimes life brings tough calls. The heart hurts, the body is dull. Even knowing this is only my own perception, I am not able to step out of the mind perceiving so.

As I met Shanti back in Mill Valley, he communicated his decision to move to Europe alone. Bluntly. Listening to him—a jolt. Our last year had been difficult, we both acknowledged. He expressed the need to be focused on his work and create time alone. Nothing that I asked for or have considered dissuaded him. It was clearly his decision and my requests had no significance. Our complicity was broken.

We had lived together for over twelve years. Our relationship had fully engaged my heart, my soul, my body, cultivating a sense of possibility that instilled tremendous joy of spirit. We had moved through different phases, difficulties, learning curves, always holding hands. This time of maturation gave me strength as a woman, as a friend, as a lover. I could stand up to the storms. Even though we were moving through a difficult moment, my love was doubtless. I was in shock realizing that we were no longer in synchronicity, that our core priorities were not the same. Maybe they had never been...

For a month I expected him to change his mind, review, find a different way to relate at a distance, make it an experiment, but keep our love and connection as priority. That was no longer important for him. At the same time, we were living with the same care and friendship we always had, and making love as often and lovingly as we always had. With a lot of tears... I felt pushed and pulled at the same time. I had eagerly been waiting for him to come back. It was not possible for me to break our bonding so abruptly. Nor did I want it. In shock, I was not ready to let him go. He stood in determination and practically got ready to leave. I helped him pack, store, mail things. I choose to stay open in my heart and body; maybe in disbelief, blindness, maybe hoping that something would change. It did not.

He waved goodbye from the shuttle to the airport. I stayed in Mill Valley. Why did he choose to leave in such tender moment? I was so delicate and just beginning to allow vulnerability to be exposed, daring to ask for support.

I understood his personal needs and difficulties, however I expected that our commitment to each other as friends and lovers, would stand exactly as the resource to bring awareness to our individual struggles and learning. His actions proved that I had missed in discrimination: that was not his priority.

The fragrance of the beloved, the care of my dear friend, my home grounding, blissful memories, sweet dreams. Suddenly gone.

Our separation threw me in the hell of the mind. The voice of caution advising to close off, defend, retreat, find a distraction; and the silence, way too penetrable to have an opinion. Red scream, hurt, continuous, pounding, nagging. Nowhere to hide.

I love the outer meeting. I am attached to the enchantment of the beloved next to me, walking hand in hand. I delight in the soulfulness of our meeting. I do not want to let go of this expression of love, and I do not want to feel the pain of betrayal that it reminds me. Can't go back, can't go forward. The sensitivity that perceives the love in form, in sharing, is the same that reveals the pain. How to keep the love alive and dissolve the pain? They seem to be two sides of one same thing.

Rawness, sadness, trying to catch a breath. Not easy. On top of it, I got sick. How did I get here? Difficult to forgive myself for such loss of sight! Inside is pain, outside is infinite futility. A blunt "hitting the wall." Clueless and tired. Somehow I geared my life to this edge, and I want to bail out! What is left? What I had so tenderly cared for was destroyed mercilessly.

I dissolve in the joy of devotion. Sitting alone I find contentment, however it is lopsided. I am attached to the subtlety evoked in my body, the gentleness that it invites in my movements, the calm that naturally bathes my heart, the luminosity I touch through intimacy. I doubt that I will ever have this richness again. I do not want to let it go! Yes, I find silence in aloneness, direct-express! However it lacks the earthiness, the vitality, the balance of opposing forces dissolving into each other, the song in the air.

The love we shared constantly pushed me beyond the edges of self-definition, our personalities so different, the background of stillness becoming more relevant, the essence of my choices.

Do I dare vulnerability without attaching any form to it? Can I stay naked in this insecurity? Do I create pain to be pushed towards a state of intensity where creativity is forced out of my guts? Can I get there otherwise? Can stillness give space to this creative life force joyfully? Can silence empty out this self-perpetuating "I" that pain reinforces?

Yes, I have skills to move beyond the pain. And yet, it feels necessary not to interfere. Life-spiral. Nothing helps the pain or reduces the tears. My heart aches. I miss his touch, his face, his body near mine.

Thousand pieces reflecting incongruent colors and shapes, dazzling or dulling my eyes. Will you ever again rest in my arms? Will I ever become the beloved within?

The wind is blowing. I cannot hold anything in my hands or intention. I feel the ground under my feet. I look at the sky and relax under the soft winter sun. There is a rightness-ripeness that shows the direction for NOW and not further. Relief, sometimes apprehension and a sense of defeat, as much as there was humming in synchronicity. Milton Nascimento sings, "Sometimes I want to cry and then the day rises and I forget… All I can give you is my own solitude and a view of the ocean…"

Can I receive this slap in grace? Spiritual bullshit! It just hurts! Is pain necessary? I do not know. I look at the mirror noticing my red, puffed eyes. I am choosing kindness these days.

Recently, an Indian man told me that in the tantric tradition, Komala represents a state of consciousness between form and formlessness. She so vividly remembers the luminosity of radiance that whatever she creates almost immediately returns to light. This image clearly describes my innermost nature. Difficult to hold on to forms. Not always easy to accept life's ride on this fine line.

Shifts are inevitable, and only loving kindness knows to avoid causing pain. Sometimes the stretch is way beyond what we can handle. And we manage it anyway. I am more keenly aware of the responsibility of love and friendship.

I do not understand the need to deny love. I sense openness that embraces without excluding. What I call love has never been any different inside, though its form of expression may have changed through circumstances.

My relationship with Shanti relaxed my heart, uncovering innocence and trust. I had offered delicacy and courage, not always in easiness, but in truthfulness. In the course of twelve years, I matured through our love and friendship. As I intentionally kept inviting my heart's softness into our relating, the inflexible aspects of my personality became more obvious. Yes, I lost it many times, and I was forced to see the covers of protection sticking out! The transparency of intimacy stirred hidden currents, challenged my mind's rigidity—occasionally it wore my crustiness to a helplessness state. Sometimes I wished to run away. And yet, decided to stay.

I write, holding on to time. Will it bring me full-circle? What difference does it make? Labyrinth. Interesting exercise, watching the one who moves through it, getting lost here and there... In the background, the gentleness of a shy voice, soothing murmur. I can hardly hear it, a feeble whisper. The place of softness that recoiled in fear is tactile. Like a caress from a young child. Flickering, then still for an instant—a tiny dot in a chaotic landscape.

Sitting for a few days in a silent retreat. The unreality of emotions is obvious. Contortions and somersaults. There is a fine line of balance, however I do not want to manipulate it to relieve the pain. I need to be in the physicality of this human body and allow equilibrium to pervade this reality as such. Not cover it up, mask it, or take turns. I foresee a moment when my actions-choices-creativity will reflect this integration, not disguise its lack.

Presence without knowing... Can I let the pushes and pulls, the winds and storms, lightning and thunders of the mind be there, and yet, stay present without knowing? I sit in front of the fire, emotions keep dissolving into translucence that absorbs heat and cold.

I want to go back. I miss my beloved, our home, our affection. I focus on small tasks. I clean my car with care.

Seeing what is, accepting what is. No complacency, nor stagnancy, or compromise. Can I stay in the openness that brings in the light while abiding in the darkness of the unknown spaces? Can I discriminate between creation that arises out of equanimity and action that arises out of fear?

Sometimes I breathe immensity, the pain and the love together. Brief moments. I do not know how it happens. The mind shouts, louder and louder! Does not like it at all. What a battle! I am tired of watching it. Is there any choice besides the madness of self-absorption, or the illusion of self-distraction?

Our truest connection happened in silence. This was the space from where we made love. That was my commitment: to go back to this peace, continuously returning to the source of openness, the heart. Shanti's presence reminded me of that suchness.

This love-opportunity was/is a priority in my life.

The bliss of aloneness does not substitute the beauty of sharing. I have not lost it. It is bittersweet. Hanging out with sadness, facts are just the way they are. Silly to say so…

Life forced me to bring the inner into expression. I have sat enough in monasteries. Now there is a pull to let the silence shine through my actions, untainted. I am not ready to let go of personal love, before I truly live it. I need to let it wash my bones, penetrate my cells, permeate my soul as I dance. Then, I may be ready to fade away…

In the last days before Shanti left, we gathered with a few friends by the ocean in Medoncino county. It was a beautiful blue sky day with the fresh rawness of the California coast softened by the haze drifting out to sea.

We were walking near the ocean, suddenly a great white osprey swooped down right in front of us, and came up with a big fish in its mouth. Our friends gasped at the wonder of the hunter bird, but I panicked inside.

"Did you see that?" Shanti asked.

"Yes, but I feel like the fish…" I replied.

Being up in the air is not easy for this ocean woman.

Since Shanti left, I have been up in the air. I don't understand how my guidance, so impeccably accurate for so long suddenly quit working. I doubt myself. I doubt our love. I question all the things that I held precious and true.

How could this shift have happened in a time when I feel most open and mature for partnership?

Like a fish out of water. I turn inside; I turn outside. There is still no peace. There are friends. There are offers. There are many opportunities, but what I cherished the most is missing.

I remember a Sufi story that I heard from Osho long ago. It is called *The Wisdom of the Sands*.

> Once there was a spring high in the mountains. Its waters were pure
> and fresh. They run downhill, turned into a brook, which was soon joined

with other brooks until there was a stream. Several streams made a river, and the water was clean, powerful, running fast towards the sea.

When the river came out of the mountains it entered into a plain. The flow slowed down, and the river widened. It lost its crystal quality and became colored with the mud of the earth.

Eventually the river approached a large extension of sand dunes, and stopped altogether. For the first time it hesitated. It didn't know what to do. Going forward meant to simply be absorbed into the sandy wastes. There was no way back. There was nothing it could do.

The longer it stood, the more stagnant it came. It felt deep grief in seeing its once proud and pristine waters turning into a dull swamp.

The situation was hopeless. The river lost heart.

In the original story, the Sufis say that the whisper came from the sands themselves. The river wasn't quite sure. However it did hear a whisper. Listening a little more intently, the river heard the message, "If you let yourself dissolve in the sun, the winds will pick you up and carry you over the sands, and further drop you in the sea."

The river was quite confused. Everything had been so smooth on its journey down the mountains. Now it had no hope of reaching the ocean. "Dissolve and the winds will carry you."

How could it trust that it would be changed back to water again? How would it know that the winds would carry it to the ocean?

The river took a chance and offered itself to the sun. It let the sun heat turn it into vapor, and then climbed as a cloud into the sky. The winds carried the cloud far over the sands to the distant ocean. There, it is said, the clouds dumped tears of joy into the sea.

I knew that if I followed my guidance, the ocean would call me. Now I am learning life in the inner desert. Certainly I am not the river I used to be. Certainly I am not the ocean. I wonder if I will dissolve once again…

Nothing sticks with consistency, except this silence that does not define or separate. New skin slowly growing, tenuous and brittle. Tears keep moistening its surface. The love of friends is a caress. Allowing the tiniest spark in my heart to expand. Not budging, not doing, not going anywhere, not changing, not looking into another direction, not trying to understand, bearing kindness throughout situations, focusing on mellowness within.

Osho's voice comes back… Your love and devotion are enough. Remember the softness of your heart… Relating with Shanti offered me a precious chance to align with the texture of my heart. What I may express through any form of work or art will never come close to the joy of sharing in intimacy.

My connection with India crystallized in the practice of Ayurveda. The wisdom that it transmits continuously opens doorways of perception and integration. This memory of sensitivity comes naturally to my voice and gestures, and translates into the practical aspects of my work.

I see friends creating homes, relationships, accumulating money, settling into places and business and new masters... My reality is aloneness and no references. A slow dance rises from my guts. The taste of freedom and sadness and exhilaration and not knowing and no-motivation served for dinner tonight! Each movement becomes fuller. Grace grows with tenderness.

My daily task is to make love visible in the little things, just the way I make my bed, cook food or drive the car. The fullness of the love we have shared enriched my life in many dimensions, and left no longing for anything new. Though my body misses his touch, as much as my soul misses his presence, I am not looking for substitution. Other people, playfulness or entertainment, do not cover this hole inside.

Presently, gentleness is not glamorous. I feel rather stupid. However, the rare drops of silence and rest that I experience nowadays still come from it. I have no energy to discipline myself inwards. The foundation has been set. Now, let's see how strong it is.

It is time for me to lounge in the empty space Shanti's absence etched. My commitment to him was unquestionable. Now I am faced with commitment to love without excuses. Not alluring, but I can't back off. I am ok staying in the hole as long as it is unclear, so that when time will come to flower into another layer, it will be real and total.

Time is misted with sadness and inquiry. Hidden inside, there is a spot... Like a thorn, its sensitivity provokes immediate reaction. My lucidity does not penetrate it. I do not have a perspective of this shift beyond distress and bewilderment. There are too many words between my reactions and what may be possible beyond them.

Unexpectedly, I met Prem during this last year. I noticed physical fear holding my sacrum, it took a while to feel safe and open my heart. We walked on the beach and rested together, our friendship and love, natural and timeless. Our lives have taken different turns. However the stillness we join in is immediately invoked. Our meeting made it explicit that I do want to live in the fullness of love's physical expression. We separated in gratefulness, open-handed.

I heard from a friend...

"Understanding is just a preparation. It gives you enough trust to dare to burst out of it. It gives you enough trust to fully love. You have developed this capacity. The explosion already happened for you. It is useless now to try to understand. Time is needed to get used to this dimension.

What you are feeling is raw pain. True spiritual guidance leads to it. When you touch this pain, spiritual guidelines become worthless. You are alone.

You came to a place where pain is unavoidable. You have experienced union that dissolves personality. It is not possible to get there through understanding.

You have rare courage. Your heart is open without reserves. You came to a state where merging in love and aloneness are inseparable. The ego structure cannot hold together.

The balance of these extremes is very subtle, the stress of its tension is uncomfortable. At this point, it is easy to run away. You have no control over your life, you are helpless, the ego suffocates. You feel that you have lost everything. To search for spiritual guidance is to miss a wondrous opportunity. The spirit is sitting inside your heart. You cannot avoid this pain, you can only postpone it.

Very few grow in maturity to stay present to this love, to hold the fragility of this balance. It is unsubstantial, and yet, it is your core strength. Specially the male mind has a difficult time here. And many women have a male mind.

The feminine knows the way of the empty heart. That is the end of spiritual search.

With this love comes the deepest pain. You are at the center of all colors. It is easier to look for distractions, or use meditation to rise above it. It is tempting to engage in relationships that maintain boundaries. This state of love burns boundaries. You cannot go back. Stay there. It is a question of time.

Commitment in relationship is only necessary to move through this moment of dissolution. Until then, excitement and attachment to the lover will be enough to sustain the bonding. When love breaks core defenses, it erases the ego's script. That is the moment when most couples separate. They do not realize that this is the beginning of true relating in love. Most men will look for another woman to reaffirm their strength and redefine their personalities, so that they will re-acquire a sense of identity. The woman needs the commitment of the man to relax into this depth.

This is the sacred meaning of marriage—the commitment to stay together through this crucial moment, when both may feel they have lost everything. The feminine merges in love naturally; the male needs conscious commitment in order to realize oneness.

The path of love requires giving it all at once. Only surrender to the feminine can lead to love. Understanding is just a preparation. If you hold on to clarity, you will live in the illusion of spiritual pride..."

In the past I have used "letting go" to escape from situations that made me feel vulnerable, insecure, unbearably open. Now, I sense maturity that sustains what truly nurtures my soul.

Letting life take me by the hand, a sense of urgency still prevails. Not much time left...

Underwater

Events vanish into the unchanging. Observing impatience, irritation, calmness, craze, anger, clarity, perplexity. I bounce from left to right, up, down and sideways. The ground gets more stable with each shake. References come and go. Something untouchable stays.

Fragmented thoughts, lingering experiences mumbling, pushing and pulling in different directions. Opinions, allusions from the past, dreams of the future. When I engage, the emptiness of each opportunity is missed.

Time of integration, recognizing expansion that merges separations, either-or-choices. Multidimensionality, invisible-indivisible. The spiral is enlarging, bringing the same elements in a different dimension. I am forced to be unreserved, not a split second ahead of time.

I am choosing, setting intentions, and yet, bowing down to what is greater than my fondness and aims. Recognizing my preferences, steering directions, and yet life plays its way. Both sides equally potent, finding the verge of harmony.

Revealing disguised gradations, receiving crispness. The sensitivity necessary to recognize this evolving process comes out of stillness. My only guidance.

The essence has never been scratched. However, it is not bright enough to flood reticent places of contraction, sadness, doubt. It is not sheer fleshy vitality. I can't lie. I wait.

I am surrounded by an environment that constantly denies everything I value, that destroys what I gently care for. Responding to practical demands in a sensible way, mediating human relationships with patience. Becoming more porous...

Grateful to the friends who hold my hand while I am underwater.

THE RIVER

What sustains the capacity to bear the magnanimity of love? What strengthens the commitment that bursts the mind, emotions and body needs? What encourages the soul to claim this love that aches for manifestation? What keeps aflame the constant reminder of love over fear, inviting merging and embracing over separation and confinement? What nurtures softness while free falling? What enhances trust instead of personality? What dissolves the pain of the mind fighting ferociously against earthy love? Is this quest for love just another facet of my ego structure? What is not?

How can I stay open to the universe's mystery while still guided by strong preferences? Will fear and pain ever stop telling my heart to be careful, knowing its nature is daring? Will this tension ever liquefy?

Learning to maintain the integrity of being without references. Life is the school, in all forms and shapes, straightforward, capricious.

I do not know what gratitude is, or what forgiveness reveals. The grace I invoke has not yet fully blossomed. Its visits are flaming though not constantly afire. Where is the fine line between all-embracing love and the illusionary expansion of longing trying to reach for it?

I have no answers.

I look at the river, stunningly emerald green.

THE OCEAN

Skin shed. I shiver, softness underneath.

A spot in my heart standstill tender. Flickering sweetness. Memory contains sadness. I avoid it.

Learning to discriminate more accurately, distinguishing potential from present reality. What is latent may never manifest. Responding with the sword of empathy, rather than with its hopes and fears.

Seeing what I see, not disguising with what may be. More ruthlessly sincere.

The ocean came closer and tidal waves ate some of my assumptions. I still grab arrogance to protect my thin skin and to mask the impatience that speaks loud when I feel unsafe and cannot relax in nakedness.

Infinite time has become now or never.